SERIOUSLY MAD

Seriously Mad

MENTAL DISTRESS AND THE
BROADWAY MUSICAL

Aleksei Grinenko

UNIVERSITY OF MICHIGAN PRESS

Ann Arbor

For questions or permissions, please contact um.press.perms@umich.edu

Published in the United States of America by the
University of Michigan Press
Manufactured in the United States of America
Printed on acid-free paper
First published October 2023

A CIP catalog record for this book is available from the British Library.

Library of Congress Cataloging-in-Publication data has been applied for.

DOI: https://doi.org/10.3998/mpub.11863498

ISBN: 978-0-472-07644-4 (hardcover : alk. paper
ISBN: 978-0-472-05644-6 (paper : alk. paper
ISBN: 978-0-472-22133-2 (ebook

Library of Congress Control Number: 2023934620

"For my part, I can speak neither as mad nor as not mad."
—Shoshana Felman

Contents

Digital materials related to this title can be found on the Fulcrum platform
via the following citable URL: https://doi.org/10.3998/mpub.11863498

Acknowledgments

This book would still be living only in my head had I not encountered a number of extraordinary people who supported or otherwise influenced my research. I am indebted to my great teachers Judith Milhous, Evelyne Ender, Jean Graham-Jones, Daniel Gerould, Annette Saddik, and David Savran, who helped me find my voice during my doctoral studies at the Graduate Center of the City University of New York. Many other brilliant minds contributed to my thought process over the decade swallowed up by this book. Some of them I have never met or spoken to, but the glow of insights radiating from their scholarship lights my way in these pages. I have also been lucky to receive timely words of advice or surprising acts of kindness directly from my colleagues, acquaintances, and friends, especially Gerard Perna, Saeyoung Park, Anne Ellis, Chris Haines, Gwendolyn Alker, Michael Clifford, Terri Palmer, Stephen Stahl, and, of course, Bess Rowen.

I am thankful to everyone who listened and gave me feedback at various meetings of the Harvard-Princeton Musical Theatre Forum, the Song, Stage and Screen Conference, the American Society for Theatre Research, and the Association for Theatre in Higher Education. An early version of Chapter 5 was published in *Theatre Journal*, and some passages from Chapters 1 and 7 originally appeared in *The Routledge Companion to the Contemporary Musical*. The editorial suggestions I received while working on both of those publications added clarity to this research project. And I am especially thankful to LeAnn Fields at the University of Michigan Press and her world-class panel of anonymous reviewers for seeing promise in my book and influencing the development of the manuscript in a considered, organic way.

I also owe a huge debt of gratitude to my academic mentors and dear friends, Elizabeth Wollman and William Cohen, not only for showing interest in my research but also for inspiring me, through the brilliant example of their own writing, to take risks and aim higher. I thank Liz for the countless lunch hours she spent listening to my anxious monologues and still more hours reading early and late drafts of the book. And my thanks to Bill for embracing my writing generously and reading so closely (even though it is all about musicals!).

Looking back to how it started, I might not have been here writing these lines if it had not been for the foresight of my old chum, Caroline Savage, who, despite my protestations to the contrary, insisted that I was brave and capable enough to jump into the unknown.

But at its heart of hearts, from its very scene of origin, this book is my love letter to two most important people in my life:

Nina Grinenko, my mom and one of the best teachers in the world. Your love has taught me to live.

And Laurence Schwartz, you are my light and my meaning, yesterday, today, and to the edge of time.

Introduction

Madness moves. On a conceptual and historical level, it is a migrating, shape-shifting phenomenon. It takes up different forms, appearing simultaneously in a preponderance of heterogeneous experiences and expressions across numerous practices and discourses, yet never fully enough to be seen in its entirety. The remarkable ability of madness to evade complete capture within any conceptual or representational framework is manifest in a staggering multiplicity of meanings and functions attached to it in various enclaves of the cultural and clinical landscapes. To follow its presences and absences even in one location, the Broadway musical, is to chase after plural histories. To write an account of madness in an art form—or of an art form in madness—is always to speak from a seat with a partially obstructed view.

In this book I follow the movements of madness through American musical theater by considering different attempts by creative teams to envision and represent it. At the heart of the historical processes I trace lies the dynamic relationship between conceptual and institutional developments in and around mainstream psychiatry and the changing representational strategies and reasons for breakdowns or inner crises in production texts written for Broadway audiences. During the twentieth century, when musicals developed their own distinct identity as an art form, mainstream and experimental stages functioned as important creative sites for working out ideas about human minds, emotions, and bodies. As cultural spaces for articulating and contemplating the ways one is expected to feel, think, or act, theatrical renditions of madness probed, defined, and debated the parameters of normalcy and pathology on the stage and in the audience. Like other aesthetic genres drawn into this epistemological project, musicals popularized and contested authoritative medical models of mental illness and health, reflecting and contributing to historical change in commonly held suppositions about human subjectivity, sociality, and difference.

Focusing in particular on the vicissitudes of the brain/mind and nature/nurture dichotomies in psychiatric thought and parallel public debates about the mental health system, I tell the story of the art form's engagement with the shifting cultural investments in different paradigms for thinking about mental distress or illness in the United States. Does madness arise from an unconscious conflict, an adverse external environment, or brain pathology? I argue that at different historical moments creators of Broadway musicals respond and contribute to the prominence of a specific paradigm in clinical and cultural settings by organizing their representational emphases and techniques around one of these possibilities. That is not to suggest that there has ever been a moment when all theatrical renditions of madness on New York stages have been ideologically and philosophically homogeneous. A broad synchronous view of cultural production within any interval of time easily disproves that notion. But following the work of historians of madness and mental health, I delineate cultural moments, or, to borrow Ian Hacking's notion, "ecological niches," characterized by a groundswell of ideas, images, sounds, and narratives catalyzing around shared clinical and artistic emphases and strategies in envisioning and accounting for mental distress.[1] During such periods, certain facets of madness appear to eclipse others, lingering at the center of public discourses long enough to signal an ascendant trend in mainstream culture and, for my purposes, the Broadway musical.

Set against the background of this main story is a concurrent narrative that explores the enduring hold of the psychoanalytic imagination over creators of musical theater, critics, and, more broadly, American culture. I argue that from the midcentury on, the stage musical has exploited the symbolic capital of psychoanalytic views of interiority to shore up its aspirations to the domain of "serious" art theater. During the 1940s and 1950s, a period that marks the so-called golden age of popularity for both musical theater and psychoanalysis, the cultural construct of "psychological depth" emerged as a tool for elevating the critical profile of the Broadway musical.[2] This construct was part of the modernist aesthetics of inner crisis, which operated as a truth discourse whose authority was bolstered by the clinical and cultural prestige of psychoanalytic postulations of mental life. The stage vocabulary of "depth," which drifted into the art form during the golden age, has continued to play a central role in the creation and reception of the "serious," "intellectual" musical to this day.[3] In conceptualizing and representing human interiority and distress, the contemporary stage musical, like much of our culture, remains beholden to the psychoanalytic imagination. It is as if the art form, having once pictured people's minds through the eyes of psychoanalysis, cannot think itself out of that vision.

DEFINING MADNESS

The word "madness" has carried derogatory, stigmatizing connotations at different points in history, yet it has also been the *mot juste* for much critical writing on the subject across various academic disciplines. I choose to use the term to align this study with the work of scholars who focus on the historicity of madness, particularly as a cultural phenomenon, and its heterogeneous conceptual and representational frameworks.[4] This designation, often qualified by actual or implied scare quotes in critical literature, is thought to elide or transcend contemporary psychiatric determinations, encompassing other historically and geographically specific paradigms for understanding what is predominately seen as a mental illness in North American and Western European cultures today. The word has also been reappropriated by some mental health awareness and self-advocacy groups and initiatives like Mad Pride, with the understanding that, "following other social movements including queer, black, and fat activism, madness talk and text invert the language of oppression, reclaiming disparaged identities and restoring dignity and pride to difference."[5] A serviceable companion to this term, particularly in the wake of antistigma discourses, has been "mental distress." As Stephen Harper notes, it is presumed to be a more neutral descriptor, capable of drawing attention to the suffering experienced by the mad and facilitating "discussions of conditions which are nebulous or lack a clear definition (such as many of those featured in media and film texts)."[6] Modeling my terminology on a combination of sociological and historiographic texts with the above considerations in mind, I mine "madness," "mental distress," and their derivatives for these critical shades and valences of meaning and reserve words like "mental illness" or "mentally ill," as well as specific nosological formulations (e.g., bipolar disorder), for allusions to medical or psychiatric frameworks and contexts.[7] My references to the psychoanalytic lexicon áre likewise meant to acknowledge its historicity and limited range of application.

Proponents of the social model of mental health and distress in the humanities and social sciences trace the origins of madness to unequal power relations determined by race, gender, sexuality, and class in North American and Western European societies. As Harper argues, "Under capitalism—and particularly, it might be suggested, in the neoliberal moment—the notion that there exists a collective responsibility for the psychological well-being of individuals is unpopular, both in the media and among many psychiatrists."[8] In writing this book, I join the ongoing efforts in academic scholarship to acknowledge and investigate the social, political, and economic determinants of mental distress and its representational practices in popular culture. Yet while my investment in the social model of mental health and distress governs my choice of contexts and methods, I proceed with care so as not to let madness disappear by way of metaphor into one or more of the above categories of differentiation. Although the first decades of the twenty-first century have seen a steady stream of excellent scholarship bringing race, gender, sexuality, and class to bear on the stage musical's technologies and ideologies of entertainment, madness—with its own distinct sociocultural, intellectual, and institutional history in the United States—has yet to be factored into our accounts of the genre. In this book, it inhabits a conceptual terrain of its own, overlapping with but not identical to those of race, gender, sexuality, or class.

My terminological and methodological preference for madness must necessarily be defined in relation to disability. As conceptual categories, axes of social differentiation, objects of aestheticization in the arts, and coordinates for activist work, madness and disability have been conjoined metonymically and put to fungible ends in the critical literature concerned with human health and difference.[9] Both madness and disability, Bradley Lewis writes, have been central to critical projects and social initiatives "call[ing] attention to the fact that much of the suffering of different bodies comes from social exclusion, isolation, and lack of opportunity, along with the often pernicious side effects of a medical industry bent on aggressive intervention to achieve 'normal' bodies," feelings, and behaviors.[10] Today disability activists, Mad Pride, and similarly oriented groups affiliated with the c/s/x/m (consumer/survivor/ex-patient/mad) movement are fighting a common battle against the hegemony of ableist and sanist norms of human health, pathologizing standards routinely reified not only through medicalization but also through cultural discourses that individualize psychic difference as a random "personal tragedy."[11]

I share and respond to these epistemological, ethical, and political priorities by highlighting the varied ways in which madness and cognitive or mental disability have implicated each other in the theatrical arena as sites of representation, conceptualization, and activist contention. Here I am particularly concerned with the historical interface between locations of fictive and lived distress, diagnosed or not, in the context of critical debates and institutional reforms and transformations within and around the mental health care system. Thinking through the abundance of stories about "disorderly minds" in academic and other locations of public life, Margaret Price stresses that "recognizing their appearance is not a yes-no proposition, but rather a confusing and contextually dependent process that calls into question what we mean by the 'normal' mind."[12] In my study, this process entails taking a broad historical view of some of the intellectual paradigms driving the field of disability studies in this contemporary moment. In particular, I am interested in how historical change in conceptions of mind, emotion, and madness during the twentieth century conditioned, and was conditioned by, the emergence of a political consciousness about psychic diversity in medical and creative arenas; and how these interrelated developments set the stage for the current efflorescence of cultural and scholarly interest in disability. I trace records of this change in contemporaneous circuits of speculative and documentary narratives, in which ideas of illness or impairment as a normative social construct and a pathologizing medical stipulation—concepts so foundational to the field of disability studies today—were being articulated and contested. For all their reputation as mindless entertainment, musicals were active players in this discursive field through much of the twentieth century.

In analyzing specific texts or groups of texts, however, I do not assume disability to be an automatic referent of madness. Rather, I trace the ways madness moves through different positions of meaning across artifacts or cultural moments. In some positions, it comes to denote cognitive or mental disability directly; in others, it attenuates this meaning and reconstitutes itself as an expressive means serving other immediate goals and signifieds. Thus, in my analysis, the nomadic figure of the Beggar Woman in *Sweeney Todd* instantiates the ontological coincidence of madness and disability, the fictions of the musical's text gesturing toward the contemporaneous histories of the mad and disabled populations on the streets of New York City. By contrast, the madness of *Oklahoma!*'s Laurey, as conveyed through her famous dream ballet, operates primarily as an abstract rendition of her mind in distress. The self-contained choreographic study of her interior does not provoke her further medicalization or stigmatization in the musical's main, external narrative: Laurey is not characterized as afflicted with a pathology or impairment, nor is she shown to be an object of scorn or fear on the basis of her mental constitution or behavioral patterns. Yet because the stage picture of her reverie is expressed through a symbolic system moored in and authorized by a clinical paradigm of mental functioning, the construction of her character is still haunted by images of illness. In other words, Laurey's psychological economy is defined through her capacity for disability. In this book, I endeavor an analysis of how such dispensations and possibilities of meaning arise and interact with one another within certain historical moments, and what is at stake epistemologically and politically in the varying rhetorical strategies and emphases proliferating through different productions.

These dynamics attest to the stage musical's participation in the broader cultural project of using madness and disability to draw and redraw the parameters of what constitutes the human subject. To suggest, as I do in certain passages, that Broadway's creative teams, in constructing the psychosocial worlds of their characters, have contributed to the circulation of exclusionary and pathologizing concepts of mental health might be old hat. But the story I tell is also about stage musicals putting these very concepts in question, disrupting by degrees the rationalism of orthodox scientific criteria for normality and abnormality. From the long-term perspective that I elaborate, the crises of repressive civilized norms of behavior and emotions replayed on the lyrical stages of New York broadened audiences' horizons of expectation by disseminating, over several generations of theatrical production, innovative conceptions of the human subject that incorporate madness and disability into the spectrum of the (new) normal. These developments can be attributed not only to progressive systems of beliefs or radical political agendas espoused by some theater-makers, but, beyond that, to the effects of what Shoshana Felman theorizes as the rhetorical performance of madness, the imprint of its formal presence and operation within and upon an artistic text and its interpretations. Applying the spirit, if not the letter, of Felman's analysis of literature (*la chose littéraire*) to musical theater's multimedia systems of communication, I think of madness as an element of dramatic structure and performance that acts as a work's internal interruption, an expressive and philosophic force that can frustrate or alienate the meaning of the production's verbal statements, "unhinging the very epistemological foundations which they presuppose and postulate, and upon which they are built."[13]

The principle of "nothing about us without us" has been a key element of self-advocacy by disenfranchised groups, including people with disabilities, in political and cultural arenas.[14] In the realm of mimetic arts, the campaign to enable authors and performers from misrepresented and underrepresented communities to take the lead in telling stories about themselves serves as an effective mechanism for increasing their visibility and assuring the authenticity of the experiences represented on the stage. Yet when it comes to theatricalizing mental distress, the embattled question of who tells whose story can be difficult to investigate or organize into a workable program for parity and ethical accountability. Because so many people diagnosed with a mental disorder and/or identifying as mentally disabled can keep their condition secret, passing as "sane" or "able" in professional life, some of the metrics commonly used to gauge the authenticity of stories about more visible forms of difference cannot be easily applied to stories about madness.

Creative artists who have known distress—and it is safe to suppose that their numbers are vast—can still get things wrong by failing various standards of accuracy. They may, for example, misrepresent or underrepresent mental illness in the sense of not adhering to a formal description of a specific disorder or syndrome as codified in the Diagnostic and Statistical Manual of Mental Disorders or other manuals. Yet the search for psychiatric verisimilitude can itself often be a problematic mode of creating and verifying experiences of distress for the stage or evaluating these portrayals in academic scholarship. Our theatrical past teaches us that stage endorsements of the most current of scientific knowledge about mental illness can at times do more harm than good. If we accept, for example, that uncritical dramatizations of hysteria as a female disorder caused by uterine dysfunction, or of homosexuality as a pathological "inversion" requiring a medical cure, are bad ideas, we should also exercise caution about the truth claims and ideological underpinnings of the authoritative biomedical diagnoses of today.

In selecting musicals for this book, I have sought out stories with characters identified as mad, crazy, disturbed, disabled, or mentally ill by creative teams, members of the theater industry, critics, fans, and, more rarely, mental health professionals.[15] For my part, I am not concerned with getting to the bottom of what the depicted experience or disorder might actually be in a medical sense. After all, the characters in a musical are not real people but purely theatrical entities, fictions of the stage. But they come to be written, embodied, seen, and heard in a specific cultural climate that fashions them as mad, psychically atypical, disabled, or sick. In exploring these dynamic, historically contingent economies of signification and meaning, I am primarily concerned with the questions of what madness authorizes in theatrical texts and performances; what factors are at play in the construction of its constituent parts; what rhetorical, expressive, and representational functions it carries at different moments in time; and how these moments fit into the broader history of ideas about human emotions and mental distress. My ultimate aim in this book is not to produce an exhaustive catalog of the stage musical's historical emphases and strategies in dealing with madness, but, rather, to foreground what these emphases and strategies have enabled the art form to do.

MUSIC AND DRAMA OF MADNESS

The work of the creative teams featured in this book relies on a range of mimetic and expressive means to dramatize or stage mental distress. Consequently, theorists of music theater and spoken drama are of equal importance to my analysis. In some cases, music plays a key role in the articulation of the mad experience, but there are also works whose investment in mad themes operates mainly on the levels of verbal or visual, rather than musical, communication. In identifying and describing the formal characteristics of staged madness in different pieces, I generally highlight the combined effects of mise-en-scène, dialogue, movement, dance, and music, recognizing the genre to be a synthesis of many arts and emphasizing the leading expressive means in each specific case.

As objects of theorization, madness and music tend to meet in discussions of the ineffable, operating from a shared space where the laws of linguistic signification and rational discourse break down. Whether examined in isolation or in tandem, these two phenomena have been conceptualized as orders of experience that are qualitatively different from that which can be represented by language.[16] The polemics within musicology about music's tendency to make itself inaccessible to logocentric forms of analysis have paralleled Jacques Derrida's and Michel Foucault's debates over the feasibility of capturing the essence of madness in written text.[17] As John T. Hamilton observes, "Every linguistic encounter with either music or madness thus seems poised on the brink of two abysses: the emptiness of the abstract concept or the awed silence before the ineffable."[18]

These challenges, however, have not preempted musicological inquiry into nonsemantic modes of communication in musical performances of madness. In her seminal essay on the operatic tradition of the mad scene, Susan McClary argues that dramatic music articulates "knowledge beyond the lyrics, beyond social convention,"[19] transcending the meaning of the sung words. The destabilizing impact of mad vocality on the repressively normative content of the opera, as McClary shows, stems from aesthetic devices embedded in the score and the libretto and from the materiality of the singer's performance. The singing madwoman does not only "give voice to symptoms of insanity" but also musicalizes her "subjective feelings." Operating in the space of affective encounters between the performer and the audience, her "music delivers a sense of depth and grants the spectator license to eavesdrop upon the character's interiority."[20]

Analyzing the relationship between dramatic structure and representations of hysteria in spoken theater, Elin Diamond asks if by containing the madwoman's symptoms, the play also "catches her disease."[21] Diamond observes that theatrical realism at the end of the nineteenth century attempted to obscure its apparatus of representation by naturalizing its visual articulations of the world within the box set and emphasizing psychological motivation and retrospective action. The formal characteristics of this new theater first prefigured and then paralleled those of emergent psychoanalytic inquiry and practice: both set up human relations within the space of a private room in order to explore someone's past for purposes of resolution or cure. Christina Wald adds that this type of play shifted the focus of representation from image to words, just as Sigmund Freud's and Joseph Breuer's conceptualization of *petite hystérie*, an alternative to Jean-Martin Charcot's *grande hystérie*, emphasized verbal utterance over the melodramatic spectacle of bodily symptoms.[22] From this perspective, realist modes of dramatic writing attempt to naturalize expressions of inner experience and distress within a commonly recognizable if historically contingent register of everyday life, banking on the audience's lay familiarity with verbal and visual signs culturally coded as madness. Yet Diamond's consideration of hysteria as a site of embodiment also unsettles claims about realism's ability to contain its representations of mental distress hermetically within a specific medical or psychoanalytic ideology. In her analysis, the performance text of the actor's body is capable of overriding the spoken word by means of physicality. In a staged environment where "traces of melodrama's irrationality and its hallucinatory effects still cling to the teacups and upholstered divans," Diamond's hysteric achieves through her body language what McClary's singing madwoman achieves through her voice.[23]

Such tensions between texted and performed dimensions of madness, along with the interplay of verbal and nonverbal means of expression, become even more apparent in musical theater, where technologies of realism have a limited practical use. While this hypertheatrical genre may attempt to pursue a realistic course in terms of plot, dialogue, acting, or scenic design, particularly since the advent of the so-called integrated model exemplified by shows like *Oklahoma!*, the conventions of song and dance inevitably pull the action into a nonrealist register. Echoing McClary's ideas about operatic madness, Raymond Knapp and Zelda Knapp write about the ways in which vocal and instrumental music predisposes the medium to expressions of distress. In their view, "Musicals are likely to push representations of nearly any mental state to the extreme, launched by the already extreme act of singing what would normally be spoken or left unstated."[24] Similar effects, I would add, are also produced through the imaging of madness in tableaux, dancing, and other spectacular means of lyrical communication so common in musical theater.

On a very broad level, then, madness can be regarded as an aesthetic quality of an art form given to reproducing reality hyperbolically. The spectacle of people singing and dancing their way through times of peace and war, while an apt metaphor for the creativity and the resilience of the human spirit, presents our world through extraordinary forms of embodiment and envoicing that suggest a certain loss of reason in all its inhabitants. From this viewpoint, which has flourished in the fields of opera and melodrama studies, musical theater can be regarded as a structurally mad or "hystericized" genre to the extent that its copy of reality is not naturalistically faithful but always somewhat bizarre or topsy-turvy.[25]

This perspective on the place of madness in musicals has the utility of foregrounding the theater as a longtime ritualized practice and institution for individual and collective fantasizing. The hypnotic impact of the music and the striking visuals of the performance downgrade the process of rational identification with the drama on the stage and stimulate one's receptiveness to truths of an irrational or arational order, insights communicated and absorbed affectively rather than cerebrally. D. A. Miller writes that a well-executed musical number is "destined to be, as we say, 'infectious': to be caught and reproduced by the spectators who at a certain moment cease to be simply watching it (with all the distance, the evaluative superiority, that such watching implies) and begin, like the orchestra conductor who rises on tiptoe for a dramatic high note, or flings his arms out with a sudden expansion of sonority, to *imitate it*."[26] The wild improbability of the stage environment refracted through the fun-house mirrors of the musical's aesthetics ushers the willing audience member into a daydreaming mode, in which they are free to entertain and inhabit fanciful realities and fantastic alternatives, nurturing their wishes and nursing their wounds, and testing out the limits of their greatness and weakness as individuals and as a society.

These mimetic interactions between the stage and the audience become still more intriguing when a musical number directly portrays people breaking down or losing their mind. Behind the spectator's identification with characters like Norma Desmond or Mama Rose, there is often a kind of surrender to the viewpoint of madness. When the audience rises in the middle of Glenn Close's performance of "As If We Never Said Goodbye" in response to her declaration that "this time we'll be bigger"—as I witnessed her fans do more than once during *Sunset Boulevard*'s 2017 Broadway run—they no doubt applaud the artistry of their beloved diva. But they also go along with the character's perception of reality, which they know to be skewed.[27] In the musical's grotesquely cruel narrative, Norma is heading for humiliation; in the space of her fantasy, she stands victorious on the precipice of a long-overdue return to her "glory days."[28] The prodigious cheers during and after the number suggest that her outlook may be more captivating and meaningful to the audience, more *real*, as it were, than the actualities of the punitive story within which she is confined.

"Rose's Turn" in *Gypsy* raises analogous questions. Stephen Sondheim explains that while the heroine's show-stopping finish, programmed to solicit a "thunderous ovation," may not suit "the psychological situation" of the book, the number's (and the show's) spectacular success demonstrates that "sometimes a theatrical truth takes precedence over a logical one."[29] The distinction he draws has intriguing implications for the ontological status of madness in relation to the genre. In affirming the ability of theatrical artifice to trump rational logic as a mode of persuasion, he allows the illusion of a character's delirium to displace forms of communication presumed more reasonable and establishes delusion as the sine qua non of dramatic storytelling. This position endorses the phenomenology of a mind in disarray as the more compelling way of making sense on the stage. Madness, endowed with a preeminent power to articulate and transmit insights and sway the audience, comes to stand for theater par excellence.

Such ideas about madness as a bedrock element of musical theater performance that is always already there have greatly influenced my thinking. Yet rather than approaching the art form as mad a priori, I consider the structural changes that the presence of mad characters and experiences provokes in the aesthetic and social content of specific productions and in the medium as a whole. Inspired by McClary's, Diamond's, and Felman's complementary tactics, I wonder: What happens to the fictional universe after it has passed through madness, or after madness has passed through it? What happens to the art form itself?

MAPPING THE MOVES

The history of madness as an object of medical inquiry has been shaped by the brain/mind divide. In the context of US mental health care, it correlates to two conceptual paradigms writ large: the *biological* and the *psychodynamic*.[30] The former attributes madness to physiological activity in the organic structures of the brain and the nervous system, the latter to psychological activity across conscious and unconscious strata of the mind. These conceptual lenses have encouraged different priorities in the choice of therapeutic regimens. The biological impulse in psychiatric thought backs up somatically based treatments, which, depending on the historical context, have ranged from physical restraints and rest cure to trepanning, lobotomy, and shock therapy to psychoactive medication; the dynamic impulse, whose single, most influential expression and carrier has been psychoanalysis, underwrites various forms and modes of talk-based therapy.[31]

Although psychiatry and psychoanalysis are by no means identical fields of thought and practice, they have deeply entangled institutional histories in the United States. The formal introduction of Freud's psychodynamic vision of mental health to this country's medical-scientific establishment is usually traced to 1909, the year of his lectures at Clark University in Worcester, Massachusetts, and the first publication of his work in English.[32] While the growing visibility of psychodynamic ideas in the specialist and lay literature generated in the United States during the decade immediately following Freud's visit is not necessarily—or not only—an index of the dissemination of his theories, it becomes progressively difficult to separate such ideas from his expanding influence in the cultural products of the interwar years. During the 1920s and 1930s, multiple direct and indirect exchanges between and among analysts, neurologists, physicians, asylum psychiatrists, and modernist avant-garde thinkers and artists sustained and promoted the cultural assimilation—or Americanization—of Freudian psychoanalysis. With the medicalization of Freudianism in the late 1930s and early 1940s, when my narrative begins, psychoanalytic models of the unconscious mind entered a period of unprecedented authority in American psychiatry and mainstream culture, a golden age of popularization that lasted well into the late 1960s.

With the midcentury absorption of Freudian ideas into psychiatry, somatic models of mental illness, which had previously dominated the field, moved to a position of secondary importance. Yet biological determinism came roaring back in the last quarter of the twentieth century, as psychiatry disengaged itself from psychoanalysis. Theories of the unconscious mind did not vanish from clinical spaces; their application and development were offloaded to social workers and clinical psychologists, chief providers of long-term psychodynamic treatment today. Yet it is psychiatrists who enjoy high prestige as the supreme authority on mental illness and set the tone for public policy and attitudes in matters of mental health in the United States. If at midcentury, they worked to convince Americans to embrace the psychodynamic paradigm of human behavior and feelings, at the end of the century, they helped swing the pendulum of mainstream cultural opinion to the biological paradigm. As long as mental distress is thought of as falling exclusively in the purview of medical sciences, a brain scan will always win more votes of confidence than a psychodynamic analysis of a behavioral pattern, even though the epistemology authorizing the former cannot capture or access much of what the latter does.

During the years of American psychiatry's romance with psychoanalysis, the question of nurture versus nature outlined itself as another urgent field of contention in the clinical project of conceptualizing madness. In the first three decades of the Cold War, cultural and clinical discourses on mental distress were overwhelmed with a newly formulated, though not unprecedented, social determinism, which presented powerful correctives and challenges to the dogmas of mainstream psychiatry. This period's *sociogenic* paradigm of madness had eclectic origins and expressions both within and outside the medical-scientific establishment. Among its leading internal advocates were psychodynamically and psychoanalytically oriented investigators who did not support the idea of psychic processes as strictly endogenous forces but rather directed psychiatry's attention to underlying environmental causes, laying the groundwork for psychosocial approaches in conceptualizing and treating mental distress. The cultural conversation about madness in the 1960s and 1970s was also dominated by the antipsychiatry movement, whose intellectual leaders developed and promoted the notion that mental illness is not only caused by a hostile social environment but is, perhaps more intriguingly, constructed and even fabricated by it. The deficit of nurture, rather than acts of nature, took center stage in explanatory frameworks promoted by environmentally oriented clinicians and many writers of classical antipsychiatry.

This book's tripartite structure emulates the above trajectory of change in the cultural reworking of ideas about madness, tracing Broadway's creative responses to psychodynamic (Part One), sociogenic (Part Two), and biological (Part Three) paradigms in the arena of musical theater. Part One focuses on the golden age for both psychoanalysis and the American musical. My main historical context here is the centrality of psychodynamic psychiatry and depth psychology to midcentury cultural institutions of selfhood and emotional life in the United States. During this period, which was marked by the commanding power of psychoanalysis in psychiatry, the private space of the protagonist's mind, staged as unconscious fantasy, served as a fertile location for artistic renditions of madness. I flesh out this trend by considering *Very Warm for May*, *Lady in the Dark*, *Oklahoma!*, and *The Day before Spring*. In engaging with authoritative depth-psychological models of the mind through forms of discourse ascribed to the unconscious, these musicals relied on modernist epistemologies and vocabularies of interiority, which were increasingly consecrated by critics and academics as authentic and truthful. The creative teams behind these golden age musicals responded and contributed to the prominence of psychoanalytic forms of selfhood in popular culture and, in doing so, helped launch the project of elevating the art form in critical estimation. Of particular importance to this part of the story is the gradual drift of critical discourses of "psychological depth" into the genre. I examine the assumptive power of these discourses during the midcentury period and afterward, paying attention to the coupling of two categories, "serious" and "psychological," by critics and producers.

Part Two historicizes an emphatic reorientation in the stage musical's representational and conceptual apparatus for madness from the late 1950s through the 1970s in a climate of clinical and cultural opinion overtaken with a tendency toward social and political analysis. Central to this part of the story are the intersecting contexts of socially oriented psychiatry and activism within the specialty; national reforms of mental health care entailing the comprehensive adoption of community psychiatry and deinstitutionalization policies; and the heyday of antipsychiatry. During this period, marked by an explosion of cultural interest in the environmental etiology of mental distress, Broadway's creative teams made increasingly varied attempts to aestheticize madness at the intersection of psychic and social processes, extending the dramatic focus from the interiorized psychoanalytic subject to an externally situated group of people, from the individual to the system. I trace defining features of this trend in *Reuben Reuben*, *Anyone Can Whistle*, *Man of La Mancha*, *Dear World*, *Prettybelle*, *King of Hearts*, *Sweeney Todd*, and *Ain't Supposed to Die a Natural Death*. All these musicals are preoccupied with politically charged questions about the social sources of and collective responsibility for mental distress. Madness is often metaphorized and enlisted in the expression of a liberal agenda, which in some cases assumes a signally antipsychiatric stance.

Part Three situates the art form's reconfigurations of inner conflict and distress in the context of newly urgent biomedical imperatives at the turn of the new millennium. With the reinvigoration of brain-centric thinking in mental health care from the late 1970s onward, the stage musical, like other popular art forms, has preoccupied itself with the biological basis of emotional life and madness. As part of this process, Broadway's creative teams have charted somatic pathways to characters' mental states, conditions, and behavioral patterns. I point out these directions in several musicals, but my case studies are *Charlie and Algernon* and *Next to Normal*, two seem-

ingly unrelated shows that upon closer inspection reveal a formal and discursive kinship. Both address the ideological priorities of brain science and
the politics of illness and personhood under the conditions of biological
determinism. Positing a dichotomous relationship between biological and
psychoanalytic epistemologies of mental and emotional life, the authors of
these shows articulate a rift between matter and spirit and situate the lead
character's crisis within that rift. These dramatic case histories, as well as
other, more recent productions, some of which I bring up in the conclusion
to the book, exemplify the lasting popularity of the psychoanalytic semiotics of depth and madness among theater-makers striving to display the
admixture of aesthetic complexity, psychological nuance, and philosophic
ambition that was once considered the exclusive domain of highbrow literature, drama, and opera.

PART ONE

Madness in the Mind

ONE

"Make a Date with a
Great Psychoanalyst . . ."

Gazing Inward in the Dual Golden Age

"Musical Comedy—or Musical Serious?" deliberates George S. Kaufman
in a *New York Times* essay published in 1957.[1] In a tone of mock outrage, the
indefatigable humorist bemoans the season's taste for "musical versions of
O'Neill [*New Girl in Town*] and teen-agers fighting each other with switch-
blade knives—and killing the hero, to boot [*West Side Story*]." While granting that both pieces are "excellent entertainments and highly successful,"
Kaufman commiserates with the old-fashioned theatergoer longing for "a
show that makes no attempts to delve into either psychological or sociological depths." Reflecting on the art form's changing sensibilities, he wonders if Broadway audiences, "having grown accustomed to crying at musical comedies in recent seasons," may soon move to declare jokes and
laughter altogether inappropriate for this increasingly somber genre. An Al
Hirschfeld caricature accompanying the essay riffs on the theme, imagining the gruesome outcomes of the tragic turn in musicals. In the foreground
of the drawing looms a dreary spectacle in which a shackled showgirl,
escorted by a blindfolded executioner, ascends a scaffold topped with a
guillotine while another performer, the next likely candidate for behead-
ing, fights off his captor, a medical doctor. In the meantime, a thinning
ensemble corralled on a proscenium stage in the background delivers high
kicks and jumps, their last hurrah. The caption under the caricature reads:
"The dire occurrences, awful agonies and aberrations of the new musicals
are pushing the old song-and-dance shows off the stage."

With Broadway producers searching for stories "sufficiently grim and
unhappy to form the basis of a musical show," Kaufman muses, where will
it end? "Will *Long Day's Journey into Night* be next on the list?" As if impelled
by his own reference to O'Neill's tragedy, Kaufman concludes his essay by
conjecturing that creative teams might soon start mining the subject of

mental health. The first such musical drama, the writer ventures, could be a contemporary boy-meets-girl story set in "a sanitarium, naturally," where the slim possibility of romance hinges on the odds of the couple meeting each other between their inconveniently timed onsets of insanity.

Kaufman's projections for a musical with mentally ill characters are less a harbinger of an unprecedented trend than an appropriation of the mad images and themes that had been infiltrating the art form over the preceding couple of decades. The audiences of New York and other American cities had already seen a few singing protagonists in situations involving mental health care settings, whether it be in an asylum, as in *Johnny Johnson* (1936, Broadway), *Reuben Reuben* (1955, Boston), and *The Rake's Progress* (1953, Metropolitan Opera), or in a private analyst's office, as in *Lady in the Dark* (1941, Broadway). The libretto for the latter had in fact been penned by Moss Hart and Ira Gershwin, Kaufman's longtime collaborators and respective cowinners of the Pulitzer Prize for Drama in 1937 and 1932. Yet while his prediction for the musical's turn to mental health issues, overlooking these antecedents, arrives somewhat late, the evolution from tragedy to psychiatry over the course of his tongue-in-cheek tirade aptly underscores vital connections between the theatrical and clinical domains at midcentury.

Kaufman's associative slippage from "musical serious" to images of madness, far from coming out of the blue, is in fact emblematic of the changes occurring in the art form from the 1940s to the time of his writing. It is during these years, which comprise the medium's so-called golden age, that the histories of the stage musical and psychiatry begin to converge and intertwine in substantive and, in hindsight, consequential ways. Two overlapping complaints in Kaufman's mock diatribe set the initial coordinates for my narrative about these interactions. One has to do with creative teams' accelerating predilection for "grim and unhappy" stories, identified with the notion of serious theater, the other with their pursuit of psychological dimension. Both artistic tendencies, in Kaufman's view, were responsible for a new kind of high-minded musical entertainment, which was disrupting and eroding the industry's time-honored norms: "no drama, no tragedy, no deep thoughts."[2] Both tendencies, I argue in this chapter and the next, opened up stage musicals to madness, with all its "agonies and aberrations," while at the same time being catalyzed and shaped by it.

The interaction between psychiatric and theatrical notions of mental distress at midcentury occurs most prolifically in the space of the psychoanalytic imagination. The years from the mid-1940s to the mid-1960s, roughly coinciding with the golden age of musical theater, mark the heyday of psychoanalysis in the United States. During this era, Freudian thought, chiefly in its Americanized variants, was at the height of popularity and prestige among the country's mental health professionals, artists, intellectuals, and cultural critics. Nathan G. Hale writes that as psychoanalysis was being absorbed into psychiatry and refashioned as a legitimate medical institution in the 1930s and 1940s, "the smart tongue-in-cheek skepticism of much of the 1920s publicity was replaced by a new seriousness in keeping with the rising status of the specialty." During and after World War II, Freud grew into a figure of such enormous cultural power that texts by both journalists and analysts tended to employ his name as a shorthand not only for all of psychoanalysis but also for "an entire, complex cultural development, such as 'modern psychiatry.'"[3]

Many of Freud's advocates among clinicians took great pains to construct him as "the most famous psychiatrist of all time," who subjected his methods and concepts to the rigorous "logic of natural science" in the noble pursuit of medical progress, establishing a "new science—which we now call psychodynamics, or 'deep psychology.'"[4] Meanwhile, his proponents in university departments, scholarly journals, and other intellectual arenas recast him as a great modernist philosopher with an unprecedented gift for unlocking the deeply buried mysteries of human nature.[5] Celebrating him for proto-existentialist insights into the current impasses of modernity, William Barrett, like many others writing in this vein, insisted that Freud "holds the key" to "how authenticity is to be achieved either in art or life" and teaches us, "creatures of the divided and self-alienated consciousness, to wrestle with the problem of how we are to live truthfully."[6] The consolidation of psychoanalysis as a legitimate medical field through its marriage with psychiatry on the one hand and its institutional alignment with high culture on the other fortified its reputation as a "serious" and "noble" pursuit, in both scientific and aesthetic terms. While repudiations of Freudianism appeared with regularity even in the thick of the golden age, they were largely eclipsed by massive endorsements in medical journals, highbrow periodicals, mass magazines, creative fiction, and Hollywood movies.

The fascination with depth psychology permeated theatrical activity in New York City during these years, informing newly influential styles and techniques, critical standards, and audience expectations. To establish a credible claim to dramatic depth and substance on the midcentury Broadway stage frequently meant to affirm, explicitly or implicitly, psychoanalytic postulations of inner life. That does not mean that the clinical authority of psychoanalysis was uniformly and openly embraced by all artists, critics, and spectators. Yet productions aspiring to a tragic human-ist dimension tended to psychologize characters through terms and methods of personal individuation stemming from the same basic assumptions about the mental organization of the human interior that were being propagated by psychoanalysts, psychodynamic psychiatrists, academic and public intellectuals in process of establishing the high canon of modernism, and journalists covering Freudianism in newspa-pers and magazines. At the heart of these assumptions lay the idea that unconscious conflict was the great motivator of people's thoughts, feel-ings, and behavior. From this standpoint, the relations of depth to surface and of interior to exterior were configured as the relation of truth to lie. Theatrical and literary road maps to human psychology were predicated on the existence of a deeper-lying inner self, to be revealed in contrast to a surface self, and on the belief that it is this deeper, inner self that con-tains a true or truer essence of the person.

That this view of the human subject was an article of faith in the mid-century theater scene was exemplified by the high prestige accorded to per-formers, directors, and teachers associated with the Actors Studio and playwrights like Tennessee Williams and Arthur Miller. With their pro-grammatic insistence on producing authentic emotions and situations, they devised increasingly sophisticated uses of subtext and other means of theatricalizing truth-lie, depth-surface, interior-exterior oppositions so cen-tral to the psychoanalytic imagination. This orientation was in turn encour-aged and consecrated by theater scholars, reviewers, and prestigious award jurors—professional arbiters of taste who determined what counted as serious art theater in the United States.

Creators of musical theater were drawn into this ideological field. By investing characters with a dynamic unconscious, they responded and con-tributed to the ascendance of a psychoanalytic self in American culture and, in doing so, brought the form a step closer to the increasingly coveted if ultimately unattainable status of highbrow art. While traces of this trend are discernible in many musicals, I will focus on four produced right before or during the 1940s: *Very Warm for May* (1939), *Lady in the Dark* (1941),*Okla-homa!* (1943), and *The Day before Spring* (1945). Historians and critics single out this decade as a paradigm-shifting period during which creative teams begin to develop more sophisticated modes of characterization, moving the art form from types to individuals and from musical comedy to musical drama. At the core of the emotional and mental suffering assigned to the deep, tragically tinged character model in these shows is inner conflict, a foundational theatrical concept made clinically relevant and culturally chic through psychoanalysis. These shows update the age-old dramatic question "To be or not to be?" by relocating its origins and operations, as did Freud and the Freudians, to the unconscious. As if to literalize this geography, at certain points in the narrative the action turns inward, as the stage fills with people, objects, sounds, and images collectively representing the mental landscape of an introspecting or daydreaming protagonist in crisis. Articulated in the psychoanalytic register of fantasy, these scenes of mental distress show the characters to be divided within themselves, struggling with the puzzling contradictions of their desires and dreads. The injunction to make up one's mind, an imperative sung or spoken at some point in all of these musicals, promises release from the anguish, but the state of indecision is protracted by psychic defenses. The daily maintenance of a coherent, rational self is undermined by an irrational Other within. The characters, ensnared by the unconscious, are prevented from fully knowing or fully wanting to know what *really* troubles them, even as they seem to be looking for answers to resolve this conflict.

The attractiveness of the psychoanalytic vision of inner life to makers of theater during this period and well beyond is not always the upshot of deeply held beliefs in its scientific accuracy or clinical efficacy. Because psychoanalysis is itself rooted in concepts and techniques native to the creative arts, it always thrived and continues to thrive as an interdisciplinary enterprise with one foot in the realm of aesthetics. In rethinking the parameters of the human mind, creative teams not only borrow popularized clinical concepts but also avail themselves of what is already there as tools of the artistic imagination about the soul or the self, conventions that Freud himself admitted were more useful in obtaining insight into mental affliction than neurologically based diagnostic formulas available in his time.[7] For example, prominent in the organization of dreams, memories, and other psychic experiences and states in the golden age fantasy sequences are allusions, displacements, juxtapositions, condensations, and other forms of abstraction that Freud made central to the scientific study of the unconscious. At the same time, these formations have always been part and parcel of the figurative diction of literature and theater. In this light, as Fredric Jameson writes, "The Freudian topology of the mental functions may be seen as the *return* of a new type of allegorical vision."[8] Other key structural commonalities between psychoanalysis and major forms of twentieth-century drama, both mainstream and avant-garde, include the recursive scrutiny of one's past as a kind of forensic scene laced with clues to the puzzles of one's emotional present; the excavation of repressed feelings or a forgotten traumatic incident as a method of breaking through to self-knowledge, which in turn precipitates a cathartic release and catalyzes a meaningful change or resolution; the presentation and construction of the individual self through narrative and role-playing; and the speaker-listener, encoder-decoder dynamic. From this perspective of mutuality between the two domains, scenes of the interior I discuss in this part of the book not only point to the prominence of psychoanalysis in American culture but also function as incidents of historical activity in the field of artistic production that show off the lyricism and sheer theatricality of the psychoanalytic imagination.

In psychoanalysis and psychoanalytic psychiatry, the primary locus of illness is not the organic structures of the brain but a more abstract entity called the mind or the psyche. The clinical gaze is drawn away from somatic markers of distress to the more nebulous processes in the realm of subjective experiences often identified with the soul or the spirit. As a theatrical counterpart to this epistemology, creative teams situate or discover madness in the delirious swirl of images, sounds, ideas, and narratives comprising the discourse of the deep psyche. These scenes hold a wide interpretive potential in terms of clinical and cultural meaning. Within the register of unconscious fantasy, the borders between psychosis and neurosis on the stage, as in much psychoanalytic theory, are undecidable. The inner experience on display in these theatrical tableaux can signify an uncommonly severe disorder or a kind of generalized suffering characteristic of the human condition. The character may be hallucinating or dreaming, raving or merely introspecting, crying out for medical attention or simply brooding on philosophic themes. This representational elasticity corresponds to the large-scale ambition of psychoanalytic psychiatry in the mid-twentieth century. By bringing together atypical and mundane mental phenomena under the unifying rubric of unconscious conflict, presumed to be a universal affliction, psychoanalysis helped extend the reach of the mental health system to an ever-widening range of feelings and behaviors. Adopting from psychoanalysis the patient's personality as its new unit of interest, American psychiatry turned its attention to discontent, sadness, and other ordinary forms of brokenness and expanded its field of oversight from those deemed severely mentally ill to virtually anyone.

In practice, however, psychoanalysis, despite its capacious view of mental distress, was slow to democratize itself as a therapeutic resource available to all. As one of the characters in *On Your Toes* quipped sarcastically, "fancy nerves" were "for a fancy class" and "not for the mass."[9] The high costs of private analytic treatment kept away members of historically underserved classes, especially communities of color, during much of the golden age. On an ideological level, the American institution of psychoanalysis, especially its reigning medicalized orthodoxy represented by ego psychologists, had yet to develop a keener awareness of Freud's and its own racialized formulations, just as it had yet to reckon with its pervasively dogmatic, restrictive attitudes toward gender and sexual variance. Nor was psychoanalysis well equipped to deal with chronic psychotic patients, most of whom were confined to asylums where the somatic style of biological psychiatry prevailed. These limitations correspond to a deficit of inclusivity in the representational profile of madness in the golden age musicals I discuss. As originally produced, the mad sequences in question center on characters representing high-functioning affluent urban white Americans or, as in the case of Laurey in *Oklahoma!*, characters implicitly modeled on this class.

As the internally divided characters of the Broadway shows featured in this part of the book wrestle with the injunction to make up their minds, so do their creators have to weigh risky decisions about the balance of comedy and tragedy on the stage. For a genre of theatrical entertainment so flagrantly commercial, the philosophic outlook of the psychoanalytic tradition, starting with Freud, is a hard sell. It leaves little room for enthusiasm about the human capacity to hold on to the kind of unreserved, everlasting happiness that seizes the population of a musical comedy right before curtain fall. The depth-psychological interior is inherently tragic. Freud and Joseph Breuer's *Studies on Hysteria* ends with the harsh conclusion that the talking cure can do no more than help the patient move from "hysterical misery" to "ordinary unhappiness."[10] Freud's later concept of the Oedipus complex, itself derived from classical tragedy, is no less pessimistic: it reconstitutes the adult self as fallen from the paradise of childhood, estranged from the world and itself, damned to a lifetime steeped in self-doubt and haunted by irreversible grief. Freudian theory is, of course, far from monolithic. It tends to question and revise itself within the space of one text as well as from one text to another. In dramatic terms, however, it adheres invariably to the modernist sensibility, which Allen Thiher links to a "postromantic matrix in which conflict, loss, and alienation are the essential themes to characterize the self in relation to the world that always deceives it."[11] Whether one reads the Freud who linked psychopathology to sexual trauma or the Freud of the Oedipal scene or the death drive, one finds variations on the same bleak vision of a constitutionally mad subject frantically fending off disillusionment or capitulating in hopeless despair. Tragedy is the organizing sensibility of the psychoanalytic imagination, which the golden age musical struggles, with mixed results, to integrate into its comedy-driven affective economy.

The art form's acclimatization to this increasingly authoritative vision of the human interior in medicine and culture just before and during the decades of the golden age occurred on different, if crisscrossing, tracks. The comic impulse behind classical musical theater conventions accommodated the perpetual suffering and alienation of the psychoanalytic subject through satire. The generation of creative teams working in the 1930s and 1940s tended to concoct humorously bizarre situations in which patients acted as gullible fools in thrall to the wily word games of an analyst, or, less frequently, as shrewd operators with the common sense to get out of treatment. This includes shows by several of the artists behind two of my case studies, *Lady in the Dark* and *Oklahoma!* For example, the out-of-town version of *Pardon My English* (1933), with lyrics by Ira Gershwin, burlesqued the analytic scene in a pair of linked songs, "Freud and Jung and Adler" and "He's Oversexed!" Both *Johnny Johnson* and *One Touch of Venus* (1943), for which Kurt Weill wrote the scores, featured the trope of a grandiloquent analytic doctor spouting nonsense. Oscar Hammerstein's book for *Very Warm for May*, which I discuss in more detail in this chapter, also contributed to this trend.

Yet as psychoanalysis continued to ascend to clinical and cultural power during the 1940s, it also began to gain purchase in the stage musical as an engine for generating a grim, melancholy portraiture of a human interior that had the cachet of critical respectability and highbrow superiority. An authentic self at midcentury is a divided self. When it comes to sympathetically designed, vulnerable characters, as in *Lady in the Dark* and *Oklahoma!*, psychoanalysis helps supply the necessary pathos, furnishing the stage with a modernist aesthetics for a heroically tragic depth.[12] The images and sounds of a chaotic mind in these musicals, as well as in *The Day before Spring* and many others that followed, code conflicted characters as more layered and truthful than their musical comedy counterparts and, therefore, much closer to the prestigious models of character complexity associated with serious drama, opera, and ballet. The impact of psychoanalysis is also felt on the level of dramatic structure and mood. To the extent that scenes of mental distress persist in these 1940s production texts, they tend to erode the comedic element with depressive qualities of a tragic order. Once established, the discourse of the unconscious, rippling the surface, undermines the musical's narrative progression to the marriage trope and casts a lingering shadow over the conventionally triumphant finale.

As Adam Phillips suggests, "The true havoc of tragedy, from a psychoanalytic point of view, is of disillusionment avoided. . . . When the ordinary catastrophic disillusionments are repressed, they return with a vengeance.

When Paradise is lost, people can't just move on."[13] The joint effect of psychoanalysis and madness in the 1940s and beyond is to frustrate, by delicate degrees, the dominant narrative traditions in musical theater. Madness, serving as the text's internal interruption, teases oppositional scenarios inhering in the space of brooding introspection, ambivalence, and disenchantment. These qualities, manifest in character, structure, and tone, have been the bedrock of regnant definitions of "good" literature and drama. They are also what made psychoanalysis, in significant ways, good *as* literature and drama.

"SERIOUS" THEATER, PSYCHOLOGICAL DEPTH, AND THE MADNESS OF THE MODERNIST PSYCHOMACHIA

There is a remarkably persistent conjuncture of the terms "serious" and "psychological" in the critical writing about the golden age of the Broadway musical. The authors behind many of the era's landmark productions—*Lady in the Dark, Carousel, Oklahoma!, The King and I, My Fair Lady, West Side Story, Gypsy*, and *Fiddler on the Roof*, to name just a few—are said to take up serious subjects and vie more aggressively for the status of serious artists no less worthy of the critics' respect than their peers in more legitimate genres like drama and opera. While a handful of similarly minded collaborations from the 1920s and 1930s, such as *Show Boat* and *Porgy and Bess*, are duly acknowledged, it is the 1940s that is routinely extolled as "the first decade to produce an impressive amount of undisputed classics regularly performed today" and "the decade in which the musical's artistry changed most decisively."[14] As one historian puts it, "a thoughtful public" could now count on musical theater for "dramatic satisfaction" because of a notable transformation in the form's "conception of character." Unlike the "cardboard" stage population of the "never-ever land of happy endings" in the earlier decades, the new heroes and heroines of the 1940s "take on a lifelike dimension. They are—in the best of our shows—motivated human beings."[15] During this belle époque, another historian opines, we begin to see "three-dimensional character[s] in an art form where such depth had not appeared before."[16] To hear another tell it, "Suddenly musical comedy characters weren't cutouts: they had ids, egos, and superegos," a sure sign that the lyrical stage had moved from "mere entertainment" to "a genre of drama."[17]

Even historians who throw into question some of the cornerstones of the golden age mythology tend to adduce character depth and tragic content as a self-evident mark of improvement. Thus, in Scott McMillin's account, "the Rodgers and Hammerstein era" was a time when "serious composers" like Kurt Weill, Frank Loesser, Leonard Bernstein, and Frederick Loewe teamed up with expert dramatists who were unafraid to pursue projects with "a serious line" and "continue the musical's advance into challenging plots." What stands as the triumphant end product of these collaborations in McMillin's analysis is shows with a "*better* book," which leaned into grave moods and themes (e.g., "violence and grief") and "deepened the psychology of the characters."[18] While some, like George S. Kaufman, found these dramatic tendencies disorienting and antithetical to the tried-and-true entertainment formulas of the musical theater industry, other, more numerous commentators writing during and after the golden age have treated these changes reverentially as a symptom of the art form's evolutionary progress toward sophistication and a benchmark for gauging the aesthetic merit of all subsequent musicals.

Such critical assessments are structured by a circular logic: psychological depth on the stage makes for serious art, and serious art is distinguished by psychological depth. These equivalences in the American theater scene were consolidated during the 1920s, when the critics hailed the work of avant-gardist playwrights like Susan Glaspell, Eugene O'Neill, and Elmer Rice as the long-awaited birth of dignified and consequential national drama. As Joel Pfister and David Savran have demonstrated, the newly prestigious formula for a play, derived in part from Ibsen, hinged on the protagonist written as a psychological puzzle.[19] Such characters were enigmatic and often mad figures, withdrawn and brooding on something unseen in their psyche or soul. The fascination with inscrutable inner forces plaguing people's emotional lives, causing them pain and driving them to inexplicable actions is, of course, not a new thing in the theater. But during the first half of the twentieth century, as psychic conflict became the object of the psychiatric gaze, melancholic, ambivalent, and introspective characters got psychologized in a "scientific" sort of way. New mad protagonists like Claire in Glaspell's *The Verge* were written—and classical ones like Hamlet or Lady Macbeth were reevaluated—as tragic creatures at the mercy of the unconscious. These characters are internally torn not only by what they openly acknowledge but also by ideas they do not know they hold and feelings they do not know they are feeling. There is a hidden design to their motivations, hidden not just from those around them but from themselves. The unknown or the repressed torments the soul, leading to suffering, breakdowns, and other distressing outcomes. This model of interiority, Pfister writes, encoded such stage characters as possessing "psychological and aesthetic 'depth,'" which signified to the critics that dramatists in the United States were finally "capable of producing recognizably 'literary' material and expressing distinctively 'modern' themes."[20] As Savran adds, the "teasing use of enigmatic situations, characters, and themes," decorated with modernist stylizations, has since proven to be an enduring and ubiquitous feature of "a commercial theater in the United States that has attempted to pass as an art theater."[21] Scenes of a mind unraveling in a state of crisis became an emblem of lofty, tragic, and authentic national drama on and off Broadway.

Christopher Herbert observes that "'deep' is a radically metaphorical value word, a rhetorical intensifier, rather than the descriptive one which it claims to be." He stresses that by exploiting the trope of "depth" to "define as most authentic that which is least accessible to direct observation," psychoanalytic, sociological, and literary texts have routinely "grant[ed] a royal privilege" to what is essentially a "category of invisibility."[22] The psychologizers of the American stage, artists and critics alike, accordingly invested a great deal of prestige in dramatic mechanisms for investigating and exposing the unseen. In novels, as Herbert remarks, depth is "closely correlated with the narrative of solitary individual character, particularly at moments of crisis or even a breakdown . . . that bring secret facets of the mind into view." In the theater, these conditions and effects arise in the act of soliloquizing, which, as Herbert might aver, produces "the illusion of individuality generating itself before our eyes."[23] Over the course of the first half of the twentieth century, such self-narrating techniques in plays by O'Neill, Glaspell, and other experimental writers painted verbal pictures of an invisible interior rooted in ideas and practices resembling psychoanalytic postulations of mind, emotions, and selfhood. The playwrights and actors working in this dramatic mode amplified the role of the subtext, utilizing the unsaid and the half-said as a passkey to the unconscious. Without necessarily alluding to analytic terms or staging the analytic situation, they subordinated the words of their characters to the conflictual traffic of irrational urges periodically gridlocked by ambivalence, suggesting repression, the Oedipus or other complexes, and other such formulations rising to prominence in psychiatry and mainstream culture.

During the golden age, musical theater's analogue to this kind of psychologizing came in the form of songs like "If I Loved You," "Soliloquy," "Shall I Tell You What I Think of You?," "A Puzzlement," "I've Grown Accustomed to Her Face," "Is It a Crime?," "Rose's Turn," and "Tevye's Monologue." The narration of selfhood by the singing characters in these numbers gives a rhetorical picture of a mind grasping for truths that it at the same time evades and delays. Music annotates the characters' thorny progression to self-knowledge, now complementing the semantic content of the lyrics, now disrupting it. A fuller understanding of what is at stake psychologically in such numbers is made available more readily to the spectator than to the character. Conceived as miniplays, these publicly intimate confessions seem to call for a round of psychoanalytic interpretation to complete or enliven their meaning. Their ideal spectator is a shrewd in-house observer who joins in the game, taking a broad, dispassionate view of the individual psychological struggle on the stage from a seat in the dark, while at the same time gathering insight experientially, by feeling with the singing character.

Tracing the consolidation of this approach to the musical number in Richard Rodgers and Oscar Hammerstein's works during the golden age, Andrea Most positions the "psychological" as the antithesis of theatrical artifice. She explains that the influence of naturalistic writing, acting, and staging techniques in the theater scene of the 1940s and 1950s makes desirable the appearance of seamless dramatic continuity between dialogue and singing. In this model, solo numbers and duets "reveal motivations, beliefs, and personal history." The characters "do not redefine themselves each time they sing," as they did so "gleefully" and "self-consciously" in the musical comedy routines of the 1920s and 1930s. The psychologized protagonists of the new variety, when breaking into song, "are not performing, they simply *are*."[24] To be sure, what Most comments on, without naming it directly, is the effect of realism's contrivances to hide its illusionism. The psychological, filtered through the scientized priorities of naturalism, abets this trick. Verisimilitude in this mode of mimesis is maintained in large part through the reproduction of emotional and mental life consonant with the logic of psychoanalysis, which at midcentury enjoys the status of an expert medical science. The word "logic" in this context does not rule out departures from the rational or the linear. On the contrary, the psychoanalytic imagination embraces—and makes oddly coherent and meaningful—what seems senseless, fragmented, and disjointed. It renders psychic conflict logical by giving it a motivation and a history so that any seeming incongruities in individual behavior add up to the sum of a total narrative of the self—a story that, once reconstructed, has a remarkable degree of continuity and consistency. During the golden age, forms of personhood patterned on the truth claims and values of psychoanalysis serve to upgrade the level of perceived accuracy in the imitation of life on the stage and, when extended from book scenes to musical numbers, help smooth out the fault lines between the planes of speech and song, with the result that the psychologized characters Most writes about, even when singing, *seem* less artificial than their vaudevillian precursors.

It can be suggested, then, that the staging of a deep self is enabled through a relation of reciprocity, rather than antagonism, between psychoanalysis and theatricality. While this cooperation may be somewhat obscured by modes of representation masquerading as naturalistic, it proceeds spectacularly in the open when creative teams opt to externalize the internal through abstract, nonrealist methods associated with aesthetic modernisms. Just as in many "straight" plays (e.g., *Death of a Salesman*, *Dream Girl*) and motion pictures (e.g., *Carefree*, *Spellbound*) during the period, the view of the fictive world in such musicals alternates between a measure of pictorial realism and, to use Savran's description, "a kind of psychic mimesis that allow[s] for the projection of psychological forces upon both the environment and the entire *dramatis personae*."[25] The tableau, in which the character's inner world is mapped aurally, visually, and kinetically onto other people and objects appearing in the playing area, comes to mimic what might be happening in unconscious fantasy. The action splits and takes a detour into the metaphysical realm of memories, reveries, dreams, delusions, or hallucinations, promoting and delaying the progression of the exterior plot. This set of techniques literalizes "depth" by translating the spatial imagination inherent in this category, with its necessary correlate, introspection, to the three-dimensional apparatus of theatrical production.

Such techniques have come to define much aesthetic production by the historical avant-gardes in Western Europe and North America, yet they can also be seen as a continuation of the longer history of psychomachic forms of theater. *Psychomachia*, as a form of theatrical presentation in which visual, sonic, and spatial elements of the stage environment, populated by bodies and objects, are employed collectively to represent different aspects of a protagonist's interiority, takes its name from the title of an allegorical poem (c. 405) by Latin poet Prudentius. Scholars of medieval and early modern theater have consistently stressed structural similarities between the morality play (e.g., *The Castle of Perseverance*, *Everyman*) and Prudentius's poem. Both dramatized the battle for the soul of mankind as externalized warfare between various allegorical figures representative of Good and Evil. As Emma Smith explains, "Psychomachic theater saw the play's characters representing not complete and separate individual human beings but qualities or personifications, giving the whole drama the sense of taking place within a single mind pulled in different directions."[26]

By reanimating psychomachic forms of theater and adapting them to the new technological capabilities and cultural imperatives of the fin de siècle stages, modernist proponents of psychic mimesis actively partici-

pated in the period's reworking of ideas about the inner space. In Prudentius, *psyche* (from Greek *psychē*, "life" or "soul") referred to a distressed
human soul, whose "normative state" had been "one of struggle" (*machē*,
"fight") and whose inner architecture had been defined by narratives of
Christian salvation and conversion.[27] Yet the modernist epistemologies of
interiority, shaped by the intensified medicalization of the human mind in
the nineteenth century, privileged scientized over theological modes of
inquiry, reimaging the soul as a secularized container of somatic and mental events. As David Lubin points out, "Previous religious and romantic
conceptions of the soul were besieged, and in many cases, overwhelmed by
mechanistic views" that now located it in the body's nervous system and,
especially in the last decade of the century, by the "experiential" turn in
psychology toward a focus on "a patient's emotional history, filtered
through the proper hermeneutic lens."[28] As various cross-currents of European and American modernisms, such as symbolism, expressionism, and
surrealism, developed new ways of looking inward, fin de siècle articulations of the psychomachia, both artistic and clinical, figured increasingly as
a war within and for the human mind.

As Mark Micale stresses, the art-science relations within modernism
were "*mutually originative* and *reciprocally enriching*."[29] This field of cross-
pollination evinced an inward turn in studying and representing the subjective realm of human perception and thought as opposed to the kinds of
external, objective evidence sought by the positivist gaze of the neurological school of psychiatry and the naturalistic trend in the arts. The granular
portraiture of interiority by modernist novelists, dramatists, composers,
and visual artists was strikingly analogous in texture and design to the
topographies of the mind proposed by dynamic and depth-psychological
theorists, who "posited models of human mental functioning with multiple
strata of consciousness and an interplay of energies and activities between
the different levels." Forged by "creative, selective, and distortive" encounters among clinical and artistic projects, the modernist mapping of interiority proved an extraordinarily prolific and far-ranging cultural practice.[30]

As part of the larger turn in psychiatry toward experiential or depth
psychology, Freudian psychoanalysis emerged as a remarkably originative
site within the modernist project of aestheticizing the inner space.[31] On the
level of textuality, Freud's inquiry into the mind combined modernist innovations such as narrative unreliability and fragmentation with traditional
dramatic structures, most famously in his influential interpretation of
Sophocles's *Oedipus Rex*.[32] While Freud did not create the idea of the
"unconscious," his writing about it helped promulgate general aesthetic

principles that shaped representations of subjectivity in a variety of cultural artifacts associated with early twentieth-century modernisms, including the newly rediscovered, overtly psychomachic forms of theater. Closely allied with the representational practices of inward-looking literary and theatrical avant-gardes were Freud's topographic descriptions of the unconscious. As Françoise Meltzer observes, Freud's theory maps the psyche through rhetorical devices concerned with space, "as if there were a geography of the mind, with the unconscious lying as an area within it."[33] This area is populated by "mental impulses" that "jostle one another like separate individuals," acting out collectively the stuff of dreams, memories, and fears.[34] The topography of interiority in Freud's model thus mirrored the conditions of psychic mimesis developed contemporaneously by modernist avant-garde playwrights, directors, and scenic designers. In the psychoanalytic imagination, the human mind appeared as a kind of theatrical stage; in the theater, the stage resembled depth-psychological models of the mind.

Clinical and artistic hypotheses of the unconscious posited dreams as one of its central forms of discourse. Extending and revising the romantic tradition of dream-writing, psychological and aesthetic modernisms incorporated oneiric images and techniques into their models of interiority. In Freud's epistemology dreams were "the royal road to a knowledge of the unconscious activities of the mind."[35] The new emphasis on dream interpretation had methodological and stylistic consequences for articulating subjective experience and defining the patient's mental landscape in the clinical situation and in the writing of case histories. By identifying the distortions of the dreamwork in manifest dream content, the analyst attempted to unveil the latent content, extracting an underlying stratum of repressed wishes from the depths of the analysand's psyche. The use of free-associative techniques became a prolific means of envisaging the temporal and spatial fragmentation and rupture, so common to dreams, as integral to the structure and texture of the patient's mental organization and lived experience. Similar techniques, such as the "stream of consciousness" method, were characteristic of literary representations of the daydreaming mind in modernist texts by James Joyce, Virginia Woolf, Marcel Proust, and many others.[36]

These shared stylistic features of psychoanalysis and modernist fiction had theatrical counterparts among the avant-garde movements, particularly in symbolist, expressionist, and surrealist performance texts, where the protagonist's subjectivity, like that of the analysand, often took the form of a psychomachic dreamscape. In this kind of theatrical dream-writing, as August Strindberg expounds, "Time and space do not exist; on an insignificant basis of reality the imagination spins and weaves new patterns: a blending of memories, experiences, free inventions, absurdities, and improvisations. The characters split, double, redouble, evaporate, condense, scatter, and converge. But one consciousness remains above all of them: the dreamer's."[37] Exploring continuities between waking and dreaming at the heart of the psychodynamic model of interiority, the modernist aesthetic prioritized depictions of "psychological" realities over those external to the mind. What the audiences saw on stage was not a copy of the observable "objective" world, with its "natural" laws, but a representation of how this world might be perceived by characters in conflict or distress.

The modernist inquiry into unconscious ways of thinking and feeling often unfolded in the space of slippage between dreams and madness. Freud's theory was motivated by "the points of contact where the problem of dream-formation intervenes in wider problems of psychopathology." Quoting Schopenhauer, who had called "dream a brief madness and madness a long dream," Freud was intrigued by the ways in which "the general correspondence between the phenomena of both" blurred distinctions between neurotics and psychotics, the "worried well" and the severely mentally ill.[38] The theatricalization of dreamscapes by the modernist avant-gardes was structured by the same set of affinities. Not restricted to dreams proper, mental landscapes akin to that formulated by Strindberg dramatized a perpetual interplay of reveries, nightmares, memories, delusions, hallucinations, and other psychic processes unfolding in the register of fantasy.

This form of stagecraft had the capacity to stimulate the spectator's identification with a mad character by collapsing the distinctions between quotidian elements of individual fantasy life and the symptomatology of serious mental illness. As O'Neill once commented on his use of the modernist psychomachia, "I want to see whether it's possible to make an audience go mad too."[39] To achieve this effect, "straight," avant-gardist plays like *The Emperor Jones, The Adding Machine, Roger Bloomer,* and *Machinal* animated the phenomenological environment of private fantasy and distress through vocal and instrumental ambient sounds, pantomimic and dance vocabularies, and other tools intrinsic to musical theater.[40] A comparable stage technology of inner life could be traced in a proliferation of dream sequences and ballets in musical comedies and revues in the early decades of the twentieth century.[41] From the late 1930s and throughout the 1940s, however, as the Broadway musical was more actively celebrated for its integration of music, dance, and drama, such tools came to be deployed more systematically to service the new depth-psychological character model of, to quote McMillin again, the "better" book. In light of this formalized dramatic function, the modernist psychomachia was reorganized around an increasingly transparent focus on psychoanalytic views of the human interior. While some of these portrayals trafficked in the light-hearted silliness of the earlier musicals, others began to invoke madness in earnest as a vehicle for pathos and depth. The struggle between these directions is manifest in *Very Warm for May*, the musical I turn to next.

BETWEEN SPOOF AND SINCERITY IN *VERY WARM FOR MAY*

Oscar Hammerstein II occupies a uniquely prominent space in the scholarship about the golden age. The subject of countless accounts brimming with superlatives, he has been canonized as the progenitor of serious musical theater and the great psychologizer of the lyrical stage. In the opinion of Stephen Sondheim, who was trained by Hammerstein in the precepts of musical theater writing, his mentor's innovations in *Oklahoma!* were responsible for a seismic shift in the medium. In lockstep with the dominant historiographic tradition, Sondheim maintains that, with one or two exceptions, there had been "no characters in musical comedy" before *Oklahoma!*, "only personalities." Following the astounding commercial success of the show, however, "'musical comedy' morphed into 'musical play,'" as songwriters and playwrights, emulating Hammerstein's dramatic recipe, began to develop stories with "singing characters who are more than skin deep."[42] Some of the more skeptical scholarly voices have pushed back against such straightforward narratives of historical change, questioning the originality of Hammerstein's "inventions" in *Oklahoma!* and presenting incisive counterarguments to the idea of one work of genius single-handedly transforming the field. Yet even these revisionist histories cannot deny Hammerstein's consistent track record as an author who "psychologized his characters."[43]

Oklahoma! was not the first musical with a book by Hammerstein to stage the unconscious in a series of psychoanalytic tableaux. A narrative ballet doubling as a mad scene in *Very Warm for May*, which opened at the Alvin Theatre (now the Neil Simon) on November 17, 1939, prefigured Laurey's dancing dreams in *Oklahoma!* Designed and directed out of town by Vincente Minnelli and choreographed by Harry Losee, the premiere production, Hammerstein's last collaboration with Jerome Kern, had been overhauled for Broadway by director-designer Hassard Short and choreographer Albertina Rasch, who were well known for dream sequences employing experimental choreography and innovative, sleight-of-hand scenic and lighting solutions.[44] An abundance of talent backstage and on, however, was not enough to ensure the show's success. Poorly received, the musical stayed afloat for only fifty-nine performances.

A backstage musical comedy, Very Warm for May is not itself a "serious" piece, yet its plot centers on the making of a show aspiring to this distinction and involves copious conversation about true art and entertainment in the theater. "It seems so long since we've had a love interest," sighs one of Hammerstein's characters. "I guess you have to be more significant these days."[45] Playfully satirical, Very Warm for May assumes a critical posture in relation to the avant-gardes, highlighting, among other things, the role of psychoanalytically conceived models of selfhood and madness in theatrical hierarchies. Through a pointedly self-conscious manipulation of stage conventions codified as psychologically honest and profound, the musical, in a narrative ballet, draws attention to nervous crisis as a cultural performance, poking fun at the zealous champions of the deep, tormented psyche in the artistic and intellectual circles of New York. Yet at another juncture it also mines the modernist conception of a psychodynamic self for genuine pathos through an emotionally charged display of inner life designed to be sincere and affecting.

The show's plot, set in a summer-stock barn theater in Connecticut, revolves around a new avant-garde production by the eponymous leader of the Ogdon Quiler Progressive Playshop Theatre Guild. Ogdon, who was played by Hiram Sherman in the original production, is the musical's straw man illustrating the excesses of modernist drama. His opus, appearing in Very Warm for May chiefly as a rehearsal within a play, consists of a series of "operettes" telling the story of two eternal lovers, Adam and Hester, whose romance spans two hundred years, from the eighteenth century to the present.[46] The different eras of the ageless saga are unified through an avant-gardist scenic vocabulary and sensibility. Ogdon defines his creative method as surrealist. In Stephen Banfield's opinion, his "modernist pretensions" carry within them "a vaguely Gallic neoclassicism . . . as though Quiler were Jean Cocteau or Guillaume Apollinaire, his musical correlatives Erik Satie or Sergey Prokofiev." The performers' movement vernacular in Ogdon's production is accordingly "purged" of vaudevillian influences and styled to look "arty."[47]

That Hammerstein burlesques not only surrealist but also psychoanalytic modes of inquiry into dreams and madness is made apparent in the

1930s episode of Ogdon's play. For this contemporary sequence, called "The Strange Case of Adam Standish, or Psychoanalysis Strikes Back," the avant-gardist playwright-actor-director has "choreographed the human brain," making himself "the focus of the entire ballet."[48] Despite a glimpse of showgirls in wigs with tentacles representing "loose nerves" at an earlier point in the rehearsal, Ogdon's actual demonstration of the scene shows that what he is interested in, as he writes and performs distress, is not the organic structures of the brain but the unconscious mind. Similar to the psychodynamicists in psychiatry, he sidesteps the physical in favor of the psychic. The stage of the barn theater is strewn with seemingly haphazard pieces of scenery and props suggestive of the vocabulary of the unconscious. These "strangely unrelated things" bewilder and annoy Ogdon's cast and crew. Yet in the artist's conceit, this senseless junk pile of matter holds a plenitude of meaning waiting to be unlocked, enjoining the labor of interpretation upon the spectator: "I don't want it to be clear! . . . They must learn to find out for themselves what a play is about."[49]

The psychoanalytic ballet begins with the solitary figure of Adam/Ogdon sitting in the dark, his head buried in his hands. Ogdon explains that the tableau should be underscored by "ten minutes of strange, eerie music while nothing happens" and "a mood is created." A visual indication of mental anguish, his brooding posture and attitude invite the audience to contemplate his enigmatic depths. Introspection doubles here as madness, madness as introspection. Both are staged as a fetishized aesthetic, a modern ceremony of cultivated psychological suffering to be enacted by an elite class of people initiated into its intricate protocols. As he raises his head, a dancer dressed like him appears on stage and is soon joined by other dancers who will act out bits of the inner drama narrated by Adam. An offstage soprano begins "In the Heart of the Dark," a melancholy song about the mystical, private domain of the mind's nocturnal visions. "Silent, waiting while the romances of fancy fill the world that I own, when I'm alone," sings the voice, charting the inward turn of the action and setting the stage for Adam's chronicle of madness.

His medical history, he confesses, began with a sudden onset of inexplicable "jitters." After trying a slew of ineffective cures, including stimulants, the advice of his astrologist, and Dale Carnegie, and analysis by a local psychiatrist who failed to make sense of his condition, Adam traveled to Vienna to be treated by two renowned analysts, Dr. Schlim and Dr. Squirtschlager. The Austrian specialists only produced a maelstrom of conflicting diagnoses as they struggled to keep apace of the patient's changing symptoms. Yet one morning, just when all seemed lost, Adam woke up "clear eyed, strong in limb and free from fear," because there were no more phobias left for him to experience ("I'd had them all!").[50]

Modeled on the stagecraft principles of the modernist psychomachia, the ballet splits Adam into multiple stage figures who represent inner forces struggling for control over his mind. The dancers parallel the speaking Adam's frenetic narration in a physical rendition of claustrophobia, delusions of grandeur, split personality, the persecution complex, and other conditions germane to the psychoanalytic praxis of the day. The psychodynamic imagination at work in the staging of Adam's interiority is discernible in the functions assigned to the choreographed bodies, particularly in the Dance of the Split Personality, where they perform his multiplying different selves. The mounting tensions between them serve to dramatize Adam's inability to move forward, as he articulates the quintessential statement of the analytic trend in the midcentury musical: "I could not make up my mind." As the battle for his psyche reaches an apex in the Dance of the Persecution Complex, where all "hell breaks loose" and Adam "is beaten into insensibility," the physical confrontations between the dancers and the narrator incarnate the unconscious/conscious duality that informs the entire sequence.[51]

"The Case of Adam Standish" lampoons the fascination with depth psychology among purveyors of art theater and high culture. As Pfister observes, the psychological in the period between 1910s and 1930s was constructed and perceived as a site of personal mystique and sophistication. It became "a value, an identity, and a performance of the self," available mostly to middle- and upper-middle-class white consumers. In the 1920s and 1930s, when much of the modernist counterculture of Greenwich Village was swept away with the iconoclastic, rebellious side of psychoanalysis, highbrow artists and intellectuals "reinvigorated 'individuality' by giving 'psychological' conflict and weakness a sophisticated, 'modern' subjective potency and by making 'psychological' identity fascinating."[52] Ogdon's drama reflects this contemporary vogue. As Brooks Atkinson recognized in the *New York Times*, the musical's "ballet of psychological phantoms" could have hailed from "any number of Broadway playwrights."[53] The modernist psychomachia comes into play as a well-known theatrical vocabulary associated with rarefied forms of "serious," "truthful" emotionality that appeals to white, upper-middle-class East Coast sophisticates like Ogdon. The mad scene does not engage psychoanalysis to shed light on the patient's condition but to enfold his anguished character in the aura of an impenetrable, glamorously transgressive mystery.

The splitting technique that dominates the psychomachia in "The

Strange Case of Adam Standish" also underpins Ogdon's intentions for other sections of the opus, including "All the Things You Are," a ballad enshrined in the American Songbook as one of Kern's masterpieces. Ogdon's staging ideas for the number instantiate modernist priorities of scale with regard to the externalization of the interior. Except in this instance Hammerstein takes deliberate care to tone down the spoof. As if to wall off the potential hit from the show's satire, the script dictates that the part of the rehearsal involving "All the Things" should be "done 'straight' and sincerely." Ogdon explains to his cast members that since the "two lovers are too shy to express their feelings, . . . the duet is sung by their heart voices." The song begins with a verse in which Adam and Hester, played by Ogdon and Liz (Frances Mercer in the original cast), ill at ease around each other, take turns venting their frustration about being unable to reveal their deepest feelings. "If my heart could only find a voice," they muse, setting up the rationale for the number's subsequent shift into psychic mimesis. At this point, two singers come forward and, stationing themselves behind Adam and Hester, sing the chorus, sounding out the concealed, inner dimension of the characters' interactions. The song's lyrics exalt an amorous longing whose gratification is projected into an indefinite future, as the principals sit on a park bench in bashful silence. The music heightens the tension between anticipation and delay through tonal ambiguity, holding off a clear statement of the tonic until the final chord. As the two "heart voices" reach the vocal climax, Adam and Hester, overcome by "the intensity of their unexpressed feelings," are "swept into each other's arms."[54] The song's search for the tonic, its deepest heart, complements the stratification of visible and invisible dimensions in the architecture of the psychological self, as staged by Ogdon. The picture of mental life, amplified and physicalized through psychic mimesis, depicts a dynamic rivalry between an authoritative voice of the interior and a resisting, if overdetermined, exterior, a vision rooted in spatial and hydraulic metaphors echoing psychodynamic theories of mind and emotion.[55]

The musical's vacillation between spoof and sincerity with regard to the dynamic unconscious can be seen as an effect of the art form working through the different creative options afforded by the joint aesthetics of modernism and psychoanalysis. The contrasting ideological positions emerging from the divergences in tone and attitude between "The Strange Case" and "All the Things" are echoed in the tacit competition between Ogdon and Johnny Graham (Jack Whiting in the original cast). Ogdon is described in the script as "pale, aesthetic, intense, and up to a point talented, beyond that point phoney." Johnny is "a real showman," steady and solid. "Sincerity on the stage is his religion," adds Hammerstein.[56] This contest of personalities is further expressed through polarizing constructs of gender and sexuality. Lines are drawn between an "effete" Ogdon, styled as a "mauve-tinted" queer, and a heteronormatively masculine Johnny, a romantic lead.[57] Ogdon's histrionics define what the reviewer for *Time* magazine called the "hysterical side of summer theatres."[58] He is guilty not only of the overkills of avant-gardist abstractionism but also of the excesses of psychological realism. "I want dimension . . . I want method . . . Each line must be dissected," he insists at the first reading of his abstruse play, urging his perplexed performers to "analyze" their given circumstances, no matter how absurdly unrealistic.[59] Having antagonized everyone around him with his incomprehensible directorial demands and "will o' the wispy" writing, the self-indulgent, self-dramatizing modernist throws up his hands and quits the theatrical profession.[60]

Johnny's clarity of judgment and pragmatism, by contrast, make him ideally suitable to the demands of the industry. He is sympathetic to Ogdon's frustration, suggesting that "nearly every man who has written a play" would "rave like that." Yet stepping in as director, he proves Ogdon's opposite, the paragon of common sense and the antidote to "phoniness." The play, in his view, has "some swell ideas," but must be purged of affectation, which he proceeds to do by teaching the performers how to act through song and making a few adjustments to the script and scenery.[61] *Very Warm for May* ends with the cast of Ogdon's play performing "All the Things You Are" on opening night. The choral explosion into song engineers the sense of a triumphant performance on the fictive stage of the barn theater, equating the show within the show, as reshaped by Johnny, to good art.

As a curious parallel, what Hammerstein praises his hero for—his show business savvy, his wholesome wisdom, his fealty to the methods of psychological realism, his mainstreaming of avant-gardist experimentalism—is what the historians will say of Hammerstein's gifts and accomplishments in the next decade. Starting with *Oklahoma!*, his 1940s collaborations with Richard Rodgers remix components of Ogdon's agenda into an effective and influential formula for a sincere, psychologically probing musical theater. Yet the production text of *Very Warm for May* points to a conceptual reorientation already underway on the popular lyrical stage. With regard to psychological depth, at this historical moment musical theater is not just on the precipice of change, as *Oklahoma!*'s hagiographers might insist, but is already changing. In a little over a year, such changes will be made abundantly clear by the success of *Lady in the Dark*, the first "serious" Broadway musical about psychoanalysis.

TWO | **"Make Up Your Mind! Make Up Your Mind!"**

The Neurotic Interior and the Dynamic Unconscious in the 1940s and Beyond

As psychoanalysis entered its golden age of popularization in the United States, the articulation of personal selfhood through unconscious conflict became a salient feature of musical theater. In this new midcentury model, a character's psychological profile is not complete without a potentially harrowing encounter with the storms of inner contradiction. The material extracted from the unconscious, as one confronts the Other within, serves to authenticate the "real" person behind the mask, revealing deeper and, as a rule, darker truths that expose the falsehoods of a surface self. Echoes of mad predecessors from a more "serious" class of theatrical productions—Hedda Gabler, Lucia di Lammermoor, Giselle—help animate and legitimize the aesthetics of mental distress in the golden age musical. But this popular medium does not simply reuse techniques imported from drama, opera, or ballet. It blends them into innovative combinations, developing its own set of conventions for staging a troubled interior. Thriving on the plurality of expressive media and styles involved in musical theater writing and performance, the art form inaugurates its own tradition of madness as a site of psychological depth, intellectual gravitas, and artistic virtuosity.

Intriguingly, the multimedia conventions of musical theater performance make it a suitable vehicle for illuminating the literary and dramatic basis of psychoanalysis. Words play a key role in the semiotics of madness on the stage, but just as pregnant are breakdowns in verbal discourse, displays of eloquent physicality and sonority whereby the body intervenes prolifically, if enigmatically, in the narrative of the self, as it does in psychoanalysis, to express unspoken or unspeakable truths. Leaning at times into metapsychology, the scenes of madness I discuss in this chapter can be said to historicize the predication of the talking cure on language and narrative, as well as its struggles with the limitations and challenges of both.

Some of these struggles unfold in the contentious space of gender and sexual difference. The master plot within which midcentury fantasy sequences are enclosed tends to subordinate psychoanalytic thought to the same kind of apolitical hermetic applications that defined the clinical project of the ego psychologists in the 1940s. As Eli Zaretsky observes, this project "stressed the strength and adaptability of the ego in the practical world, while also maintaining that the deeper experiences of life were to be found in the private realm." It routinized self-contemplation, schooling patients in the art of getting in touch with their personal depths, but "it also aimed at keeping emotionally charged or so-called moral issues out of politics."[1] As if in lockstep with the Freudian orthodoxy, the 1940s musicals I consider next relate neurotic flare-ups to instinctual and sexual foundations of individuality, amplifying the role of desire and repression in familial and conjugal situations. The madness of the private interior, while tenuously linked to interpersonal and other contributing factors in the outer milieu, is isolated from the larger societal issues at stake. Not surprisingly, there are more madwomen than madmen in the musicals of the 1940s. For these variations on the damsel in distress, the road to salvation entails an analytic assessment of the repressed sexual problem and culminates in that fossil of a musical theater ending: the heteronormative marriage. When it comes to the implied sources of distress, the obstacles to mental health or happiness are to be discovered within the psyche, in the cryptic schemes of the unconscious rather than in the flaws of the political system or the rigors of the oppressive culture.

But psychoanalysis also has a parallel, arguably more consequential history as a discipline that, prefiguring the legacy of poststructuralism and postmodernism, radically questions the stability of any system of truth, including its own. To the extent that psychoanalytic thought, as Stephen Frosh writes, tends to "unsettle situations by revealing the unconscious elements that feed into them," exposing "existing powers of domination," the scenes of mental distress in these 1940s musicals can be said to serve a latent socially critical function.[2] From the vantage point of contemporary hermeneutics animated by the priorities of feminist and queer theory, the reading of the effects of psychoanalysis in these works as restrictive can also be flipped on its head. Indeed, does a musical like *Lady in the Dark* only reinforce the patriarchal master narrative that shapes its story, or does it also throw it into question? This is particularly important given the long and rich history of queer labor in the musical theater scene and the nearly cultlike status of the art form among queer audiences. The formation of intimate affective bonds between theatrical stories hostile to otherness and the actual historical referents of this otherness cannot be explained away as a passively complicitous concession to the hegemony of heteronormativity. To explore these interrelations, my discussion of *Lady in the Dark* outlines some ways in which a musical that appears to endorse the scientific rationalism of a white patriarchy can also be recognized as a historical site of battle with it. Here I follow Eve Sedgwick's notion of reparative reading. As she stresses, "What we can best learn from such [reparative] practices are, perhaps, the many ways selves and communities succeed in extracting sustenance from the objects of a culture—even of a culture whose avowed desire has often been not to sustain them."[3] The excess of meaning generated through the images of the unconscious on the stage underscores a multiplicity of viable identificatory positions that could, in turn, be appropriated toward critical ends in new productions. Such opportunities abound in *Lady in the Dark*, a musical riven by the same internal antinomies that have shaped the cultural and clinical history of psychoanalysis.

THE INNER CONFLICTS OF *LADY IN THE DARK*

Unique in making psychoanalysis its central subject, *Lady in the Dark*, with a book by Moss Hart, music by Kurt Weill, lyrics by Ira Gershwin, and decor by Harry Horner, was the most extensive and focused dramatization of a clinically defined madness by musical theater artists in the golden age. The story's protagonist, Liza Elliot, is a fashion magazine editor who suffers from depression, anxiety, insomnia, and other seemingly inexplicable symptoms. Her distress escalates as she struggles to figure out the elusive nature of her shifting desire in her relationships with men. Alternating between three locations—her psychiatrist's office, her workplace, and the mazelike landscape of her dreams, reveries, and memories—the action traces the steps by which the heroine, in the course of analytic treatment, comes out of the "dark" of repression into the light of self-knowledge, which appears to have a salutary effect on her mental health. The original production, which opened at the Alvin Theatre on January 23, 1941, was an instant critical and popular hit. The show played 467 performances, went on a national tour, and returned to New York for an additional 83 performances at the Broadway Theatre in 1943.

Lady in the Dark is a cultural product shaped by the far-ranging ambitions of medicalized psychoanalysis, which was just entering the most influential—and the most dogmatic and moralistic—period in its institutional career in the United States. Baked into the musical's book is a cultural campaign to turn psychoanalysis into a supreme expert science that can explain all forms of human discontent through a systematic application of universalizing master narratives like the Oedipal complex. Yet the eccentric contents of one's unconscious and one's life experiences, in psychoanalysis and on the stage, show one's psyche to be singular and unrepeatable. The mad structures of individual subjectivity resist programmatic attributions to a common, one-size-fits-all tale of origin. While the psychiatrist's application of the Oedipal system in *Lady in the Dark* attempts to contain the polysemic material of the patient's unconscious within an airtight hermeneutic framework, what happens in the analytic tableaux on the stage surpasses and writes over the didactic mission of the interpretation he advances. The upshot of this dynamic is a musical at odds with itself, its internal divisions mirroring the conflicted nature of both the mind and the science presented on the stage.

The efforts of *Lady in the Dark*'s creative team to appeal to the highbrow intelligentsia without losing the mainstream entailed an anxious negotiation of Broadway's entertainment codes on the levels of form, genre, and tone. "Mr. Hart clearly wishes his new piece to be taken seriously, as a dramatic work as well as a spectacle," commented the *New Yorker*'s reviewer.[4] For much of its duration, *Lady in the Dark*, billed as "a musical play," divided the action between long, spoken scenes styled as naturalistic drama and similarly long, abstract musical sequences, which Weill envisioned as "three little one-act operas."[5] The former sections, occurring on the plane of material reality in Dr. Brooks's consulting room and Liza's office, were directed by Hart, while the latter, set in the psychical reality of Liza's mind, were staged by Hassard Short and choreographed by Albertina Rasch, who had collaborated on the mad sequence in *Very Warm for May* on the stage of the same theater just a season ago.[6] Through a judiciously measured dose of banter and comic business in the "straight" play and a proliferation of musical theater vernaculars and scenic extravaganza in the so-called operas, the creative team took steps to ensure the show's box-office success. But in marking out different portions of the action as belonging to the province of "serious" genres, they also sought to distance themselves from what Hart described dismissively as "the tight little formula of musical comedy."[7] Through identification with literary drama and opera, *Lady in the Dark* staked out a claim for inclusion in a higher class of theatrical productions, which, like the works of Eugene O'Neill and Alban Berg, spoke to elite, well-educated audiences.

The show's enthusiasts among the critics welcomed the ways in which the musical's visual opulence and bursts of levity were subordinated to the larger dramatic scheme that had the weight and appearance of a brooding modernist drama with a tormented character at its center. Invoking Shakespeare, Wagner, Proust, and Pirandello, they deployed the conjoined notions of serious theater and psychological depth in positioning *Lady in the Dark* as a work of substance and sophistication. Brooks Atkinson's coverage of the show in the *New York Times* typifies this critical vein. As he sees it, *Lady in the Dark* is a modern masterpiece because of its tragic ambitions. "A dramatic story about the anguish of a human being," it deals with the "emotional mystery" of a "nervous wreck" and, in resolving the heroine's "subjective crisis," offers "terrifying insights into people's relationships." What's more, the show explores and expresses these lugubrious themes through "a new, centrifugal dramatic form," which fuses drama, music, dance, and scenography in a way that is revolutionary not only for musicals but for the whole of American theater. "Let's call it a work of art," Atkinson rules solemnly.[8] The show earns this portentous distinction in great part through its fluent command of a "depth" aesthetics modeled on canonized genres, and its inventive translation of this aesthetics into musical theater terms, which it both reforms and transcends.

The role of Liza, praised by a Boston critic for being "a perfect Hamlet of a part," opened up new expressive possibilities in the relationship between madness and musicals and set new standards for creating and judging performances of psychological depth in the medium.[9] Gertrude Lawrence, who originated the part of the neurotic analysand, was showered with love letters in the press for a performance of "extraordinary insight and virtuosity."[10] Because of the show's bifurcated mimetic style, she appeared as a modern tragedienne in the realist domain of the play and a musical entertainer in the nonrealist realm of the operas. Watching her, Atkinson exclaimed, was like "gazing in rapture at a tornado."[11] Lawrence proved herself a serious actor and a lyrical "goddess."[12] Today a mad role requiring impressive acting chops in addition to singing is a common means of demonstrating dramatic range, stylistic versatility, and psychophysical stamina in musical theater, thereby establishing one's diva credentials. Angela Lansbury, Betty Buckley, Patti LuPone, Donna Murphy, Bernadette Peters, and Christine Ebersole are all associated with their star turns as distraught heroines. *Lady in the Dark* is situated historically at the start of this trend on Broadway's lyrical stage. As *Variety*'s critic phrased it at the time, Lawrence was "the star in the full, literal cosmic sense." Impersonating the "nerve-tortured maladjusted swank magazine editor," the "British wonder woman" was "seldom off stage," now delivering a chilling, "almost psychopathic scene in semi-dark stage," now "wham[ming] across a sizzling hot song and dance."[13] By ushering the tragic mad figure of drama and opera into the realm of popular musical theater, *Lady in the Dark* inaugurated the now standard utility of nervous breakdown as a vehicle for a bravura performance in the genre. Liza/Lawrence in that sense is the ur-madwoman of the American stage musical.

Lady in the Dark earned its widespread reception as a "seriously-told story" of a woman in "soul torment" not only by appealing to the semiotic codes of more prestigious theatrical genres but also by thematizing and mimicking psychoanalysis, which was fast emerging as a leading scientific truth discourse in the mental health arena.[14] In 1938, the American Psychoanalytic Association established a new policy, according to which "only physicians who had completed a psychiatric residency at an approved institution could become members."[15] The rule was emblematic of the broader movement to scientize and medicalize the psychoanalytic enterprise, which would catapult a conservative Freudianism, identified especially with ego psychology, to a position of unprecedented power within American psychiatry over the course of the next decade. Dr. Lawrence S. Kubie, who was Hart's analyst at the time, was directly involved in this crusade to legitimize psychoanalysis as a medical field.[16] He vetted the playwright's ideas for the musical at different stages of its development, imprinting his clinical views on *Lady in the Dark*'s narrative.[17]

There was a mutually beneficial dynamic between the Broadway show and the strengthening Freudian orthodoxy represented by Kubie. Hart dedicated the musical to his analyst and, in his painstaking efforts to dramatize the modern science of the soul faithfully, promoted a reverential attitude toward psychoanalysis. Kubie, in his turn, publicly endorsed Hart's book on several occasions.[18] In his preface to the Random House edition of the libretto, for instance, the analyst confirmed that "from the technical psychiatric point of view the portrayal, both of the illness and its evolution out of her [Liza's] normal life, is accurate in the subtlest details." But he also seized on the show's utility in raising mental health awareness and educating the theatergoing public about his field. His reading of the plot in the preface extended Liza's affliction, "the neurosis of the so-called normal," to "any woman—and, with some transposition of forces, to any man." Here was a case history, he charged, that "could be the document of almost any human life." As such, it could have "profound and social significance," for thoughtful playgoers might, in time, come to admit their own unhappiness and resolve to seek "medical therapy."[19]

Pursuing a serious, clinically credible approach to mental illness, Hart furnishes the play's action with the dramatic tension and teleological drive of a classical analytic case history. His copious stage directions fleshing out Liza's movements, gestures, facial expressions, and speaking voice are unusual for a musical theater libretto from that period. The dramaturgy of her symptomatic act in the "straight" scenes requires a show of meticulously planned stage business. In the consulting room, Liza "hesitates," "fighting hard for a moment of calm before she can speak," "pulls at the cigarette nervously," "lapses into silence," starts to speak "angrily," "takes a moment to steady herself," "laughs shortly," and "looks uncertainly about." "Her hands go to her eyes and cover them," "her voice sounds strange as though she could not quite control it." The publishing office scenes are likewise punctuated with plangent signs of her "enormous effort at regaining some kind of self-control." We see her "slamming the paper cutter she has been toying with down on the desk," "exploding" and flinging a cigarette box at her interlocutor, or, lighting another cigarette "nervously," standing "quite still" and staring into space "unseeingly," "as if hypnotized." When everyone leaves, she "crumples into the desk chair, her head and her arms on the desk" and "begins to cry, violently, uncontrollably." Or she "flings herself down" on the couch, lapsing into a hypnoid state. Or paces "up and down. Up and down."[20]

In these scenes, Hart constructs Liza as the contemporary neurotic heroine of the legitimate stage, hearkening back to Ibsen's plays, which provide an enduring model for psychological drama in the United States. Elin Diamond writes about Ibsen's form of realism as a theater of knowledge that "legitimizes itself through its ability to know, to respect, to reflect the truth." It endows the female body with "the enigma of hysterical symptoms" and positions the spectator to recognize and verify the authenticity of the action and its lifelike stage signs.[21] This dramatic paradigm, in the manner of a detective story, encourages a willingness to hunt for psychological clues to the riddles of her bewildering behavior. Like Hedda Gabler, Liza "is to be watched with interest."[22] Dr. Brook and the audience look at and listen to the distraught woman as a living scientific text, sifting through subtext-laden fragments of physical action and speech to get to an underlying truth, which this form of realism both suppresses and reveals.

The dream operas hold pieces of the same psychological riddle but represent mental phenomena through a different mode of mimesis. This theater of knowledge, figured as the opposite of pictorial realism, distances us from the world of the "straight" play through the self-consciously artificial conventions of operetta, vaudeville, circus, and minstrelsy. By the turn of the rotating stage, we are transported to a stylized domain of theatrical pageantry over which presides the medium of music, its abstract properties ideally suited to the task of dramatizing the structure and texture of mental symbolization in unconscious fantasy. The dreaming interior in the operas is a fantasmatic merry-go-round of words, images, themes, and narratives, chaotic with fleeting coincidences and contradictions. These tableaux utilize the shared language of artistic and psychological modernisms to present content that does not denote itself but always refers to something else, which is beyond the grasp of the conscious mind. Each of the dreams, as in Freud's theory, is "a projection, an externalization of an internal process."[23] The discourse of unconscious fantasy, however, eschews literality. In making visible what happens underneath the realist surfaces of the drama—what is repressed by its naturalistic vernacular—the operas generate their own obfuscations, occluding the latent dream content with the fanciful distortions of the manifest content. Inside the subtext of the play is enclosed another subtext.

As Dr. Brooks (Donald Randolph in the original cast) and the audience watch these abstract, lavishly produced operas set in Liza's psyche, so does she—from the inside, as a character physically involved in the dream's action but always somewhat alienated from it, and from the outside, as analysand, temporarily offstage but invisibly present as the raison d'être for the performance on the stage. In these scenes of the interior, Liza's body is no longer the chief signifier of madness, at least not in the way it is in the spoken scenes. She may still be given to histrionic expressions of distress we have seen in her waking life (e.g., "screams," "hides her face"), yet her stage figure, as embodied by the actor, plays an auxiliary role in the larger signifying scheme of the psychoanalytic tableaux.[24] On display are fragments of her inner self caught in a kaleidoscope of dramatic arrangements engineered by fantasy. She is an imagined character still readable as herself: a chic celebrity ("The Glamor Dream"), a bride ("The Wedding Dream"), or an entertainer on trial ("The Circus Dream"). But the phenomenology of her subjectivity is also diffused through the whole of the dream world, with its multiple other players. The last of the psychomachic sequences sets this dramatic economy in high relief: it shows her simultaneously narrating, performing, and analyzing the repressed memories she is reconstructing in Dr. Brooks's office. Caught in the *mise en abyme* of a Pirandellian universe, Liza is the star, the hero, the author, and the audience of a self-referential theater of knowledge that stages her unconscious.

Wreathed together in these hypertheatrical scenes of the interior are madness and introspection. Liza is, to borrow Dianne Hunter's term, a "psychodramatist" akin to Anna O., whose amazing case history lives on the pages of Breuer and Freud's *Studies on Hysteria* and the mass of literature engendered by that book.[25] Characterized by Hunter and other feminist scholars as the mother of psychoanalysis, this famous hysterical patient, whose real name was Bertha Pappenheim, all but invented the "talking cure" when she devised and suggested to Breuer the method of narrating back piece by piece the story of each symptom to reach its source. Like Anna O. / Bertha Pappenheim, who would refer to her daydreams as "my private theater," Liza stages and play-acts her way through a circuit of hallucinatory texts as she traces the roots of her pain in order to alleviate it. These inward-gazing psychodramas are sites of self-examination, but they are also messages addressed outward to the analyst—and to whoever else is listening in the theater. What do they communicate?

At the core of the dream narratives—and of the whole musical—is Liza's disharmonious relationship to gender norms and expectations. Her performance as "the epitome of the glamorous woman" in the operas is contrasted with her exterior in daily life: "a severely tailored business suit," no jewelry, no makeup. At no point in the treatment does Liza indicate that she is unhappy with her wardrobe and styling. On the contrary, she tells the analyst that she "happen[s] to like business suits and simple dresses." Yet for Dr. Brooks the "austere" way she dresses is a key part of the medical problem, a symptom to decode and invest with psychological meaning. According to his interpretation, her appearance, so obviously lacking in "feminine adornments," is a "protective armor," a psychic defense traceable to an unconscious decision made under Oedipal conditions not to "compete as a woman."[26] Binary assumptions pile up in a rigid hermeneutic framework that holds up compliance with gender norms as the hallmark of a healthy personality. As Bruce McClung has shown, in presenting Liza's gender-nonconforming behavior as a psychogenic pathology in search of a clinical remedy, Hart's book pays obeisance to Kubie's oppressively orthodox ideas about gender and sexual difference.[27] Indeed, the conservative bias with which Dr. Brooks evaluates his patient's presentation of gender is of a piece with Kubie's record as an analyst committed to reforming queer patients. His doctrinaire reading of the plot in the preface to the libretto depicts Liza as tragically stranded in a "no man's land between the sexes."[28] The high-handed essentialist assumptions of the two American doctors, fictional and real, impose a grid of gendered scientific rationalism on the woman's subjectivity, installing conformity to societal standards as a therapeutic ideal.

Strikingly, it is by returning to the Oedipal scene of origin that this "musical *play*" comes to terms with its disavowed *musical comedy* identity. When Liza is finally able to recover her childhood memories, the pageantry of music and pantomime retrieved from the unconscious floods into Dr. Brook's office, a space hitherto reserved for the realist drama. The play and the opera—with their attendant Lizas, a straight actor and a musical theater diva—achieve simultaneity, as the analysand comes into possession of a new narrative of her past.[29] This moment of catharsis, marked by her recovery of the long-forgotten song, "My Ship," installs integration in place of conflict, mending the heroine's divided soul at the same time as it mends the musical's. The transformation is made complete in the next and final scene, as Liza—and her speedily chosen suitor—sing "My Ship" together in the middle of the publishing office as *musical theater characters*. The swelling sounds of the orchestra reframe this opaque, melancholy song as a romantic duet for the happy couple, to be sung "gaily—happily."[30] The Oedipal cure has yielded a canned theatrical conclusion. As if forced to embrace its own "essential" nature, the show has assumed a conventional form, ending as a musical comedy.

In characterizing the finale this way, however, I am not suggesting, as some scholars have, that its rote didactic message was persuasive or even important to all spectators. The Broadway musical, in part because of the interruptive nature of its storytelling aesthetics, has had a prolific history as an arena for alternative spectating practices by members of minority groups excluded from mainstream narratives. As Ralphe Locke says, "To some extent, it comes down to how much one wishes to let the outcome of a plot determine the reading of everything that came before."[31] For queer viewers, identification with the story may come from the accidental, marginal aspects of the production, glimpses of ironic displacement in the text's mainstream ideology, slips of theatrical tongues lighting up what is repressed but present on the stage. This viewing and listening position crafts of such moments an alternative supertext of counternarratives and counteraffects that affirm the lived experience and inside knowledge of otherness.

Liza's dream operas appear crowded with images and sounds, which, bypassing the overdetermined stipulations of Dr. Brooks / Kubie, can land as messages of solidarity with the queer community in the audience. How terrifying the grotesque vision of the heterosexual wedding in the second dream, for instance, with six identical brides in red wigs dancing with men like synchronized automatons, as she watches. The fantasy sequence, "winding up in a cacophonous musical nightmare," paints a frightening picture of the societal pressures to marry and "be beautiful," from which Liza is seen to recoil, "her hands pressing against her ears to shut out the accusing voices." Shortly after passing through this terror, Liza, alone in her office, attempts a makeover. In a rush of momentary capitulation, she snatches an evening dress off a dummy and changes into it with an air of defiance. As she steps into this masquerade of normative femininity, she is "crying again—wildly now." This is not an enchanted Cinderella-before-the-ball moment. No jubilant finale to act 1 follows the transformation, only a hummed snatch of a phrase from "My Ship" caught in her throat between the sobs.[32]

During the trial in "The Circus Dream," she presents her defense by performing "The Saga of Jenny." As Naomi Graber observes, this "blues number about a woman of dubious sexual morals underscores the possibility that Liza's newly awakened sexuality will take a queer turn."[33] Indeed, since Liza has been pushed to choose between two identities, Executive or Enchantress, her emphatic injunction in the song that one mustn't make up one's mind is a resistive move to treat these options as false, arbitrary constructions and the absurd legal proceedings predicated upon them as invalid. Raymond Knapp and Zelda Knapp's discussion of this eleven o'clock number pays equal attention to what precedes it, which is another showstopper, "Tschaikowsky." This patter song is performed by the Ringmaster, a fantasized figure played by Russell Paxton (Danny Kaye in the original cast), a "pansy" character who works for Liza's magazine.[34] As these writers note, the seeming irrelevancy of Russell's number to the arc of the dream "is consistent with his marginalized place within the story, where, as an 'invert,' his principal function is to provide a cautionary example regarding Liza's tampering with gender roles."[35] The back-to-back placement of these eleven o'clock numbers extends them into one another intertextually as a double act dramatizing the compulsion to speak out while at the same time circumventing the risks of self-disclosure. At the time of the original production, the pairing brings to mind a real-life duo, Noël Coward and Gertrude Lawrence, who had appeared together in several shows with a queer subtext and were part of the down-low gay and bisexual scene in New York's bohemian circles.[36] Calling up these transgressive referents (with a wink at Hart's sexual identity), the effeminate man and the butch woman on the stage burst through the pathologizing discourses of the psychoanalytic play in a coded address to "anyone with vision," a select group of spectators possessing an intimate familiarity with the valuable, at times life-saving skills of a strategically assumed indecision.[37]

Not to make up one's mind is to remain in madness. Yet in the musical this very gesture simultaneously occupies different positions of meaning. For Dr. Brooks, to linger in the space of madness is to prolong one's pathological suffering. The field of signification in Liza's psychodramas, however, also slides into another position to tell a rivaling story, in which her madness is not a blind flight from one's "essential," biological nature, as Dr. Brooks would have it, but a consequence of the intrusion of socially driven biases into medical thought; not a psychic defect, but the index of one's place in a patriarchal culture. From this standpoint, not to decide means not to accept the rules of the curative project inscribed in the libretto, to contest the imposition of pathology, to undo the definitions of the master plot. These impressions are fleeting. But the counternarrative glimpsed in Liza's dreams and solitary office scenes sabotages the machinery of the play's clinical teleology so that the formulaic ending rings a false note. "My Ship," as David Savran remarks, feels as though it "effects a resolution that does not resolve" and "refuses a happily ever after."[38] Indeed, the briskness with which the creaky marriage trope is shoehorned into the musical's closing minutes betrays a haste to cover over what occurred before, to close off the possibility of another reading prompted by the polysemic material of unconscious fantasy on the stage of Liza's "private theater."

The status of Liza as the author of her dreams is of course only an effect of the text, a fiction engineered by the joint labor of the creative team. But this effect, amplified through the rhetorical echoes of Anna O's story, points to the embeddedness of feminism in the psychoanalytic discovery of the unconscious. Toril Moi writes that "psychoanalysis was born in the encounter between the hysterical woman and the positivist man of science," setting in motion two competing impulses within the new field. On the one hand, Moi notes, endemic to classical psychoanalysis, including Freud's writing, is a tendency to resist the "irrational discourse of femininity," because of the havoc it wreaks in settled androcentric modes of knowledge making. Tripped up by what he does not understand or won't accept about women's sexuality—that area of the unknown once characterized by Freud as "the dark continent for psychology"—the "man of science" deploys rationalism to reassert his imperialist authority and keep gender hierarchy from crumbling. On the other hand, by letting the madwoman tell her story, by listening to her, this newly born medical enterprise shows a motivation to reshape its own epistemology, "a will to consider *her* discourse as one ruled by its own logic, to accept the logic of another scene. As long as this contradictory project is in place," Moi writes, "the discourse of the hysteric continues to unsettle and disturb the smooth positivist logic of the man of science."[39]

This interplay between "a colonizing rational impulse" and "a revolutionary effort to let female madness speak to male science" has structured a great deal of psychoanalytic activity, even during some of the most restrictively moralistic moments in its cultural and clinical history.[40] The production text of *Lady in the Dark* is caught up in a confrontation between these contradictory positions. As an artifact of the early 1940s, this musical—tellingly titled *I Am Listening* in early drafts—historicizes a paradoxical dialectic of exclusion and inclusion, domination and emancipation, regression and advance at the heart of American Freudianism writ large. By releasing the rhetorical machinery of the unconscious into the production text, the authors of *Lady in the Dark* produce a multivalent field of madness. Diffused through the master plot of the Oedipal book is the evidence of another story that critiques the domineering essentialism and absolutism of the Freudian orthodoxy and appeals to the other side of psychoanalysis: a discipline at peace with uncertainty and skeptical of its own truth claims in the encounter with the unconscious.

BRINGING UP *OKLAHOMA!*

Not two months after *Oklahoma!*'s historic Broadway opening on March 31, 1943, which inaugurated a record-breaking run of 2,212 performances, Oscar Hammerstein II published his account of this musical's gestation in the *New York Times*. Likening the show to a human being, he couched its biography in the popularized terms of psychoanalytic developmental theories. His psychohistory proceeds from the premise "well established by psychiatrists that what happens to us in the first critical years of our childhood is a prime determining factor in the kind of men and women we turn out to be." This grandiose framing, playful as it may be, allows Hammerstein to build a progress narrative of *Oklahoma!*'s "upbringing," tracing the work's "virtues" to "basic decisions made quite early in its life." The playwright writes that "the child *Oklahoma!*" was conceived because its future parental figures had detected in Lynn Riggs's 1930 play, *Green Grow the Lilacs*, from which the musical would be adapted, "real dramatic vitality under a surface of gentleness." What followed was an intricate adaptation process motivated by the material's alluring prospect of subterranean energies, which—once unearthed, regulated, and exploited—assured the child's maturation into the successful "adult, now flourishing at the St. James."[41]

According to Hammerstein's psychobiography of the musical, the single most important reason for *Oklahoma!* growing up to be a smash hit is that it gives the Western landscape of the past an "essentially modern" stylistic treatment. Lemuel Ayers's settings, for instance, are "Indian Territory at the turn of the century expressed in the stage-design idiom of 1943." The same principle governs Hammerstein's lyrics, Richard Rodgers's music, Rouben Mamoulian's direction, and Agnes de Mille's choreography, with the result that, "deriving from a source that is real, the whole production is lifted a plane above literal reality." Hammerstein concludes that this elevation is "almost an obligation for a musical production." Under such conditions, dancing, for instance, turns out "better" and "more exciting," because, despite "authentic figures and genuine hoe-down steps," it looks like it "might be daydreamed by a young girl who was going to a dance."[42] Embedded in the mimetic techniques through which Oklahoma! manipulates different orders of reality is the contemporaneously fashionable idiom of psychological modernism. Lining the aesthetic universe on the stage with reverie, this musical draws on the increasingly authoritative psychoanalytic postulations of human interiority and uses them to boost its own critical image as a true work of art, at once au courant and timeless.

The two people directly responsible for the inward turn in Oklahoma! are de Mille and Hammerstein. As we have already seen, Hammerstein was not new to the modernist psychomachia. In partnering with de Mille, however, he found a collaborator who had a fresh, vibrant perspective on this representational mode and its expressive capabilities. Having been in psychoanalysis, de Mille could draw on her own personal experiences as a patient. Just as importantly, coming to musical theater from the modern dance scene, which thrived on psychodynamic dramatizations of inner life, she had at her disposal a whole set of aesthetic tools compatible with psychoanalysis. Susan Jones traces de Mille's focus on the expression of psychological states and storytelling devices favoring the perspective of a single protagonist to her apprenticeship stint in England with Rambert Ballet and especially her work with choreographer Antony Tudor. It was during those years that both de Mille and Tudor absorbed and developed the modernist psychomachic aesthetic that came to define much of their subsequent work in the United States during the 1940s (e.g., de Mille's Fall River Legend, 1946; Tudor's Pillar of Fire, 1942).[43] Among other contemporary choreographers who created psychomachic ballets influencing de Mille's work were Rasch (whom she once called "the best"), George Balanchine, and Martha Graham.[44]

In its ballet sequence, "Laurey Makes Up Her Mind," Oklahoma! works out a musical theater counterpart to Freud's psychodynamic vision of dreams and neurosis. Laurey, who was played by Joan Roberts in the original cast, has trouble deciding which of her two suitors should accompany her to the box social, a typical dilemma for a leading lady in the musical shows of the early twentieth century. In the 1940s, however, the art form increasingly relegates indecision and ambivalence to the explanatory power of psychoanalysis, to be played out in the arena of the unconscious. Pulled into the interiorizing vortex of this trend, Oklahoma!'s heroine assumes a new dramatic stature. The dream ballet refashions Laurey, a farm girl from a mythologized American past, into a sophisticated midcentury analysand on the proverbial Freudian couch. She is no longer the predictably "flat" ingenue, the cliché of musical comedy and operetta that she appeared to be at the start of the show, but an intensely psychologized character that can lay claim to the tragic depth and complexity of the more esteemed, "elevated" genres.

After taking a whiff of smelling salts, Laurey closes her eyes and assumes a restful attitude. In a manner resembling self-hypnosis, she proceeds to sing about dreaming and the coming of night, gradually inducing in herself a trancelike state approaching sleep. This introduction to the psychomachia sets up conditions equivalent to those required by Freud for free association, facilitating "the relaxation of a certain deliberate (and no doubt also critical) activity which we allow to influence the course of our ideas while we are awake."[45] As Laurey reaches a threshold state between waking and dreaming, her critical functions suspended, the stage action slips into psychic mimesis to dramatize a train of seemingly unfiltered thoughts and dream structures circulating within her deep psyche. The content of these visions at once clamors for and obstructs interpretation. The plot of the sequence is tightly controlled through a meticulously selected set of abstractions and symbols, all but telegraphing the authors' predetermined interpretation. Yet incorporated into the story's fabric are distortions and exaggerations designed to cloud its transparency, bearing a calculated resemblance to unstructured, disorganized mental material emerging from a free-associating patient.

Oklahoma!'s approach to the mise-en-scène of the unconscious is in many ways similar to Lady in the Dark's. Yet unlike Liza's dream operas, which seem almost overburdened with words, Laurey's fantasy sequence does away with speech. This tactic, accommodating Freud's pictorial and auditory imagination about dream life, stages the emergence of Laurey's "involuntary ideas" and their transformation "into visual and acoustic images" without verbal discourse.[46] As the medium of modern dance takes over the stage, the singing heroine of the waking world is replaced with a dancing counterpart (Katharine Sergava in the original cast), who is in turn surrounded by other moving characters populating Laurey's mind. Performed to a collage of variations on the tunes heard in the preceding scenes, this spectacle of a wordless interior makes choreographed physicality and instrumental music chiefly responsible for the production of meaning on the stage.

De Mille always insisted that her dream ballet, which closed the first act, radically "changed the quality of the show."[47] This was a remarkable incidence, uncommon in the golden age musical theater scene, of a female collaborator substantially rescripting a portrait of a woman's subjectivity written by a male playwright. According to de Mille, Hammerstein wanted to "end the act with something gay and colorful and up, to send the audience out in the lobby with."[48] Indeed, his initial outline for the sequence states that "the treatment will be bizarre, imaginative, amusing, and never heavy," echoing his comic engagement with the modernist psychomachia in *Very Warm for May*.[49] The choreographer, however, did not share Hammerstein's apprehension about closing the first act with "gloom" and, instead, urged her collaborator to "depress the hell of out them."[50] Calling for "threat," "suspense," and "sex," de Mille redefined Hammerstein's projected treatment of "the problems that beset Laurey" through new plot details involving murder, sexual assault, and a racy saloon scene.[51] De Mille's interventions in the dream script subverted what she saw as the "innocuous gingham-aprony Sunday-school" sensibility of the preceding scenes with "a dream of Laurey's terrors."[52]

Once again, the madness of the unconscious arrives to destabilize the main narrative, derailing its comedy-driven aesthetics of character. Freud states that "dreams *hallucinate*—that they replace thoughts by hallucinations."[53] This assertion not only gets at the irrational quality of situations constructed by the dreaming mind—a quality that *Oklahoma!*'s dream ballet attempts to emulate visually and musically—but also supports Freud's conceptualization of dream life as the nexus between neurosis and psychosis, a place where everyone is mad. As Freud explains, "In dreams . . . we appear not to *think* but to *experience*, that is to say, we attach complete belief to the hallucinations."[54] The odd environment of the dreamscape, as well as everything that happens within it, seems as real to Laurey as the fright she continues to feel when she awakes. This sequence teases out unconscious ideas that have been causing her intense suffering and stages them as hypnagogic hallucinations. In so doing, it extracts from Laurey's depths an approximation of a psychotic experience.

Historical accounts of the show's development reveal differences between the male members of the creative team and de Mille with regard to the desired degree of explicitness in probing questions of sexuality. In his *New York Times* psychobiography of the musical, Hammerstein recalls his and his male collaborators' sense of unease about Riggs's "shivoree" scene, which had "a vaguely Freudian flavor" of sexuality much too risqué and dark to reconcile with the "healthy gayety appropriate to musical plays."[13] Hammerstein, Rodgers, and Mamoulian proceeded to regulate the play's "ribald," "smirky" impulses, diluting the sexually charged ritual down to a brief moment of unmistakably "good natured hazing" in act 2.[55] Contrary to her collaborators, de Mille, in her work on the dream ballet, favored much more permissive attitudes toward sexual expression on the stage. Tapping into the iconoclastic side of Freudianism, which had inspired the feminists and bohemians in the preceding decades, she insisted that "nice girls dream rather dirty dreams. You better get inside that girl's mind. She's a mess!"[56] De Mille's approach shifted the representational and interpretive emphasis of Hammerstein's earlier ballet script to the psychodynamics of Laurey's sexual desire.

Jud's collection of postcards with pornographic images, featured in the Smoke House scene preceding the ballet, inspired de Mille's notion that Laurey might be unconsciously drawn to him and his "absorption in sex, a mysterious and forbidden kind of sex."[57] To articulate this idea, the choreographer introduced a group of scantily clad dance-hall girls, which she described as "the whore parade," into Laurey's unconscious, to suggest that the heroine "somehow vaguely and secretly identifies with the postcards."[58] Employing the critical tools of psychoanalysis to conduct an inquiry into the protagonist's mind, de Mille manipulates Freudian motifs and techniques to spell out a routine psychoanalytic insight that Laurey "is not only frightened of Jud, she is frightened of herself."[59] The psychomachic splitting of Laurey into two figures, one that speaks/sings and one that dances, dramatizes an unconscious conflict over something she is not allowed to do, underscoring the contentious relationship between language and sexuality so crucial to psychoanalysis. The absolute elimination of verbal expression in this sequence suggests a theatrical analogue to Freud's "conversion" hysteria, in which a repressed idea returns as a symptom in the body rather than as a conscious entity in the mind. The dream ballet operates here as a bodily enactment of sexual desire that, due to societal prohibitions imposed on Laurey, cannot be articulated linguistically.[60]

This dynamic places the dream ballet in the broader history of modern dance as a site of feminist activity. As Felicia McCarren has argued, "in a world where men were more frequently read and heard than women," dance "effect[ed] a reinvestment of meaning in the body and its expressive forms." The "choice to speak without words" resembles the hysteric's means of dismantling the logocentric order; it is an instrument for "eclipsing the medical gaze of patriarchy while moving in it." Like many other female-identified choreographers that came before and after her, de Mille forged a dialogue between dance and psychoanalysis, making the two fields learn from each other, while "shaping a space in which to listen to and to tell, the body's story."[61]

The havoc wrought by *Oklahoma!*'s mad ballet, rather than descend on the stage out of the blue, grows out of the tonal shift introduced earlier, in the Smoke House scene. It is in this scene that the musical first manifests its brooding sensibility, zooming in on the subjectivity of Jud (Howard Da Silva in the original cast), who was regarded by critics and members of the creative team as a more obviously mad character. A *New York Times* article described him at the time as a sinister "Freudian interpolation."[62] Jud's "dark, dirty" house, with its "dust and cobwebs" and a "grimy" bed that is "never made," is transparently designed to reflect his status and his inner state as the musical's mad villain.[63] His song "Lonely Room," resembling an operatic aria, has a number of qualities that make it stand out from the rest of the score. Tim Carter observes that it is *Oklahoma!*'s only number written in a minor key and its only soliloquy.[64] To add to this list of special attributes, "Lonely Room," in which Jud recounts his fantasies of wish fulfillment, distinguishes itself as the musical's other instance of reverie that signals, in this case verbally as well as musically, the presence of madness in the dreamer's subjective experience. As such, this number, defined by Hammerstein as Jud's "self-analysis," operates in a psychoanalytic register of dream life, which de Mille's ballet picks up and extends into an amplified, three-dimensional stage picture of Laurey's unconscious.[65] The hypnagogic continuities between these two scenes posit Jud's room and Laurey's mind as interarticulated sites of madness, which tip the show's tonal balance from musical comedy to tragedy.

Describing the opening night, Lawrence Langner, one of the cofounders of the Theatre Guild, which produced the show, recalls "that electric feel that passes through the audience when it feels that it is attending something of exciting import in the theatre."[66] What this observation seems to convey, as he records the temperature of the house during the intermission, is the show's demonstrable success at being viewed as a legitimate musical drama. Indeed, as Carter's analysis of *Oklahoma!*'s early reception history shows, the musical had champions among relatively highbrow critics, who sought to "grant the genre something of the status of high art."[67] Citing a couple of earlier Broadway musicals—Show Boat, Of Thee I Sing, Porgy and Bess—as evolutionary milestones of the form's gestation, the enthusiastic critics saw in Oklahoma! what they had seen in Lady in the Dark: the genesis of a sophisticated, "compellingly native art of the lyric theatre."[68] The show was billed as a "musical play," an appellation all the more common in musical theater nomenclature in the 1940s. The term demarcated the creative team's aesthetic and ideological departures from vaudeville and musical comedy, reflecting the "serious" agenda of the Theatre Guild. Comparisons to the more privileged genres were mobilized for similar purposes. Olin Downes in the New York Times, for instance, exalted the show as "Broadway's gift to opera."[69] Even George Beiswanger, who opined in 1944 that serious drama was not and never had been an American art, conceded that the authors of musicals like Oklahoma! and Lady in the Dark merited comparison to high culture: "They come close to being Aristophanes or Molière. Increasingly they approach opera."[70] The emphasis on choreography in Oklahoma! was also praised profusely as a major development in the emergence of a forward-looking, distinctly American dance idiom. As critic Burton Rascoe exclaimed, de Mille's numbers were "such supreme aesthetic delights as to challenge anything the Met can produce this season."[71]

The use of aesthetic gestures linked to straight drama, ballet, and opera in Oklahoma!—and the critics' reinforcement of these connections—fortified the legitimization of the Broadway musical as a form well on the path to fulfilling the lofty ambitions of art theater. As demonstrated by recurring metaphors of depth in the period's effusive responses to the show, Hammerstein's project of extracting the "dramatic vitality" of Riggs's play from under its "surface of gentleness" succeeded. "Under the comedic mask and the convention of spurs, revolvers and ten-gallon hats," gushes Downes, "we recognize an ancestral memory, echo of an experience that went deep, a part of the adventure that has made us ourselves."[72] What contributes to the perceived seriousness of Oklahoma! is its expression of "genuine things that lie deep in the people."[73] Implicit in this critical language is a conviction that this brand of musical comedy presents characters and situations that, far from being conventionally flat, have an expansive psychological dimension, "triumphant of the soul."[74] The musical owes this kind of reception in large part to its vivid staging of psychoanalytic depth, especially in de Mille's avant-gardist ballet, which resonated with contemporary sensibilities by mining the impressive symbolic capital of psychologized forms of personal individuation underwritten by Freudian psychoanalysis.

SINGING WITH FREUD IN *THE DAY BEFORE SPRING*

In the opinion of book-writer and lyricist Alan Jay Lerner, "With *Oklahoma!* the musical theater began its *belle epoque* which lasted for a quarter of a century,"[75] yet it was Weill, with his "accent on good books," who had paved the way for shows that offered "something more than an evening for light-hearted entertainment."[76] Lerner credited *Lady in the Dark* in particular with inspiring *Oklahoma!* and "then the whole change in musical theatre."[77] While he got to collaborate with Weill on *Love Life* in the same decade and with Hart on *My Fair Lady* in the next one, his most direct homage to *Lady in the Dark* would come years later, in *On a Clear Day You Can See Forever* (1965), with its scenes in a psychiatrist's office employing the multimedia conventions of the modernist psychomachia. His interest in the new deep-character technique of the 1940s, however, can already be seen in *The Day before Spring*, his second Broadway collaboration with composer Frederik Loewe. Like the other shows discussed in the chapter, this musical enlists the programmatic emphasis of the golden age on the total integration of the arts to service the staging of the psychoanalytic interior.

The musical's action, set at a fictional Harrison University, tells the story of a ten-year class reunion during which the heroine, Katherine Townsend, finds herself in the throes of a difficult decision: whether to stay with her husband Peter or leave him for the famous writer Alex Maitland, her former flame. With book scenes directed by Edward Padula and numbers staged by John C. Wilson, *The Day before Spring* premiered at the National Theatre (now the Nederlander) on November 22, 1945, and ran for 167 performances. Its sophisticated, or, as the *New York Post* saw it, "pseudo-sophisticated," flavor stemmed in part from the discursive prominence of the literary culture, which the production foregrounded spatially through library and university settings, and rhetorically through sung and spoken discussions of real and fictional writers.[78] The highly subjective mental processes involved in reading served as the musical's entryway into the staging of the dynamic unconscious in several scenes. Engaging psychoanalytic formations on a literary plane, these scenes explored a series of generative encounters between literature and reader. The ballets and musical ensembles were fittingly entrusted to Antony Tudor. Praised by the period's critics for dark, psychoanalytically minded pieces, he was no stranger to modernist choreography in which, as Jones writes, "every movement represents the outward expression of a lived interiority."[79]

The Day before Spring teases a daydreaming register through the title number in the first scene, which proffers yet another 1940s image of a woman lying down on the couch, lost in contemplation. Played by Irene Manning on Broadway, Katherine, the recumbent character in question, is discovered in the library of her impressive New York City apartment—not in the analyst's office—and her immediate activity is, ostensibly, reading— not soul-searching. Yet at the precise moment that she touches the volume, a novel written by Alex, "a sweeping theme is heard in the orchestra," fleshing out her experience of the book in front of her.[80] As Katherine reads a passage out loud, her delivery shifting between speaking and singing, she transforms the prose into rhymed lyrics. The song, with its eroticized juxtaposition of a cold protracted winter and the bursting forth of spring, is less concerned with the novelist's text than with the effect of this text on Katherine and her interpretive transformation of it. In staging the heroine's encounter with literature—her falling prey to what Shoshana Felman calls "the lure of rhetoric"—this number sets in motion a psychodynamic inquiry into Katherine's semiconscious and altogether repressed desires.[81]

This number relies primarily on pictorial realism in the sense of presenting a freestanding figure in her daily environment, with her mental processes to be inferred mainly from her words, glances, gestures, and movements. It is not until scene 5 of act 1, in the sequence titled "Katherine Receives Advice," that another library, that of Harrison University, is overtaken by a full-blown psychomachia. From this point on through the end of the act, several new characters, as well as extra voices in the background, serve as a combined visual and sonic articulation of different impulses and forces within the heroine's conflicted self, as she confronts her wish to leave her husband for Alex the novelist. Katherine's entrance into the dimly lit library is greeted by the sound of an offstage ensemble chanting in "a crescendo of discord and monotony":

Katherine, Katherine, two lovers now have you;
Katherine, Katherine, what are you going to do?
Katherine, Katherine, before the night is done,
Katherine, Katherine, you must decide on one.

After she shuts out these inner voices, "putting her hands over the ears" and telling them to stop, the lights come up to reveal busts of "three philosophers"—Plato, Voltaire, and Freud—who proceed to voice the dynamics of her inner battle in the form of a sung debate. Plato urges Katherine to preserve her "peaceful married state" and "keep it platonic," arguing that a sexless marriage is a sign of personal maturity in an advanced, "civilized society." Voltaire is convinced that she ought to take a lover on the sly, while her "appetite is keen," and keep her husband for companionship in old age. Deriding such opinions as "antique," Freud (Hermann Leopoldi in the original cast) urges her to embrace her desire openly. "Go with your lover and make a fresh start," he sings to the surging tune of an opulent waltz. Emboldened by his emphatic belief that "to do a great right you must do a little wrong," Katherine sings that she can "see it clearly" now and, full of hope and resolve, runs off to find Alex as the curtain goes down on act 1 to the jubilant sound of the ensemble restating her newly gained insight.[82]

Within the literary ethos of *The Day before Spring*, a musical keenly pre-occupied with the creative experience of reading and writing, Freud figures as a modern philosopher-artist who is commemorated in the university library alongside Plato and Voltaire and, through Katherine's conversion to his perspective, elevated a notch above them. His insistence on the primacy of sexual satisfaction, to be pursued regardless of social norms and institutions, reifies the popular image of an iconoclastic Freud, which, having gained purchase on the imagination of American artists and thinkers earlier in the century, had helped weaponize cultural production against conservative values and, during the musical's moment, was being actively propagated by academic and mainstream writers as an instrument of high modernism. Lerner's Freud, by debating with Plato and Voltaire and, more generally, by being part of the musical's broad network of literary allusions and figures, is implicated intertextually in the history of the Western European and North American philosophic enterprise. Yet what helps him prevail in this scene, exposing his opponents as "a pair of dilettantes," is not just his attunement to modern sensibilities but also his presumed access to medical expertise and empirical data. The entire psychomachic sequence, in fact, can be read as a therapeutic encounter, in which the analyst frames the "solution" being sought as a cure, a way to "fix up" Katherine's mind. To Freud the scientist in the musical, the mind "not at rest" is an "ill" mind, an assessment that authorizes his medical intervention in the heroine's neurosis. "The symptoms you exhibit show emotions you inhibit," proclaims Freud as he traces the etiology of Katherine's "depression" to "a physical repression," doling out crudely formulated, widely popularized generalizations of psychoanalytic principles from his patriarchal pulpit.[83]

Dramaturgically, Katherine is not the musical's only candidate for psychomachic treatment. Her husband Peter, who was played by John Archer, gets a scene in which his interiority is likewise superimposed on the environment around him. His psyche, like Katherine's, becomes a stage. Peter's perspective invades the action in a sequence dramatizing his inner experience as a reader. As he peruses Alex's novel, with fluctuations of attention and affect, the text is embodied and enacted by live performers behind him. Choreographed by Tudor, this scene offers the spectacle of the text passing through Peter's mind, with the idiosyncratic meanings accruing through his interpretation of the pages and causing him to feel increasingly distressed. Slamming the book, he segues into a psychomachic number, "Where's My Wife?," in which unknown people with generic names (e.g., Man, Girl, College Boy), along with a handful of previously seen characters who now appear as though strained through his imagination, gather on stage, singing and dancing in a kind of feverish allegory representing the hero's mind in crisis. The arrival of madness is further telegraphed scenically with "a sort of dementia praecox" backdrop, designed by Robert Davison.[84]

Lerner's epigraph to the libretto is a quotation from Alexander Dumas: "The chain of wedlock is so heavy that it takes two to carry it—sometimes three."[85] The broken bond between the married couple is resealed in the finale, but the air of mutual disappointment lingers, the happy ending formula sagging with the weight of disenchantment. Several reviewers griped that the show floundered when it came to humor.[86] Lewis Nichols in the *New York Times* called *The Day before Spring* "likable" and "smart" yet too "austere" and "heavy."[87] In the opinion of the *New Yorker*'s Wolcott Gibbs, who lauded the show as "generally literate" and "considerably above the average musically," the authors were at their best "in their tougher moods." The "comedy sketch, involving the shades of Plato, Voltaire, and Freud," he wrote, "didn't make me laugh at all."[88] Indeed, however ironic the musical's authors tried to be in "Katherine Receives Advice" or "Where's My Wife?," the spectacles of the human interior in these scenes seem laden with signs of frustration and ambivalence too poignant to sustain a purely comic posture. *The Day before Spring* got caught in the undertow of the joyless themes that the instruments of psychological modernism tend to crack open and magnify. But it is also with the help of these instruments that the musical presented itself as a sophisticated experiment, earning, despite mixed reviews and a short run, the moniker of a "succès d'estime."[89]

AND AFTERWARD

The appearance of a singing Freud on the stage of a Broadway musical during the 1945–1946 season depicts a larger cultural process in which midcentury theater artists come to terms with the clinical and literary status of psychoanalysis as a preeminent truth discourse about the human condition.

Pushed into the limelight of the art form is the depth-psychological picture of psychic conflict, a view in which one is never master of one's self. With the rapid ascendance of this model of mind to dominance in mainstream psychiatry during and after World War II, the unconscious, with its repositories of madness, becomes a defining attribute of the average American.

The ambitious scope of the psychoanalytic paradigm of mental health enabled psychiatry's medicalization and, not infrequently, pathologization of inner states and emotions once considered natural events in the life of humans. But it also, paradoxically, opened up the medical world to viewing mental illness on a continuum, blurring traditional psychiatric boundaries and distinctions between mental health and mental abnormality.[90] This twin effect of psychoanalysis helps account for the broad representational and rhetorical capacity of madness in the golden age musical. The scenes of a mind overwrought by inner conflict in the productions I have discussed are informed by normative concepts of mental health, which position psychic difference as mentally disordered. But these scenes also, conversely, humanize madness, reframing it as a range of psychic experiences we all pass through at various points in our lives by reason of having an unconscious. This period of experimentation rewrites the human subject as constitutionally mad and lays the groundwork for empathically conceived depictions of a mentally distressed interiority in the stage musical.

Given the broadening of psychiatric definitions of mental illness during the golden age, the specter of madness becomes a discursive presence even in musicals that stay within the bounds of lighthearted comedy, as people on the stage begin to rethink their feelings in terms of medical categories. In Call Me Madam (1950), for instance, two characters singing in counterpoint ponder competing perspectives on a "strange" combination of inner states, debating whether experiencing them means you are "sick" and therefore in need of "analyzing"' or "just in love."[91] Similarly, Adelaide in Guys and Dolls (1950) contemplates the possibility that her "long frustration" over being unmarried may be the root cause of her persisting colds.[92] These droll scenes attest to the commanding power of Freudianism over the nation's medical taxonomies of mental life during the golden age. They popularize and contest depth-psychological concepts of behavior and personality, while at the same time mining them for humor.

Yet depth psychology also becomes the prime requisite for character construction in musicals aiming for the ennobling heights of literary art theater with a distinctly tragic structuration. It is not surprising that "Rose's Turn" in Gypsy (1959), often cited as a major milestone in the development of an intellectual Broadway show capable of Shakespearean or O'Neillian proportions in terms of character depth, should be the ultimate product of this golden age trend. Defined by the creative team as Mama Rose's "nervous breakdown," the song is conceived as an act of mental striptease during which she discovers and exposes a hidden dimension within herself.[93] In the contemporaneous words of Atkinson in the *New York Times*, during this moment *Gypsy* "abandons the sleazy grandeur of show business and threatens to become belle-letters," as the musical "deserts the body and starts cultivating the soul."[94] As is typical of this period, the critic maps the hierarchical distinctions between "low" theatrical forms, such as burlesque and vaudeville, and literary theater onto the split between the body and the soul, the latter entity serving as the touchstone of a work's artistic merit. In this context, the concept of the "soul," albeit not without the lofty echoes of the religious imagination, is all but synonymous with the "mind," which at midcentury implies a psychodynamic organization. Indeed, in predicating Rose's "mad scene" on the existence of a conflict between conscious and unconscious levels of action in her mind/soul, the creative team subscribes to a psychoanalytic logic.[95] At a time when both psychoanalysis and musical theater are enjoying a golden age in the United States, it is the ubiquity of clinical and artistic projections of intricate topographies of inner space within the psyche, along with the tantalizing promise of a partial reveal afforded by introspection, that makes stripping such a legible and effective metaphor for the staging of Rose's epiphany.

The subsequent consecration of Stephen Sondheim, who shaped the dramatic situation and wrote the words for Rose's mad scene, is a telling example of the far-reaching legacy of this psychologizing trend in the art form after the golden age. Critics and historians have made much of the way he steered musical theater to a new level of sophistication and seriousness by drawing on and refining the dramatic principles he had learned from his mentor, Hammerstein, and other artists of that generation.[96] In most of Sondheim's shows one finds the spectacle of introspection bleeding into madness. His characters, like those in plays by his contemporaries Edward Albee and Harold Pinter, are often disenchanted and distraught human beings, teetering on the edge or falling off into the dark night of the soul. It is small wonder that happy ever-afters are hard to come by in his oeuvre.

Over the years Sondheim's mastery of psychological subtext in songwriting—what he describes as "something to play underneath the speech, bringing a depth, a counterpoint to what is said"—earned him an extraordinary amount of symbolic capital both in the industry and in the academy, making him, as he himself admits self-deprecatingly in *Sondheim on Sondheim*, the "God" of musical theater.[97] For instance, in a recent encomium Ben Brantley maintains that it is Sondheim's supreme command of the art of ambivalence that got him to "his rightful place on an Olympian peak that no subsequent songwriter has ever been able to ascend." As the critic sees it, the master's "complex dialectic of words and music" paints "confusing" but "exhilarating" pictures of emotions. Hidden between the lines of his "paradoxes, puns and declarations of uncertainty, all etched into deep-burrowing grooves" is the truth of "life as we know it, if we're being honest with ourselves."[98] Brantley—like countless other critics and artists he echoes—speaks of the surface-depth dialectic as a natural good on the stage, a self-evident merit that needs no further defense. Thus distinguished, Sondheim emerges as the eminent creator of intellectually stimulating musical entertainment. What is more, his oracular pronouncements on life and emotions cannot be disproven. If we do not agree with him, it only means that we are not *being honest with ourselves*. In this rhetorical move, which recalls all too well the canonization of O'Neill a century ago, the image of Sondheim the artist merges with the image of an old-fashioned analyst resembling Dr. Brooks.[99] His insights are hard to swallow but to resist them is to run away from yourself, opting for, in the manner of Oedipus, a self-inflicted blindness. As Jesse Green puts it, "In words, and onstage, [Sondheim] was Freud himself, bringing to the American musical theatre its most fully realized psychological portraits."[100]

Such worshipful accolades showered on Sondheim and his creations bespeak the invisible power of psychoanalytically derived concepts of personality and behavior in American culture. As he once stated shrewdly, "Every time you can write a self-deluded song, you are ahead of the game, way ahead."[101] Sondheim's deification has been conditioned by a tacit acceptance of the depth-psychological model of the mind, along with its attendant representational techniques, as a conduit to artistic and philosophical truths about the human condition. He is, of course, not alone in reaping the spectacular benefits of the psychoanalytic imagination as a commanding method of theatrical persuasion. Many other musical theatermakers working today, especially those with an emphatically intellectual, arty reputation, put Freudian and post-Freudian technologies of depth to compelling creative uses. The authors of pieces like *James Joyce's The Dead*, *Spring Awakening*, *Fun Home*, *Preludes*, or *First Daughter Suite*, to name only a few, create moving emotional landscapes through the dynamic language of unconscious conflict and often profit by it in being perceived as creators of serious, sophisticated musical drama.

These technologies of depth go back to the modernist experiments of the golden age teams who used madness as a prolific medium for peering inside the character's soul. But the golden age also saw the beginning of another conceptual trend in the art form's relationship with mental distress. During the first three decades of the Cold War, American culture would be overtaken with a quest for the social meaning of madness and mental illness. A number of New York theater artists, including Sondheim, would group themselves around this epistemological project. Looking for a more productive relationship between individual psychology and political analysis, they would experiment with new ways of looking outward through madness, amplifying and cementing its rhetorical role in theorizing and critiquing society.

Madness in Society

THREE | "There Are Heroes in the World . . ."

*Psychiatric Activism, Antipsychiatry, and
Political Consciousness*

Holding fast to a mobile suspended from the ceiling of the nightclub, Reuben soars ecstatically over the crowd. He is an aerialist and a barker in a traveling circus conjured up in his mind. With a crescendo of calliope music, the stage around him has been transformed into a big top, a kaleidoscope of dancing lights revealing a picturesque procession of lion tamers, snake charmers, jugglers, freaks, clowns, and balloon vendors. These people are in fact some of the nightclub staff and patrons, who act and move the way Reuben, "transfixed in his dream-world," sees them. "Oblivious to everything but his vision," he pays no heed to the clamor of onstage observers who, pronouncing him "crazy," send for the "nuthouse wagon." Climbing higher and higher, Reuben serenades "the circus of his childhood," until, at the very top, "his wild elation freezes" as he imagines seeing his father, a trapeze artist who committed suicide many years ago by leaping to his death. "Don't, Pop. Don't do it. There is no net," Reuben pleads. Yet in an instant he changes his mind and, taking the place of his father, cries, "Make way for the human dart!" He jumps, everyone screams, and the first-act finale of Marc Blitzstein's musical *Reuben Reuben* dissolves to a blackout.[1]

The original production of *Reuben Reuben*, directed by Robert Lewis, choreographed by Hanya Holm, and designed by William and Jean Eckart, received mostly unfavorable reviews and never made it to Broadway, closing after a handful of tryout performances in Boston in October 1955. Whatever its merits or failings, the musical's detractors and advocates seemed to agree on one point: Blitzstein's creation was nothing if not highly experimental and intellectual.[2] As was typical in the dual golden age of psychoanalysis and musical theater, the modernist language of amplified interiority in the mad scene above performed its double trick: it supplied the author with avant-garde techniques still registering as innovative and, through its identification with the fashionably sophisticated, helped encode the musical as a serious work of art. Yet while *Reuben Reuben* may have tapped an established Broadway trend as a source and marker of experimentalism and depth, reifying the psychomachic conventions of the mid-century, it also inaugurated a new direction for musicals concerned with mental distress, a route connecting it to a number of Broadway shows that would be created over the subsequent two decades.[3]

Components of Blitzstein's innovative approach, while already visible in Reuben's breakdown, are fully fleshed out in the next scene, which reviewers characterized as shocking and frightening.[4] After the intermission, Reuben and his date Nina are discovered in the wards of a mental institution. This "nuthouse" is "one helluva place," sings Reuben. Discernible on the dimly lit stage are the asylum residents, "some in introvert poses and states, others in constant motion, but very little, and very slow." Two more inmates are confined to cages. Played by the ensemble, these people, each in their "own private world," express their "fantasies of contact" through a song and a ballet, which Blitzstein intends as a "reductio ad absurdum of all non-communication," underscoring the musical's theme of social alienation embodied by Reuben and the inmates. Moved by the pitiful sight of the lonely, neglected patients, Reuben and Nina offer whatever help they can. In the women's ward, Nina goes to comfort a Black woman, who "instantly curls up like a baby in her lap." In the men's, Reuben assists a young resident named Ury to a bench, draping a blanket around him soothingly in counterpoint to the ensemble's increasingly agitated dancing. After a brief moment, Ury gives in to the music's desperation. Before Reuben can stop him, he draws out a large iron spike from under his shirt, gashes his wrists, and, turning his hands out, displays his wounds to the climactic sounds of the ensemble's "dream-like tune." He stands there "grinning foolishly" as two members of the hospital staff arrive. With detached, bored looks on their faces, they discharge Reuben and Nina, ushering them out and relocking the doors. One of the attendants then turns to the bleeding Ury, uttering: "Why you no-good sonofabitch." As the lights go out on the asylum scene, we see him reach "his arm backward to strike Ury across the face."[5]

The nightclub and asylum scenes represent a crucial shift in the structure and location of mental distress, introducing a different kind of madness into musical theater. In a departure from the dominant conceptual and aesthetic model of the golden age, this musical, in its approach to Reuben and the inmates, turns to states and behaviors suggesting a loss of contact with reality, which, from a clinical standpoint, read as psychosis.[6] As I indicated in the previous chapters, psychotic thought patterns had always been present, however tenuously, in scenes of the interior during the 1940s, but they remained strictly circumscribed within the realm of the dreamer's or the patient's fantasy. Blitzstein's musical, however, takes psychosis out into the open, making it part of waking reality and social life. Significant in this relocation is a broadening of conceptual focus from the anguish of the singular psychoanalytic subject to the material plight of an externally situated group. The turning of the critical gaze outward raises a new set of issues. These characters are not the high-functioning "worried well" working through their life problems on the analytic couch, but the more vulnerable mad committed to mental hospitals. Bypassing the art form's preoccupation with neurotic fragility, the musical confronts the audience with urgent rhetorical questions about chronic patients locked away in asylums. What has psychiatry done for such people? What have we as a society?

The field of contention outlined in this example is part a broader reorientation in the debate about the nature of madness in the United States. In the time between World War II and the civil rights era, newly urgent agendas within psychiatry and the social sciences prioritized directions of thought that recast mental illness in social and political terms. The joint impact of, on the one hand, environmentally oriented, activist psychiatry and, on the other hand, the antipsychiatry movement of the 1960s and 1970s was the redefinition of madness as a sociogenic phenomenon. According to this newly dominant paradigm, mental illness was produced and determined by society. Far from being represented by one unified philosophy or movement, the social turn in conceptions of madness encompassed a confluence of heterogeneous and, not infrequently, mutually antagonistic theories and practical actions. Yet the buildup of internal tensions within this paradigm was responsible for a tremendous outpouring of clinical and cultural energy that repositioned madness as coming from the outside rather than the inside.

Prompted by *Reuben Reuben*, in this chapter and the following two I explore the social turn in the Broadway musical's renditions of madness in the 1960s and 1970s. My main thesis is that just before and during these decades some creative teams begin to rethink and stage madness in emphatically collective terms. In musical theater histories, this period is predominantly characterized as the beginning of a new era of political consciousness, when the art form's articulations of discontent with America's past and present grow more numerous and more trenchant. Madness is drawn into political messaging across a cluster of new shows that express solidarity with the protest movements of the turbulent decades, magnifying the rallying cries for justice and equality heard across the culture. While components of this trend show up in different guises in a number of musicals featuring mad or mad-adjacent states and experiences, the main players of my story in this part of the book are *Anyone Can Whistle* (1964), *Man of La Mancha* (1965), *Dear World* (1969), *Prettybelle* (1971), *King of Hearts* (1978), *Sweeney Todd* (1979), and *Ain't Supposed to Die a Natural Death* (1971). These musicals are invested in exploring the role and status of sociogenic factors in what is experienced as extreme distress or thought of as a mental pathology. The causes of psychic pain and rationales for diagnoses, medical or popular, are found in the hierarchical order governing the fictional universe. Madness becomes the site of opposition between personal conceptions of self and reality and those of the larger, dominant environment, which takes the form of agonistic encounters between marginalized individuals and powerful mainstream groups and institutions, including psychiatry. As the preceding chapter shows, this current of social theorizing may already be gleaned in the psychoanalytic reflections of the 1940s musicals, but not without effort; one has to search for it. The shows I discuss in this part of the book wear their polemical passions on their sleeves. Madness in them is, invariably, a political banner.

This period in the history of madness sets the stage for the increasing visibility in popular culture of people diagnosed with schizophrenia and major mood disorders. At the center of this part of the story is the postwar crisis of the public mental hospital system, which had traditionally been the locus of care and treatment for chronically mentally ill or disabled Americans. The nation's attempts to deal with the crisis through the closure of asylums, the release of inmates into the community, new therapeutic regimens, and other means unfold against the backdrop of social and political activism within and without psychiatry. In the first decades of the Cold War era, popular periodicals, documentaries, fiction, movies, and plays seize on the subject of patient abuse and neglect in psychiatric settings. The stage musical likewise contributes to a cultural fascination with the life of mental patients, previously locked away and largely unseen. Starting with *Reuben Reuben*, ostensibly psychotic characters, long a staple of the dramatic stage and opera, begin to find their way into the art form. In the 1960s and 1970s, a new generation of musical theater artists, imagining how asylum residents or candidates for committal might think or act, attempt to depict states and behaviors more atypical or extreme than those exhibited by the "worried well." From this point on in my narrative, and in the context of this trend, madness in musical theater relates to the category of "serious" on two planes. It can be "serious" not only in the sense of generating a tragically tinged spectacle of artistic and psychological depth, with its aura of critical prestige, but also in the sense of alluding to severe conditions featuring psychosis and traditionally viewed by mental health professionals as "serious mental illness."

Yet despite the period's explosion of cultural interest in those diagnosed with chronic, disabling conditions, this musical theater trend is, for the most part, unconcerned with pursuing psychiatric verisimilitude. In these texts, madness is less a representation of a medical condition than a reflection on the sociopolitical organization of human life that results in the marginalization and suppression of psychic difference. This attitude dovetails with the basic tenets of antipsychiatry, a formidable intellectual movement that rose and flourished internationally in the 1960s and 1970s. Among thinkers whose work formed the backbone of classical antipsychiatry were Thomas Szasz, Erving Goffman, R. D. Laing, and Michel Foucault. Despite marked differences in disciplinary origins and methodology, they advanced comparable arguments for demedicalizing mental distress, interrogating the methods and objectives of psychiatric interventions in modes of being which society deems deviant. Collectively, they contributed to a corpus of influential critical texts defending the notion that "personal reality and freedom were independent of any definition of normalcy that organized psychiatry tried to impose."[7]

As historians of mental health point out, antipsychiatry, which constituted a kind of psychiatric counterculture, grew out of the postwar social theorizing within psychiatry. During the late 1940s and the 1950s, psychoanalytic and psychodynamic clinicians were instrumental in turning mainstream psychiatry's attention to sociogenic factors. In response to the limitations of both biological and purely intrapsychic models, they developed and consolidated a psychosocial view of mental health in the field, and, in their activism, represented a socially oriented, liberal psychiatry.[8] The origins of mental illness, they contended, were to be found in the external environment, and the path toward the optimization of mental health lay in the amelioration of adverse societal conditions. Antipsychiatry, however, pushed the conversation about environmental etiologies much further, in the direction of a social-constructionist vision of mental illness. From this perspective, psychiatric diagnoses were for the most part based not in empirically proven, objective facts but in societal prejudices against behavioral and ideological divergences from the norm. While the heyday of antipsychiatry waned by the 1980s, the lasting purchase of its ideas on the artistic imagination comes into view in a great deal of contemporary dramatic writing, whenever attempts are made to

show madness or disability in the process of being constituted and recon-
stituted by society. In this part of the book, I show how the drift of social-
constructionist ideas into mainstream culture plays out in the musicals of
the 1960s and 1970s. Antipsychiatric motifs are especially strong in *Anyone Can Whistle* and *Man of La Mancha*, but they inform the representational profile of mental distress, in different degrees, in all of the musicals
I discuss here and afterward, in the rest of the chapters.

During the 1960s and 1970s the art form continues to mobilize psychologized discourses of inner depth inherited from the golden age. Yet while
cooperating with the psychodynamic imagination, the medium also shows
signs of reservation, if not outright discontent, regarding the ethical components of the analytic enterprise. These decades mark the end of a golden
age of popularity not only for the Broadway musical, but also for psychoanalysis, whose authority is undermined by a strengthening biological psychiatry, antipsychiatry, powerful critiques from the feminist and gay liberation movements, and other cultural and institutional factors. Drawn
into the ongoing conceptual and clinical challenges to and revisions of
Freudianism and other theoretical strains, the shows discussed in these
chapters attempt, with varying degrees of involvement, to discipline psychoanalytic structures into deeper engagement with the social. By embed-
ding depth-psychological formulations in the stories of collectively produced or experienced mad states and conditions, these texts exploit the
insights of psychoanalysis and test the limits of its applicability to the
urgent concerns of the 1960s and 1970s.

Prettybelle is the most obvious example of this dynamic in that it dramatizes a sociogenic etiology by means of involving the heroine, an asylum
resident, in a quasi-analytic procedure that takes the form of the modernist
psychomachia. The other musicals, by contrast, can be said to minimize the
interiorizing effects of the classical psychoanalytic imagination, employing
staging solutions that fix the audience's gaze on the realities external to the
mind. At the center of the spatial economy in these musicals is not the
amplified phantasmagoria of memories, dreams, and reveries, but the
social geographies of a mad subject—or, more frequently, a proliferation of
mad subjects—in institutional and urban settings. Yet even "antipsychiatric" musicals like *Anyone Can Whistle* and *Man of La Mancha* seem unable to
un-psychologize their protagonists. While they appear critical or, at the
very least, ambivalent about the value of psychoanalysis, they end up cir-
cling back to its utility as an epistemological foundation for apprehending
the workings of the human psyche or prying open the deeper recesses of
the soul.

The absorption of madness into various models of social theorizing and action in the 1960s renewed its discursive function as a polemical tool and a vehicle for allegory. Michael Staub writes that the cultural profile of madness assumed a "double aspect" during this historical moment: "On the one hand there was unquestionably an impetus to foster more humane and sympathetic treatment of the mentally ill. Yet on the other hand, and often simultaneously, all through the postwar period, representations repeatedly released 'mental illness' from any reference to actual psychic disorder, which permitted attention to madness to serve usefully as political critique."[9] The public outcry over the abysmal conditions of asylum psychiatry served as a flashpoint for broad-ranging debates about the precarious status of the individual in modern society, which made the ethics of mental health especially well suited to the countercultural projects of the 1960s. This is evident in the classical texts of antipsychiatry I discuss. While working toward the ostensible goal of liberating those designated mentally ill from institutional mistreatment and social stigma, their authors invariably exploit the rhetorical utility of madness to buttress overarching arguments about the government's encroachments on personal freedoms, the policing of difference, the steady rise of totalitarianism, and other such tendencies. In the context of these broader agendas, the images of psychiatrically managed patients, while serving to illustrate the historical suppression of psychic diversity, cannot help but function simultaneously as totalizing metaphors for the plight of all marginalized groups. Similarly, the creative teams behind the musicals discussed in this part of the book use figures of madness, defined with a strategic vagueness, to enliven their commentary on domestic and global ills endemic of capitalist modernity. As Staub notes, "The critical reflections on mental illness and social conditions put forward in the postwar decades eventually came to offer the counterculture an invaluable vantage point for articulating profound disgust at society-wide hypocrisies and cruelties."[10] Rallying around poignant, at times sensational, images of madness, the new generation of musical theater writers participated in the same broad-ranging oppositional project that conjoined advocacy on behalf of the mentally ill with other progressive causes. In certain moments and scenes in their productions, the sensory and affective fabric of living with mental distress came through with remarkable vividness, especially when the experiential dimension of the institutional and social conditions was amplified through the combined effects of music, poetry, and movement. But just as often, the mad or disabled on stage appeared as generic, distancing emblems pointing to the evils of modern societies or the virtues of nonconformism.

The embrace of the semiotic utility of a manacled or freed madness for political commentary is largely characteristic of the theater scene during the period. The fashionable literary and artistic trends of the 1950s—such as existentialism, the beat movement, the theater of the absurd—had been shot through with valorizations of psychopathology as the hallmark of a dissenting individual and denouncements of the mainstream's pragmatic rationalism. With the eruption of the theatrical experiments of the 1960s and 1970s, these themes acquired multiple new expressions. For many of the avant-garde and underground artists identified with the off-off-Broadway movement, as well as innovative playwrights and directors working with the mainstream stages, madness was a guide and a method for breaking free of the dogmas, taboos, and clichés of the past. The sacralization of Antonin Artaud, whose *Theatre and Its Double* was published in English in 1958, best illustrates this point.[11] His darkly poetic vision of the primitive conflict between the human psyche and civilization and his ruthless aesthetic program for a Theater of Cruelty intrigued and inspired multiple creative artists and collectives working or presenting their pieces in New York City, such as Jean Genet, Peter Brook, Jerzy Grotowski, Karen Finley, John Cage, the Living Theatre, the Performance Group, and the Wooster Group, just to name a few. A visionary theorist, director, and playwright with a long, tortuous history of coercive psychiatric treatment, Artaud embodied and championed, in his own words, the "authentic madman . . . to whom society did not want to listen and whom it wanted to prevent from uttering unbearable truths."[12] This kind of reverential attitude to the insights of mental distress characterized a great deal of experimental theatrical fare in the 1960s and 1970s, from *The Apple* and *Dutchman* to *Marat/Sade* and *Every Good Boy Deserves Favor*. Turning madness into a method of social knowing and a source of aesthetic novelty, the new avant-gardes mobilized its extremes as expressions of unadulterated individuality and political radicalism. These trends were integral to the networks of mutual influence in which creators of musical theatre were operating in New York.

The shows discussed in this part of the book do not only examine society for answers about the sources and nature of mental distress or pathology but also look to mental distress or pathology to explain society.[13] The programmatic allegorization and politicization of madness by the creative teams stretches its referential field in polarized directions, often within the same text. On one end is the alarming condition of contemporary society imagined as a world "off of its hinge."[14] Racism, gender and sexual discrimination, prejudice against perceived disability, poverty, wars, consumerism, mob mentality, totalitarianism, and environmental dangers are all symptoms of the civilization's precipitous decline into insanity. On the other end stands a sentimentally conceived individual or group of individuals traditionally designated as "mentally ill" or "crazy": residents of mental institutions, lunatics, or eccentrics at large. Portrayed in an array of romanticized, ennobling attitudes, they are social outcasts who won't go along with the ruling ideology of the majority. As such, they constitute an antidote to the world's loss of reason. This bifurcation in the referential field of the word "madness" or its synonyms is especially true of *Anyone Can Whistle, Man of La Mancha, Dear World*, and *King of Hearts*. Overdetermined by the polarizing romanticism of the sixties imagination, these shows divide the stage population into clear-cut representatives of malevolent and benign sociopolitical forces. The basic premise is that Western civilization is so far gone in the insanity of its self-destructive ways that the only way to reverse its course and save humanity—or, as Jerry Herman puts it in *Dear World*, to take the "sick world" off "the critical list"—is by resisting the status quo through the redeeming folly of nonconformism.[15] Madness, thus metaphorized, becomes a drifting, elastic concept that toggles freely between the two ends of the hero-villain binary.

The invocation of a heroic madness makes listening to the mental patients or lunatics a dramatic priority. This theatrical trend revives age-old tropes of madness as the locus of prophetic wisdom and spiritual enlightenment and projects them onto quasi-messianic outsider figures from different times and places. Philosophizing on the impasses and malaises of the modern condition, Hapgood, Cervantes / Don Quixote, Countess Aurelia, and other "loonies" serve as a sort of leverage for the stage musical's entrée into the high realm of humanist debates. At certain points in the narratives, these characters, invested with the burden of introspection and authenticity, espouse a kind of solipsistic detachment from the social milieu. Like the psychological man of the 1950s, championed by social theorist Philip Rieff, they cleave to "a self-concern that takes precedence over social concern and encourages an attitude of ironic insight on the part of the self toward all that is not self."[16] Such moments bring into view a postwar mix of Freudian, neo-Freudian, and existentialist ideas that, as Jean-Christophe Agnew writes, enthralled American intellectuals and provided American highbrow culture with a "tragic sense of itself."[17] Yet while such grand philosophic associations may have the desired effect of legitimizing these shows as "serious" drama, fostering the continued project of elevating the art form in the critical hierarchies, a sustained commitment to navel-gazing proves impossible in the worlds on the stage. The attempts to establish an ironically apolitical, alienated stance get compromised or entirely outweighed with a competing ethos attuned to the revolutionary impulses of the 1960s. Madness in these musicals yields an activist program. To borrow a line from *Prettybelle*, "Adjusted people never change anything. It takes a bunch of 'nuts' to change the world."[18] Assuming the mantle of leadership, the mad visionaries and iconoclasts, endowed with a special mission to teach, mobilize, or vindicate the rest of the outcasts represented on stage, raise their voices, speaking or singing back to power and compelling those who will listen to join their cause. As part of this collectivizing trend, madness becomes a romanticized participatory practice open to anyone marginalized and radical enough to join.

The foregrounding of an insightful madness and the concerted attention to environmental and social-constructivist explanations in this cluster of musicals are shared across multiple quarters of clinical, legislative, sociological, journalistic, and activist arenas. Some of the theatrical texts are implicated in the push across these arenas to stimulate institutional reforms and social change in response to the failures of asylum psychiatry and other areas of societal neglect and misconceptions around mental distress. Yet madness has a much broader reach and utility, serving the purpose of explicating and defining social systems and relations. Its representational profile consequently remains plastic and often operates in the slippery distinctions between materiality and metaphor. Whatever the end goals and results, it is a time when Broadway musicals, like much of the culture, persistently make the words and silences of the mad into something worth paying attention to.

MENTAL HEALTH REFORMS AND *ANYONE CAN WHISTLE*

On February 5, 1963, President John F. Kennedy delivered a special message to the Congress, calling for a "new bold approach" to mental health care. Over half a million "mentally ill" Americans, he stressed, "are confined and compressed within an antiquated, vastly overcrowded, chain of custodial state institutions," a situation that "has troubled our national conscience—but only as a problem unpleasant to mention, easy to postpone, and despairing of solution." The time had come to establish a comprehensive national mental health program aimed at "prevention, treatment and rehabilitation," lifting the social quarantine imposed upon "the afflicted" and supplanting their "reliance on the cold mercy of custodial isolation" with "the open warmth of community concern and capability."[19]

President Kennedy's speech and the accompanying legislation marked a rapid expansion of the federal government's role in the field of mental health. The cornerstone of "the wholly new national approach" was the transfer of the responsibility for the mentally ill from asylums to local communities through the process of deinstitutionalization, which entailed the discharge of patients from public mental hospitals and their (re)integration into society.[20] The passage of the Community Mental Health Centers Act of 1963 established a legal and economic framework, with allocated federal funds, for setting up local care centers, which were meant to provide former asylum residents—and those yet to receive a diagnosis of serious mental illness—with treatment on an outpatient basis. The new federal entitlement programs such as Medicaid and Medicare, as well as the gradual, if limited, inclusion of psychiatric services in third-party insurance plans, facilitated the provision of ambulatory therapeutic care to these dependent population groups. Some states, such as New York and California, had been developing and implementing community-based outpatient programs as alternatives to psychiatric hospitalization since the 1940s. Yet with the federal government's involvement, deinstitutionalization became a nationwide phenomenon in the 1960s. As a result of the sweeping reform, the number of resident patients in the country's public mental hospitals fell from 559,000 in 1955 to 132,000 by 1980.[21]

In painting the picture of the crisis of institutional psychiatry, President Kennedy's message invoked harrowing images of asylums that had been circulating in the popular imagination with mounting urgency since the 1940s. During the postwar years, a proliferation of newspaper and magazine articles, as well as novels and Hollywood movies, had brought to light the disastrous state of the nation's understaffed and overcrowded mental hospitals. One such exposé, "Bedlam 1946," published in *Life* magazine, chronicled the dehumanizing conditions in state mental hospitals, stating that these institutions had "degenerate(d) into little more than concentration camps" through public indifference and "legislative penny-pinching." Indicting photographs of restrained, naked, and undernourished asylum inmates all but incarcerated in unsanitary, claustrophobic spaces vividly illustrated the article's charge that "thousands who might be restored to society linger in man-made hells for a release that comes more quickly only because death comes faster to the abused, the beaten, the drugged, the starved and the neglected."[22] The dreary state of the mental ward in Blitzstein's *Reuben Reuben* pointed to the same institutional issues. The composer-playwright intended this scene to be a depiction of New York City's Bellevue Hospital.[23] His choice to end the scene on the cusp of violence, with a freeze-frame of an attendant about to hit a bleeding inmate, posed a pointedly unresolved question about the fate of chronic patients at public hospitals. As Gerald Grob stresses, the authors of the postwar "exposés of institutional defects . . . were better at portraying problems than offering concrete and workable solutions," yet "the cumulative effect of their work was to give mental health a more prominent position on the political agenda."[24] The accelerating traffic in chilling images of institutionalized madness across products of popular culture in the years leading up to the 1960s amplified the affective charge of the president's clarion call for reform, in which he characterized the treatment of severely mentally ill citizens as "a prolonged or permanent confinement in huge, unhappy mental hospitals where they were out of sight and forgotten."[25]

The closure of public mental hospitals in the United States was the last step in the consolidation of a new institution: community psychiatry.[26] The relocation of the locus of psychiatric practice from the asylum to the community began in the years immediately following World War II, as a growing number of psychodynamic and psychoanalytic clinicians turned to environmental explanations for mental distress, tracing the roots of psychopathology to external stresses associated with combat experiences. Reflecting on the insights American psychiatry had gained from working with soldiers and war trauma, William C. Menninger, one of the most influential voices within the specialty at the time, concluded that "the force of factors in the environment which supported or disrupted the individual" was far more important than the "history of personality or the personality make-up or the internal psychodynamic stresses."[27] The growing emphasis on the causative impact of the outside milieu led to a questioning of the therapeutic gains of institutionalization. Psychodynamic psychiatrists maintained that treatment both in the military and in civilian life was more effective when offered in a private setting, closer to home and family, rather than in the isolation of a cold, impersonal mental institution. This opinion was of course in part predetermined by the traditional ambulatory organization of psychoanalytic treatment and its privacy requirements. But on a conceptual level, the preference for the community model also stemmed from the psychodynamicists' belief in a smooth continuum from health to disease, from the normal to the abnormal. If there was such a continuum, then "the possibility existed that before the process had run its course *outpatient* psychiatric interventions could alter the outcome."[28] Menninger stressed that the wartime practice of offering psychiatric services to soldiers in "out-patient clinics" and "battalion aid stations" had proven highly effective in preventing the onset of psychoses. It followed that a similar structure for early treatment in civilian life would "materially increase the present rate of recovery of mental illness" and reduce the need for hospitalization.[29]

The goals of prevention and rehabilitation projected onto the outpatient model reflected psychiatry's increasing engagement with "the broad field of social interests." Increasingly optimistic about "the potential opportunities of helping the average man on the street," psychodynamic community-oriented clinicians worked to reorganize the specialty's institutional structure and its underlying philosophy from a narrow focus on "dementia praecox" or the "oedipus complex" to the kinds of "grief and sorrow and suffering" that have to do with "individual struggles, community needs, state and national problems and international concerns."[30] If madness was primarily a product of the rigors and stresses inflicted by external life experiences, then curative and preventive measures should begin with the task of improving adverse social conditions. As the authors of West Side Story phrased it, being "psychologically disturbed" now meant being sick in a sociological sense. "I'm depraved on account I'm deprived!" yells one of their juvenile delinquent characters on his way to the "headshrinker."[31]

The environmental outlook directed clinical attention to such causative factors as poverty and racism, energizing psychiatric advocacy for disenfranchised population groups. To be sure, most clinical services to underprivileged communities were provided by social workers (whose training by this point was largely psychodynamic in nature), since the overwhelming majority of psychoanalytic and psychodynamic psychiatrists chose office careers and saw a limited number of patients, mostly white and well-to-do. Yet due to the inordinate prestige of their specialty during this period psychoanalytically trained doctors were instrumental in influencing public policy changes in the direction of liberal welfare ideals. According to statistical data cited by Grob, psychiatrists, both as private citizens and in their official capacity as members of advisory boards for state and federal governments, "tended—unlike their colleagues in other medical specialties—to support legislation designed to assist less fortunate individuals and groups."[32] In the years leading up to the 1960s, psychodynamic psychiatrists collaborated with social scientists on research and specific recommendations to lawmakers, helping reshape local and national mental health policy toward community-oriented models of treatment.[33] During the civil rights era, the identification of community psychiatry with political and social activism only deepened. "If we are to make any substantial progress in promoting mental health," insisted advocates of a socially oriented, liberal psychiatry in the Ameri-

can Journal of Psychiatry, "we must involve ourselves in informed activism to change our national goals and priorities. We cannot afford to have health, welfare, and education programs cut to give higher priority to highways, wars, farm support, and missiles."[34]

While the philosophy of social psychiatry was spearheaded by environmentally oriented psychodynamicists, the practical implementation of the community-based program was greatly facilitated by the introduction in the early 1950s of psychoactive drugs, such as chlorpromazine (brand name Thorazine), which alleviated symptoms attributed to schizophrenia and other severe conditions and disorders. Such new drugs held out the promise that many of those confined in mental institutions could now be restored to sustainable levels of functioning in the community. Grob notes that by the end of the 1950, the majority of psychoanalytically trained psychiatrists incorporated some form of psychoactive medication into their practice, reinforcing a belief that the internal differences between biological and psychodynamic paradigms "that had threatened the unity of psychiatry" just a decade ago "were fast disappearing."[35] President Kennedy's rationale for deinstitutionalization reflected the period's optimism about the integration of somatic and psychological interventions, as he stressed time and time again that both "tranquilizers and new therapeutic methods now permit mental illness to be treated successfully in a very high proportion of cases within relatively short periods of time, weeks and months, rather than years."[36] Despite such hopeful prognostications, the rift between biological and dynamic thinking in psychiatry would only widen in the last quarter of the twentieth century (Chapter 6). But in the late 1950s and the early 1960s, public arguments for the superiority of community treatment and care—along with the ensuing reforms on local, state, and federal levels—were contingent not only on the environmentally driven vision of then-dominant dynamic psychiatry but also on the availability and perceived effectiveness of new biological remedies in the form of psychoactive drugs.

The civil rights era endowed community psychiatry with "the character of a social movement," which paralleled other "melioristic social policies" expected to "reshape welfare and health systems, diminish poverty, and end discrimination."[37] The investment of a liberal, socially oriented psychiatry in the rehabilitation of the mad, especially those diagnosed with severely disabling conditions, from the early 1960s on became coextensive with the intensifying movements for social justice and civil rights. Michael Dear and Jennifer Wolch point out that "instead of spatial isolation of deviant, dangerous, and dependent classes," mental health professionals now increasingly prescribed "spatial integration, engagement in community activities and interaction with the nondependent population in the course of everyday life."[38] Advocacy efforts by various citizen pressure groups and professional organizations coalesced in a movement against traditional asylum practices, which were decried in the aforementioned presidential message for "a desultory interest in confining patients in an institution to wither away."[39] As political and social activists within and without psychiatry mounted public challenges to involuntary commitment, coercive therapy, and extant legal definitions of insanity and criminality, deinstitutionalization came to be seen as a long-overdue corrective to the flagrant abuses of psychiatric power. In this context, patient rights became central to the rhetoric of mental health. The mad confined to the state mental hospital system were citizens and as such were entitled to full participation in society.

The activist focus on patient rights defined a new field of contention in the cultural conversation about madness. *Anyone Can Whistle*, which opened at Broadway's Majestic Theatre on April 4, 1964, participated in this discourse. The critical response to the original production recalled *Reuben Reuben*'s reception in Boston. The reviewers in the press and other commentators on record objected to the show's "heavy" material and confrontational tone. While many appreciated the show's "high intentions" and experimental ambition, most found it "too sophisticated," "too cerebral," or too "smart-ass" for its own good.[40] Yet unlike *Reuben Reuben*, *Whistle* survived its tumultuous out-of-town tryouts, made it to Broadway, and, despite shuttering after a painful nine performances, became something of a cult musical in its afterlife.

Whistle can be said to develop the same line of critical inquiry we have glimpsed in *Reuben Reuben* with regard to sociogenic sources of mental illness and advocacy for social and institutional change. Yet whereas the politics of institutionalization is of a cursory interest to *Reuben Reuben*, it becomes a matter of central concern in *Whistle*. Members of this new musical's creative team were aware of Blitzstein's depictions of the defects of institutional psychiatry during the preceding decade. William and Jean Eckart, who designed *Whistle*'s sets, had created the physical environment of *Reuben Reuben*, including its mental ward scene; Stephen Sondheim, who wrote the score and lyrics, had reportedly attended a backers' audition for Blitzstein's musical.[41] Perhaps even more consequential for *Whistle*'s socially conscious take on madness was the track record of its director and book writer Arthur Laurents, who had participated in the postwar wave of sensational exposés as a script writer for *The Snake Pit* (1948), a film adaptation of Mary Jane Ward's semi-autobiographical novel (1946), which described horrific conditions inside a mental institution.

The agenda of a liberal, socially oriented psychiatry acquires a voice in the initial scenes of *Whistle* through the character of Fay Apple (played by Lee Remick in the original production). Head nurse at Dr. Detmold's Asylum for the Socially Pressured, she refers to her forty-nine patients lovingly as Cookies from the Cookie Jar. Throughout the musical's action, Fay builds a campaign for their release into the community, where they can be "free to be happy or unhappy any way *they* want."[42] On a dramaturgical plane, the idea of integrating the mad into society takes the form of crowd scenes in outdoor public places, a common tactic for this musical theater trend. Like *Man of La Mancha, Dear World, King of Hearts, Ain't Supposed to Die a Natural Death,* and *Sweeney Todd, Whistle* is preoccupied with the place of the mad in urban social geographies. By getting the inmates out of the asylum and onto the street, the musical sets up conditions for the staging and interrogation of ideological conflicts at the heart of the period's discourse on institutionalized madness.

Early in act 1, Fay brings her charges out to a town square where droves of pilgrims are congregating around a rock spurting water purported to have healing powers, a miracle fabricated and marketed by Mayor Cora Hoover Hooper and her coterie. In Fay's opinion, the longer the town's corrupt public officials go on selling this myth, the harder the consequences for those duped by them. The fallout from the disillusionment, once the pilgrims realize the miracle is fake, is likely to take the form of en masse admissions to the Cookie Jar, which is already precariously overcrowded. "Every bed is full and they are sleeping in shifts," she remonstrates, echoing contemporaneous critiques of public mental hospitals.[43] Fay hopes to stop the local government's scheme before it causes an epidemic.

But the site of the miracle is also Fay's opportunity for the advancement of her patients' rights. When Comptroller Schub refuses to sell tickets to the "loonies," she cuts him off indignantly: "NOT—THAT—WORD! . . . Nor any word like it!" Delivered over the ostinato of an "angry" piano and punctuated with loud exclamations of brass, her protestations, which constitute the longest spoken monologue in the musical, are a matter of principle: if the miracle is open to the public, then her patients should be admitted to "that leaking drain pipe," because "Cookies are people, Schub, they are human beings and they are to be treated as such and have the same rights as everyone else!" With further references to "segregated sections" in movie theaters and other manifestations of systemic inequity, Fay's forceful speech on behalf of her patients mobilizes the arguments for social

equality that went into the making of the period's antidiscriminatory legislation, including the Civil Rights Act of 1964, which was being considered
by the Senate at the time of the show's opening and would be signed into
law in July of that year.[44]

Fay's speech reveals ontological conflicts at the core of the sociogenic
paradigm of madness. In framing the asylum inmates as "socially pressured," the musical, at this initial point, straddles two competing, if overlapping, directions of thought within the debates about environmental etiology writ large. On the one hand, madness is an illness that is caused or
aggravated by material and psychological hardships resulting from the
unequal distribution of privilege in society and other external factors. On
the other, it does not appear to be an illness at all but only a social label for
those who are uncomfortably or inconveniently different. As Fay puts it,
her patients have been "quarantined out of fear their disease may be conta-
gious"; they have been put away because they "made other people nervous
by leading individual lives." Madness, then, is not only *caused* by the power
of "groups and systems" but is also *constructed* as such by them.[45] The latter
position begins to gather force in the next scene with the arrival of another
principal character, J. Bowden Hapgood. By the end of the first of its three
acts, *Whistle*'s reflections on madness settle into an unambiguously social-
constructionist mode, anticipating a string of similarly minded musicals in
the 1960s and 1970s.

ANTIPSYCHIATRY AND *ANYONE CAN WHISTLE*

David Savran and Daniel Gundlach write that "*Whistle* attempted to bring
the kind of theatrical and political provocation that was flourishing Off-
Off-Broadway to Broadway audiences who were quite unfamiliar with
experimental idioms," including absurdist modes and methods of storytelling, breaks to the fourth wall, and a metatheatrical commentary on the
passivity of the bourgeois spectator. Madness, too, though "daring" for a
Broadway musical, was a theme at once "highly regarded" and "well-
worn" in an intellectual climate saturated with a range of sociological and
political treatments of the subject, as well as existentialism, absurdist plays,
and Artaud's manifestos.[46] As Laurents tells it, *Whistle*'s distinctly experimental aesthetics took shape "not by design" but as a logical consequence
of his and Sondheim's belief that "content determines form": since "in
Whistle, the content was insane, when I wrote the book it came out insane
and the numbers were crazy."[47] To be sure, madness and avant-gardism

were mutually intertwined in the 1960s, as both were both being championed as creative alternatives to the rational, the conservative, the linear, and the realist in the realm of theatrical performance. It was not that madness preceded experimentalism or the other way around but, rather, that the two tended to accompany, complement, and inform each other within the theatrical and cultural zeitgeist of the 1960s.

The boundaries between literal and metaphorical madness in *Whistle* are extremely porous. Sondheim himself admits that it "wasn't clear" to him or Laurents what Cookies actually were: "Are these loonies? They're called 'Cookies,' but, in fact, they're non-conformists. But they're in an asylum. What is going on here?"[48] This definitional and conceptual indeterminacy, which brings madness into the shared space of mental illness and nonconformism, was symptomatic of much antiestablishment art. In the 1960s, such questions were also being actively reformulated and popularized by the antipsychiatry movement. The varied intellectual projects that are usually grouped by historians under the umbrella of antipsychiary had a shared investment in theorizing the social "constructedness" of mental illness, laying bare the arbitrary ways in which behavioral conventions have been codified into systemic hierarchies that support and are supported by unequal power relations. For Thomas Szasz, Erving Goffman, R. D. Laing, Michel Foucault, and other proponents of these ideas, madness is a product of governing ideologies. Psychiatry, in this context, is usually an agent of social control and coercion; mental illness less a real disorder than a diagnostic label for people society considers deviant and abnormal.

In some ways, a Foucauldian reading of *Whistle* and the other musicals of the trend would be more than justified here. After all, Foucault must exercise an a priori influence on my narrative not only because of the formative role his *Folie et dérasion: Histoire de la folie à l'âge classique* (1961) has played in the modern history of intellectual projects about madness, difference, and disability but also because of the staggering amount of prestige accorded to his ideas in the US academy. Yet the Foucauldian interpretive paradigm has been well established in the extant scholarship on representations of mental distress in theatrical performance. I have therefore chosen to engage texts by Szasz, Goffman, and Laing, which were widely popular among intellectuals, academics, social activists, and countercultural figures during the decades of the social turn in the musical's renditions of madness. While comparable to Foucault's in many ways, these writers' arguments about the social construct of mental illness preceded the publication of the first English translation of his tome in 1965.[49] Additionally, as Staub reminds us, their projects were distinctly different from their French counterpart in that they were "based on direct ethnographic and clinical encounters."[50]

Szasz argued in his book *The Myth of Mental Illness* (1961) that while medicine proper discovers diseases (e.g., paresis), psychiatry merely invents them (e.g., hysteria). The broader implication of his thesis was that psychiatric diagnostic categories served the purpose of explaining, regulating, and policing the behavior of nonconforming members of society. Goffman interrogated the medical model from a sociological rather than a psychiatric standpoint, arguing that patients in asylums, which function like prisonlike total institutions, "distinctively suffer not from mental illness, but from contingencies."[51] Similarly, Laing spoke out ardently against the medical construct of mental illness, insisting that psychiatric nosology passed moral judgments on individuals who failed to meet conventional standards of normality. "There is no such 'condition' as 'schizophrenia,'" he wrote, "but the label is a social fact and the social fact a *political event*." In Laing's view, the bias against and persecution of schizophrenics made our "enlightened epoch . . . a veritable age of Darkness." Like Szasz, Laing, and Foucault, he posited and showed by example that in conducting inquiry into the sources and nature of madness, it was "the social system, not single individuals extrapolated from it" that "must be the object of study."[52]

Whistle's affinity with the social-constructionist model of madness promulgated by antipsychiatry becomes evident in the final scene of act 1, a long, musicalized sequence called "Simple," in which Hapgood, a newly arrived Cookie Jar patient mistaken for a psychiatrist (Harry Guardino in the original cast), is asked to identify the Cookies among the Pilgrims at the site of the town miracle. On one level, by making the mad and the nonmad completely indistinguishable, the scene interrogates the very existence of mental illness. The sight of the asylum inmates blending in with the presumably "well adjusted" is in keeping with Szasz's and Laing's ideas about the pathologization of individual conduct in mainstream psychiatry: as long as they continue to look and act like the majority, there is nothing actually wrong with them, no signs of antisocial behavior for psychiatrists to turn into a medical condition.[53] In this context, the madness of the Cookies is not an occasion for contemplating the internal structures of lived experience specific to those designated mentally ill but a rhetorical device for asking questions about the plenary use of state power over precariously situated citizens and the civic limits to one's freedom in defining one's personal reality and living according to it. The figures of inmates are thus predisposed to function as metaphors for nonconformism and political dissent.

If the asylum residents are not mad but only labeled and treated as such by the mainstream, what does this scene say about society? In a commonplace twist of allegorization, madness is repurposed as a descriptor of the absurdity of American life. In the words of Angela Lansbury, who played the part of the mayoress in the original production, Laurents's dramatic premise is that "the 'Cookies' in life are the only sane members of society, and the so-called silent majority belonged in the nuthouse."[54] To dramatize this thesis in the "Simple" sequence, the authors resort to a traditional satirical use of insanity to create a sense of a world gone topsy-turvy, keying up their targets and messaging to the priorities of 1960s antiestablishment politics. Sondheim's music, Savran and Gundlach write, creates a disorienting effect through a kind of "rhythmic undecidabilty," equivocating in duple and triple times, "oscillating back and forth between simple and compound meters," and "including sections in which the two meters become entangled or overlaid." At home in this unstable soundscape, Hapgood, in a fashion "closer to free association than deductive logic," conducts a series of sung and spoken interrogations, encapsulating some of the country's urgent problems, including gender inequality, racism, fearmongering, standardization and commodification of life, and the proliferation of weapons of mass destruction.[55] Those who participate in the system without questioning the status quo, he implies, are the really mad ones. This viewpoint is made explicit in the number's finale, in which everyone charges downstage and, lining up across the stage in the "weird glow" of the footlights, "chant[s] fast and shrill, with mounting intensity" until a blackout plunges them into darkness, abruptly ending the cacophony. Picked out by a single light, Hapgood "looks at the audience with a smile and, breaking the dead silence, says quietly: 'You are all mad.'"[56]

As in the texts of classical antipsychiatry, which apprehended a specter of encroaching totalitarianism in every major institution, the staging of a standardized, automatized society in Whistle brings into view the stealthy involvement of psychiatry in the mass production of the model citizen. In Szasz's theory, committal practices were a salient feature of the "Therapeutic State," a concept he proposed in 1963 and developed in much of his subsequent writing. This modern form of polity, he explained, supplanted "the rule of law and punishment" with "the rule of medical discretion and 'therapy.'"[57] "Simple" can be said to dramatize a version of Szasz's Therapeutic State in which "medical symbols" have taken the role of "patriotic symbols" to the extent that "words like democracy or mental health may be waved about like flags on the Fourth of July, and for the same reasons." In such a society, people have given over their lives to psychiatrists, who, under the pretext of patient welfare, "act as agents of social control, compa-rable to policemen, judges, or prison personnel." Hapgood's tongue-in-cheek manipulation of a docile, if brittle, crowd hints at the insidious effects of psychiatric hegemony and its veneer of "do-goodism," which trouble radical critics like Szasz.[58] The hero, dishing up a series of pointedly non-sensical diagnostic rationales couched in mock-syllogistic patterns, pokes fun at the scientism of psychiatric orthodoxy, whose determinations of mental illness, as Szasz would say, only serve "covert preferences of indi-vidualistic or collectivistic ethics and their attendant notions concerning the duties and privileges of citizen and state in regard to each other."[59] The townspeople are shown to be blindly dependent on Hapgood for direc-tions to their proper place in society, demanding anxiously: "Doctor, what Group am I in? Where do I belong? Where am I? Tell me where I am?"[60] One by one, these cries are absorbed into an exuberant waltz swelling over "an accompaniment that, superimposing simple and complex meters, sounds like it is tripping over itself."[61]

The supreme governing function of the medical-scientific establishment within the town's sociopolitical system reaches its apotheosis in the next scene, in which we see Hapgood being carried around the town square on a litter, cheered and besieged for autographs, to the sounds of a chanting crowd rhyming "well-adjusted" with "trusted" and "not neurotic" with "patriotic."[62] As in Szasz's vision of a mental health system abetting totali-tarianism, the implication of psychiatry in the machinery of social engi-neering on the stage is so complete that members of this community cannot be sure of their own identity or their common standards of citizenship without being adjudicated by psychiatric experts.

While the musical assumes a clearly oppositional stance to the field of psychiatry, its attitude toward psychoanalysis proper is more ambiguous, which also has its parallels in antipsychiatry. The mid-1960s marked the end of the institutional and cultural reign of psychoanalysis, as the spe-cialty's clinical authority within mainstream psychiatry began to dwindle. That is not to say, however, that antipsychiatry's leading figures rejected psychoanalysis in toto. On the contrary, much of their theorizing exploited the socially oriented insights developed by postwar psychodynamic psy-chiatrists and neo-Freudian philosophers and was written in a loosely psy-choanalytic register.[63] For Szasz and Laing, who were themselves psycho-analytically trained medical doctors, the main target was asylum psychiatry, which was identified with a biological view of mental health and somati-cally based treatments such as lobotomy and shock therapy. When it came to the analytic enterprise, these writers rejected medicalized, dogmatic iterations of Freudianism, such as ego psychology, for underwriting the pseudoscientific rationalizations of psychiatric orthodoxy, promoting conformity and adaptation, and facilitating America's hegemonic project of social engineering and control. Yet in exploring the idiosyncrasies and contingencies of the individual psyche, they remained attracted to what Eli Zaretsky characterizes as the "charismatic, anti-institutional" aspects of psychoanalysis.[64] Seeking to resurrect from the analytic tradition its originary skepticism, shorn of diagnostic and curative imperatives, Szasz and Laing cleaved to the same antinomian strains in psychoanalysis that inspired much political theorizing in the 1960s among members of the counterculture and the New Left.[65]

The distinction between psychoanalysis as a homogenizing and coercive therapeutic force and an emancipatory source of radical individualism plays out in the musical's treatment of the specialty. Laurents's partiality to psychoanalytic thought had shown up in his prior work. *The Snake Pit* had served as an indictment of institutional psychiatry yet endorsed the principles of psychoanalytic treatment. His 1946 play *Home of the Brave*, dealing with soldiers' experiences of wartime trauma, likewise presented the efforts of psychoanalytic psychiatry in glowing terms. *Whistle*, by contrast, takes jabs at psychoanalysis in the "Simple" sequence and in scenes with Dr. Detmold, a medically trained analyst shown to be ridiculously ineffectual and thoroughly indifferent to his patients' needs.[66] Yet at the same time, *Whistle* attempts to salvage an iconoclastic, antinomian Freud from the rubble of medicalized psychoanalysis. When Fay is forced to identify her patients to the authorities (one of several allusions to McCarthyism in the musical), we find out that they share last names with trailblazing historical figures like Gandhi, Ibsen, Mozart, Brecht, Jorgensen, and Kierkegaard. As the recaptured Cookies "march off in the direction of Dr. Detmold's Cookie Jar," singing wistfully with defiant grins on their faces, a patient named Freud is among them. In this symbolic act of locking up the creator of psychoanalysis along with other individuals who "made people nervous by leading individual lives," the musical typifies the period's renewed interest in going back to the charismatic, anti-institutional origins of psychoanalysis as an alternative to American Freudian orthodoxy, which many countercultural and New Leftist figures viewed as complicit in the Cold War state ideology.[67] Retaining a link to the artistic intelligentsia's continued fascination with psychoanalytic thinking as a conduit for subversive thought and political radicalism, *Whistle* wrestles with the contradictions of a historical moment that, in the words of Zaretsky, found it necessary, yet again, to refashion Freud as "a theorist of suppressed longings, utopia and desire, surrealism and the Situationist International, in a word, of revolution."[68]

The musical's indebtedness to psychoanalysis also manifests itself on the level of individual characterization. Here the authors differentiate between somewhat flat, unsympathetic characters like the mayoress, deliberately written as a superficial musical comedy type singing pastiche numbers, and the more dimensional protagonists, Fay and Hapgood.[69] The latter express themselves within a musical stylistic register that Stephen Banfield describes as "symphonic. That is [their numbers] have dramatic pretensions: they enhance our sympathies and forward the protagonists' aspirations in terms that go beyond the simple generic image."[70] Fay and Hapgood's long scene in a hotel suite in act 2 is a case in point. Laurents and Sondheim's writing here is moored in psychoanalytic conventions of interiority, which they themselves helped popularize in their previous collaboration, Gypsy. As part of this psychological mode, the action moves from a public square, dominated by what Sondheim describes as "show biz style," into a private room, which he associates with a "more personal musical language."[71] Withdrawing from the world of outside appearances into the realm of interior substance, we find out that Fay's character is constituted by a crippling neurotic tension between two halves of her self: her easily accessible, highly operative "nurse" side, dominated by "control and order," and her latent "French soubrette" side, characterized by sexually uninhibited behavior.[72] On the face of it, her inner conflict is presented in terms of a humorously reductive psychoanalytic reading and, as such, provides much material for comic business and banter in the scene. Yet the effect of Fay's troubled duality is also to lay the groundwork for her song "Anyone Can Whistle," which, reversing the sensibility from the frivolous to the melancholy, ruefully aestheticizes her repressed character through her inability to whistle.

Over the years the titular ballad has garnered much praise from critics, performers, and fans as a prime example of psychologically deep musical theater writing. In Joanne Gordon's opinion, which is typical of the song's reception history, "Anyone Can Whistle" gives "the clearest exposition of Sondheim's emotional priorities": "profound angst and sensitivity" expressed with "subtlety, anxiety, and fundamental seriousness."[73] As moments like this show, Whistle, despite its attempts to sound both critical and blasé in relation to psychoanalysis, cannot disentangle itself from the psychologized forms of personhood that infiltrated the art form earlier in the century, nor from the lure of depth they tease and the critical prestige they bestow. When it comes to creating authentically flawed modern characters, Laurents and Sondheim invariably fall back on depth-psychological views of the human psyche.

Hapgood's solo, "Everybody Says Don't," by contrast, paints a rather uncomplicated picture of saying no to personal reservations and societal restrictions. He is not the only mental patient to express himself through song in this musical. Cookies have a short march-like theme, "I'm Like the Bluebird," which, repeated several times over the course of the performance, makes their dissident sentiments transparent in the second verse: "I should worry, I should kick, I should be a heretic."[74] But as an incidental number sung by a group of dimly delineated, abstract characters, more theatrical than human, it does not aspire to the flesh-and-blood vitality of the "I am" or "I want" song type, remaining an impersonal, distant gesture. Hapgood's number, however, not only rearticulates and amplifies the links between mental illness and nonconformism Cookies stand for but also delivers a brash affirmation of personal grit and defiance with the kind of aggrandizing panache that is all but synonymous with Broadway musicals, a quality that helps account for the song's continued appeal to recording artists and nightclub performers. Singing "low, with tight anger at first, then with mounting passion," Hapgood attempts to sway a reluctant Fay to his rebellious lifestyle, to inspirit her to "tilt at windmills," "laugh at the kings," and "make a noise." Though performed in the intimate setting of a hotel room, "Everybody Says Don't" straddles the private and the public, and, building from a "ripple" to a "wave," spills into a program of social and political mobilization for radical change. His ambitious vision invokes social-constructionist views of mental illness circulating in America's intellectual circles in the 1960s, expressing and popularizing the same kind of antiestablishment ideas we have seen in antipsychiatry. As Hapgood says to Fay before launching into song, "The world made those Cookies, you didn't. . . . Fix the world, not them!" A spirited exchange between the two characters following "Everybody Says Don't" evolves into a three-part ballet in which they tear up medical records and symbolically release Cookies from their status as mental patients, "setting them free, in dance, to be what they want." The hotel suite gone, the stage erupts into a utopian image of a jubilant street, where the joy of the dancing, liberated mad is so catching that "Fay herself is infected and begins to dance freely and happily."[75]

Whistle's dramatic universe, Sondheim suggests, is powered by a vigorous dialectic between the forces of cynicism and idealism.[76] Hapgood, who acts as an agent of cynicism in "Simple" and an agent of idealism in the sequence described above, is himself caught up in this conflict. In the course of the show, he stakes out dueling positions, now pronouncing himself "a retired Don Quixote" no longer "responsible to or for anything or anyone," now resuming his "bad" habits as "a practicing idealist" and recruiting Fay into a mass movement. "I can't just turn it off in one day!" he explains. His attitude toward being institutionalized is similarly riddled with contradictions: the asylum is at once a haven where one might contemplate the world at an ironic remove and a terrifying place of confinement for the disaffected that has no place in a free society. Leaving these paradoxes in play, the musical's finale implies that Hapgood chooses the freedom to live at large the way he wants. Whether this choice means going back to the "mad" activism of his idealist years or tuning out is unclear, but it does indicate a life without "pretending to be like everyone else." Fay, who is converted to his romantic philosophy by the end of act 3, concludes that Hapgood and "all the crazy people" like him are "the hope of the world."[77]

FOUR | **"To Dream the Impossible Dream . . ."**

Communities of Madness in the
Musicals of the Long Sixties

As new questions about the social predication of madness continued to multiply across American culture, more and more artists engaged with them in portraying human affairs on the stage. Exemplifying this trend, creative teams behind the musicals in this chapter develop and expand the dramatic strategies we have seen in the previous one: the attribution of madness to a handful of sympathetically portrayed like-minded people, who are marginally placed within a larger negatively depicted society; the valorization of an insightful madness and its coupling with nonconformity; images and discussions of an insane world, sinking in crises of its own making; and deep-seated, if at times obscured, psychoanalytic modes of selfhood in the service of dramatizing pivotal moments of individual epiphany and confession. The portraiture of a distressed interior balancing between self-scrutiny and self-evasion indexes the enduring utility of psychodynamic models of madness in aggrandizing the art form's serious aspirations. But the period's preoccupation with sociogenic forces and processes also animates the notion of madness as an outsider's coign of vantage, a countercultural positionality that enjoys high prestige as the locus of theater making considered consequential in the zeitgeist of the sixties. Moving across these two frequently conjoined valences of meaning, madness bridges individual awakening and social transformation. This leads to different outcomes for the ruling system portrayed as in need of change: it can be dismantled, reformed, or condemned. But the end results of these stratagems matter less vividly on the stage than the extravagant talent of madness for arousing, through poetry, music, and dance, all those who will listen, emboldening them to believe and dream the impossible together.

MAN OF LA MANCHA: A MADMAN'S PROTEST

Man of La Mancha, with a book by Dale Wasserman, lyrics by Joe Darion, and music by Mitch Leigh, opened at the ANTA Washington Square Theatre on November 22, 1965. Directed by Albert Marre, the musical won five Tony Awards and ran for a total of 2,328 performances. Although contractually *Man of La Mancha* enjoyed the legal status of a Broadway show, the downtown location and unconventional appearance of its first New York venue, which would house the show until its move to the Martin Beck Theatre in 1968, linked it to the city's alternative theater scene. From a creative standpoint, the production substantiated these associations through the use of anti-illusionist techniques on a thrust stage configured as an abstract platform with adaptable props. The simulations of improvisation by a company of players in the musical recalled the aesthetics of *The Fantasticks*, which was playing at the Sullivan Street Playhouse located in the same neighborhood. The forbidding prison set, designed and lit by Howard Bay, established an oppressively grim environment nearer in spirit to Peter Brook's production of *Marat/Sade* than to traditional musical theater fare. All these factors imbued *Man of La Mancha* with the atmosphere of an experimental off-Broadway event.

In its plotting and philosophic outlook, *Man of La Mancha* closely follows Wasserman's earlier teleplay, *I, Don Quixote*, which was broadcast in November 1959. Like its source script, the musical uses a play-within-a-play technique to conjure up equivalences between the Spanish writer Miguel de Cervantes awaiting trial by the Inquisition and his world-famous mad character Don Quixote. When the jailed author, who is first and foremost a "poet of the theatre" in the musical, is prevailed upon to expound his worldview, he devises a piece of entertainment, casting himself in the role of his starry-eyed creation, Quixote, and distributing the other parts to his fellow prisoners. This dramatic structure, in which the action shuttles between the two realms of the double narrative, works like an optical instrument with two alternating lenses. The stage picture and its narrative setting transform periodically before our eyes, but, despite the changes in detail, we are still looking at the same thing. "We are both men of La Mancha," confirms Cervantes during the final minutes of the musical as he exits to face the Inquisition after playing Quixote's death scene. Having merged into one stage figure, the madman and the playwright are celebrated as fearless visionaries inspiring small groups of disaffected, victimized individuals to follow their valiant, if impractical, example.

There are, however, notable formal differences between the two universes of the double narrative in the musical. The outer play, set in a Seville prison, is stylized as spoken drama, in which singing or dancing, if any, Wasserman explains, must be "motivated realistically." The inner play, which channels the action to "various places in the imagination of Miguel de Cervantes," has "musical style and form" and is envisioned as representative of a poeticized, heightened reality. This world, in contrast to the external, framing setting of the prison, is presented openly and self-consciously as a live performance, a provisional existence in the process of being constructed, a creative act. The outer scenes thus retain the basic aesthetics of I, Don Quixote, which, by Wasserman's own admission, cleave to the "assertive naturalism" of television. The inner scenes update the earlier iteration of the project by giving it a form that the author characterizes as "disciplined yet free, simple-seeming yet intricate, and above all bold enough to accomplish that ephemeral objective which is called 'total theater.'"[1]

It is within the inner play's aesthetic and metaphysical realm that the story of madness comes to life. Cervantes begins his musical charade facetiously, disclaiming its serious intent. Yet by degrees, he unspools a thread of grave metaphysical reflections from a show of Quixote's antics and, by raising the stakes of his protagonist's staunch idealism, accrues to his madness a distinctively heroic pathos. Richard Kiley, who originated the twofold part, received ecstatic reviews for his performance, winning a Tony Award. As critic Howard Taubman observed, when "shading into Quixote . . . his eyes take on a wild, proud, otherworldly look. His posture is preternaturally erect. His folly becomes a kind of humbling wisdom."[2] The iconography of Kiley's performance within the performance instantiates the idealistic spirit of the knight's status as visionary within the musical's narrative. This "mad, gallant, affecting figure," who sees life not as it is but as it should be, is presented by the character of Cervantes as a remedy for the ills of a "lunatic" world blinded by the surplus of pragmatism and reason.[3]

The merged identities of the writer and the knight errant, embodied by a single actor, make both of them into emblems of dissent, highlighting the terms of equivalence between the story of imprisonment in the outer play and the story of madness in the inner performance. Like the writers of antipsychiatry, Wasserman invokes the Inquisition as a readily legible and spectacular allusive framework for his case about the state-sanctioned persecution of nonconformism and psychic diversity. In the years that elapsed between the teleplay and the musical, Wasserman explored these themes in a contemporary context by penning a stage adaptation of Ken Kesey's famous novel *One Flew over the Cuckoo's Nest* (1962). This play, like its controversial source material, which was instantly adopted by the counterculture as a manifesto of individuality, offered a lurid story of hair-raising abuses of psychiatric authority in a mental institution. Before rendering Kesey's novel to the stage, Wasserman recalls, he set out to learn "as much as possible about the insane and the asylums that housed them, . . . starting with a posh clinic in New York City and sliding down-scale to the abysmal asylum at Milledgeville, Georgia," which he remembers as "a classic snake pit where patients spent their days chained to radiators." Wasserman's stage adaptation of Kesey's novel premiered on Broadway in a 1963 production starring Kirk Douglas and was revived off-Broadway in a new 1971 staging that would run for over two thousand performances. The playwright explains that thematically *Cuckoo's Nest* and his Quixote project can be regarded as the same play, in which the protagonist, "a rebel against society, sets out to right wrongs." Both heroes, Randle McMurphy and Quixote, are "stubborn individualists who won't conform. Both are punished and eventually crushed by the society against which they rebelled."[4]

These themes in Wasserman's work tracked with the ideas driving contemporaneous analyses of mental hospitals in antipsychiatry. In his sociological study *Asylums* (1961), Erving Goffman compared asylums to prisons on the grounds that both functioned as total institutions, controlling and predetermining the inmate's self-image and behavior. Presenting the results of his observation at St. Elizabeths Hospital in Washington, DC, he outlined a complex network of social procedures by which civilians with distress are transformed into chronic patients through hospitalization, as they enter into the interpretive scheme of the total institution. The scheme begins upon the inmate's arrival, which the staff takes to be "*prima facie* evidence that one must be the kind of person the institution was set up to handle. A man in a political prison must be traitorous; a man in a prison must be lawbreaker; a man in a mental hospital must be sick. If not traitorous, criminal, or sick, why else would he be there?"[5] This initiation process is replayed in the opening scene of *Man of La Mancha*. Mirroring the institution's presupposition that one's presence within its walls must mean one belongs here, Cervantes's fellow prisoners subject him to a mock trial. "But what have I done?" the playwright begs. "We'll find something," one of the inmates replies impassively.[6] The ad hoc courtroom drama the prisoners improvise parrots the attitudes from which they themselves have suffered; their play-acting reenacts the rote moral determinism accorded to the inmates by the system.

Folded into the framework of the prison as a total environment in *Man of La Mancha* is a meditation on madness, with a set of interlocking antipsychiatric themes centering on the pathologization of psychic diversity through medicalization and coercive therapy. At the core of the inner play, presented by Cervantes for the mock trial in the outer play, is a question about the source and nature of Quixote's behavior: has he merely "been carried away by his imagination," or has he "lost his mind and is suffering from delusions?" The former formulation belongs to a priest character named Padre, the latter, a mental health expert, Dr. Carrasco. According to the first interpretation (shared by Cervantes in the outer play), Quixote need not be viewed through a medical framework. He is to be thought of as an original, erudite thinker who, not unlike *Anyone Can Whistle*'s Hapgood in his younger days, deliberately "lays down the melancholy burden of sanity and conceives the strangest project ever imagined . . . to become a knight-errant and sally forth into the world to right all wrongs." Wasserman's metatheatrical conceit helps dramatize this point of view by framing madness as a personal choice of conduct in relation to society. Putting on the costume and makeup of Quixote in full view of the onstage spectators and the real audience, Cervantes assumes his hero's frame of mind with a certain "tongue-in-cheek" distance: "an actor aware that he's performing." The musical's unraveling of Quixote's "gentle insanities" as a theatrical identity, which one can step in and out of, stages madness as a deliberate expression of personal philosophy, an ideological script rather than a medical condition.[7]

The second alternative, promoted by Dr. Carrasco (Jon Cypher in the original cast), frames Quixote's madness as a mental illness requiring therapeutic interventions. In this medicalized interpretation, the errant patient, whose real name is Alonso Quijana, thinks he is someone else, may present a danger to others or himself ("Who knows what violence he has committed!"), and must therefore be handed over to a medical authority for treatment. Goffman's analysis in *Asylums* shows that a person's transition from civilian to patient status requires the involvement of their "next-of-relation." The curative project in *Man of La Mancha* is accordingly facilitated by Quixote's family and household members. In a scene bookended by the musical number "I'm Only Thinking of Him," Quixote's niece and housekeeper, ashamed about "having a madman in the family," threatened by his unconventional behavior, and seduced by thoughts of an inheritance, sing of longing to "lock him up and throw away the key."[8] Dr. Carrasco, as the mediating mental health professional in the institutionalization scheme outlined by Goffman, assures the family that the course of action he has defined "involves no betrayal but is rather a medical action taken in the best interest of the pre-patient."[9] Armed with the excuse of moral duty, the household members reprise the song, this time joined by the doctor, to restate their role as disinterested parties motivated solely by whatever may be of help to the sick person close to them. The hypocritical motif of "I'm Only Thinking of Him" sets in motion Dr. Carrasco's quest to "wean this man from madness" and "turn him from his course," the prospect of confinement looming over the hero.[10] The medical concern with the patient's welfare in the world of Man of La Mancha carries within it a menace, a built-in mechanism of state- and family-sanctioned coercion threatening one's individual autonomy and freedom of self-expression. Such sinister prospects fueled the countercultural antipathy toward psychiatry across the political, clinical, and artistic domains in the 1960s and 1970s.

In order to administer a "cure" to Quixote's "sickness," Dr. Carrasco sets up a therapeutic ambush. Disguising himself as a knight, he appears before his unwitting patient, wearing "a chain mail tunic on which are mounted tiny mirrors" and wielding a shield of polished steel, whose "blinding and bewildering" reflective effect is further multiplied by a group of attendants with "similar mirrors." Thus armored, he engineers conditions for Quixote's epiphany in a kind of choreographed analytic session, shocking him with a view of "things as they truly are." Endorsing the primacy of "objective" reality reflected in the mirrors, a reality in which Quixote is not a "gallant knight" but "an aging fool," the doctor's coup de théâtre invalidates his patient's fantasy life and furnishes correctives to his "disordered" thinking. The moment literalizes the theatricality of psychoanalytic procedure. "Drown—drown in the mirror," the doctor intones, guiding Quixote, with a hypnotic insistence, to peel off the surface of his daily "masquerade" and "go deep" where his true self ought to be found. As lights dim on the sight of a "beaten" Quixote "huddled weeping on the floor," the setting alters back to the prison, where the Captain of the Inquisition arrives to summon Cervantes to trial, reinforcing the links between the church's persecution of religious dissent and psychiatry's policing of personal opinion and conduct.[11]

Man of La Mancha's staging of the psychoanalytic intervention echoes contemporaneous antipsychiatric attacks on ego psychologists' therapeutic ideal of social adaptation, with its emphasis on identifying and correcting "deviant" thoughts and behaviors in the name of narrowly defined, rigid norms of mental health. Dr. Carrasco's terms of treatment have far-reaching restrictive implications: "Thy freedom is forfeit and thou must obey my every command." At the beginning of his next and final scene Quixote is seen on his deathbed under the watchful supervision of his household and the doctor. The "I'm Only Thinking of Him" leitmotif returns in a "melancholy" rendition. With his eyes "open but deep-hollowed and remote, windows on a mind that has retreated to some secret place," the hero appears aware of his words and actions being under rigorous scrutiny. His apparent difficulty in recalling the events of his quest has less to do with a failure of his memory than with his surrender to psychiatric power: "In my illness I dreamed so strangely . . . no . . . I dare not tell lest you think me mad." As Padre feared, the "cure" turns out to be "worse than the disease." Robbed of the daily sustenance provided by his fantasy, Quixote dies. "Don't you think I did right?" demands a strident Dr. Carrasco. "Yes, there is the contradiction," sighs Padre.[12]

The organizing function of musical expression in the articulation and performance of a noble, enlightened madness in *Man of La Mancha* is best exemplified by Quixote's anthem, "The Quest" (aka "The Impossible Dream"), which explicates and glorifies the idealistic principles of his impractical mission. As Darion, the musical's lyricist, recalls, the creative team saw this number as "the fulcrum of the whole show. It was the point . . . where the audience would begin to admire him (Quixote) rather than finding him an old fool."[13] The song's memorable opening lines, "To dream the impossible dream / To fight the unbeatable foe," come from a short poetic statement declaimed by the knight in the teleplay. Enlarging Wasserman's thesis to the scale of a Broadway song, Darion's lyrics depict a lifelong climb, tragically hopeless yet unyielding, to "reach the unreachable star." Leigh's tune mimics the vicissitudes of the quest, descending to a near standstill at the point of the hero's narrative death ("when I'm laid to my rest") yet soaring up again to project a fantastical, if posthumous, victory in a grand, solemn conclusion at the top of his register. The skyward aspirations of the melody are buoyed by the march of a bolero in the accompaniment. As Raymond Knapp observes, "The rhythms of the bolero are eminently suitable for the building strategies of the inspirational Broadway number, establishing an ostinato rhythm as an emblem of obsession yet controlling it" steadily, with a "hypnotic effect," to the end.[14] This musical expression of a madman's mission to "fight for the right" resonated with the vigorous idealism of political and social activism during the years of the antiwar protests and the civil rights movements.[15] Echoed across the nation in countless recordings by celebrated vocal artists, it became a popular manifesto of quixotic resistance.

For every idealistic expression of hope in the text of *Man of La Mancha* there is a grim affirmation of existential despair. Yet a comparison of the teleplay's and the musical's endings shows that the story's capacity to project an optimistic outcome inflated between 1959 and 1965, as if to better accommodate the heady promises of the new time. The closing shots of *I, Don Quixote* single out one convert, an incarcerated woman who "stands apart from the others, in her own dream." Visually, she is to be read as someone poised to take the mantle of the madman's vision. Yet musically, the spark she might carry forward is all but extinguished by the augmenting roll of the drums and the chanting of the Inquisition, which concludes the teleplay. *Man of La Mancha*, however, ends with the image of a group of united prisoners, who, one by one, enter into a reprise of "The Quest," twice nudging the song's key upward, until the fervor of their voices, "swelling in full chorus, overwhelms the 'Inquisition theme.'"[16] Quixote's music collapses the distinctions between the inner and the outer settings of the show. The representational mode associated with the story of his lunacy in the inner performance has carried over into the outer play, for nothing about the polished, harmonized singing of the prisoners or the sweeping sound of the omniscient orchestra is realistic. The inmates, having passed through a musical about a madman, have adopted his song as their protest credo, and, in a sense, become like him, causing a shift in the metaphysical structure of their world, as if to rewrite it for a revolution.

DEAR WORLD: A MADWOMAN'S PROTEST

Dear World, with a score and lyrics by Jerry Herman and a book by Jerome Lawrence and Robert E. Lee, opened at the Mark Hellinger Theatre on February 6, 1969. A musicalization of Jean Giraudoux's 1943 play *La folle de Chaillot*, this philosophic anticapitalist fable tells the story of an eighty-year-old woman called Countess Aurelia, "considered by most people to be mad," who "stops a group of greedy, unscrupulous businessmen from destroying Paris."[17] *Dear World* did not do all too well critically or commercially, closing after 132 performances. However disappointing the reception was, Herman and other members of the creative team had regarded the idea of a musical based on Giraudoux's drama as a daring proposition, an occasion for creating an offbeat Broadway show that would be both socially conscious and aesthetically elevated. The early drafts of the book evince meticulous attempts on the part of Lawrence and Lee to flesh out a fervent didactic message about the evils of capitalist greed and consumerism, including an expansive choreographed sequence staging the mob mentality of a "Plastic Society." While various revisions in the course of the protracted tryout and preview period softened the more abrasive portions of the libretto, shrinking its list of targets, the original production, as directed and choreographed by Joe Layton and designed by Oliver Smith, still conveyed, with a nearly agitprop directness, the anticapitalist critique at the heart of the original play.

For Herman, who viewed Giraudoux as the author of "challenging literary material," the play suggested a need for more legitimate musical solutions in the form of "art songs." According to his memoir, he deliberately moved away from the "show-biz sound" of his 1960s smash hit musical comedies, Hello, Dolly! and Mame, and composed a score that he describes as being "of a higher caliber": "It's more mature, it's more classical, it's more inventive, it's more daring."[18] Angela Lansbury, who originated the part of Aurelia, also entered into the project with a measure of high-cultural aspirations predetermined, in part, by the dramatic pedigree of Giraudoux's play. The acting challenge offered by the material appeared to hold out the promise of raising her Broadway career to a level of critical prestige still somehow unattainable to her, despite her Tony Award–winning tour de force performance as the eponymous leading lady in Mame. As she recounts, Herman offered her the role of Aurelia after it had been turned down by Katharine Hepburn (who starred in the film adaptation of the play). Lansbury accepted enthusiastically because she "wanted to play a serious role" and prove to everyone that she was "more than that madcap polly kind of thing," Mame.[19] Her madwoman of Chaillot would be lauded as "one of the great portraits in the history of American musicals," earning her a second Tony.[20]

Unlike Anyone Can Whistle and Man of La Mancha, Dear World is not in the least concerned with the flaws or conspiracies of the medical-psychiatric establishment, but, similar to these two musicals, it pits the foresight of a wise madness against an ailing society. Once again, the stage population is divided into two camps, both designated mad but to diametrically opposed ends. As the titular song spells out, the planet has been rapidly declining into ill health. The perpetrators of this crisis are the oil-hungry corporations and banks, whose moneygrubbing schemes, posing a grave danger to the environment, are enabled by a pleasure-seeking, politically inert mainstream. This world, in the musical's estimation, is "out on a binge" and "out of its mind."[21] Contrasted with the negatively mad, capitalist society are the madwoman Aurelia and her community of fellow eccentrics and vagabonds, who aid her in the ambitious task of rescuing the city and, by extension, the planet. One of the more detailed drafts of the libretto explains that "there is a warmth, beauty, understanding, camaraderie about the group which inhabits this enclave of Chaillot: a quiet rapport among them that gives them a special vividness, perhaps even enchantment—somehow missing in the President [of the corporation] and his automated allies."[22] Bringing together a sewage worker, a street entertainer, a deaf-mute, and other kinds of marginally situated denizens of Paris, Aurelia's hippie-like tribe collectively represented the redeeming force of a status-quo-defying madness. Critic Martin Gottfried quipped in *Women's Wear Daily* that the musical might as well be titled *Queer World*.[23]

Dear World shares *Man of La Mancha*'s interest in the ability of the mind to "weave a dream" protecting one from "despair."[24] The subject takes center stage when Aurelia is visited by her two friends, Constance, the Madwoman of the Flea Market (Carmen Mathews in the original cast), and Gabrielle, the Madwoman of Montmartre (Jane Connell). The relocation of the action from the public exterior of the Parisian neighborhood to Aurelia's private sewer-adjacent apartment, where she receives her guests for tea, complements the scene's interior turn in characterization. Musically, "The Tea Party," divided into five musical sections with intermittent dialogue and singing ("Memory," "Pearls," "Dickie," "Voices," and "Thoughts"), is an intricate chamber piece, which, in Herman's opinion, "could have come straight out of classical opera."[25] The three madwomen, drifting off into reverie, express themselves in stream-of-consciousness patterns that command a view of their prolific fantasy lives. Sifting through elusive snatches of old memories and new, made-up ones, they cannot seem to agree on a uniform account of the past, nor of the present. In the final section of the piece, however, a reprise of the last three themes laid contrapuntally on top of one another bands the varied sounds of their subjective experiences into a harmonious coexistence, without endorsing any one perspective as more valid than the rest. These musico-dramatic forays into depth-psychological territory elicited the critics' compliments, despite otherwise unsympathetic reviews. Walter Kerr conceded in the *New York Times* that "quite often there is something strangely authentic, in a rich legitimate sense about [the musical]." During the tea party, "The stage is in repose and can afford to be because the women are *there*. The moment is close to the best in Giraudoux, close to light opera, and close to perfect."[26]

As in the case of Quixote's illusions in *Man of La Mancha*, the contradictions apparent in the madwomen's accounts can be conceivably apprehended as a symptom of age-related cognitive changes. Yet while this reading is certainly available, *Dear World* aestheticizes these narratives not as a frailty to be pitied but as a rigorous survival strategy, a productive space in which these women hang on to life. "Everything that was . . . is / Everything that lived . . . lives," insists Aurelia in "Thoughts."[27] Echoing *Man of La Mancha*'s "espousal of illusion as man's strongest spiritual need, the most meaningful function of his imagination," the tea party scene reflects on the generative role of fantasy in equipping these women with mental images and ideas that keep them from breakdown in the experience of loss and grief.[28] Such themes are also diffused through other moments in the musical, resurfacing in Aurelia's ballads "And I Was Beautiful" and "I Don't Want to Know."

The latter number stages a defensive act of denial, situating its mechanism in the slippery distinctions between conscious and unconscious strata of the mind. Herman says that "I Don't Want to Know" is one of his "'statement songs' like 'I Am What I Am' and 'Before the Parade Passes By.' It's the Madwoman's statement that she is angry with the misery and the ugliness and the cruelty in the world, and she's not going to put up with it anymore."[29] Yet the song is also distinctly different from Albin's and Dolly's fairly unambiguous hymns of empowerment in that it contrives a plan of attack by disavowing rather than coming to terms with a newly revealed truth. Aurelia is not about to move out in front, daring all to take a look at her proud poise. She turns away from the challenge and, burying her head in the sands of her memories, tries, unsuccessfully, to "live in a world full of lies."[30] Written in triple time, the song begins gently, the enchanted murmurs of the harp and the concertina conjuring up nostalgic images of carefree summers, blissful lovers, and laughing children. The lyrics, however, proceed by negation, establishing that none of these things are happening. By degrees, the music catches up to Aurelia's disclaimed anger, accelerating into a fully orchestrated frenzy. It is as if one part of her mind is clinging desperately to the waltz as a reservoir for the reassuring memories, while another, more potent part is interfering with this object, straining and overwriting the semiotic codes of the music. As Kerr reported in a rapturous coverage of Lansbury's performance, "Moving to the footlights, eyes hurt with the years and angry with mascara, jaw tight and every feather aquiver, she pushes [the truth] away with nervous energy, a will of steel and a rhythm she has caught by the throat. The words say, sharply, 'I will not have it!'"[31] The lighting during this moment altered "from the pale blue of a Paris sky to a deep red sunset that looked like fire," illuminating the fierce battle inside her mind.[32]

The political agendas that 1960s musicals like *Dear World*, *Man of La Mancha*, and *Anyone Can Whistle* pursue are riddled with a certain sense of unease around the balance of ethical priorities in relation to the individual and the collective. This ambivalence stems in part from the contradictions of liberal individualism during these years, which, David Savran and Daniel Gundlach write, "was both redemptive, because it opposed standardization and conformism, and egocentric, because of its tendency towards an arrogant and selfish solipsism." The progressively minded creative teams behind these musicals, torn between sympathy for the growing civil rights movement, on the one hand, and a deep-seated distrust of the collective "as a conformist herd," assign different values, positive and negative, to the potential of groups represented on stage and negotiate the precarious place of the individual within them.[33] The anxiety underlying the interactions between one and many on stage is carried over into the varying uses of the trope of enlightened madness. What should the moral and ethical responsibilities of such a madness be with regard to the collective? Should the mad luminary withdraw from society and observe the impasse from a distance? Or should the wisdom of an idealist madness be directed out into the social, its insights converted into activist coalitions that might help "straighten out the world"?[34]

If the psychoanalytically inflected realm of the mad tea party scene, with its high-art pretensions, promotes a certain detachment from the world of politics, the epiphany of "I Don't Want to Know" is a turning point that prefigures Aurelia's conversion to mass movement politics. "As the story progresses," noted *Variety*'s reviewer, "Miss Lansbury has to become more emphatic," shedding "the boobyhatch vagueness of the eccentric Countess."[35] To accommodate this transition, Herman abandons his experiments with art music and reverts to his winning trademark song type, a stirring march with radiantly optimistic lyrics. Modeled on group numbers like "Before the Parade Passes By" and "Open a New Window," *Dear World*'s title song and "One Person" build affective pathways to collective mobilization through a current of sanguine energy emanating from the leading lady to the ensemble.

Assembling a small group of sympathetically drawn people on stage and pitting them against a larger, more powerful group (represented physically or implied by the narrative) is a common musico-dramatic solution that helps the creative teams assure some equilibrium between their responsibilities to the individual and the collective in a socially conscious away as they develop their antiestablishment themes. The numerical sparseness of an onstage minority—Cookies, prisoners, eccentrics, and vagabonds—helps mitigate liberalist fears of the loss of individuality in a mass, preserving, visually and aurally, the autonomy of "one" amid "many." The individualist priorities—and risks—of the small-group solution rise into high relief in the early drafts of the first-act finale, which completes the process of Aurelia's radicalization. "There is no number larger than one," she proclaims. "Once you know that, figures can't frighten you." A white parasol and the top of a garbage can aloft, she begins singing "One Person" as she rallies a posse of oddballs "in a march against the ugly realities of today." Infused with the madwoman's enthusiasm, each member of the newly formed tiny collective proceeds to declare an "individual independence" from the "regime" in a resounding unison. The size of this "odd parade," however, starts to dwindle, when the marchers, one by one, get lured away by the agents of the corporations or drawn off in the general confusion of the city until a larger crowd representing a negative mob sweeps the rest of them offstage. Deserted yet unfazed, Aurelia stands tall, a physical expression of the stolid "one person" principle behind her philosophy of collective action. Her solitary figure silhouetted against the glow of a flaming red sky, the madwoman, a quixotic "knight-in-armor," begins to pound her umbrella against the top of the garbage can and, in "a lone voice of defiance," brings the song to a resolute finish:

> If one person can beat a drum
> And one person can blow a horn
> If one person can hold a torch
> Then one person can change the world![36]

The stirring quality of songs like "One Person," "The Quest," and "Everybody Says Don't" parallels the urgency of the mad protagonist's moral and political mission and adds an extra dose of uplift that helps sell a seemingly far-fetched scenario as an affectively credible program. Mushrooming into choral or balletic production numbers, these compositions rehearse the romantic convictions of sixties culture. The sentimentalism of these songs is so unabashedly absolute that in hindsight they appear to kitschify the period's antiestablishment crusades. Yet during their original moment, they were staged and performed in earnest, as rousing calls to action.

PRETTYBELLE AND OTHER ASYLUM INMATES

For the creative teams writing in the 1960s and 1970s, the art form's built-in capacity for conveying extravagantly sized emotions provided an engine for amplifying the urgency of a narrative's antiestablishment telos. As we have seen, this generation of progressively minded musical theater artists contributed to the cultural rediscovery of a newly relevant type of outsider, remaking the figure of the lunatic or the asylum inmate into a contemporary symbol of political dissent and protest and using it to champion social causes, which occasionally included but, mostly, far surpassed the problems specific to the lived experience of those diagnosed mentally ill. The appropriation of a prophetic madness in the classical texts of antipsychiatry by writers like Laing and Foucault entailed a similar amalgam of countercultural allegory and romantic sensibility. Laing, for example, wrote passionately that "so-called schizophrenics" should be accorded "no less respect than the often no less lost explorers of the Renaissance," for their voyage through the unconscious holds lessons for all of us. The future generations, he proclaimed, would see that "what we call schizophrenia was one of the forms in which, often through quite ordinary people, the light began to break through the cracks in our all-too-closed minds."[37] Such breathless, poetic treatments of psychosis in the popular texts of the antipsychiatric literature mirrored the celebration of the mad visionaries and iconoclasts in the theater. The musicals that participated in this trend encouraged one to lean into madness—recited, sung, danced, or mimed— not for the purpose of landing on a diagnosis or cure but for the sake of gaining insight into oneself and society.

Still, amid the persisting abstractions and metaphors animated by the phenomenological properties of the art form, listening to madness along with these musicals also involved reflection on the material conditions and experiential realities of living with mental distress or illness, both as a medical condition and a social label. The authors of *Prettybelle* and *King of Hearts* expanded this representational angle by focusing on the lives of asylum patients. Unlike Cookies in *Anyone Can Whistle*, the inmates in these musicals have an adequately legible history of mental distress. Theirs is not a dramatic universe in which, as in Szasz's absolutist theories, asylum patients are only nonconformists wrongfully incarcerated, and psychic suffering, like mental illness, is only a myth. Instead, the worlds of *Prettybelle* and *King of Hearts* are conceptually closer to the work of Goffman and Laing, who expose the limitations of the medical model without denying the existence of psychological affliction. Their creative teams still use madness to signpost the ideological asymmetries between the patient's worldview and that of the mainstream, but they also endow it with affective and experiential qualities pointing to the patient's difficulties in navigating themselves through life's challenges. Laing's writing about psychosis is a particularly fitting framework for the dramatic composition of distress in these texts.

Coalescing around models of a sociogenic madness that integrate environmental and social-constructionist explanations, both musicals share their critical and rhetorical apparatus with community psychiatry and antipsychiatry. Tokens of the cultural animus toward asylums surface periodically in these shows through references to involuntary commitment. Yet the authors of *Prettybelle* and *King of Hearts*, while grazing this politically charged terrain, avoid dwelling on the defects of institutional psychiatry and, instead, put the asylum setting to other uses. Since the source of the inmates' distress is traced to their precarious position in the social milieu, which is shown to be intolerant of difference and hostile to mental affliction, the dramatic function of the asylum moves from that of a sinister repressive institution to that of a shelter. This conversion is not without precedent in musical theater. The sane hero of Kurt Weill and Paul Green's *Johnny Johnson* (1936), for example, when granted a release after an involuntary ten-year stay in a mental hospital, contemplates staying on among his mad friends. His reasons are similar to those we hear at the end of *Prettybelle* and *King of Hearts*: the outside world is much too cruel. Yet if the institutionalized patients surrounding Johnny were broadly comic figures with not a hint of psychic pain in their past or present, the dramatic makeup of the new generation of psychiatrically managed mad characters emerging in the 1970s, while not impervious to the levities of the genre, has a tragic spin, evincing markers of psychological "depth" through the experiential realities of distress.

These emergent emphases are shaped by robust public discourses about the ongoing reforms and enduring areas of concern in the mental health system. But they also absorb critical content from the cultural proliferation of patient perspectives in the form of biographical and semibiographical accounts (e.g., *The Bell Jar*, *Will There Really Be a Morning?*). The steadily increasing visibility of first-person accounts in the 1970s is further stimulated by the rise of activist groups and campaigns led by mental patients themselves. Akin to Black, women's, and gay liberation movements, this movement comprised self-advocacy efforts by a disenfranchised, commonly silenced sector of the population. Variously identifying as expatients, ex-inmates, and survivors, members of this movement insisted on the importance of defining their experiences on their own terms and speaking for themselves.

That is not to say that *Prettybelle* or *King of Hearts* aims to represent the voices of historical patients. As fictional texts, they have a remote, dim connection to the real-life experiences shared publicly by members of the ex-patient movement or other individuals who were choosing to make their personal stories of distress heard in the 1970s. But as historical documents, these works provide a window into a time when musical theater writers are developing new access points for envisioning and listening to madness, inventing dramatic situations in which asylum inmates relate their personal experiences with mental distress. In virtually excluding asylum custodians and medical staff from the action, *Prettybelle* and *King of Hearts* can be said to rehearse a structural reversal of power that is gradually taking place in the therapeutic relationship between doctors and patients in US mental health care. Rather than being passively constituted by the asylum onstage, the inmates are seen to engage creatively with their environment, as they manage their mental health on their own, a move that subtly mimics the gains of patient liberation in the new era of community psychiatry and anticipates the broadening of creative approaches to dramatizing the individuality and agency of characters receiving psychiatric treatment in the early twenty-first-century musical (Chapter 7).

Prettybelle began its out-of-town tryout performances at Boston's Shubert Theatre on February 1, 1971. Based on Jean Arnold's 1970 novel *Prettybelle: A Lively Tale of Rape and Resurrection*, this dark musical, with a book and lyrics by Bob Merrill and music by Jule Styne, indicted and satirized the racist, patriarchal order of the American South in a complexly conceived avant-garde production, directed and choreographed by Gower Champion. "Every Broadway show I've done has been a cotton candy, never-never land kind of thing," said Champion during the rehearsal process. "*Prettybelle* says things I would like to say on brutality, racism, a father's relationship to a son, but most of it is done in outrageous comedic terms, with sharp, acid comment." For Champion and Merrill, this dramatic material afforded an opportunity not only to make a "statement on today" but also to create a show with "an unusual concept," combining the avant-garde techniques of modernist theater and auteur cinema.[38] Elliot Norton, one of the most revered regional critics at the time, applauded the aspirations of the creative team. "This bold new show at the Shubert," he wrote, "could become a memorable American musical play. It could and it should."[39] Yet the other reviewers, as well as, reportedly, the majority of the Boston audience, found *Prettybelle* unpalatable. Disturbed by the production's abrasive sensibility, its "collection of ethnic slams and four letter words," flashes of nudity, and depictions of violence and sexual assault, they castigated the new musical for being "foul," "vulgar," even "immoral."[40] Despite Champion's undying enthusiasm for the material and his relentless efforts to reshape it during the tryouts, the producer, Alexander H. Cohen, abruptly canceled the production's move to New

York two weeks before the booked opening at the Majestic Theatre, ending its life in Boston.[41]

The musical's heroine, "a demented but gracious southern lady," Prettybelle Sweet, who was played, yet again, by Angela Lansbury, is a mental patient residing at the Piciyumi State Hospital in Louisiana. "Everybody up here has a story," she confides to the audience during her first solo routine, a comic patter song entitled "Manic-Depressives." In this number, she self-identifies as an alcoholic schizophrenic and refers teasingly to her two fellow residents, Howard Baines (William Larsen), described in the production notes as "an intelligent and gentle manic depressive" and coded as queer, and Cybil Mae Asch (Barbra Ann Walters), "a hopeless paranoid."[42] Advised by her psychiatrist to try writing as a form of therapy, Prettybelle sets out to reconstruct the sequence of events that brought her to the institution and serialize them in the *Piciyumi Gazette*. As she begins to piece together her autobiographical account, her thoughts and memories are rendered physically present on stage through the scenic elements and the bodies of other actors. Oliver Smith's skeletal, multilevel set and Nananne Percher's tight area lighting in the Boston production facilitated the swift interplay of the past and the present in Merrill's book.[43] Similar techniques were employed by Harold Prince and Boris Aronson in *Follies*, which was having its out-of-town tryout run at the Colonial Theatre, just a few blocks away from the Shubert. Like *Prettybelle*, this soon-to-become legendary musical, with a score by Stephen Sondheim and a book by James Goldman, theatricalized the internal economy of mental distress through psychoanalytically inflected dramatic conventions and a cinematically fluid, avant-gardist staging, but did so without an overtly clinical narrative framing.[44]

With the medical staff offstage except for a brief appearance in the first scene, *Prettybelle*'s asylum setting effectively morphs into a simulacrum of a patient-controlled environment in which those designated mentally ill act as though they have taken treatment into their own hands. (Even the *Piciyumi Gazette* appears to be patient-run.) Structurally, the show mimics the format of the analytic session. Prettybelle, the figurative analysand, narrates and comments on the past events as her present self, maintaining an intermittent dialogue with Howard and Cybil, who, noting down her story, assume the position of the analyst. Walking into her materialized recollections, the heroine relives key incidents, which she painstakingly curates and attempts to arrange into a straightforward narrative. Her itinerary through these reconstructions of the past, however, starts to meander, splitting into alternative paths that cast doubt on the reliability of her account. It soon becomes clear that presented on the stage is the story of a mind in the grip of self-evading ruses. Howard and Cybil, in their symbolic function as the analyst, address her omissions and contradictions with leading questions, which, even when left unanswered, disrupt and reconstitute portions of the history she crafts. Like no other musical before it, *Prettybelle* maps the narrative experience at stake in the analytic situation onto the mise-en-scène of amplified interiority, staging minute recalibrations and adjustments to a self that is being perpetually authored by patient and analyst.

Although much of the action is set inside Prettybelle's mind, the show articulates a psychosocial, rather than a purely intrapsychic, view of distress. To quote from Laing, "Something is wrong somewhere, but it can no longer be seen exclusively or even primarily 'in' the diagnosed patient."[45] As Lansbury tells it, her heroine is "nuts" because "How would she be otherwise? She was a sensitive, dear little woman. And she wanted everything to be golden and gorgeous. And here she was married to this brute. And you saw a lot of that brute in action."[46] Her husband, LeRoy (Mark Dawson), who is dead at the time of her "analysis" but vividly alive in her thoughts and memories, is a sheriff. His acts of aggression signify a collective mentality inscribed in the social order of the musical's dramatic universe. To show a system of violence operant in the community, the musical flashes back to visually and verbally disturbing recollections in which LeRoy and his deputies assault women and terrorize and murder people of color in different localities on and off stage. The reenactment of Prettybelle's halting memories from that period reveals that she was able to proceed with her daily life by drinking heavily and suppressing her awareness of her husband's and the town's hate crimes. But the "blocked out" knowledge gnawed at her defenses, transmogrifying into depression and nightmares, symptoms of distress that, in addition to being alluded to verbally, were marked scenically, musically, and choreographically in the production.[47]

The musical's take on Prettybelle's history of distress is not modeled on the most up-to-date clinical descriptions of her diagnosed condition, schizophrenia, in mainstream psychiatry. Instead, it bears remarkable correspondences to Laing's alternative views in *The Politics of Experience* (1967), in which he argues that "the experience and behavior that gets labeled schizophrenic is a special strategy that a person invents in order to live in an unlivable situation."[48] Reformulating ideas that go back to Freud, Laing writes about the protective function of the unconscious in carrying a person through a time of trauma or crisis. As if reading from Laing, Prettybelle explains to Howard, "I only go mad when I choose to go mad. I, like you,

Mr. Baines, am one of creation's small furry animals, pursued by the fiery hounds of hell. If caught, life can eat us up and spit out our bones. When faced with our pitiful defenses, we are forced to retreat into a hole. The hole *we* choose is *madness*."[49]

This mechanism applies not only to Prettybelle and her fellow residents at the hospital, but also to her son, John, who was institutionalized at the age of thirteen. Flashback scenes show him being pressured to adopt the violent behavior expected of white men in his community until his resistance to the toxic, "grossly male" culture, represented by LeRoy, takes him into the space of psychosis.[50] Climbing up a tree, he fires a volley of bullets from a rifle, killing three men conspicuously resembling his father. A choreographed sequence, not so much dance as "dramatic movement" in Champion's production, portrays the capture of the "maddened boy," a "cornered animal," for subsequent institutionalization.[51] His madness is a mental response to what Laing describes as "a position of checkmate," a "can't win" situation in which "no move is possible and making no move is equally unlivable."[52]

Typical of this cultural moment, Prettybelle's tale of madness doubles as a story of political awakening. This narrative thread comes to the fore when the heroine, no longer able to keep Leroy's crimes out of her conscious awareness, faces up to the facts and, to her dismay, also realizes that she may have been "a party to victimizing them poor people." The turning point is marked by an explosively energetic song, "How Could I Know What Was Goin' On?," which, rhythmically and melodically, echoes Merrill and Styne's "Don't Rain on My Parade" from *Funny Girl*. Belting her way out of a tight knot of dread, denial, and guilt, Prettybelle rues the years she has wasted "baskin' in the bright shine of the universe of [her]self," insensible to the darkness of the outer world.[53] Following the epiphany, she launches into a flurry of reparative efforts, some of conceivable value to the civil rights organizations in her vicinity, some woefully misguided.[54] The immediate effect of her entanglement in progressive politics is to provoke the rage of the white supremacist townsfolk: "You're either for us or against us down here. Even a sick head oughta know *that*."[55] Yet Prettybelle, defying the ensuing threats, continues her quest to right the wrongs. After she refuses to give a false testimony against a Black man in a court of law and, instead, publicly accuses a white man of sexual assault, she is deemed a danger to the community and herself and sent away to the Piciyumi State Hospital.

The conflict between Prettybelle and her community casts into relief the organizing function her "mental illness" plays in the maintenance of the civic order. She is, in Laingian terms, like a plane flying out of formation.

Even though she may be the only person heading in the right direction, when we look at her position in relation to the image of the whole community, it is she, not the rest of them, who appears to be straying off course. Given these optics, her behavior, "strange and incomprehensible to most people," is "liable to be diagnosed as subject to a condition called schizophrenia."[56] On the one hand, Prettybelle herself admits she has had credible bouts of "nerves," which were first triggered off by the incident with her son. On the other hand, she is made into a "cuckoo" and a "lunatic" because, her community tells her, "only a crazy woman would send checks" to the NAACP.[57] The stigma of her prior record of institutionalization makes it that much easier for the town to recertify her as mentally ill, whether she is presenting legitimate medical symptoms or not. Madness in this musical is, then, not only a real experience of distress or a diagnosed medical disorder, but also "a political event," which "imposes definitions and consequences on the labelled person."[58] Her community needs her to be "disturbed and incompetent" so its members can remain in the position of rationality and order, validated by the optics of staying in formation.[59] In this social scheme, Prettybelle is forever a madwoman.

The show musicalizes Prettybelle's "can't win," double-bind situation in a poignant scene during which she, looking "dazed and irrational," is discovered sitting in the tree that formerly held John, dangling her shoes on her fingertips. As if prompted by the lonely call of the harmonica, very quietly and slowly, she begins to sing a strikingly simple tune, reflecting on her fragile state of mind ("I'm in a Tree"). While sitting in a tree is "a strange place to be," Prettybelle muses, "being down there is even stranger."[60] With a few more instruments joining in, the melody and the lyrics, both pointedly uncomplicated, are slightly undermined by subtly dissonant, sliding intervals in the accompaniment. But the overall effect remains that of a song that is delicate, sparse, and a shade mechanical like an old music box. According to an original cast member, Lansbury's performance at this moment enacted a kind of psychological regression into a younger age: "No makeup. No lighting. Nothing. You believed she was seventeen. She just *tore* your heart out."[61] Her interpretation, keyed up to the deliberately childlike simplicity of the song, brings out a common bond between her and John, not only as mother and son, but also, experientially, as people driven mad by the system. Prettybelle, like her child, chooses to hide out in the hole of madness, with "sparrows in [her] hair" because life below is "too frightening."[62] Her identification with John, reinforced through the doubling of a mad scene in the tree, positions both of them as casualties of white patriarchy.

At the end of the show, having reconstructed and published her personal narrative, Prettybelle is free to leave the asylum. The idea of release after a period of involuntary commitment offers a ripe dramatic opportunity for a cathartic exit to freedom. Yet Prettybelle decides to stay on in the hospital. Far from merely hiding out or confining herself to solitary self-contemplation, she transforms the mental institution into a would-be headquarters for grassroots activism on behalf of abused women designated mentally ill.[63] "How could I leave in the midst of a collaboration?" she exclaims, embarking on a new writing project: Cybil's history of sexual assault and madness. A pad and a pencil in hand, she sits down in Cybil's chair, assuming the role of the figurative analyst, while Cybil, another woman driven mad by the patriarchy, "enters proudly," takes the symbolic position center stage as analysand, and begins her account.[64] Through this final gesture, the musical broadens its agenda from individual to collective empowerment. The second patient narrative, yet to be told in the fictional universe now passing out of sight, implies an infinite succession of other such stories, imagining prospects of self-representation and community building for other formerly muted voices beyond the space and time of the theatrical performance.

KING OF HEARTS AND THEATER OF ESCAPE

The theme of asylum as refuge was also an essential feature of *King of Hearts*, which opened at the Minskoff Theatre on October 22, 1978. The musical, with a book by Joseph Stein, music by Peter Link, and lyrics by Jacob Brackman, was a stage adaptation of the 1966 French antiwar film *Le roi de coeur*, with a screenplay by Phillippe de Broca, Maurice Bessy, and Daniel Boulanger. The film had flopped upon its initial US release in 1967 but reemerged in the 1970s, achieving something of a cult status among the audiences of college towns and other centers of liberal thought. The story, set at the end of World War I, concerned a Scottish soldier who, during a covert operation, encounters a community of asylum inmates on the streets of an abandoned French town and, in the end, chooses to stay with them. In the words of a contemporaneous critic, *Le roi de coeur* was a cockeyed fairy tale, "with a patina of intellectual content," whose appeal to the countercultural audiences lay not in "the comedy or the plot but the philosophy."[65] The film's simple thesis, that life and love are better than war, was demonstrated through the contrast between innocent, fun-loving lunatics standing in for a pacifist minority and absurd-acting German and English soldiers, representing a self-destructive and murderous, if allegedly sane, mainstream. The musical's creative team attempted to recreate and update this conceit. The reviews during the tryouts in Boston were promising. "It's not just another mindless musical. It has something to tell us," enthused the *Boston Globe*'s critic, noting nevertheless that some cuts and alterations were still needed if *King of Hearts* was to realize its glimmering potential to become a hit.[66] Yet upon opening in New York, the production, directed and choreographed by Ron Field, received uniformly unfavorable reviews and stayed around for only forty-eight performances.

The creative team's approach to the mad borrowed some of the film's representational strategies, which were already theatrical, and involved other techniques, prompted in part by the conventions of the Broadway musical and in part by the changing climate of cultural attitudes toward madness. According to the production notes in the script, the "delightful, zany, and attractive" asylum inmates live in a world "totally different in texture and performance" from the menacingly "realistic" world of the soldiers.[67] The show's designer, Santo Loquasto, expressed the whimsical quality of the mad through the various locations in the town of DuTemps, displayed on a turntable. The set for the town's exterior, with its "dozens of toothpick balconies and matchstick stairways" converging upon one another, looked like a "birdcage hung from a mountain-top."[68] The stage then spun to the interior of the Asylum of St. Anne, where the inmates, clad in patient gowns, delivered their first musical number, "Stain on the Name," from a jungle gym of teetering beds, "arrayed in an almost Chagallian defiance of gravity."[69] This vaudeville-like routine, in which they expressed their outrage at being deserted by their caretakers, the nuns, established the idioms of early twentieth-century musical comedy and operetta as the principal stylistic register of madness in the show. As the inmates spilled into the streets, the show literalized the film's commentary on the theatricality of everyday life by turning them into a "Company of Players." Each "choosing their one role," they picked up props and donned costumes to assume the identities of "the characters they once were in reality or [had] come to believe they were."[70] The transformation set in motion the Company's transition into a diegetic performance mode, which they sustained throughout the evening in big production numbers: a religious chorale on a sloping cathedral roof ("The Coronation"), a can-can at a bordello ("Turn Around"), and a circus sequence in a big top, complete with acrobats, trapeze artists, and snake charmers ("Le Grand Cirque de Province," "Hey, Look at Me, Mrs. Draba").

All these representational choices are typical of the allegorical function attached to madness in the cultural products conditioned by the anti-establishment drive of sixties culture. To the extent that the authors of *King of Hearts* follow the basic plot of the 1966 film, they exploit the trope of a childlike lunacy unspoiled by the corrupting influence of civilization to restate the antiwar message of the source material. This dramatic conceit, especially when imbued with a brashly comic sensibility, tends to drain the dramatic profile of madness of discernible connections to emotional pain. Yet the musical also departs from the representational politics of the film in ways that transcend the function of the inmates as mere abstractions. On the screen, the lunatics, signifiers of a pacifist philosophy, are nearly always blissfully unperturbed. Neither does the film burden itself with the question of how they got to the asylum in the first place. It is as if they had always been there, fixed in a sort of universal time, ready to oblige a passerby with witty aphorisms and sentimental platitudes. Stein's libretto, however, takes some steps to de-metaphorize the inmates, attending to the place of distress in their lives, its etiology, and the history of their institutionalization.

The inmates' backstories are woven into the soul-searching by the musical's nominally principal, initially nonmad character, a US Army private, Johnny Perkins (played by Donald Scardino). As he gets to know the asylum residents, he wonders why and how they came to be institutionalized. The first answer comes from Demosthenes (Gary Morgan), who uses a combination of sign language and mime to indicate that he was committed at a very young age for being mute. The other inmate accounts, presented verbally in four monologues, relate different configurations of the same recurrent situation, in which expressions of extreme distress attendant on grief or psychosexual trauma are misunderstood and dismissed as pathological by society. Each story replays a Laingian scenario: a "brokenhearted" person goes into a breakdown mode in an attempt to defend the self or to heal. But the "experiential drama" they are undergoing and expressing is misinterpreted as a disease requiring medical intervention and segregation from the mentally healthy population. At the heart of all these personal stories presented to Johnny is a unifying commentary on society's profound indifference to the outcries of mentally distressed people around them and unwillingness to accept the "unusual" behavior of madness as a valid language by which the mad communicate their inner experiences.[71]

If *Anyone Can Whistle*'s Cookies were written as generic, abstract types whose primary function on stage was to fulfill a specific signifying role in the political commentary of the production text, the asylum inmates in

King of Hearts are afforded individualized markers of "depth" that signal psychological personhood in contemporary drama. The monologues and other comments dispersed through the two acts endow each of them with a soupçon of subjectivity and a critical agency beyond their group identity as institutionalized patients. Stein's attempts to thus humanize the mad and allude to the reality of their distress and precarious social standing did not go unnoticed. For some reviewers, the inmates' somber confessions were not enough to "develop a sense of urgency about the fate of the characters."[72] The cheerful spectacle of the singing and dancing mad prevailed on the stage, diverting attention from the attempted pathos of their personal tragedies. Yet others were apparently moved. As the *Boston Globe* reviewer noted, "The lunatics are like small glittering flames briefly shining in the oppressive dark. They matter. They matter not in the Big Scheme of Things, not as world-shakers or world-beaters, but as simple harried, in most cases, bent (if not broken) human beings." In this reviewer's critical scheme, the inmates' monologues constituted the main ingredient of the musical's humanistic philosophy, which, buoyed rather than derailed by the score and the performances, raised *King of Hearts* from the category of "mindless" entertainment to intelligent theater with a serious message.[73]

While some moments in the musical would seem to follow an anti-institutional logic with regard to the inmates, the overall plot trajectory relinquishes or, at the very least, rescripts this logic. On the one hand, *King of Hearts* expresses solidarity with the countercultural and public opposition to the asylums, as the inmates, humming an enchanted waltz ("Déjà Vu"), step out joyfully into the town streets for a "day of freedom." Here the musical performs a variation on a classic 1960s–1970s theme as it rehearses the iconography of the mad being liberated from the proverbial chains of institutional oppression. On the other hand, *King of Hearts* romanticizes the asylum as a refuge for the abused and disenfranchised. Commended by one of the inmates as a "lodging for the lost, happy home for the homeless and mansion for the mildly mad," St Anne's harbors no menacing presence within its walls. After the romp on the town, the mad cannot wait to resume their daily routine in the asylum's cocoon of safety. Johnny, shedding all his prior attachments, follows them there to spend the rest of his life in their company, as one of them. In the end, *King of Hearts*, like *Prettybelle*, reimagines the institution as a haven where society's rejects can forge an alternative community and, sheltered from the punitive, dehumanizing gaze of the mainstream, live a life of validation and acceptance. This asylum is not the dreaded end point of one's descent into madness but a fortunate escape from an insane world.

| "Is That Just Disgusting?"

Filth, Madness, and the City in
Sweeney Todd and Other Musicals

"Spit it out, dear. Go on. On the floor. There's worse things than that down there," urges Mrs. Lovett with a mixture of relish and revulsion as she watches Sweeney Todd choke on a mouthful of stale pie.[1] On the one hand, her words are a first-aid gesture, a way of proffering relief to senses invaded by a dirty, decaying substance. On the other, they are an invitation for active assimilation into a filthy universe populated by foul objects and practices.

As directed by Harold Prince and designed by Eugene Lee, the original Broadway production of Stephen Sondheim and Hugh Wheeler's *Sweeney Todd, the Demon Barber of Fleet Street*, which opened at the Uris Theatre (now the Gershwin) on March 1, 1979, lavishes attention on the materiality of dirt and pollution in nineteenth-century London. The onstage cityscape in this macabre show is contained within the skeletal outlines of a giant factory, whose begrimed glass roof diffuses any promise of clear sunlight. The action down below, whether physically represented or imagined, teems with scenic and textual filth. Polluting substances—a pile of dirt, a cloud of dust, a heap of trash, a belch of smoke—insinuate themselves at one point or another into the production's visual field of unclean images.[2] Feeding on the plot's predilection for death, *Sweeney Todd* befouls its articulation of urban ecology with suggestions of sickening smells associated with decay, from decomposing rats "gone home to Jesus" to putrid urine ("What's that awful stench? . . . This is piss.").[3] In this relentlessly bleak environment, where life seems to entail constant encounters and negotiations with unpleasant, contaminating matter, characters are seen to recoil in revulsion, pinch their noses at foul odors, and spit out suspicious-tasting food. Giving visual form to disgust-inducing aspects of corporeal mortality, spurts of blood gush from open wounds, and dead human bodies are frequently displayed. Some of them are dumped into the ground; the rest are chopped up, baked in pies, and consumed. According to Sweeney's pungent précis, this place is "like a great black pit, and it's filled with people who are filled with shit."[4]

The nauseating cityscape serves as the setting for a politically charged story of madness. While almost all the characters in this musical have been discussed as "mentally or morally challenged" or "warped in one way or another," most of the critical attention has focused, understandably, on the eponymous hero.[5] As Bruce Kirle, among others, concludes, while Sweeney is a "victim of a corrupt society, he in turn has been corrupted and has lost his mind in the process."[6] Indeed, following the trend described in the previous two chapters, this musical's creators dramatize environmental etiologies of mental distress, formulating a multivalent madness that both typifies and critiques the social order that produces it. According to Prince's elucidation, the industrial factory, whose steel beams prop up and enclose the human world on the stage, "make[s] Sweeney Todds."[7] The musical's overarching theme—what David Savran aptly describes as "the crisis of the subject, marooned in capitalist modernity"—is expressed through the figure of a madman manufactured by his milieu.[8]

I want to suggest that the musical's anticapitalist critique finds its expression not only in madness but also in filth, or, rather, in the kinship between the two. This strategy is not an entirely new development. In some ways, the tight proximity of distress and disgust at the heart of *Sweeney Todd* is an upwelling of entanglements already present in the politically conscious musicals of the 1960s and 1970s. Indeed, Sweeney's précis referenced above echoes Aldonza's in *Man of La Mancha*: "The world's a dungheap and we are maggots that crawl on it!"[9] Yet *Sweeney Todd* amplifies what was more cautiously sketched in the earlier mad musicals and pushes it to the center of the affective and political economy on the stage, filth and madness pulsating together in the dense, juicy textures of extreme feelings, sounds, and images. As the distance between "dung" and "shit" indicates, *Sweeney Todd*'s world is angrier, madder, and dirtier than those I discussed in the previous chapter.

While various manifestations of the musical's dirtiness are duly mentioned in the extant scholarship, the ontology of its filth has yet to be examined adequately. Critics and historians have traditionally been drawn to this musical as a variation on Brechtian themes and aesthetics. Responding to the musical's critique of the Industrial Revolution, they have highlighted various ways in which the musical uses its nineteenth-century Victorian setting to comment on the underside of modern-day America.[10] Despite Sondheim's and Prince's disclaimers about the German director-playwright's influence over their creative process, a somewhat abstracted

Brechtian framework can indeed be ascribed to the musical.[11] Yet I would suggest that in focusing on the musical as a political allegory, scholars have unwittingly consigned its filth to the realm of the metaphorical, skirting the significance of its materiality. There is a kind of disavowal at play in this critical trend, arising from historical prohibitions that have banned waste matter from public places and confined discussions of excrement to the periphery of public discourses. My aim is to counter this trend by reconsidering *Sweeney Todd* as a musical that is centrally concerned with and largely constituted by filth, "shit" being not only the most extreme but also the most important of its manifestations. In doing so, I do not and cannot avoid the dimension of figurality, for filth points as much to conceptual structures as it does to material phenomena. But an unflinching focus on the latter helps extend my analysis from ideas to concrete objects, spaces, practices, and institutions, all bound together by the charge of affective urgency that filth generates.

William A. Cohen employs the word "filth" as a capacious umbrella term for all manner of material and symbolic manifestations of a complex phenomenon conceptualized by other scholars in terms of pollution, contamination, dirt, waste, impurity, and abjection.[12] Sorting through correspondences across a vast range of scholarship from different intellectual traditions, he interweaves existing perspectives on this broadly conceived topic by situating filth at a "theoretical crossroads" that "represents a cultural location at which the human body, social hierarchy, psychological subjectivity, and material objects converge."[13] Taking my cue from Cohen, I posit filth as a material presence, as well as an ideological construct, that operates at the intersections of the social and the psychic in *Sweeney Todd* — that is, at the same strategic junction where the musical locates and articulates madness. The tight overlap between structures of disgust and distress in the production text takes different forms and occurs on different planes of individual and collective experience. My interest here is in how this multiplicity of inner and outer relations involving filth and madness comes to be part of the show and what it accomplishes for the musical's investment in environmental etiologies and social disparities.

Filth is not only foul but also fecund. Cohen writes that "while filthy objects initially seem utterly repulsive and alien, . . . they also paradoxically bear potential value."[14] This principle of conversion from refuse to reuse supplies a conceptual basis for my discussion of the different functions and qualities of filth in *Sweeney Todd* and two other musicals, *Ain't Supposed to Die a Natural Death* and *Dear World*. As an artistic strategy, representations of figurative and literal dirt help define a social system onstage by marking and transgressing its borders. On the one hand, people's negative reactions to what is dirty foreground acts and methods of marginalization and exclusion at play. On the other hand, objects, actions, and ideas traditionally deemed polluting or impure can also be celebrated for challenging oppressive cultural hierarchies or offering a means of sustenance and survival. The effect of the proximity of madness to filth in these musicals is not only to articulate the pain of living in the social and psychic spaces of abjection but also to demonstrate inventive, life-affirming strategies through which individuals or groups can fortify themselves. In parsing these dualities, I draw on theories from anthropology and cultural sociology (Mary Douglas) and psychoanalysis (Melanie Klein), as well as critical projects that blend these modes of thought (Eve Sedgwick, Julia Kristeva).

Dirt in the artistic arena can be instructive when we view it as a vehicle whereby heterogeneous relations between material realities and psychological subjectivities are historicized. Michelle Allen observes that in the mid-Victorian middle-class imagination "the problem of filth was at once a physical danger (defined as such by an emergent scientific authority), a demoralizing influence, and a social threat; moreover, it was inextricably tied to perceptions and anxieties about the urban poor, who were themselves insufficiently contained."[15] Naturalistic images of pollution, poverty, and squalor in the original production of *Sweeney Todd* have been discussed by critics as a scenic realization of the Victorian urban environment particular to the living conditions of underprivileged classes. From this perspective, the visual concept of the production can be linked to nineteenth-century bourgeois conceptions of filth as aestheticized and popularized by writers like Charles Dickens. Stephen Banfield's use of the term "Dickensian musical" underscores a well-established scholarly approach to thinking about "the dirty, wicked metropolis" in Sondheim studies.[16] Yet my discussion of *Sweeney Todd*'s urban ecology deliberately bypasses the show's indebtedness to the nineteenth-century legacy of filth. As Dominique Laporte reminds us, "That which occupies the site of disgust at one moment in history is not necessarily disgusting at the preceding moment or the subsequent one."[17] Keeping in mind the unstable, ever-changing nature of social conceptions of and reactions to filth, I am concerned with the ways in which *Sweeney Todd*, a late 1970s show created by Broadway artists for Broadway audiences, can be understood in relation to its own historical moment.

That *Sweeney Todd*'s route to madness must cut through different orders of substantive and figurative filth is in part determined by the material realities of the early postasylum moment. In Chapter 3, I described the mental health system's move to the community psychiatry model, which entailed the closure of large mental hospitals and the reintegration of institutionalized patients into society. In this context, the vision of the asylum inmates in *Anyone Can Whistle* jibed with the idealism of the calls to free the mentally ill in the 1960s. By the late 1970s, however, public assessments of the reform's outcomes revealed some damaging consequences for the lives of the service-dependent mad or disabled population. Sondheim's recourse to images of asylum inmates in *Sweeney Todd* occurred during a decade when many of those reassigned to community care were being virtually abandoned to fend for themselves in an increasingly hostile socioeconomic environment. In my reading, a fluid interface between staged and actual manifestations of mental distress in the city foregrounds the original production as a site for grappling with social anxieties about the physical presence of the mad on the streets.

On a conceptual level, the links between madness and filth in the 1960s and 1970s are also a product of an intellectual climate overdetermined by theories of cultural relativism. Antipsychiatry's key texts on mental illness and sociological studies of dirt, such as Mary Douglas's *Purity and Danger*, both approach their subjects as cultural constructions. Overriding the realm of the biological, such theoretical frameworks elaborate madness and filth as relative ideas formulated through a classificatory process by which society establishes and policies its morals codes. In the musical theater arena, distress and disgust likewise run on parallel tracks in that they both can be used to aestheticize perceived disruptions to a sense of order and logic within categorically defined hierarchies, drawing attention to what appears anomalous to the privileged classes. The phenomenology of filth and madness in *Sweeney Todd*, as well as the other musicals discussed in this chapter, contributes to the art form's narrative and rhetorical emphasis on how arbitrary systems of labels organize relations of power in society.

The authors of *Sweeney Todd* were intentionally going for an unsettling effect. Len Cariou, who created the part of Sweeney, admits that when he first started reading the script he was shocked by the hero's song about people filled with shit. "Well, we aren't endearing them to us, are we?" he griped, wondering if Sondheim and Prince might have "gone over the edge" and "lost their minds completely."[18] The extremity of the material, of course, goes back to the melodrama by the British playwright Christopher Bond, which served as the basis for the libretto. What I focus on in this chapter, however, is the new dimensions and qualities of disgust that the story of madness acquired in the process of being converted into a Broadway musical. In my reading, the original production of *Sweeney Todd* becomes a theatrical event that refracts the sociocultural practices in and around Times Square in the 1970s. That is not to suggest that the immediacy of *Sweeney Todd*'s relationship to the theater district is unique. A number of musicals and plays that opened on Broadway during that period can be and have been analyzed as actively drawing on and contributing to the look and feel of the Times Square area.[19] Neither is the coupling of filth and madness characteristic of *Sweeney Todd* alone. It appears in different forms and degrees in other artistic texts, some of which I include in this chapter. Rather, in tracing the ways in which the original production of *Sweeney Todd* maps its locale's "vortices of behavior" over the London setting of the source material, I want to demonstrate that the convergence of socially produced filth and madness in this musical is not just a matter of quirky aesthetic choices made by a group of theater artists but also a cultural event that is deeply rooted in the overlapping histories of mental distress and sanitation in the United States.[20]

REWRITING THE FILTHY CITY

The developmental process of what would become one of the dirtiest musicals on Broadway in the 1970s absorbed articulations of material and metaphorical filth from a wide range of cultural influences. Some of the show's filthy properties, particularly bodily excretions, mutilation, and decay featured in moments of staged or narrated violence, have been linked by members of the creative team and the critics to the traditions of the Théâtre du Grand-Guignol. The French theater, active in Paris between 1897 and 1962, was famous for its naturalistic simulations of gruesome acts. Richard Hand and Michael Wilson's study of the Parisian "Theater of Horror" shows that much of the Grand-Guignol's aesthetic programming centered on production techniques designed "to shock or disgust the audience."[21] Although Sondheim envisioned *Sweeney Todd* as a much more serious, "purer" melodrama than the Grand Guignol horror shows he had seen in Paris in the 1960s, the audience reception of bloodletting in the original production echoes the history and mythology of that French theater.[22] Angela Lansbury, who originated the role of Mrs. Lovett in the musical, recalls, "I never, ever realized how put off people would be by the blood.... [F]rom the very first of the previews, the gasps and the general reaction of the audience was stunning. They didn't like ... what they were being asked to stomach."[23] The detailed, often prolonged staging of other potentially nauseating moments in the show produced a similar effect. According to the *New York Times*, "squealing noises" were heard among the opening night audience when Tobias (played by Ken Jennings) discovered a human hair, then a fingernail in his food.[24]

Yet just as the Grand-Guignol's production style, according to Hand and Wilson, was influenced by the spatial restrictions of the stage as well as the specificity of the venue's neighborhood, so the original production of *Sweeney Todd* was rooted in the material and social geographies of its own place and time. What Sondheim had initially intended to be an intimate "story of personal obsession" became an epically conceived tale about the "breaking down of society."[25] The idea of scaling up the project's sociopolitical concerns, of turning its environment into an oversized urban hellscape, belonged to Prince. In pursuit of a more expansive staging concept, Prince and Lee at first explored nontraditional spaces as a way of breaking out of the confines of the proscenium frame.[26] "We looked everywhere," reminisces the designer. "We looked at the docks, we tried to find any other possible location to do *Sweeney Todd* other than a theater."[27] Eventually, however, they settled on the Uris Theatre, one of the largest Broadway houses.

Prince was, admittedly, uncomfortable with staging *Sweeney Todd* as a straightforward period melodrama until he and his collaborators found a solution for what the show's "'motor' was going to be. That's how I always think of it, as the motor—it has a lot to do with the way the scenery is going to look, and how the people are going to move around in the telling of the story."[28] In many of his previous productions (e.g., *Cabaret*, 1966; *Company*, 1970; *Follies*, 1971; *Pacific Overtures*, 1976; and *Evita*, 1978, West End), Prince had utilized the stage set and the topography of the characters' lives within it to highlight and enhance the social and political dimensions of the dramatic action. The "motor" of *Sweeney Todd* assumed the shape of a foundry, roaring and hissing, with a hemmed-in city within. "The effect of this monstrously beautiful setting," wrote drama critic Jack Kroll, "is to body forth the Industrial Revolution as a portentous, ambiguous edifice—part cathedral, part factory, part prison—that dwarfs and degrades the swarming denizens of the lower orders."[29] This oppressive environment shaped the population's actions and, as the director implies, mediated their apprehension of the world: "They never saw daylight. We built a set so that daylight never shone. All you saw was dirt."[30] The contrasting look of the white walls of the Uris, which had opened in 1972 and still retained the characteristic sheen of a brand-new construction, only accentuated the unsettling view of a sunless, filthy city on the stage. Lee's enormous set edged out beyond the proscenium as if threatening to spill the musical's grisly action into the auditorium, diminishing the symbolic boundaries between the drama and the real world.

As the musical acquired a definite shape, its music, lyrics, and book, along with the scenic environment of the production, became overlaid with a complex geography of urban pollution and sanitation. As a New Yorker, Sondheim was able to connect to Prince's politicized vision through a shared "sense of the city," which resulted in ideas for new musical sequences like "City on Fire."[31] Bits of dirty action already present in some form in the source play grew in detail and scope. Describing his work on Mrs. Lovett's introductory number, "The Worst Pies in London," Sondheim recounts, "The first thing I thought of was: it's fun flicking the dirt off the pies. And then I thought: why isn't the whole shop alive with roaches and flies and dust? It would be fun to punctuate the song with her constantly wiping her greasy hands on her apron and blowing things off the pies and slapping cockroaches."[32] Stephen Banfield highlights in this number "the elaboration of Bond's single reference to stage business (flicking dust off the pie, with its verbal aside) into a virtuoso comic routine of making pastry and squashing bugs."[33] Indeed, Mrs. Lovett's vocal line is constantly interrupted with spasmodic rests in which she combats the incursion of dirt and vermin in the kitchen, gasping for air. But the expansion of attention paid to the daily march of material pollution in this song also showcases the priorities of scale in the musical's inflections of urban filth. Implicit in the genesis of this and other unsanitary sequences in the show is a creative process that mines the authors' real or imaginary experiences of city living. Furthermore, since Lee's design incorporated found and reconstructed pieces (e.g., an actual iron foundry), environmental filth encroached on the stage of the Uris in material ways. According to Lansbury, one piece of scenery, which Lee "had gotten from some junk yard," turned out to be "full of the biggest wood lice you've ever seen. And they were crawling all over the stage and all over us at the first performance."[34]

The spread of literal and simulated filth through this and other theatrical events of the 1960s and 1970s paralleled the intensification of interest in filth in cultural sociology and anthropology. Mary Douglas's *Purity and Danger*, published in 1966, offered an influential account of the role of commonly held ideas about pollution, uncleanliness, and contagion in the symbolic ordering of social hierarchies. Douglas demystified unclean things through the lens of "the old definition of dirt as matter out of place." From this vantage point, "There is no such thing as dirt; no single item is dirty apart from a particular system of classification in which it does not fit."[35] The function of such a system is to organize experiences into predictable patterns that lend a sense of order to the world. Consequently, when something slips out of its culturally assigned location within the hierarchy and appears in the wrong place, it is perceived as anomalous, dangerous, and disgusting. Embedded in our ideas of pollution and sanitation, then, is a powerful impulse to reject objects, bodies, and practices that threaten the integrity of the physical, social, and moral boundaries we have drawn as a society.

The disgust affect that inflects the setup of the cultural and moral hierarchies in *Sweeney Todd* slithers between material substances and social practices, inanimate matter and human lives, within an intricate system of power relations. While the stage picture purports to represent nineteenth-century London, with its class system depicted in a honeycomb on the front drop, there is a historical contingency to the musical's renditions of filth, a specificity that aligns the production with the time and place in which it was created.[36] The 1970s was a period of urban blight for the American metropolis, characterized by a slumping economy and surging crime rates. During this bleak era the area in and around Times Square and, in particular, Forty-Second Street was notorious for its profusion of sex trade, adult entertainment, drug dealing, and other transgressive practices. The social ecology of this neighborhood, continuous with the theater district, was perceived by many as threatening and pathological. "Theater tourists who spill onto the Eighth Avenue sidewalk are safe, so long as they keep a steady pace," warns Josh Alan Friedman, as he recounts his experiences in Times Square in the early 1980s. "Stagger from a few intermission drinks and you're fodder for lowlife scramblers keenly interested in reaping the Broadway audience's wallets, watches, and earrings."[37] As Elizabeth L. Wollman clarifies, the real dangers of the neighborhood were somewhat exaggerated, yet "the growing fear of random street crime, which was apparently shared by locals and tourists alike, was keeping a growing number of potential spectators home, especially after dark."[38]

In addition to unsought encounters with sleaze and criminality, many theatergoers associated a walk through the neighborhood with assaults on the olfactory and visual senses. *West 42nd Street: "The Bright Light Zone,"* a 1978 sociological study, provides a glimpse into this dynamic in interviews with predominately middle-class respondents. Complaining about "obvious safety hazards which have nothing to do with OSHA [Occupational Safety and Health Administration]," they describe "the filth and stench that is perpetually there" and decry the "unsightliness" of the "undesirables" and "derelicts."[39] Reactions to biological stimuli bleed into determinations of moral distinctions in a chorus of offended sensibilities cited as the evidence of a collective need for a "revitalization" of the theater district. As Cohen points out, filth functions in modern culture as a "term of condemnation, which instantly repudiates a threatening thing, person, or idea by ascribing alterity to it."[40] The opinions gathered by the sociologists around the southern border of Times Square represent the voice of a dominant class, seeking wholesale sanitization of a confluence of diverse practices, objects, and bodies perceived as "matter out of place."

The organizing function of dirt in the social stratification of the urban landscape on the stage of the Uris cannot be fully understood apart from these processes. In the domain of public policy, the tendency of dirt to "confuse and contradict cherished classifications" has inspired an onslaught of sanitizing actions affecting the city's marginalized communities.[41] The development of Broadway's *Sweeney Todd* occurred at the same time that New York City, as Samuel R. Delany writes, "anticipated and actively planned [its] redevelopment."[42] Social reactions to the homeless played a significant role in the emergent efforts to clean up and renovate the Times Square neighborhood. As a text belonging to this cultural moment, *Sweeney Todd* plugs into the tensions and anxieties about the rapidly growing problem of homelessness, mapping them onto the plight of the Beggar Woman and other vagrant mad characters.

THE HOMELESS MAD AND DEINSTITUTIONALIZATION

As the city grafted its presence onto the musical, the story was infused with an amplified interest in the homeless mad, a topic that, in the context of the 1970s, increasingly involved debates about the crisis of community psychiatry. The distribution of madness across *Sweeney Todd*'s metropolis was in implicit conversation with the social ecology of New York's theater district. Drifting across the musical's and the city's public spaces were the homeless mad, whose presence in the Times Square neighborhood increased exponentially in the 1970s. The surge in the number of those deemed mentally ill on the streets of New York and other cities across the United States was, in many ways, an outcome of the deinstitutionalization reform.[43] As the American Psychiatric Association would concede in a 1984 report on the homeless mentally ill, the concept of community psychiatry was "basically a good one," but eventually, through flaws in design and implementation, became a "major societal tragedy."[44] The new community centers, which supplanted the old system of state mental hospitals, were supposed to provide therapeutic services. Yet in terminating the custodial function of asylums, the architects of the mental health reform did not provide adequate alternatives for people unable to take care of themselves, with the result that, as Gerald Grob writes, "the social and human needs of the most severely and especially chronically mentally ill—particularly the assistance in dealing with the subsistence tasks of daily life—were often ignored and overlooked." Moreover, "caring and support services . . . were affiliated with a welfare system that by the 1970s and 1980s was under attack by a political constituency bent on diminishing governmental responsibilities and activities," a constituency that believed that "dependency was self-inflicted, and that poverty, misfortune, and illnesses were consequences of character deficiencies rather than environmental and biological circumstances."[45] As the alarmed authors of the APA report observed, "The ragged, ill and hallucinating human beings, wandering through our city streets, huddled in alleyway or sleeping in vents . . . are now regarded as an eyesore at best and the victims of a moral scandal at worst."[46]

Most communities were not adequately prepared for the fiscal and logistical burden of inheriting discharged mental patients, many of whom had nowhere to go and no one to assist them in the complex, long-term process of reintegration into society. Among those similarly affected by this crisis of mental health care were service-dependent mad or disabled people who had never been institutionalized. Unable to receive the help they needed, a staggering number of mentally distressed people wound up on the street, concentrating "in inner cities where many public and commercial services were readily available and where local opposition was weak and fragmented."[47] New York City became a particularly notorious urban harbor for the homeless mad during this period. According to a 1980 report by Governor Carey's office, in the course of the deinstitutionalization reform New York State "reduced the population of its 23 psychiatric hospitals from 89,000 in 1960 to . . . less than 23,000" in 1980.[48] Consequently, the Department of Mental Health estimated a near total of six thousand formerly hospitalized mental patients on the streets of New York City.[49] While public opinion about the massive reorganization in national mental health care remained divided, with the negative outcomes blamed alternately on federal, state, and local governments, psychiatrists, and patients, by the time of *Sweeney Todd*'s premiere the homeless mad had become a staple of the visual imagination about the metropolis.[50] "It is hard not to notice the mentally ill as they wander the streets of New York," reflected the *New York Times* in the fall of 1979. "Some act strangely, embarrassingly; some are pitiful. . . . [T]hey permeate some areas, particularly Times Square and parts of the Upper West Side, with their own weird ambiance."[51]

In this context, much of what happens on the streets of London in *Sweeney Todd* becomes coextensive with the streets of New York City. The first person Sweeney and Anthony encounter, as they disembark in London, is the Beggar Woman, who was played by Merle Louise in the original production. This character's unpredictable behavior, musicalized through abrupt transitions between the themes of begging ("Alms") and soliciting ("'Ow would you like a little squiff, dear") and further amplified by a combination of screams, muttering, spitting, and contrastive body movements, signals her status as a madwoman.[52] Anthony, who, unlike Sweeney, has not been missing from the city for the last fifteen years, readily identifies her as "only a half-crazed beggar woman. London is full of them."[53]

On a basic level, the attribution of madness to this character is traceable to the source play. In Bond, she goes mad as a result of rape. Sondheim dramatizes this traumatic connection by underscoring the flashback to the scene of the sexual assault with the Beggar Woman's soliciting theme "in a different guise. The justification for this is that . . . the symbol of that rape is the music which is always playing in her mind," he explains.[54] Yet in Bond's play, this character, while nominally referred to as "mad" and "deluded," does not sound confused or act erratic; the logic of her lines is not muddled; her conduct is not socially disruptive; neither is she seen to make attempts at selling sex.[55] She is constructed sentimentally, in keeping with the melodramatic parameters of a wronged yet dignified Victorian heroine in need of help and retribution. The marked distance between the play and the musical with respect to the Beggar Woman's madness points to the local priorities and influences affecting the process of cultural adaptation. The accretions of iconographic and ideological content involved in the Americanization of this character contain traces of material structures and affective experiences that make her, unmistakably, a product of 1970s New York City.

The dramatic organization of the Beggar Woman's madness in Broadway's *Sweeney Todd* makes visible the dynamic interrelation between structures of disgust and social exclusion. Of all the characters in the original production, the Beggar Woman looks the filthiest. Her face and hands are covered in smudges of dirt, her hair is unwashed and tousled, her clothes are a bundle of soiled rags. When accosting potential clients, she sings in "dirty Cockney slang" and, pulling up her skirts, reveals that she is wearing nothing underneath.[56] The staging of the social reactions to the Beggar Woman emphasizes the quotidian discomforts of sharing the urban space with this "crazy hag": the passers-by are "clearly revolted by her" and, on seeing her, "move away."[57] As Cohen's theory would suggest, she earns associations with filth not only by the uncleanliness of her physical body but also by the "perceived attributes" of her identity that "repulse the onlooker."[58] In addition to being literally dirty, she is tainted with her vagrant status and her transgressive sexual behavior in public spaces.[59]

Throughout the musical Mrs. Lovett makes repeated attempts to drive the Beggar Woman out of the neighborhood. As the pieshop owner worms her way toward wealth and middle-class respectability, she gets all the more vociferous about her perception of this "loony" as "trash from the gutter." Her main motivation is, arguably, to keep the Beggar Woman (Lucy) from revealing herself to Sweeney as his long-lost wife. Yet her calls to "throw the old woman out" of the community assume the tone of an ad hoc sanitizing campaign, done for a public good, which, ironically, correlates to her improving social status as a result of capital accrual.[60] The Beggar Woman's homelessness, poverty, gender, and perceived madness coalesce here within a complex ideology of filth, which, as a set of geographically and temporally bound notions, operates in dialogue with contemporaneous anxieties about the mad on the streets. The precarious configurations of her life trajectory on the stage of the Uris, located in a neighborhood characterized by a large influx of mentally distressed homeless people, position her in the overlap between the bag lady and the "smut" of the Time Square district.

Sweeney Todd's Beggar Woman joined the imaginary company of other homeless madwomen in the contemporary musical theater arena. For some audience members, the image of a singing madwoman on the street might have awakened memories of Countess Aurelia in *Dear World*, yet the Beggar Woman had a closer counterpart in the figure of a bag lady in *Ain't Supposed to Die a Natural Death: Tunes from Blackness*, which opened at the Ethel Barrymore Theatre in 1971. Written by Melvin van Peebles and directed by Gilbert Moses, this musical confronted America's racism in a series of choreographed monologues about Black lives in an urban ghetto. Unlike *Dear World*, which, despite being steeped in discourses of filth, had a sort of precious, viewer-friendly quality to it, *Ain't Supposed* adopted an in-your-face approach to portraying people and practices that society condemns as deviant and disgusting. The show's map of urban filth covered scene locations (e.g., community toilet), characters (e.g., dirty-looking homeless, pimps, sex workers, junkies), and actions (e.g., public urination, sexual acts, nudity, lewdness, profanities). As critic Clayton Riley noted, the dramaturgy of this "dazzling theater experience" fused naturalistic and surrealist registers to shape a social universe in which "behavior and appearance" were "taken past the perimeters of respectability, taken outside." The geography of the inner city was delineated by Kert Lundell's "hideously effective" set, "a stark metal and mortar fortress rising above so many Black streets in the land."[61] Performed by a large cast of actors and six musicians, this experimental musical gave a vivid account of how it felt to be seen as matter out of place in the United States.

Among the denizens of the block in the musical was a Crazy Old Scavenger Lady, played by Minnie Gentry. Like the nonconformist mad characters of the 1960s, she follows the beat of her own drum and, in the end, paves the way for a revolution. The inhabitants of the inner city are shown to be manipulated by a grinning figure in a white mask who hovers above the block, leading them like puppets by multicolored ribbons. Habituated to the system, the "poor black people on a string" carry on "as if nothing happened, as if [they] were masters of themselves." Yet the Scavenger Lady, like Countess Aurelia or the Beggar Woman, is "too nuts to take her ribbon and get in line."[62] A variation on the old trope of a mad visionary, she possesses a special insight into the hidden machinations of evil. With her "shopping bag of a bric-a-brac," she silently drifts in and out of view, stooping down every now and then to pick an abandoned item or a piece of trash, as if to preserve a memory about a nearby event or experience she has witnessed.[63]

The Scavenger Lady breaks her silence at the end of the show. Following an agonizing sequence in which a Black teenage boy, Junebug, dies of gun wounds inflicted by a cop, the block is transformed into a prison, a Foucauldian panopticon of a city, with a searchlight sweeping "back and forth across the camp grounds." Taking in the sight of Junebug's crumpled, lifeless body and a row of puppetlike prisoners "frozen in mid-cringe" against the wall, the Scavenger Lady "lets out a wail from the bottom of her soul" and, in a voice that "comes from somewhere most people have never been," launches into the show's closing monologue, "Put a Curse on You." Pouring out her anger and grief over the intensifying pulse of the drums and occasional improvisatory riffs coming from the brass and the electric bass, the madwoman "floats back and forth across the prison yard-street-stage-block, twirling and working her words." Leveled directly at the audience, her curses are fantasies of recrimination teeming with various orders of filth:

May the block gobble up your futures too
And them rats come slipping out your trash

And sliding into your children's cribs too
Put my curse on you

Van Peebles writes that her filthy words are "words that no one wants to hear," "crazy words." In the staged universe, they have the power to break the spell of the oppression. As the Scavenger Lady delivers a final refrain of curses, waving a monkey's tail and spinning like a dervish in her raggedy dress, the white mask dissolves, the ribbons stretch and snap, and the "ex-puppets," charging downstage, "advance on the world."[64] Similar to mad characters like Aurelia and Quixote/Cervantes, the Scavenger Lady emerges as the leader of a resisting community.[65] But the pictorial vision of her despondent movements across the staged metropolis—as well as her status as a mad seer among the blind or the ignorant—also prefigures *Sweeney Todd*'s Beggar Woman, scurrying through the streets and alleys, casting curses with her fingers and calling out "Mischief!"[66] The inconsolable voices of these two homeless women overlap in the common soundscape of crisis reverberating across different cultural artifacts of the decade. Their disparate life trajectories intersect in the space of protest against a hidden machinery of systemic manslaughter devouring their communities.

As *Sweeney Todd* continued to draw Broadway audiences at the end of 1979, one of many *New York Times* articles on deinstitutionalization during this time concluded that "too many people who are out belong in. Too many others, who belong out, have instead been abandoned."[67] Such statements about the problem of the homeless mad in the city help rethink the social concerns of Prince's production within a broader network of the period's anti-institutional discourses and movements. Commenting on the unjust power relations implicit in a system that seeks to punish/reform its criminals and restrain/cure its mad by keeping them in jails and asylums, *Sweeney Todd* constructs a tense dialectic between incarceration and release and extends it beyond the fate of the eponymous hero, a wrongly accused convict at large, to the whole population of the onstage cityscape. Philip Jenkins observes that "by the mid-1970s . . . [i]n the wake of multiple court decisions, extended involuntary commitment became difficult to impose except where individuals posed a grave and immediate danger to themselves or the community, and that became even harder to prove."[68] In keeping with these contemporary debates, the musical interrogates the moral principles underlying the practice of locking up marginalized members of society and insists on the ultimate impossibility of keeping anyone in for good. Judge Turpin's success in committing Joanna, his ward, to Mr. Fogg's Private Asylum for the Mentally Deranged is short-lived: she shoots the warden and escapes, as we watch the inmates "tear down the wall and rush out of the asylum, spilling with euphoric excitement onto the street."[69]

The magnitude of the breakout is indicative of the creative team's strategy of expansion in adapting the source play (in Bond, only Joanna's escape is shown). Reconceived on a massive scale, this scene is at once a striking reenactment of the process of deinstitutionalization and a refraction of the cultural anxieties surrounding the urban crisis of homelessness in 1979. Joining ranks with the Beggar Woman and other formulations of human and animal filth outside, the dirty, ragged ex-inmates race through the night, chanting in a panicked canon:

City on fire!
Rats in the streets
And the lunatics yelling at the moon![70]

Within the sociocultural moment of the original production, London's public spaces on the stage body forth the mad, homeless geographies of the Times Square neighborhood, its illuminated signs doubling as blazes of fire. New York's bright light district is the musical's other city, where sanitizing social policies threaten to wipe out the last hope of shelter for those consigned to neglect in the sweep of deinstitutionalization.

PSYCHIC AND SOCIAL ECONOMIES OF SHIT

After an intense 4:00 p.m. to midnight shift in Manhattan's Midtown South Precinct, an exhausted patrol officer says to his partner, "I don't know, Andy, but I have to get out. This job's like shoveling shit against the tide."[71] In terms of intent, this simile, recorded by sociologists from the City University of New York in the late 1970s, might be little more than a figure of speech employed in private by a frustrated law enforcement officer. The framework of municipal administration, however, complicates his remark with inevitable social implications.

In light of the patrolman's duties, which, according to the graphic account in West 42nd Street, bring him into regular physical contact with nauseating sights and foul smells, literal shit acquires at least as much significance as metaphorical shit does. Waste matter here has the common utility of providing a phenomenological baseline for social definitions of what is experienced as disgusting and threatening. The institutional practices of social regulation in Sweeney Todd's cityscape are likewise fraught with the materiality of filth. The Beadle comes to inspect Mrs. Lovett's pie-shop because it stinks up the neighborhood: "They say at night it's something foul."[72] Sensory reactions also play an influential role in the courtroom as Judge Turpin recapitulates his day at work in terms of his bodily experiences with unpleasant odors: "The stench of those miserable wretches at the bar was so offensive to my nostrils I feared my eagerness for fresher air might well impair the soundness of my judgment."[73] Such encounters between the city's disgust-inducing properties and its officials are part of the musical's elaborate approach to the mise-en-scène of hierarchized urban sociality. However, it is Sweeney Todd—the show's ultimate "Sword of Justice"—that articulates the most vivid use of filth in defining the polluted metropolis and its population.[74]

Upon arriving in London, Sweeney proclaims:

> There's a hole in the world
> Like a great black pit,
> And it's filled with people
> Who are filled with shit.[75]

He reprises and further elaborates this description—what Joanne Gordon calls "his excremental vision of the world"—toward the end of act 1 in "Epiphany," a number that, as Sondheim explains, dramatizes the moment at which Sweeney goes mad.[76] I want to suggest that the reappearance of "shit" at his critical moment plays a central role in the dramatic economy of Sweeney's madness, which the musical defines in large part through the hero's relation to the social order represented by the city. Characterizing his perception of the urban population and of himself, this manifestation of filth is a narrative and affective linchpin that holds together the social and the psychic in the dramaturgy of Sweeney's mental distress.

Sondheim recalls that in plotting "Epiphany," a song that took him the longest to write, he was determined to remedy "the one weak moment" in Bond's play: Sweeney's instantaneous conversion "from someone who kills only for specific and justifiable reasons into a mass murderer."[77] The composer-lyricist "never believed why Sweeney would turn from frustration at an individual killing, to wanting to kill the human race."[78] Bond's explanation that now Sweeney had "a taste for blood" did not suffice.[79] "The real problem," he reminisces, "was to find: what is it that turns him—exactly what is it?" Pursuing this line of questioning, Sondheim elaborated a more layered rationale for the psychological transformation in Sweeney and mapped it onto different sections of the song, with the result that the hero now "alternate[d] between his fury at the world and his yearning for his dead wife, and his frustration at just having been cheated of his revenge."[80] All these and other inner states written into the scene were meant to paint a more convincing picture of the onset of madness, which Sondheim imagines as a kind of psychotic breakdown and, ignoring the diagnostic standards of psychiatry, defines as "schizophrenic."[81]

On a clinical plane, the excavation of the psychic material underlying and setting in motion Sweeney's breakdown corresponds to the emphasis of the psychosocial paradigm of mental health, which prioritizes not the external symptoms of a disorder but what lies behind them. As a dramatic strategy, Sondheim's insistence on a more variegated—and more *truthful*—map of inner motivations affirms his abiding commitment to the modern dramaturgical principles of psychological depth, which is a well-established characteristic of his writing by this point in his career. The difference in this instance, however, is that Sondheim intensifies and reorganizes the familiar features of an internally preoccupied, neurotic character from his earlier musicals (e.g., *Company*, *Follies*) into what he understands to be a "schizophrenic personality."[82] By bringing his psychotic character into closer compliance with the strictures of psychological realism (despite the psychiatric misreading), Sondheim updates Bond's Sweeney, making him more legible as a conflicted protagonist to the contemporary audience.

The attempts to make Sweeney's slippage into madness plausible, to justify it as a psychologically possible event in the context of his social circumstances, are animated by the ubiquitous dramatic conventions of a psychoanalytic self (which, in the space of fantasy, almost always appears psychotic). On the level of scale and affect, the ferocity of his psychic economy—and of the musical itself—recalls Melanie Klein's formulations of mental life. Kleinian psychoanalysis tends to envision the inner experience in terms as oversized and graphic as those we encounter in *Sweeney Todd*. As Eve Sedgwick writes, there is an "almost literal-minded animism" to Klein's vision of fantasy (or, as Klein spells it, "phantasy"), which she populates "not with representations, knowledges, urges, and repressions but with *things*, things with physical properties, including people and hacked-off bits of people."[83] At its darkest, Kleinian theory of object relations presents the mind as a vicious scene of defensive and punitive investments in cannibalized and mutilated bodies; a violent economy of inner warfare in which the self is propelled into attack mode by its own sense of impotence and dread. To be sure, the chief analogy I am drawing here between Klein and the musical is of a literary-philosophic order. For me, they are primarily twentieth-century cultural artifacts sharing in and (re) constructing the textures of extreme mental distress arising under the conditions of Western modernity. Jacques Lacan once referred to Klein as an "inspired gut butcher."[84] She is, indeed, the Sweeney Todd of classical psychoanalysis.

Indispensable to her Grand Guignol accounts of distressed interiority are propositions about the fantasized relations between the ego and bodily excretions. In Klenian thought, the infant, plagued by paranoid anxieties and fears, projects poisonous excrement onto and *into* the mother, who is perceived to be bad. These attacks may be attempted literally, but they reach their full potential in unconscious fantasy, in which the child fills the mother with explosive substances in order to harm and control her. This process is complicated by Klein's original concept of projective identification: the child's missiles contain "bad" parts of his/her split-off ego. Thus, the mother, as well as the father and any other people who may be incorporated into these fantasies later, "is not felt to be a separate individual but is felt to be *the* [child's] bad self."[85] This psychic state represents the extreme of the paranoid-schizoid position, which, in Klein, begins with infancy and continues to be a regressed, fragmented mode that we slip in and out of as adults. When in this state, we see the world and ourselves in violently exclusive, absolute terms. Things appear either "magically good or bad — where those are not in the first place ethic designations but qualitative judgments perceived as involving life or death."[86]

Rather than being nurtured by his society, Sweeney is expelled to a penal colony and returns full of rage. Like the Kleinian child in a state of extreme vulnerability he feels that all the goodness has been taken away from him, rendering him an abject, marginal thing. Sweeney's mind enacts a sadistic fantasy in which he is filling his perceived enemies with explosive excrement in order to disarm and destroy them. His fecal weapons, as Klein would suggest, also contain his own badness. "People filled with shit," the external persecutors, double here as carriers of the internal sense of shame that Sweeney has incorporated into his self in the long process of being punished and excluded from society for crimes he never committed. Once an honest tradesman, Sweeney becomes transformed into a vengeful madman, railing at the city he now sees as a pit of excrement packed with inhabitants who "all deserve to die!"[87] Sweeney's "Epiphany" marks his entrance into the all-or-nothing space of Klein's paranoid-schizoid position. His vacillation between "they" and "we" in the song confirms the rubric of "people filled with shit" to be inclusive of himself.

One of the common approaches to conceptualizing filth inside or outside of psychoanalytic formulations is through its relation to cleanliness.

Theorized at various points in history in terms of opposition, imbrication, or equivalence, the interrelations between these two categories have animated modern Western discourses of sanitation. The filth-versus-cleanliness dynamic inflects the dramaturgy of the musical's social environment and, in an especially insistent way, shapes the architecture of Sweeney's actions and fantasies of moral purification. As a barber whose job it is to clean up people's appearances by way of cutting, trimming, and shaving, Sweeney is part of the social machinery of sanitation from the beginning. "Epiphany" expands his cleansing functions to include homicide, which the hero is able to justify as a natural activity within the logic of capitalism. Sondheim explains, "I thought his insanity would be wonderful if I could somehow make it so that Sweeney thought that he now knew what he should do in the world—which is to kill everybody—and that, in his mind, it was work."[88] For Sweeney, this moment translates his "determination to be a Sword of Justice"[89] into a legitimate job that targets material and moral dirt in the "great black pit" of London. Parallel narratives of 1970s New York City, in which the Times Square neighborhood similarly figures as a "hellhole" and "the pits,"[90] realign Sweeney's work with the production's historical moment, when a patrolman's job in the theater district could be compared, on phenomenological grounds, to shoveling shit against the tide.

Sondheim's use of the so-called Herrmann chord connects Sweeney's breakdown in "Epiphany" to the Beggar Woman (the "Alms" section in "No Place Like London") and the asylum inmates ("Fogg's Passacaglia"), while simultaneously gesturing toward multiple representations of madness underscored by Bernard Herrmann in such Hollywood classics as *Hangover Square* (1945), *Vertigo* (1958), *Psycho* (1960), and *Taxi Driver* (1976).[91] Sondheim traces the origin of his interest in Herrmann to his fascination with *Hangover Square*, a thriller about a composer who lived in turn-of-the-century London and who, "whenever he heard a high note . . . went crazy and ran around murdering people."[92] The musical's Sweeney likewise hears "music that nobody heard."[93] Yet in the context of the late 1970s, the phenomenological and ideological tensions between dirt and cleanliness in the musical acquire a striking affinity with *Taxi Driver*, whose hero, Travis Bickle, a former marine, enacts his fantasy of social purification by committing a slew of brutal murders in New York City. For this Vietnam War–era veteran, Manhattan, in the words of Michael Fleming and Roger Manvell, is a "paranoiac nightmare of the mean streets in which he moves and feels an overwhelming sense of defilement from the degenerate society around him."[94] Driving his taxi through the Times Square district, he launches a fantasized attack on filth, muttering, "Someday a real rain will come and wash all the scum off the streets."[95] The original production of *Sweeney Todd* belongs to this moment in the history of the city and similarly superimposes themes of moral cleansing and regulation upon the mental distress of its hero. Murder by razor eventually becomes Sweeney's externalized way of dealing with what he perceives to be foul and contaminating. His impeccable execution of the sanitary mission earns him "a nod" for "neatness" in the opening chorus.[96]

As Cohen points out, "Human excrement instantly taints anything it touches, but it is also the subject of countless schemes and fantasies for self-sustaining agricultural cycles."[97] Historically associated with ideas of recycling and renewal, shit can be turned into gold, whether in the form of fertilizer or capital. Cohen interprets this potential for conversion through the ability of filth to "cover two radically different imaginary categories, . . . *polluting* and *reusable*."[98] This duality has implications for the operations of filth in the ordering of social and cultural life. No classificatory system, no matter how widespread, is monolithic; neither are people's experiences with dirt homogeneous. What is contaminating to some may be rewarding to others. As Cohen adds, "When people who understand themselves to be degraded, dispossessed, or abjected by a dominant order adopt and appropriate (sometimes even celebrate) what is otherwise castigated as filth, there is a possibility of revaluing filth while partially preserving is aversiveness."[99] Attending to how the mad and the unclean on the stage interact with what is traditionally coded as impure shifts the focus to the existence of alternative systems by which they might apprehend and organize their worlds.

Sweeney Todd is not the only one among the cluster of mad musicals from the 1960s and 1970s to dramatize this side of filth. *Dear World*'s Aurelia, for instance, lives in a home that has an entryway to the city's sewage system. Inscribed at this symbolic divide between the city and its waste, she moves effortlessly between the "clean" and "dirty" spaces and is not at all concerned with the risks of defilement that her contact with the latter might pose to her body and social image. What Aurelia fears, however, is the risks of economic disparity and environmental pollution posed by the expansion of big industry and the interests of big banks. It is manifestations of uncurbed capitalist greed and want of empathy that appear out of place and therefore threatening within the madwoman's classificatory system. In the end, Aurelia defeats her adversaries by luring them into the labyrinths of the sewage and sealing the exit. The triumph celebrated in the fable's finale is achieved through a tactical repurposing of the city's entrails for the good of the planet.

What appears as "matter out of place" to the rich and the powerful in *Dear World* is a source of prospective succor to the mad-affiliated community. In the musical number "Garbage," Aurelia and her cohort reminisce about the good old days "when garbage was a pleasure, when you found the sound of good and plenty gurgling in your drain." This ode to trash piles of yesteryear plugs into the city's recent memories of the Sanitation Workers' Strike, which took place in February 1968, while the musical was being created. From this perspective, "Garbage" indirectly dramatizes New Yorkers' encounters with an unprecedented abundance of material trash in the city. Yet rather than echoing public outrage at the offensive consequences of the strike, *Dear World* celebrates garbage as a repository of reusable matter. For the madwoman's community, garbage once had the utility of providing physical and psychological sustenance; it held the prospect of finding "the joy of gracious living underneath your sink."[100] In holding up to scrutiny the production and accumulation of urban waste, *Dear World* injects the Paris setting of its source play with concerns specific to the American metropolis. At a time when New York City is fast approaching one of its bleakest periods, what worries Aurelia about her city's economy of trash is not its threat to cleanliness but the depleting of its sharing force, the diminishing of its nourishing capacity.

Sweeney Todd's production text likewise mines filth as a fertile resource for reuse and recycling. Except, in this musical, the embittered hero does not only reject but also embraces the dominant system. As I have suggested, Sweeney's fantasized interactions with excrement implicate his self and the external world in hostile, contaminating exchanges. Yet the Kleinian child is also capable of repurposing shit as a gift to the loving mother.[101] The productive side of Sweeney's foul fantasy is lodged firmly in the economy of capitalism. With the aid of Mrs. Lovett, Sweeney exploits the regenerative capacity of filth by starting a lucrative business based on the principle of the consumption *of* "people filled with shit" *by* "people filled with shit." This cannibalistic enterprise becomes the show's central descriptor of the profit-driven human ethics in the staged socio-economic order, where, as Raymond Knapp writes, people are "both the ultimate commodities and the ultimate consumers."[102] Within the musical's extensive vocabulary of dirty practices, the unsavory principle of "man devouring man"[103] can be traced to the utility of shit. The machinery of Sweeney's fancy barber chair, which initiates a sort of assembly line introducing raw materials into processing, suggests technological parallels to the water closet. Like Travis Bickle in *Taxi Driver*, Sweeney flushes the city "down the fucking toilet" and, at least for a while, gains access to a mode of social functioning that feels productive and congruent with the system.[104] The musical thus formulates its critique of the United States as a capitalist empire by exploiting the contradictory capacities of human waste, alternating between pollution and reuse. The schema of cannibalism enacted in *Sweeney Todd* begins and ends with excrement, implicating the entire population of the onstage metropolis in the mechanized loop of production, distribution, and consumption. Before the parting words of the chorus in the final scene, we are once again reminded of the causal relationship between these conditions and madness, as we watch a prematurely white-haired Tobias cut Sweeney's throat and make his way back to his job at the grinding machine amid the carnage. "There's work to be done, so much work," he mutters eerily, turning the handle.[105] Sweeney's factory within a factory has made another Sweeney.

The psychoanalytic path of "bad affect" I have followed in exploring the dramaturgy of Sweeney's distress leads out to a view of the musical's broader definitions of psychosocial experience.[106] Replayed incessantly within the frame of "The Ballad of Sweeney Todd" is a story that offers little in the way of redemption or reparation and distances itself from the common emotional landscape of the majority of Sondheim musicals. The painful ambivalence that characterizes the psychological structuration of *Company* (1970), *Follies* (1971), *Merrily We Roll Along* (1981), *Sunday in the Park with George* (1984), *Into the Woods* (1987), and *Passion* (1994) resonates with Klein's idea of the depressive position, a psychic state entailing integration of good and bad within one whole object. This state, Klein warns, will always be fraught with nagging "feelings of mourning and guilt" arising from "the synthesis between the loved and hated aspects of the complete object."[107] But it also offers us the comfort of hoping that we might be capable of undoing some of the damage we have inflicted, of repairing what we feel we may have destroyed, of recovering some part of what we have lost. While these Sondheim musicals are steeped in a grim acceptance of melancholy as an ineluctable part of living, the pain of human mistakes they contemplate is ultimately mediated, albeit with varying degrees of clarity, by the promise of reparation. As if reaching for the Kleinian depressive position, these shows settle on "sorry/grateful, regretful/happy" as emotional resolution and the hallmark state of adulthood.[108] As Phyllis Stone, one of the principal characters in *Follies*, offers, "Hope doesn't grow on trees. We make our own. And I'm here to tell you it's the hardest thing we'll ever do."[109] *Sweeney Todd*, by contrast, is Sondheim's only musical that, from beginning to end, operates in the Kleinian realm of the paranoid-schizoid, which has no place for ambivalence. In this hopeless, violently polarized universe of fragmented selves and dismembered bodies (Klein's "part objects"), no integration or reparation is possible.

Klein's theory, while lacking in systematic attention to environmental etiological factors, has nevertheless proven a fecund resource for thought in cultural sociology.[110] Julia Kristeva, in her biography of the psychoanalyst, observes a critical tendency in late twentieth-century scholarship "to theorize a socialism attentive to the inner universe and the depressive self by drawing from Klein as a way to lessen the blows of the globalization we are currently experiencing."[111] In these texts, the conciliatory, integrative potential of the depressive position serves as a basis for a more empathic system of social relations. It is not surprising, then, that *Sweeney Todd*, in its critique of a system that turns "beauty into filth and greed," should affix itself, instead, to a psychic mode that resembles the dark, unrelenting economy of the paranoid-schizoid position.[112] In cultural and sociological analyses featuring Klein, this position has come to figure as "a social structure, a placement and deployment of power, a combination of real persecutory forces."[113] As Kristeva puts it, this more "disquieting" dimension of Klein's thought represents "a perpetual return to the negative . . . that functions as a sort of *a black hole* in her systematization." Yet despite its fractal horrors, it provides "fertile ground for exploring human and social darkness."[114] In *Sweeney Todd*, the paranoid-schizoid mode, "characterized by a tendency toward possession and domination," becomes a means of dramatizing— more on the level of affect than linear exposition—the workings of unbridled capitalism, with its "'instrumental reason' imposed by ultraliberalism, the speculations on the part of the financial markets, the unchecked exploitation of nature, and the wholesale mastery of society."[115] The register of extreme negativity overhanging the "great black pit" of capitalist modernity in *Sweeney Todd* is strikingly fitting and perhaps even intrinsically necessary for a musical that focuses on the reification of human beings as objects in the process of being turned into shit.

CLEANING UP

As noted by Richard Eder, a *New York Times* critic, the early reception history of *Sweeney Todd* was tainted with a "note of critical reserve that attached itself even to some enthusiastic reviews—and with the decided aversion a number of sophisticated theatergoers felt on seeing it."[116] Like many critics in the 1970s, Eder considered the physical presentation, "the lavishness of the effects and the density of the texture," to be "too much for whatever there is of ironic or tragic intellectual purpose in the show."[117] John Simon of the *New Yorker* griped, "Is it necessary to have a four-letter word—in rhyming position yet!—recurring in a lyric strong enough without it?"[118] Such reactions were often voiced in tandem with vehement objections to the musical's finale, in which the company, pointing their fingers at the audience, sing in a shrill counterpoint: "Isn't that Sweeney there beside you? . . . There! There! There! There!"[119] As critic T. E. Kalem summed it up in 1979, "The general impression there is, 'You're debased; I'm debased; you're degraded; I'm degraded; we all do the same thing.' . . . It's an attempt to outrage the audience in a way that I, as a member of the audience . . . don't accept. I don't think that I've lived my life in that way."[120]

In an attempt to rebuff this line of criticism, Sondheim explains that, far from accusing everyone in the audience of complicity with the barber's murderous acts, "what the lyric very clearly states is that Sweeney—the spirit of Sweeney—is all around us."[121] Transcending critical analyses that pursue one-to-one correlation, Sondheim's clarification points toward a broader spectrum of psychosocial experience embedded in the work. The implied production method, as we have seen, is to draw the spectator into a theatrical reality composed of vivid and often aggressive encounters with filth and simultaneously signal a route toward collectively shared emotional and sensory experiences outside the walls of the Uris.

In keeping with the sanitizing movement in and around the Times Square neighborhood, much of the "smut" and dirt that flourished on the stages of the theater district in the 1970s would be cleaned up or toned down over the next few decades.[122] For *Sweeney Todd*, this would manifest in revivals that bypassed much of the original's graphic emphasis on the filth and the city, which, in turn, meant a loss of the trenchant political vision that these two dimensions transported. To carry out the makeover of Times Square, Delany writes, New York City "instituted not only a violent reconfiguration of its own landscape but also a legal and moral revamping of its own discursive structures, changing laws about sex, health, and zoning, in the course of which it has been willing, and even anxious, to exploit everything from homophobia and AIDS to family values and fear of drugs."[123] Ironically, *Sweeney Todd* was among the Broadway shows featured in the "I Love New York" publicity campaign designed to improve the city's image as a safe and wholesome tourist destination. In the television ad, Cariou and Lansbury can be seen cautiously approaching the camera in a calculated attempt to appear mysterious yet nonthreatening. Their performance here seems uncharacteristically hesitant, as if expressing ambivalence about the place the show's urban vision occupies in a video promoting New York as a fun, family-friendly city. The stark nonalignment between *Sweeney Todd*'s dirty contents and the official goals of this public campaign captures a moment in the history of the Broadway industry when its musical theater fare gets sucked into the vacuum cleaner of political conservatism. The ad documents the end of a creative era responsible for the birth of musicals like *Sweeney Todd* and *Ain't Supposed to Die a Natural Death*. As such, it is a record of the art form's capitulation to the new normative standards of the rebranded city.

As an artifact of the 1970s theater scene, however, *Sweeney Todd* revels in the creative—and instructive—capacity of filth. In this context, the twice repeated lyric "Freely flows the blood of those who moralize!" might be reinterpreted as a statement of resistance to the encroaching sanitization of the entertainment district, the slogan of the musical's polemical passion against the advent of a cleaner Times Square and a cleaner stage musical.[124] As Cohen stresses, "By appealing to their audience's experiential, sensory, and emotional apprehension, accounts of dirt in even the widest contexts connect such experiences to the lives and worlds of others—whether or not readers or viewers want to imagine themselves sharing those others' existences."[125] The musical's inducement of the disgust affect makes visible social practices and material histories that might otherwise slip our notice; it makes us pause at the sight or thought of lived realities that, in our discomfort, we hasten past and leave behind. Echoing Mrs. Lovett's invitation to Sweeney, the original Broadway production beckons its audiences in the late 1970s, with a kind of morbid fascination, to acknowledge and embrace the overwhelming presence of filth all around them. "Spit it out, dear. Go on. On the floor. There's worse things than that down there."

PART THREE

Madness in the Brain

SIX | "What a Lovely Cure!"

*Staging the Interior in the New Age of
Diagnostic Psychiatry*

During a tense debate at the annual meeting of the American Psychiatric
Association in 1982, one of the critics of the new edition of the Diagnostic
and Statistical Manual of Mental Disorders argued that, "like it or not, psychiatry *is* dynamic. It has more in common with the inevitable ambiguity of
great drama than with DSM-III's quest for algorithms compatible with the
cold binary logic of computer science." He warned that the field's newly
formulated adynamic, biologically driven vision of mental health, inscribed
in the manual, would in the long run diminish psychiatrists' technical
capacity for understanding and dealing with the challenging complexities
of deep emotional and psychic wounds. By privileging somatic data, the
"visible flame of unseen combustion," and turning away from epistemological and therapeutic principles rooted in Freud's "poetic science" of
inner life, psychiatry was losing sight of the problems of the human spirit,
the compass of its empathic mission.[1]

That this doctor's defense of psychoanalysis should allude to poetry is
not surprising. Depth psychology had been shaped by a process of cross-
pollination between medical sciences and imaginative arts. Like the works of
"great drama," psychoanalysis and dynamic psychiatry explored the vicissitudes of a mind undone by "a series of catastrophes" at a nebulous border
of the personal and the social.[2] Indeed, as we saw in Chapters 1 and 2, Freud's
project, invested with the properties and techniques of a literary and theatrical imagination, was instrumental in directing the psychiatric and cultural
gaze from the distressed patient's somatic symptoms to thoughts, memories,
and dreams; from the tangible and visible to the speculative and invisible;
from the putatively objective to the patently subjective.

In the last quarter of the twentieth century, however, the medical-
psychiatric establishment rang down the curtain on the analytic theater of
the unconscious, reinstating the physical structures of the body as the pri-

mary origin and location of madness. As Rick Mayes and Allan Horwitz write, "In 1980, at one stroke, the diagnostically based DSM-III radically transformed the nature of mental illness."[3] The massive overhaul of the manual inaugurated a systemic pivot to the biomedical paradigm, "which stresses the neurosciences, brain chemistry, and medications—superseding the psychosocial vision that had dominated for decades." In the wake of this "cataclysmic change," somatic conceptions of mental distress regained their long-lost authoritative status in psychiatric settings, putting nature, rather than nurture, back at the center of etiological theorizations.[4] As Horwitz sums up, by the early twenty-first century—and "over a very short time"—the biological study of human behavior had "evolved from a marginal and discredited enterprise to the dominant model of mental illnesses" in psychiatric curricula, research, scholarship, and popular culture.[5]

In this part of the book I focus chiefly on two Broadway productions, *Charlie and Algernon* (1980) and *Next to Normal* (2009), which extend the theatrical trends and conventions outlined in the previous chapters into the new era of biological determinism. Echoing the brain/mind, body/soul divide within contemporary psychiatry, these shows plug into long-standing philosophical tensions between somatic and psychological models of mental life and distress, tensions that prompt the central questions of these two chapters: What are the implications of the biological turn in conceptions of mental distress for the stage musical's established relationship to the psychoanalytic imagination and its dynamic concepts of inner conflict? How does the sweeping cultural move to absorb madness and psychic difference into the biomedical model affect the theatrical conventions of a deep self grounded in the vernacular of the unconscious? What does the tension between somatic medicine and psychoanalysis at the turn of the new millennium effectuate in artistic terms? In clinical terms?

While classical psychoanalysis borrowed ideas from the biological sciences, its significance lay in the break from the dominant nineteenth-century medical tradition of studying madness as a product of organic life. In this respect, as Allen Thiher reminds us, "Freud is on the side of the writers who have contested the hegemony of medical discourse, and, in spite of himself, . . . can be considered a part of the modernist revolt against psychiatry, a revolt let by poets and seconded by psychoanalysis."[6] Originally a neurologist and anatomist with a passionate interest in Darwinian thought, the father of psychoanalysis would never fully relinquish his originary supposition "that there must be a biological 'bedrock' to all psychological conditions and theories."[7] Yet this idea grew exceedingly marginal to his actual theorizations and clinical work in the 1880s and 1890s, a period that laid the foundation for psychoanalysis, and would remain conceptually vague throughout his writing afterward. As Jean Laplanche emphasizes, Freud's theory uses biological concepts analogically, not to imply an empirically viable organic reality but to use them as metaphors for the psyche.[8] While his references to biological principles have themselves been rightfully criticized as moralistically loaded and linked to harmful clinical dispositions and modalities across different historical locations, they never amounted to any kind of systematic program on Freud's part to construct out of psychoanalysis a somatically grounded psychiatric practice.

The rift between psychoanalytic and biological views of psychopathology, between mind-thinking and brain-thinking, is manifest in the changing balance of power between psychodynamicists and somaticists in US mental health care over the long twentieth century. During the postwar years, when Freudianism was at the height of its authority, the genesis of mental disorders was predominantly ascribed to "an untoward mixture of noxious environment and psychic conflict."[9] The biological project within psychiatry was relegated to an auxiliary role. The somaticists thrived best when their efforts were subordinated or in some way reconciled to the research agendas and goals of the psychodynamicists (as in, for example, the postwar boom of psychosomatic medicine), or when they operated in clinical settings where psychoanalytic psychiatry had a limited presence (as in the treatment of severe mental illness in asylums). While somatic interventions like shock therapy and lobotomy continued throughout the midcentury period, as did research into genetic, neurological, and other organic pathways to psychopathology, the dominant intellectual paradigm in mainstream psychiatry was one that recognized the brain but prioritized the conscious/unconscious mind.

The resurgence of biologism in mental health care in the last decades of the twentieth century put a newly urgent emphasis on symptomatology and reorganized psychiatry "from a discipline where diagnosis played a marginal role to one where it became the basis of the specialty."[10] Of particular importance to this side of the story is the process of re-scientization and re-medicalization through which psychiatry, caught up in the aftermath of the asylum crisis and the antipsychiatric hostilities of the 1960s and 1970s, refashioned and rebranded itself as a research-based medical field. Courting a tighter alliance with the natural sciences, DSM-III inaugurated psychiatry's de-Freudianization, which, on a deeper level, constituted a repudiation of psychological or "cognitive" modernism and a stringent reembrace of positivist standards and methods.[11] By distancing themselves from the psychoanalytic models of the unconscious, seen as too open to speculation and ambiguity, and seizing, instead, on brain research, with its reputable basis in organic empiricism, psychiatrists reasserted themselves in the medical and cultural arena as legitimate physicians and scientists engaged in the production of judgment-neutral, "objective" knowledge.

Musical theater has been involved in the cultural re-turn to the biomedical model of mental distress. The intensification of biological thinking in the art form between the late 1970s and the present is traceable not only through *Charlie and Algernon* and *Next to Normal* but also other new shows produced during these years, including *Passion* (1994), *Jekyll & Hyde* (1997), *A New Brain* (off-Broadway, 1998), *The Light in the Piazza* (2005), and *Be More Chill* (Broadway, 2019).[12] In working out a rationale for characters' feelings, choices, and actions, creative team members behind these musicals, especially the librettists, probe the role of biological circumstances in the mental functioning of the human subject and project different psychological scenarios involving somatic events and interventions. Depicting states and behaviors coded as irregular, extreme, or disordered, they adopt a range of historical models for conceptualizing and aestheticizing mental alterity, including those that have traditionally been in the service of theatricalizing madness. But what makes their creations part of the same cultural trend is a novel impulse they follow collectively to outline, with varying degrees of elaboration or conviction, a biological/somatic premise as the basis of emotional and mental life on stage.

When it comes to depicting the clinical domain, musicals of this era express and promote different attitudes toward brain science and somatic interventions. Some do that in a straightforwardly positive way. For example, the life of the lead character in William Finn and James Lapine's *A New Brain*, based on Finn's own medical history, is threatened with an "arterial venous malformation."[13] A successful surgery removes this dramatic obstacle and brings the story to a close. Catastrophe averted, all characters, including the doctor, spring into a sprightly song, celebrating the restoration of health, peace, and creativity. *Jekyll & Hyde*, to which I come back later in this chapter, can likewise be seen as a lyrical tribute to brain science and somatic remedies. This musical's protagonist, a medical doctor and researcher, fails to achieve victory over mental illness and dies in the finale. Yet in poeticizing his scientific quest for cure and his fight against a backward-looking medical establishment, the production reimagines this nineteenth-century character as an unsung hero, the glowing promise of his unfinished work serving as a referent for the new hopes of the 1990s, which President George H. W. Bush declared "the decade of the brain."

The Broadway productions of *Charlie and Algernon* and *Next to Normal*, by contrast, address overarching brain-centric views of mental health from a position of skepticism. Both musicals situate a lead character, Charlie and Diana respectively, within a system of psychiatric thought overdetermined by biological priorities and then push this system to the limits of its curative capacity and ethical motivation. To deliver this blow, the authors develop a dynamic of progressive friction between the doctors' medical views of mental health and illness and the protagonist's own experience of self and the world until the medical narrative reaches an impasse. The buildup of pathos on the stage is designed to solicit empathy for the patient's perspective, which links both shows to the rhetorical strategies and goals of the patient liberation and antistigma movements. On the level of form, this perspective is verbalized directly through sung and spoken statements, but it is also conveyed, perhaps more signally, through the scenic and dramaturgical conventions of the modernist psychomachia, in which unconscious life doubles as inner depth.

The differences in the referential effects of the psychomachia in *Charlie and Algernon* and *Next to Normal* are conditioned by the nuances of the relationship between madness and illness in each clinical history. The character of Charlie is constructed explicitly to be understood as a person with a developmental disability.[14] The script locates his illness in the brain rather than the psyche. The content of his psychomachic scenes is not used to mark symptoms of a disorder but to reveal depth in his character. The stage pictures of psychoanalytic selfhood facilitate the construction of psychological complexity, which is there to buttress the evening's didactic message: that Charlie has an inner life like everybody else. The musical's creators fall back on the Freudian playbook as a theatrical technology of persuasion, which gives them the means for articulating the humanity of the patient-protagonist and for legitimizing him as a subject worthy of dramatization.

Next to Normal goes for these effects too. But its system of psychic mimesis, much more elaborate than *Charlie and Algernon*'s, plays a specific referential role in the dramatic portrait of Diana's medical disorder, which the authors define as "bipolar, with a delusional component." The psychomachia serves to map out mental processes that, from a psychiatric point of view, contain symptoms of her diagnosed condition. It is the creative team's central solution for dramatizing the psychological reality of someone who "suffers from mental illness" and their "way of bringing the audience inside this experience."[15] Yet at the same time, the phenomenology of Diana's interior, physicalized through the stage language of unconscious fantasy, aestheticizes something that transcends or bypasses the rubrics of psychopathology. As an artistic rendering of the routine flow of fantasy life, which also functions as an abstract picture of a grieving mother's soul, the psychomachia moves this character, marked out with a special diagnosis, into the register of the average. In the opinion of Alice Ripley, who originated the part for the off-Broadway and Broadway premieres, Diana is "everywoman."[16] Other members of the creative team, as well as the critics, have likewise stressed the story's appeal to the commonalities of the human experience. Once again, psychoanalysis functions as the philosophic and literary language that codes madness as an entity at once atypical and ordinary.

It is through the alternation between two forms of mimesis, quasi-realist and psychic, that both musicals work their way to the climactic moments of confrontation and impasse between patient and doctor. What is missed or dismissed by the brain-centric gaze of the medical establishment is galvanized into life in the stage pictures of the introspecting or fantasizing mind. Both musicals, in their own historical contexts, deploy the psychoanalytic imagination as a method of theatrical pathos and truth-telling that dismantles the reigning politics of illness and recovery at the heart of the clinical domain on the stage. Within the critical project of *Charlie and Algernon*, the brain scientists, who purport to mean well, are caught in the sly act of negotiating a disconcerting alliance with a culture hostile to people with disabilities, which, in the context of the late 1970s and the 1980s, tracks with the consolidation of a neoliberal economy averse to welfare support programs for the dependent population. *Next to Normal*, in its turn, draws on the techniques of the psychoanalytic imagination to challenge the hegemony of biomedical standards of illness, health, and recovery as well as to interrogate the sometimes oppressive cultural norms of happiness and well-being these medical standards codify. By making its heroine's subjective world open to observation through the shared language of aesthetic and psychological modernisms, the musical mounts a compelling defense of complex mental processes downplayed or neglected in the wake of the "diagnostic revolution" in psychiatry.[17] The conflict between Diana and the medical establishment replays and brings up to date the fears expressed by DSM-III's opponents, of whom I spoke at the beginning of this chapter. Historicizing the consequences of the parting of ways between psychiatry and psychoanalysis, *Next to Normal* grapples with the disavowal of the unconscious and a surreptitious loss of the human soul under the new conditions of bioscientific rationalism in mental health care.

Considering the critical direction of my discussion, this part of the book may give the impression of denouncing biological psychiatry in toto. That is not my intention. The intensification of neurobiological research over the last few decades has resulted in new pharmacological options for the management of various psychiatrically recognized disorders, improving the quality of life for many patients. The recent gains in our overall knowledge of the human brain hold out further hope that more effective somatically based remedies might be discovered in the future to the relief of more people living with distress. Yet the privileging of the biological has also morphed into a systemic imperative that, in quarters both clinical and political, effectively preempts sustained inquiry into the psychosocial, which leaves great numbers of people affected by mental illness, especially those in marginalized communities, in dire straits. Horwitz writes that in the first decade of the twenty-first century even those works of psychiatric literature that "emphasize the heterogeneity of possible biological, psychological, and social causes of mental disorders give pride of place to the biological roots of these disorders."[18] The continued dominance of this trend, even at the time of this writing, thrives on the assumption that forms of mental pain with a known organic etiology are somehow more legitimate, more "real," than those attributed to social or intrapsychic factors. This is made all the more ironic by the fact that the authoritative profile of mental illness as a brain disorder has managed to flourish in the absence of any significant answers from neurobiological researchers as to the causes of bipolar disorder, schizophrenia, or other major psychiatric diseases. In this part of the book, then, I am primarily concerned with the ideological implications behind the ascendance of the biomedical paradigm, especially inasmuch as its default equation with truth and objectivity has marginalized other modes of understanding distress. I concur with writers like Horwitz, who reminds us that "the view that real illnesses must have biological causes is, paradoxically, a cultural construction."[19] Despite diagnostic psychiatry's pretensions to the empirical standards of the natural sciences, the current reign of somatic paradigms of madness in clinical and cultural domains has so far been less the triumph of proof than of ideology.

The revival of biological determinism within psychiatry in the last quarter of the twentieth century was not predicated solely on conclusions of a purely scientific order. There were, as it usually goes, internal motives of expediency and outside economic and political influences. What historical factors and players catalyzed this seismic cultural shift in conceptions of madness toward organic explanations in psychiatry and culture? How did Broadway musicals participate in the dissemination of the renewed ideology of nature? How did psychiatry and politics combine, for example, in *Jekyll & Hyde*?

BACK TO NATURE: RE-SCIENTIZING THE SELF BIOLOGICALLY

One of the biggest sources of professional anxiety for American psychiatrists in the 1960s and 1970s was their precarious status within medicine. As public discourses about madness swelled with anti-institutional critique, psychiatry came to be seen by many as a pseudomedical enterprise whose determinations of mental illness, for the most part accepted on faith, failed to satisfy the standards of scientific rigor and objectivity upheld in other medical fields. While both somaticists and psychodynamicists came under attack, the former had some technical advantages over the latter. Their epistemology of mental health, concentrating on the physical, bore a redeeming resemblance to the character of medicine proper—a welcome sign of fealty to the positivist principles of the natural sciences. This methodological basis enabled them, at least in theory, to more effectively address the increased calls for empirical validity in a cultural climate of antipsychiatric opposition. In practice, biologically oriented psychiatrists could point to the successes of the new psychoactive medications. Not only did the accelerating popularity of psychopharmacology from the 1950s onward boost their influence within psychiatry, but it also helped salvage their public image, framing them as practitioners of "real" medicine.

In this context, Freudians and other talk-oriented psychiatrists found themselves in a more vulnerable position. At a time when psychiatry was desperate to secure its wobbly footing as a bona fide medical branch, psychoanalysis appeared irreversibly contaminated with a poetic subjectivism. Its humanist concerns and speculative hermeneutics, features that had once given it the title of a radical science of the mind, produced knowledge that could not be adjudicated on purely rational grounds. The imbrication of Freudianism with the literary-philosophic domain made the psychodynamic component of mainstream psychiatric praxis feel too much like an intrusion from the humanities. Furthermore, the internal critics griped, the ceaseless proliferation of diverse psychoanalytic schools, with their propensity for internecine ideological battles, weakened psychiatry's profile as a medical specialty committed to the discovery of immutable, empirically validated facts of nature.[20]

Another massive dent in the reputation of psychoanalysis was made by a surge of criticism from second-wave feminism and gay liberation movements, which attacked the universalizing, patriarchal misconceptions baked into the Freudian project and laid bare the virulently sexist and homophobic beliefs behind its Americanized applications in the clinic and popular culture. Additionally, as Dorothy Ross writes, the declining image of psychoanalysis during his period paralleled "the vicissitudes of modernism as its authority splintered on the cultural politics of the 1960s." The loss of modernism's ascendancy in the 1970s and its dissolution into postmodernist multiplicity and ideological polarization "withdrew from Freud's ideas what had been a high cultural imprimatur, and without that imprimatur, the criticisms of Freud could multiply and be more easily heard."[21]

With the cards stacked against it in the clinical and cultural arenas, it was easy to make psychoanalysis bear the brunt of the blame for the disgraced status of the psychiatric profession. The way to move forward, its institutional opponents concluded, was to denounce depth psychology and reorient psychiatry toward a research-based medical model, fostering diagnostic reliability and accountability for treatment outcomes and prioritizing the production of testable, quantifiable, and, therefore, authentically scientific data. These goals were inscribed in the new, much-expanded DSM, which was instrumental in the de-Freudianization of American psychiatry. Unlike the previous editions, which had rested on the basic principles of psychodynamic thinking, the 1980s iteration, Mayes and Horwitz write, "emphasized categories of illness rather than blurry boundaries between normal and abnormal behavior, dichotomies rather than dimensions, and overt symptoms rather than underlying etiological mechanisms."[22] For proponents of this reform, the new symptom-based system of disease classification represented a long-overdue reinstatement of the Kraepelinian tradition of medical descriptive diagnosis.[23] This paradigm, they declared, represented "a strategic mode of dealing with the frustrating reality that, for most of the disorders we currently treat, there is only limited evidence for their etiology." Under the circumstances, the best way to define mental disorders, until solid evidence was found, was through "manifest descriptive psychopathology," or, in other words, a detailed rundown of symptoms.[24] Although DSM-III did not overtly postulate a uniform etiology for mental distress, the return to descriptive diagnosis as the organizing principle of psychiatry revived the biological premise underlying Kraepelinian assumptions — "that the core symptoms of mental disorders stemmed from some form of brain malfunctioning."[25] Given this somatic default, the course of psychiatric treatment as well as research into causative factors of madness would, from this point on and into the present, be guided largely by the priorities of the biomedical paradigm.

In the words of its developers and defenders, DSM-III constituted "a significant reaffirmation on the part of American psychiatry of its medical identity and its commitment to scientific medicine."[26] As an expression of

the specialty's new professional image, the manual's expansive nomenclature for visible, tangible manifestations of disease entities, reimagined as
discrete disorders, emulated the classificatory and diagnostic approaches
common to other medical fields. Divested of equivocal psychoanalytic
interpretations of inner life, with their vexed tendency toward distortion by
the observer, American psychiatry was able to rebrand itself as an evidence-
based branch of science, reentering the charmed circle of empirically driven
producers of objective knowledge. This makeover, however, did not mean
the specialty was willing to give up its unique clinical and cultural power
over broad matters of personality and problems in living, which had drifted
within its purview during the reign of psychoanalysis. Rather than relinquish this conceptual turf packed with bountiful reserves of symbolic and
actual capital, the new diagnostic psychiatry reclassified endless numbers
of human traits, behaviors, and emotions under its jurisdiction—the spoils
of the analytic age—as bona fide medical conditions, re-scientizing the
American self as an increasingly biological entity.

As T. M. Luhrmann writes, "The argument for the medical nature of
mental illness . . . encourages psychiatrists and non-psychiatrists to sim-
plify the murky complexity of psychiatric illness into a disease caused by
simple biological dysfunction and best treated by simple biological interventions."[27] This tendency was not lost on the early opponents of the newly
re-scientized psychiatry. Commenting on the conceptual and practical
implications of "brain-thinking," many alarmed voices in and outside the
field issued warnings about the creeping erasure of the mind in clinical
approaches to distress.[28] The roots of this problem were traced to the adynamic nature of DSM-III. One of the chief criticisms of the manual, from the
start, was that its authors inaugurated a "reductionistic" view of mental
life. By avoiding basic dynamic concepts like "defense mechanisms," they
had stripped psychiatric praxis of any serious investment in "emotional
conflict," instituting a gag on the unconscious. In its valorization of "laun-
dry lists" of "transient surface phenomena," a perspective that "risk[ed]
confusing symptom with disease," the new diagnostic science turned away
from the underlying interplay of psychic and social dimensions that generates and constitutes experiences of distress.[29]

The reversal from the mind to the brain, far from being only a product
of internally driven developments within psychiatry, was encouraged
and facilitated by powerful external players. During the 1980s and 1990s,
when biomedical investigators were overwhelmingly guided by the standardized criteria of the re-scientized manual, government funding for
brain research grew exponentially.[30] The period's expansion of support

for the new psychiatric science also had ties to the interests of the pharmacological and health insurance industries, both of which capitalized on the biological turn. When DSM-III was still under development, big insurers like Aetna and Blue Cross / Blue Shield applied much pressure on its designers, pushing for the standardization of diagnostic categories and treatment procedures. From the 1980s on, most insurers would demand a medical diagnosis from the manual and reimburse only quick, "evidence-based" interventions, increasingly denying coverage for long-term psychodynamic treatment. To managed care companies, Luhrmann writes, "The ideological tension between the psychopharmacological and the psychoanalytic looked as if it presented a choice, and the pharmacological approaches seemed cheaper and more like the rest of medicine." Psychotherapy was still prescribed, especially as a complement to medication, but could only be reimbursed if administered within a "credible" stretch of time, as defined by insurer. This "new world of rationalized and rationed medicine" made prescription pills the default option for most patients with chronic conditions and problems, the new economic pressures "turning psychodynamic psychiatry into a ghost."[31] The popularity of medication proved a gold mine for the pharmaceutical industry. Underwriting the claims of the new psychiatric science, major drug companies lavished funding not only on research into major psychiatric disorders but also on grassroots mental health organizations like the National Alliance on Mental Illness (NAMI, founded in 1979), which promulgated the biomedical diagnosis.

The arrival of diagnostic psychiatry coincided with a conservative backlash against environmental concepts of mental illness. In the 1980s and 1990s, as Michael Staub writes, right-wing commentators generated a steady stream of revisionist accounts of deinstitutionalization that blamed the crisis of homelessness on liberal politics and antipsychiatry. The majority of such attacks concentrated on denouncing social-constructionist theories of madness, which, according to the conservative pundits, "had addled the brains of academics and New Left militants alike in the 1960s and 1970s" and led to social policies that released mentally ill people into the streets.[32] Ridiculing antipsychiatric theses about the myth of mental illness, such commentators mobilized biological assumptions to reassert its factual nature. After all, since madness was, as biomedical researchers declared, an illness of the brain, questions of the adverse social conditions, on which the liberals were so fixated, were hardly relevant to the scientific task of helping humankind overcome this disease. The ties between biological thinking and reactionary politics during this period extended to the arena of federal policies, as the Reagan administration and Congress—the same government that poured money into brain research in the 1980s—proceeded to slash funding for community mental health services established in the 1960s, as well as the Social Security disability benefits that helped cover them.

Psychiatry's drift away from psychosocial explanations of distress thus paralleled the consolidation of neoliberalism in the United States. In a sense, brain scientists' promise to establish, once and for all, firm, reliable distinctions between the mad and the nonmad along empirically grounded, somatic lines had the effect of downplaying such contributory forces as poverty, inequality, and individual trauma in the genesis of madness. In the nature-versus-nurture debate about the psychological makeup of the human being, conservative demagogues sided with nature. The new psychiatric science arrived just in time to provide extra ammunition for their arguments. As a result of this confluence of ideological and economic calculations and legislative action favoring the biomedical model, the availability of affordable psychosocially oriented mental health care, particularly for the poorest and most vulnerable among those living with severe or chronic forms of distress, shrank rapidly, a tendency that has continued unabated into the present.

This dynamic of mutual interaction between biological psychiatry and conservative social policies found an expression in the conceptual economy and narrative function of madness in *Jekyll & Hyde*, with a book and lyrics by Leslie Bricusse and music by Frank Wildhorn. Directed by Robin Phillips, this musical adaptation of Robert Louis Stevenson's 1886 novella opened on Broadway in 1997 and ran for almost four years, closing in 2001. The show's opening scenes establish Dr. Jekyll (Robert Cuccioli in the original cast) as a "seeker of truth" involved in experimentation with "life-altering drugs" to "illuminate the elements of goodness and evil, which are inherent in every human personality." His crusade to isolate and control these two elements, we are told in the prologue, is "not really for the furtherance of science" but "for the relief of human sorrow and suffering." The scene is accompanied with Jekyll's sentimental arioso, in which he swears to "find the answer" to the illness destroying his father, whose body is laid out in front of him, in all its human frailty, on a gurney.

"There are doomed broken souls in a thousand asylums / left there to rot for the lack of a plan," he sings passionately in the next scene, applying to the board of governors for permission to try his experimental chemical formula on a mental patient. The doctor is positioned rhetorically as a modern progressive hero fighting against a reactionary establishment, which cleaves to the superstitions of the past. "The only thing constant is change" is Jekyll's mantra. Encouraged to sympathize with the brave doctor and his valiant mission, the audience is asked to go along with the musical's underlying thesis, in which the term "madness," applied to mental patients, is equated with evil. Jekyll's plea to the board invokes asylum inmates as a self-evident example of that "dark nature" that resides in "each of us," of the "evil that all men can do," of the "dysfunctional" that must be isolated from the "functional." Soon enough, the musical's action backs up this thesis with lurid evidence, when Jekyll, injecting himself with his formula, induces that latent "streak of madness inside" him to come out and becomes a mass murderer.[33]

The creative team's retelling of a nineteenth-century story set in a world of Londoners imperiled by a serial killer on the loose would seem to make the show's approach to madness continuous with *Sweeney Todd*'s. Yet on a philosophical and moral plane, these two musicals, belonging to different cultural moments and ideological strains in the history of Broadway's relationship to mental distress, are almost diametrically opposed to each other. In *Sweeney Todd*, madness is conceptualized not as an organic condition but as a product of the social order: the hero is born into a hostile environment which eventually damages him to the point of insanity. In *Jekyll & Hyde*, the hero is born into madness as a biological reality. It is always there as a natural given, a hidden menace lodged in the body, apt to break out and lead its host to violence. The only way to stop the "curse" of madness, insists Jekyll, is "behavioral control" through somatic means.[34] The role of social circumstances or individual traumas in the etiology and progression of mental distress is irrelevant to this 1990s reimagining of the old classic.

The biological vision of madness that drives Jekyll's crusade for "compassion and medical science" has its own cruel logic appealing to neoconservative politics. The fear of the Other and lack of empathy in the musical's overblown professions of concern for the mad are there in plain sight: brain science must waste no time in discovering a remedy for the mentally ill inmates of a thousand asylums—or America's prisons, which supplanted the closed asylums as places of segregation for the mentally ill after deinstitutionalization. But until that day arrives, given the "natural" proneness of the mad to crime and violence, it is only in the interests of public safety to continue keeping them locked up and off the streets, away from the "functional" population.

Alarmed voices within psychiatry at the close of the twentieth century stressed repeatedly that the new diagnostic science left little room for sustained, in-depth engagement with the lived experience and individuality of the patient. "As psychiatrists, we are under ever-increasing pressure to provide only somatic therapies," stated an editorial in the *American Journal of Psychiatry* in the mid-1990s, when the institutional consequences of DSM-III were beginning to be felt. "We are encouraged to base our medication decisions on diagnoses made after a 'quickie' interview, which screens a few relevant symptoms and ignores that each patient is a person living in a unique environment with a unique past history."[35] Governed increasingly by biomedical investigators, rather than clinicians who work with actual patients, and shaped by the interests of the pharmaceutical and health insurance industries, the new therapeutic and diagnostic regime shrank psychiatry's capacity to attend to the intricacies of the patient's subjective experience. The end-of-millennium project of redefining mental patients biologically appeared to have come at the cost of their individuality and depth. The internal critics within the field regarded these changes as a direct expression of "the increasingly materialistic and mean-spirited social structure that surrounds us." The hegemony of somatic determinism was having a dehumanizing effect on psychiatry, as its medical practitioners were becoming "only physicians of the body" and abandoning their "responsibilities for the mind and the soul."[36]

INTO THE MAZE: *CHARLIE AND ALGERNON*

Charlie and Algernon: A Very Special Musical, with a book and lyrics by David Rogers and music by Charles Strouse, takes up little room in the annals of Broadway history. Following its Canadian and West End premieres in 1978 and 1979 respectively, the show opened in a substantially revised version at the John F. Kennedy Center in Washington, DC, in the spring of 1980. This production, directed by Louis W. Scheeder, choreographed by Virginia Freeman, and designed by Kate Edmunds, transferred to Broadway's Helen Hayes Theatre in the fall of the same year and, meeting with mostly negative notices in the press, closed after seventeen performances. The general sentiment running through the reviews, replete with adjectives like "simplistic," "predictable," and "undistinguished," was that of boredom.[37] Even the failures of the musical did not strike the New York audience as remarkable enough to become fodder for subsequent fabulation, save for glancing mentions by chroniclers of Broadway flops.[38]

Yet *Charlie and Algernon* has the exceptional status of being the first musical on Broadway to offer a speculative, dramatic exploration of the strengths and weaknesses of biological psychiatry. The musical's hero,

Charlie Gordon, who was played by P. J. Benjamin in the US production, is described in the libretto as "a good-looking man of about thirty with a mind of an eight year old." While his coworkers occasionally refer to him as "crazy" and "a nut," he is different from the patient-characters discussed in previous chapters in that his condition has an overtly defined and arguably incontestable biological origin.[39] One of the doctors in the musical explains that, as a child, Charlie suffered from phenylketonuria, an "unusual biochemical or genetic situation that caused damage to the brain."[40] This patient, then, thinks, feels, and acts the way he does because of a process that "nature began."[41] The doctors believe that their new experimental psychosurgical technique can cure Charlie and even increase his mental capacity "to the level of genius."[42] The operation does make him extraordinarily intelligent, but the change is not permanent. As the effects of the surgery wane, Charlie begins to revert to his original state. Foreshadowing a grim outcome is the death of Algernon, a lab mouse who underwent the same medical procedure before him.

Like its famous source material, Daniel Keyes's 1966 novel *Flowers for Algernon*, this science-fiction show teases prospects of giddy progress in the realm of psychosurgical experimentation only to delimit their realization. Without throwing into question the somatic etiology of the hero's developmental disability, the musical defines the failings of the psychiatric science on the stage as a crisis of human ethics. As Charlie, his mental capacities expanding, begins to "dig under the surface of things," he becomes increasingly conscious of being treated like a lab animal. His doctors, chasing after a magic bullet, are blithely unconcerned with a host of psychic and social dimensions involved in living with a psychiatrically diagnosed chronic condition. In the name of their noble mission to "give Charlie Gordon a life," the brain scientists deny and erase his personhood.[43]

The musical's book derives its critical take on the ethics of biological psychiatry from the era of Keyes's original material, when somatically oriented psychiatrists were being overwhelmingly cast as villains in movies, novels, and plays following the postwar wave of exposés about invasive treatments like lobotomy or shock therapy. This record of the inhumane side of somatic psychiatry provided one of many reasons for the broader cultural animus toward biological thinking about human behavior, a paradigm that was extremely unpopular in American culture and scientific thought in the midcentury period. Tainted by associations with the horrors of Nazism, the status of genetic and other biologically based explanations of human behavior was at its lowest during the 1950s and 1960s, when antihereditarian views dominated psychiatry and the social sciences. During this period, marked by the emergence of a liberal, socially oriented psychiatry among the psychodynamicists, somatically leaning clinicians for the most part "rejected the claim that their specialty had particular competence to resolve broad social issues."[44] Gerald Grob writes that this attitude would define biological psychiatrists for the rest of the century. Though rigorously committed to finding effective means of curing mental illness, they remained "neither involved nor concerned with psychosocial rehabilitation or community support systems."[45] This detachment from psychiatric activism matched the aura of reactionary politics enveloping the ubiquitous figure of a sinister brain surgeon across different cultural productions in the 1950s and 1960s.

As a reviewer noted, the "white-coated medicos" in *Charlie and Algernon* are demonstrably "more concerned with the clinical outcome of their experiment than with its human implications."[46] The musical articulates this dynamic by involving, on the plane of mimesis, two competing models for apprehending and defining reality in both psychiatry and art. Dr. Nemur and Dr. Strauss's undertaking has all the necessary accoutrements of a legitimate scientific experiment modeled on positivist standards and criteria. Addressing "the most distinguished scientists and neurosurgeons in America" at a special meeting, the doctors give a verbal account of Charlie's illness and then proceed to a display of "tangible results," contrasting the visual appearance and speech of their subject in his current, cured condition with photographs and audio recordings from the early stages of the experiment.[47] Lending the appearance of scientific validity to their truth claims are figures, graphs, and diagrams. Yet the most solid source of visual evidence, with which the doctors intend to buttress their case, is a maze test serving the dual purpose of gauging and showcasing their subjects' improved brain functions. In the Broadway production, it appeared as a tall, three-dimensional scenic unit constructed of Lucite bars.[48] A simulacrum of a clear, self-contained problem with a concrete number of solutions, the maze incarnates the biomedical vision of the brain as an inherently knowable, finite thing. The doctors' demonstration appeals to a scientific imagination that endorses manifestations of the physical as the single legitimate basis for a valid study of human health.

Contrasted with the gratifyingly solvable, realistically rendered challenge manufactured by the brain-oriented doctors is the insoluble, abstract maze of Charlie's psyche. As the hero, prompted by his teacher Alice to "find the answers inside," embarks on a quest of self-discovery, he travels deep into the labyrinths of his unconscious.[49] His passage through the landscape of the self takes the form of crushing, if enlightening, encounters with a host of inner presences—other characters as reimagined by Charlie, as well as repressed memories of his parents and himself as a little boy—all played by live actors. Amplified to the point of overtaking the staged environment, this vivid spectacle of psychoanalytically inflected interiority offers a competing view of reality, a world of intense subjective experiences viscerally real to Charlie but closed off to the matter-bound gaze of the biological science on the stage.

In splitting Charlie into different figures incarnating his inner world, the musical's creative team replicates and builds on Keyes's use of analogous literary devices.[50] Over the course of his writing career, he came "to strongly believe in two of Freud's ideas: the power of the *unconscious* as a motivating force directing behavior, and his method of *free-association* to plumb unconscious connection." This method, which the writer first practiced on himself while undergoing analysis, became wedded to his creative practice as a tool for generating characters and situations. Keyes says that in his work on *Flowers for Algernon* he would use "free-association like a gardener's spade to dig out connected memories, bring them into the light and replant them where they can bloom."[51] The mechanistic descriptions of Charlie's unconscious fantasy and memory in Keyes's novel mimic the processes by which he created much of his hero's mental life and, in turn, furnish a template for representing it in the musical.

Matching his use of depth-psychological literary devices in the novel, the creative team resorts to Broadway's conventions for theatricalizing the deep self in two psychomachic sequences. Integrated into the first of these are the trappings of the analytic situation. "It's opening up. There is so much. . . . I'm remembering so many different times," comments Charlie, as performers, through a mixture of song and dialogue, reenact his surfacing childhood memories of being taken care of and then abandoned by his parents ("Dream Safe with Me," "Not Another Day Like This").[52] The presence of a psychiatrist here is only nominal. He is a theatrical device facilitating the hero's narration of self.[53] In the musical's medical world, talk therapy, as a form of treatment, appears to be an empty protocol, with little clinical value. For Charlie's doctors, the patient's recovery of repressed memories matters chiefly as proof of his increased IQ, attributable to the surgery's success. They show no investment in the ample evidence of psychic pain emerging from the patient's unearthed and reported personal experiences, past or present, nor in helping him cope with this pain. The complex emotional picture of Charlie's mind in distress—a vibrant inner dimension that the musical's creators dramatize via the stage vocabulary of unconscious fantasy and to which they consistently direct the audience's sympathies—plays no role in the brain doctors' deliberations regarding what their patient might actually need in the dizzying process of maturation and socialization.

In the musical's second psychomachic sequence, which follows Algernon's death, Charlie, sans analyst, makes a last-ditch effort to figure out the flaw in the doctors' theory and stall his own imminent "deterioration."[54] Half-remembered, half-imagined people from the hero's life return, encircling him menacingly. Through a montage of sung and spoken lines gradually congealing into a single cacophonous mass, they make him relive the traumas of his past, impeding and provoking his fight to avert the "regression."[55] The battle for his soul culminates in a confrontation between Charlie and his old child self. After the little boy breaks free of Charlie's grip and runs off, the hero's specular encounter with himself continues as a solo number ("Charlie"). "I reached this height / I won't descend," sings Charlie resolutely. His melody tends to move in downward steps, as if mimicking the progress of his decline, but this trajectory is periodically reversed with an upward surge in pitch, a reflection of his struggle to stay "in control" and not to "go back into the dark, into that cage."[56] The soliloquy ends like a classic Broadway cri de coeur of a defiant self-assertiveness in the face of an impending catastrophe. Commanding the world's attention at the peak of his vocal range, Charlie belts out his own name three times amid the apotheosizing halo of orchestral sound.

Charlie's rapidly growing mental capacity after the surgery parallels his increasing sense of dehumanization at the hands of his psychiatrists. The more he learns about himself after the operation, the more he objects to being treated as "something in a test tube." When his doctors inform him that he and Algernon are to be "presented" at the meeting of scientists and neurosurgeons to secure a new round of funding, he retorts, "We'll be there. You want us in costume and makeup?" and, taking the mouse from his case, performs the title duet.[57] Composed to be delivered "in the manner of old vaudeville," this song is a rare moment of pastiche in a score whose sound is more reminiscent of the decade's hits like *Company* and *A Chorus Line* than Strouse's own *Annie* (1977).[58] In the Broadway production, Benjamin performed "Charlie and Algernon" in a follow spot, while his stage partner, played by a trained white mouse, "danced" up and down his black-clad arms and torso. Emulating the aesthetics of *Cabaret*, *Pippin*, and *Chicago*, this number, complete with foot work, jazz hands, comic asides, and a stand-up routine inserted in between the verses, presented an ironic act of razzle-dazzle commenting on the exploitative uses of spectacle in medical practices.

The political underside of the friction between the brain scientists and the patient is fully unveiled in a public rhetorical match between them at the special meeting. Taking turns at the podium on the stage, the sparring characters appeal to the medical community in a direct address to the audience. Dr. Namur and Dr. Strauss propound that Charlie "did not exist before this experiment." It was not until the successful application of their psychosurgical technique that he was born as a real person, transformed from "a mentally subnormal shell," "a burden" on others, into "a man of dignity and sensitivity, ready to take his place as a contributing member of society."[59] The argument the doctors make in their bid for the renewal of grants is not only strictly biological but also political. Their experiment harbors a crusade to lift the weight of collective responsibility for dependent citizens designated mentally ill—and considered less than human—and to increase their productivity in the capitalist market. As the specter of a sinister cooperation between medical and political power begins to outline itself here, the musical replays antipsychiatry's hermeneutics of suspicion from the time of the novel, fears that psychosurgical experimentation might be used as a state tool of social engineering and behavioral control. But these connections between psychiatry and politics also acquire a new, uncanny resonance at the time of the musical's premiere. Dr. Nemur's and Dr. Strauss's rhetoric appeals to ideological and institutional forces that welcome an overdetermined biomedical view of mental health as a means of deflecting the attention from the environmental sources and determinants of mental distress. Produced at a period when the welfare system charged with the task of caring for the seriously mentally ill was under attack by voters and legislators bent on shrinking the reach of the government's activities, the musical adaptation of the novel draws attention to the increasingly precarious living conditions of Americans with psychiatric diagnoses and disabilities.

Charlie, taking his place at the podium, condemns the ethics underwriting the psychiatric praxis in the staged world. He rejects the doctors' dehumanizing claims that science "gave birth" to him and that people with developmental disability, unless cured, are merely "burdens on society": "I had, like everyone else, retarded or not, feelings, emotions, and a personal dignity, whether I knew it or not." Looking out into the audience, he warns the medical-scientific community that "knowledge, research, and education that have not been tempered with human feelings ain't worth a damn."[60] Yet his plea for empathy falls on the deaf ears of a psychiatric institution that reifies recovery and well-being into regulatory standards serving the needs of a capitalist market, standards that, if unmet, push one off the grid of social acceptance and security into the blind alleys of disenfranchisement in the ever-widening peripheries of American life.

The musical's sociopolitical critique is further articulated in a song titled "The Maze," in which Charlie, standing under the translucent maze hovering above him, introduces a new referent for the show's central metaphor. In this song, the maze is not a tool for assessing his brain function, nor an analytic picture of his mind, but a vision of capitalist modernity, described as a kind of race in which we are all trapped running, from birth to death, with no choice or means of escape. The music, reminiscent of a Jacques Brel ballad, moves in a loop, suggesting the motion of a carousel spinning inexorably in triple time. Similar to Brel's "La valse à mille temps" and "Fils de," the song teases an ethereal, somewhat precious atmosphere in the opening measures, then grows progressively ominous, depicting life sonically as a kind of mad circus. In the end, Charlie sings, "We are all the sum of the way that we pass through the maze." As if sealed rhetorically within this unstoppable machine, the musical's story hurtles to its anticipated ending. The Broadway production's final image, that of Charlie reverted to his original state—"posture, voice, smile"—sitting alone on a playground, implicates the overstated claims of brain science in America's entrenched systems of ableism, even as the consolidation of the neoliberal state injects a new vigor into political conservatives' hostility to social support systems.[61]

Mel Gussow, one of the few New York critics, if not the only one, to express enthusiasm about *Charlie and Algernon*, praised the creative team for turning "this seemingly unlikely musical material" into "a show with heart about our minds." In his review of the musical as performed at the Kennedy Center, he applauded the "intelligence" with which the show tackles "the abuses of science and technology, the blindness of do-gooders and the problems of those who are rejected by society."[62] While the critical notices after the Broadway opening ranged from much less generous to downright scathing, none of them missed the main point the musical was making about Charlie's "humanity." The modernist language of a conscious/unconscious self helped theatricalize this point by commanding a view of the hero's subjective world written off by the "smug scientists."[63]

To be sure, the psychomachic spectacle of epiphanies occurring in Charlie's mind was not there to make an argument about the virtues of psychoanalysis, nor to adjudicate the brain/mind controversy in psychiatry (of which the creative team were very likely unaware). More conceivably, it was yet another instance of twentieth-century artists recycling theatrical conventions of psychological depth, imagined to be timeless and universal, to dramatize inner conflict as a symptom of the human condition. In pursuit of this chronically ill-defined, grand target, they turned Charlie into a sympathetic, psychological everyman, giving him an analyzable self. The expansive, vivid staging of his inner life brought into view a psychodynamically inflected picture of his mental processes as evidence of his humanity. The stark contrast between the affecting truths of Charlie's deep self and the flat, sterile reports of the biomedical investigators, who are unable to see those truths, articulated a dialectic of incompatibility between his soul and brain science.

While the time of *Charlie and Algernon*'s fleeting appearance on Broadway has a curious correspondence to the time of DSM-III's publication, the musical arrived years before the full impact of the new diagnostic regime on the status of psychodynamic thinking could be felt in clinical settings and before the implications of the somatic turn spilled into mainstream cultural awareness. During the following decades, the rising prestige of biological explanations of mental distress and the increasing visibility of cultural movements for and against them galvanized a host of urgent, eclectic responses to psychiatry in public discourses. *Next to Normal* became a touchstone text of this cultural moment. Barely a few minutes into the new musical's opening number, an allusion to *Flowers for Algernon* flashed through the dialogue.[64] The ensuing stage action would soon reveal vast differences between the case history at the center of *Next to Normal* and that contained in Keyes's classic and its stage adaptation. Yet the life trajectories of the patient-protagonists depicted in these two musicals would crisscross in the critical space of biological subjecthood. Almost three decades after Charlie Gordon's brief stint on Broadway, Diana Goodman, the bipolar "everywoman" of the early 2000s, would traverse the staged medical world looking for answers about her soul. Like Charlie, she would find biological psychiatry soulless.

| ## "Sing a Song of Forgetting . . ."

*Listening to the Unconscious
in* Next to Normal

There is a momentary lull in act 2 of the 2009 Broadway production of *Next to Normal*. During a number called "Better Than Before" the musical seems to peek out timidly from under the debris wrought by the surge of unrelenting emotional pain in act 1. At this point in the narrative, Diana Goodman, the bipolar protagonist of *Next to Normal*, has returned home after a course of electroconvulsive therapy (ECT) to a life she does not remember living. As her husband Dan and daughter Natalie sit with her at the kitchen table and sift through family photos in an effort to bring back some of the memories she lost as a result of ECT, they begin to sing of going back to normal, a possibility that somehow, for the first time in a long while, does not seem far out of reach.

Perhaps the clearest sign of improvement is that Diana is no longer delusional. Gone are her fantasies that her son Gabe, who died when he was eight months old, is still around and almost eighteen. Throughout the action leading up to ECT, Gabe—or rather Diana's idea of Gabe—is played by a live actor. We can see him on stage fully integrated into the family's daily routine the way she imagines he would have been, had he lived. Yet in the days following ECT, Diana does not even remember ever having a son. In terms of representational style, the production here abandons the abstract device of using the stage figure of Gabe to dramatize the dynamics of Diana's inner life and shifts toward a more "realist" optics. The readjusted stage picture in front of us, just like the carefully pruned photos in front of the characters, is wiped clean of Gabe's presence. As we watch Diana, Dan, and Natalie peer at the photos, their ocular experiences correspond with ours. Just like us, they are all seeing a family of three, not four. This number models and endorses as wholesome a "realist" kind of seeing—that is, seeing only what is exterior and anterior to the mind, a world of matter rid of the fabrications of the unconscious. The sight of three bodies in "Better Than Before" reinforces with phenomenological eloquence the Goodman family's progress toward a semblance of normality and parallels their emerging, if fragile, optimism about Diana's chances of full recovery, as she learns a new script for her subjectivity, one that precludes fantasized interactions with the now-forgotten Gabe.

With the reappearance of Gabe on the set in the next number, "Aftershocks," the production reverts to its former abstract mode in the mise-enscène of Diana's subjectivity. Perched on the second level of the three-tiered set, Gabe addresses Diana, as she sorts through the photos and old papers at the kitchen table below. The heroine's character is once again split into two figures, Diana and Gabe, who at this precise moment represent, respectively, conscious and unconscious activities of her mind. The distance between the two actors placed on different levels of the stage furthers the idea of a barrier separating these two domains of her mental life. Having forgotten all about Gabe, she no longer communicates with him directly. Yet, "though she doesn't hear him," she feels the pressure he is exerting from his place in her deeper unconscious: "It's like it's tugging at me. I can almost see it." ECT has erased Diana's son from her conscious memory yet failed to sear him out of her "soul." Gabe's physical presence onstage in "Aftershocks" undermines the cures teased in "Better Than Before" and signals Diana's imminent relapse. As Gabe puts it, he is "a scar no treatment can erase."[1]

In giving divergent pictures of reality, these two numbers, positioned back to back, replay the historical friction between positivism and cognitive modernism. "Better Than Before" offers a tutorial in trusting only "objective," empirically verifiable facts, as it trains the characters' eyes on the evidence of three physical bodies in the photos and ours on the evidence of three physical bodies onstage. "Aftershocks," in its turn, mounts a challenge to the excessive realism of such externally based accounts of the world and, by looking inward, amplifies the mediating role of subjectivity in perceiving and describing reality. The return of Gabe brings us back to the metaphysics of fantasy, restoring the reign of psychic mimesis that was temporarily upended by positivistic demands and naturalistic priorities in "Better Than Before." The reinstatement of the visual language of the unconscious in "Aftershocks" is in keeping with the dominant philosophical current that powers the musical's epistemological machinery for knowing and showing the heroine's self. As such, the number makes a broader statement about the relativity and fallibility of "external" truths in scientific models of the world.

The competition between "Better Than Before" and "Aftershocks" as two modes of seeing and representing reality corresponds to the brain/ mind, somatic/dynamic rift in modern psychiatry, a conflict traceable to the historical tensions between positivist and modernist thinking in scientific and artistic arenas. The development of *Next to Normal* took over ten years, from 1998, when composer Tom Kitt and playwright and lyricist Brian Yorkey presented its first iteration as a ten-minute exercise in the BMI Lehman Engel Musical Theatre Workshop, to the final Broadway version, which opened at the Booth Theatre on April 15, 2009, and ran for 733 performances. Coming out of the "decade of the brain," *Next to Normal* reflects on the heady promises of neurobiological research into the sources of serious mental illnesses like bipolar disorder. In interviews, Kitt and Yorkey have made supportive, if not giddy, statements about "the huge strides" being made in the field over the recent decades.[2] Yet their specific creative choices situate the story within a discursive framework charged by contemporary debates about the limitations of psychiatric knowledge. By organizing the drama of the interior as a classic trauma narrative, which attributes psychosis to unconscious conflict rather than organic causes, and by using the side effects of ECT and psychopharmacology as obstacles impeding the resolution of the dramatic problem, they focalize the action around what Yorkey defines as the vexed "question of what lies in the brain, what's in the chemistry, what's in the circuitry, and what's in our soul."[3] The show's exploration of this question cracks open the biomedical model of distress, illuminating the levels and textures of lived experience flattened or erased by soma-centric definitions of mental life and personhood.

Gabe, who sings of memories forgotten, heartache unnamed, words unuttered, knowledge dreaded, is the show's raisonneur, and simultaneously, a metaphor for an ever-vigilant unconscious. The arational discourse he embodies and voices is deployed as a rhetorical mechanism and a mode of reasoning within the musical's philosophic and medical economy of madness. Through the stage pictures of Diana's fantasy, the production text marshals the persisting tendency of the unconscious to escape from and disrupt overscientized notions of the self, to render essentializing truth-claims unstable, a tendency that frequently comes into play in clinical stage narratives using psychic mimesis. We saw traces of this destabilizing effect on the production text of *Lady in the Dark*, where the arational discourse of Liza's dream world, intended to endorse a prefixed interpretation, generated a surplus of meaning that subtly counteracted the efforts of the Oedipal plot to master the unconscious and to suppress sexual and gender difference. Yet whereas in *Lady in the Dark* the narrative of the unconscious questioned biological essentialism within psychoanalysis

itself, in *Next to Normal* it comes into contention with the biomedical paradigm and its norms of illness, treatment, and recovery. Articulating an
unrepeatable individual self within a diagnostic regime overdetermined by
somatic priorities, it allegorizes the erasure of the subjective experience in
brain-centric views of the human mind and positions the psychodynamic/
psychoanalytic paradigm as the empathic school of the soul, a clinical and
philosophic practice whose modes of truth formation and truth telling cannot help but clash with those of biological psychiatry.

In the pages that follow, I discuss the operations of the unconscious in
Next to Normal in two overlapping senses: as a formal element and a clinical
category. In the former sense, it shapes the show's dramatic structure and
characterization techniques, and, as a depth language cherished by critics,
aids the musical's reception as a serious drama. In the latter sense, it is a
carrier of persisting, if historically contingent, forms and means of knowledge about mental life and distress. Though threatened with obsolescence
as a clinical category in the new age of biological empiricism in psychiatry,
the idea of the unconscious builds a bridge to more empathic, nonpatholo-
gizing models for thinking about madness and illness in and through *Next
to Normal*.

THE FAMILIAR ART OF PSYCHOLOGICAL DEPTH

In 2010 *Next to Normal* became the recipient of the Pulitzer Prize in Drama,
an honor rarely bestowed on works of musical theater. This highly coveted
distinction, coming on top of other significant awards like the Tonys, as
well as glowing reviews from the nation's leading theater critics, was the
culmination of the show's tremendous critical success since it opened on
Broadway. According to the nomination criteria for the Pulitzer, the piece
should be "a distinguished play by an American author, preferably original in its source and dealing with American life."[4] *Next to Normal* meets the
last two requirements with obvious ease: it is not based on any preexisting
material, and the scope of its main preoccupations, circumscribed by the
geography of the action, the dramatis personae, and the casting choices in
the original production, is largely defined by the concerns of the white
middle class in the United States.[5] The "distinguished play" component of
the description, however, represents what has arguably been the biggest
roadblock to any musical's potential win. Indeed, then only the eighth
musical to earn the distinction in the long history of the prize, *Next to Normal* had to have fulfilled certain preconditions to be seen as a legitimate

contender in a category overdetermined by the critical hegemony of literary theater.

The Pulitzer board singled out Kitt and Yorkey for writing a "powerful musical that grapples with mental illness in a suburban family and expands the scope of subject matter for musicals."[6] Bipolar disorder, ECT, and psychopharmacology were indeed novel topics for the genre. Yet, on a broader level, these thematic paths all led to the old terrain of madness, which has a long, venerated history of granting access to interior life on stage and a repertoire of psychologized devices that have been consecrated by theater critics and scholars as the hallmark of serious drama in the United States. I want to suggest, then, that Next to Normal's broad critical recognition and its success in superseding the historical bias against musical theater in the case of the Pulitzer Prize are in many ways due to its firm moorings in the canonized theatrical conventions of inner depth.

For an overwhelming majority of reviewers, one of the show's greatest achievements is, as one of the critics defined it, its "high emotional involvement."[7] Next to Normal garnered high praise for its relentless focus on the "pain that cripples the members of a suburban family," for disinterring from underneath the "all-American averageness" the hidden "anguish at the core of their lives."[8] Alice Ripley's performance as Diana, in particular, was lauded as a "fearless" feat of "astonishing . . . theatrical intensity,"[9] "beautiful in its complexity, as authentic a portrait of a personality divided against itself as you'll encounter in a musical."[10] In Ripley's own words, this role is "full-frontal emotional trauma." As one of the reviewers put it, "Watching her unravel is a harrowing experience."[11] Repeating words like "honest," "authentic," "daring," and "complex" with a grueling consistency, the critics commended the creative team and the cast for creating a musical steeped in a "dangerous cocktail" of extreme, uncomfortable feelings and "never releasing the audience from the captivity of [the] characters' minds." As Ben Brantley summed up in a representative rave in the New York Times, "Such emotional rigor is a point of honor for Next to Normal"; it is not "your standard feel-good musical," but "a feel-everything musical, which asks you, with operatic force, to discover the liberation in knowing where it hurts."[12]

The role of music in amplifying the characters' feelings, often to a point of extremity, has long been seen as foundational to musical theater, which in Kitt's opinion makes this story of "mental illness . . . filled with many heighted emotions . . . a natural fit to sing."[13] As members of the creative team, as well as the critics, have noted, the characteristic quality of emotional rawness in Next to Normal comes by way of rock aesthetics. Constructed and marketed from inception as a medium of exceptional authenticity, rock has historically been celebrated as a form of artistic expression more spontaneous, unreserved, and personal than older traditions of popular music, including show tunes of the Tin Pan Alley variety. In the musical theater arena, its utility for articulating an edgy affective ethos at the turn of the twenty-first century is apparent in such musicals as *The Who's Tommy*, *Rent*, *Hedwig and the Angry Inch*, and *Spring Awakening*. Kitt and Yorkey situate *Next to Normal* within this lineage, citing *Rent* especially as an inspiration.

Rock communicates and maintains its foundational, if intermittent, presence in *Next to Normal* through a combination of aural and visual signifiers.[14] On the level of sound, starting with the eloquent burst of a power chord within the first few opening bars, the Broadway production signals rock's centrality to the sonic environment of the performance through the timbral connotations of electric guitar, electric bass, and drums; musical gestures from a variety of rock types (e.g., arena rock, folk rock, piano rock, heavy metal); and characteristic vocal stylizations (e.g., labored voice production, uneven phrasing, mixing between registers, pitch variation, melismata). Visually, rock's signifying properties are manifest in Michael Greif's *Rent*-like staging of the performers' movements. The actor playing Gabe, for instance, spends a lot of his stage time singing in a bent-knee position reminiscent of *Rent*'s Roger.[15] Among other visual signifiers are the flashy rock-performance effects of the lighting design by Kevin Adams, the metal rails and scaffolding of the set by Mark Wendland, the casual wear costumes abundant in denim and T-shirts designed by Jeff Mahshie, and, perhaps most importantly, the physical presence and visibility of the musicians on the stage. All these sonic and visual gestures cultivate and sustain an underlying framework of a rock concert, which ultimately takes over the stage in the final tableau. With play-specific properties removed to the background and lighting and sound systems amped up to full capacity, *Next to Normal* ends with the image of singers and musicians performing a "rousing anthemic number," a rock musical convention that, as Elizabeth Wollman observes, "pay[s] direct homage to rock concerts, many of which conclude in much the same way."[16]

Yet while rock's angst-ridden sonic and iconographic properties in the Broadway production are no doubt instrumental in enhancing the stage effect of uncharacteristically honest feelings being unleashed, I want to consider a different route by which this musical, as its director, Greif, puts it, "goes to a very deep place."[17] This route consists of theatrical technologies—words, gestures, and images—that have supported the mise-en-scène of internal and invisible mental processes in US theater since the first waves of dramatic modernism in the early twentieth century. It is by exploiting familiar theatrical formulas of the unconscious—conventions that despite their staggering ubiquity in the contemporary artistic domain still retain a faint aura of provocation and sophistication—that *Next to Normal* achieves its status as intellectual, art theater. Yorkey accurately observes that his musical "presents naked human emotion and dysfunction in a way that a play might."[18] Indeed, to a great extent, *Next to Normal* gains admission to the upper strata of the middlebrow culture by *passing* as a straightforward psychological play. The sleight of hand is carried out by following a popular dramatic recipe that combines two classic preoccupations of American drama: nuclear family and psychic conflict. This beloved admixture defines a wide array of plays on the historical list of Pulitzer Prize finalists and winners, such as *Death of a Salesman*, *Cat on a Hot Tin Roof*, *Long Day's Journey into Night*, *Who's Afraid of Virginia Woolf?*, *Buried Child*, *Fences*, *How I Learned to Drive*, *The Clean House*, and *August: Osage County*, to name just a few.

The show's visual profile in the theater district during its Broadway run projected these associations through advertising choices. As spectators gathered outside the Booth Theatre, a pair of disembodied eyes displayed on the marquee signaled the musical's conditions of amplified inwardness. In the fuller versions of the logo hung above the theater's main entrance, these proverbial windows to the soul hovered over a disproportionately tiny suburban house, announcing the production's priority of scale with regard to the subjective, inner dimension. The collocation of the domestic and the psychological as tightly interarticulated, if metaphysically different, private realms of interiority was further articulated through elements of the stage design. During the performance, the eyes from the poster reappeared on a pair of shutters within the set to intensify the action's introspective register during Diana's sessions with Dr. Madden. The set itself, an abstract three-tiered structure representing the Goodmans' house, doubled as a physicalization of Diana's and at times other characters' mental landscapes. Vaguely reminiscent of Jo Mielziner's renowned design for the domestic psychomachia in *Death of a Salesman*, this scenic solution moored the nuclear family in *Next to Normal* to an architectural metaphor that splices modern American notions of the interior of both the mind and the home.

The musical's rootedness in established theatrical conventions of depth, as well as traces of their historical cooperation with the psychoanalytic imagination, can also be observed on the level of the libretto's dramatic structure. Like much of the American theatrical canon of the twentieth century, *Next to Normal* follows a traditional well-made plot formula influenced by the domestic dramas of Henrik Ibsen. In this musical, as in the abovementioned dramas, a tense dialectic between concealing and revealing events buried in the past propels the action forward until the secrets are brought out into the open, resolving the play.[19] Praised in the *New York Times* for its "sly staggering of information about its characters," *Next to Normal* is a faithfully executed exercise in Ibsen's psychological teleology, a consecrated dramatic logic traceable in a significant number of Pulitzer Prize–winning plays.[20]

Next to Normal is driven by an archaeological preoccupation with the heroine's past as a clue to her present, an interest that was cultivated contemporaneously by fin de siècle modernist playwrights and psychoanalysts. Discernible in the shape of the musical's narrative is the retrospective direction of self-scrutiny integral to analytic treatment, with expectations of progress to be achieved through reconstructions of a repressed past. Yet in its buildup and release of hidden internal pressures, the musical's dramatic structure can also be seen as a theatrical counterpart to the hydraulic models of the psyche in classic Freudian theory. Such models picture the unconscious as energy, which, "like water exerting pressure against the weak wall," eventually "must find an outlet."[21] *Next to Normal* establishes a comparable sense of the invisible/internal seeking imminent eruption from the outset. Starting with the first number, "Just Another Day," which crafts the impression of a family dynamic strained by internal pressures, the authors of *Next to Normal* manipulate the subtext to agitate the flows of disclaimed resentment, aggression, and despair in the characters' words and actions. Following the hydraulic logic, the pent-up feelings begin to push up against and leak through the barriers of concealment or repression, until the dam comes crashing down, dragging the characters into a verbal vortex of deadly confessions and confrontations. Replaying this teleological pattern so familiar to Broadway audiences, *Next to Normal* identifies itself with a long catalog of canonized American plays. Edward Albee's *Who's Afraid of Virginia Woolf?* is an especially obvious prototype for the musical's book, not least because the underlying interdictions building up to release over the course of the action in both pieces revolve around a nonexistent child. Ripley says this play inspired her work on the role of Diana.[22] Marin Mazzie, who took over the role in 2010, and her husband Jason Danieley, who starred as Dan opposite her, were admittedly drawn to the musical, at least in part, because of their long-standing desire to play the lead couple in *Who's Afraid of Virginia Woolf?*[23]

Lodged snugly within this popular dramatic formula, the Broadway production of *Next to Normal* infuses its realist base with avant-gardist theatrical styles externalizing the subjective experience. Like a slew of Pulitzer Prize winners in drama (e.g., *Death of a Salesman*, *Angels in America*), this musical exploits a combination of abstract visual devices to peer inside the mind. As I argued in the first two chapters, this approach to representing inner life in Broadway musicals was formalized in the midcentury period, as creative teams experimented with new ways of conceiving characters in dialogue with Freudian metapsychology. Similar to the population of Liza Elliot's dreams in *Lady in the Dark*, the presence of Gabe on stage signals a register of unconscious fantasy, ushering the audience inside Diana's psyche. According to the medical opinion expressed by the doctors in the musical, he is a delusion, a symptom of Diana's mental illness. Yet dramaturgically, Gabe is a psychomachic extension of her character, a stage figure that embodies parts of Diana's subjectivity hidden from others and, frequently, from herself.

The musicals of the 1940s tended to signpost transitions between internal and external orders of reality on stage, leaving little room for ambiguity at any given moment as to whether the action is taking place within someone's mind or in the outside world. *Next to Normal*, however, eschews clean-cut separations between its interior and exterior narratives—between that which happens only in Diana's fantasy and that which happens on the level of "objective" reality shared by the other characters. Instead, the musical merges both experiential dimensions visually, presenting them simultaneously. After explicating the dual nature of the events to the audience in the number "He's Not Here," the musical invites a spectating mode attentive to the tug-of-war between its interior and exterior narratives. If we accept this invitation, we spend the next couple of hours watching the two levels of action collide, overlap, and cross into each other, making competing claims for authority and credibility. At some moments, the inside takes precedence, invading and shrinking the outside, running over, under, and through it. With the appearance of Gabe in the number "I Am the One," for example, the internal comes to dominate the external, as the visible, live action on stage comes to mimic Diana's perspective. At other moments, however, the dynamic is completely reversed, as the outside expands and causes the inside to contract or disappear from view (as in "Better Than Before"). The incessant ebb and flow of energies and tensions between the inside and the outside in *Next to Normal* results in a blurring of boundaries between the conscious and the unconscious, making these realms appear continuous and discontinuous simultaneously, as they do in psychoanalytic texts and much modernist and postmodernist fiction.

While indebted to midcentury precursors, Kitt and Yorkey's approach to psychomachic mise-en-scène incorporates subsequent stylistic innovations in the genre. Despite the vicissitudes of psychoanalysis in cultural and clinical settings after its golden age of popularity, creative teams continued to proffer embodied visions of inner experience in dream or fantasy sequences through the rest of the twentieth century and into the twenty-first. Yet from the 1950s through the 1970s the formal solipsism that characterized this device in its midcentury uses began to splinter as the cultural engagement with madness shifted toward collective-based etiologies and solutions. During this period, some creative teams repurposed the device to accommodate scenes of communal interiority such as the shared dreamscape in *West Side Story* ("Somewhere") or the group breakdown in *Follies* (the "Loveland" sequence). Similarly, the psychomachic portrayal of the unconscious realm in *Next to Normal* is not always limited to one mind. While granting primacy to the mise-en-scène of Diana's subjectivity, the musical also uses Gabe, albeit more sparingly, to flesh out the interior life of the other members of the Goodman family (e.g., Dan's in "I Am the One Reprise," Natalie's in "Superboy and the Invisible Girl" and the bathroom scene during "I'm Alive"). As Aaron Tveit, who originated the part of Gabe, explains, "I was kind of the manifestation of everyone's problems in the show, depending on where the show was at and what everyone was doing."[24]

The collective character of the psychomachia in *Next to Normal* draws distinctions and builds alliances. By involving Gabe, a figure of the unconscious, in the visual and aural composition of three different minds on stage and by leaving interrelations among these interior proceedings largely open to interpretation, the musical proposes that there is an infinity of divergent ways in which the psyche can spin the same set of shared or witnessed life experiences. Yet by staging the daily convergences of these three minds within a unified realm of fantasy, the musical also hints at the notion of the family itself possessing an unconscious, a connective tissue of mutuality that holds these people together, despite the divisive idiosyncrasies of discreet subjectivities.

These and other aesthetic permutations and dramatic functions of the unconscious traceable in the production constitute an essential part of the musical's technology of depth. Though not the only reason for the success of *Next to Normal*, the symbolic capital of the psychoanalytic imagination carried over from the twentieth century—and the enduring prestige of artistic forms through which this capital circulates—is instrumental in the work's having been inducted into the pantheon of art theater. What makes

Next to Normal, in the words of its champions among the critics, a "rare recent example of Broadway integrity" is that it confronts "issues normally reserved for serious drama" and instead of "sugarcoating its depiction of bipolar disorder" finds "provocative ways of representing its seismic emotional fallout on stage."[25] What passes as aesthetic provocation is the upshot of the musical's basis in techniques that are traditional yet still capable of extracting a residual sense of daring experimentalism from their critically fetishized avant-gardist genealogy. On the one hand, the amplified tensions between the outer and the inner, the conscious and the unconscious, in the musical adopt psychologized conventions associated with traditional spoken drama, giving it firm grounds for recognition as a distinguished American play. On the other, they mark *Next to Normal* as a stand-out piece within its own genre, a "startling," "revolutionary" work that, "unlike the frivolous fare that all but defines the modern American musical," is "serious," "substantial," "dignified," and "uncompromising."[26]

For its unflagging commitment to depth, *Next to Normal* approached the kind of reception accorded to "intellectual" or "boutique" musicals by innovators like Stephen Sondheim, William Finn, Michael John LaChiusa, Dave Malloy, and Adam Guettel. Elevated into a small, perhaps even elitist class of their own within the genre, such works tend to benefit from the long-standing equivalences between the psychological and the serious in theater criticism. *The Light in the Piazza*, for instance, in John Lahr's opinion, defies the "anodyne commercial formula" of "frenzied Broadway-style forgetfulness" and rouses us to "reflect on our own unexplainable wounds . . . the mysterious things that hold us back from embracing life or allowing it to embrace us."[27] The critic admires Guettel's piece for rising above the "cheap-and-cheerful" sensibilities of most musicals: it "doesn't want to make theatergoers feel good; it wants to make them feel deeply." A similar logic permeates the enthusiastic responses to *Next to Normal*, the "feel-everything musical." The cult of inwardness in artistic and critical quarters concerned with musical theater dates back to the modernist experiments with madness in the midcentury scene. In some sense, the depth-psychological vernacular of the soul accomplishes for *Next to Normal* what it once accomplished for *Lady in the Dark*. Just as Hart, Weill, and Gershwin's "dramatic story about the anguish of a human being" was hailed as the coming of a new form of musical theater, so, in the representative words of an early twenty-first-century reviewer, Kitt and Yorkey's "honest account of the trials of a tormented mind" represents no less than "the future of sophisticated musicals."[28]

"STAY OUT OF MY BRAIN": TREATMENT AND RESISTANCE

Kitt and Yorkey have repeatedly offered assurances that *Next to Normal* is not meant to be an indictment of modern psychiatry. In one of the many interviews staking out this position, Yorkey explains that they wanted "the medical professionals in this show to behave as competent, well-meaning medical professionals would. It's easier I think . . . to write a show about a doctor who is incompetent and what a problem that is. It's more of a challenge, and I think more interesting, to write a show about what's really more common, which is, a doctor who is very competent and very well-meaning runs up against a disease he or she still can't cure. And that's often the case with mental illness."[29]

Inventing a clinical drama at a cultural moment characterized by a renewed public trust in psychiatry and a preponderance of antistigma and mental health awareness discourses, the creative team focused the attention of the narrative on the difficulties of living with a chronic mental illness. As part of this approach, they devoted a great deal of poetic energy to steering the audience toward a compassionate apprehension of Diana's lived experience. Yorkey recalls: "What we really wanted was to try and bring about empathy, to have people sort of actually walk a little bit in her shoes." To ensure a high degree of referential precision in this theatrical effect, the creative team undertook "a tremendous amount of research," which entailed, on the one hand, regular consultations with mental health experts, who gave them feedback on drafts of the show, and, on the other, listening to "people who came to us and told us their stories and talked about what their families went through, as many, many people did."[30] The authors' reading list likewise ran the gamut from medical and psychoanalytic texts to confessional literature about mental illness by patients, which proliferated exponentially in the 1990s and the 2000s: "Often every new plot point would send us off for more research. We read first-person accounts like Andy Behrman's *Electroboy*, Kay Redfield Jamison's *An Unquiet Mind*, Kitty Dukakis's *Shock*, Terri Cheney's *Manic*, and William Styron's *Darkness Visible*, among others. An invaluable resource was Andrew Solomon's *The Noonday Demon*. We also looked at more clinical texts like André Green's *On Private Madness* and seminal works like *Listening to Prozac*, by Peter Kramer."[31] The creative duo's sense of responsibility in crafting the story was also conditioned by their personal relationships and connections to mental distress: "We both have people in our lives who struggle with mental illness and I think that part of our wanting to write this and our wanting to get it right was that we wanted to do justice by their experience and also we wanted to understand their experience more ourselves."[32]

The musical's affecting score and theatricality shot through with empathic didacticism, as well as its cultural prominence as a Broadway hit, help account for its absorption into the field of consciousness-raising, antistigma activism. NAMI, in particular, embraced the show as a useful resource for "expand[ing] public awareness about mental illness and its impact on ordinary individuals and families." A frequent sponsor for public events featuring talkbacks with cast members of the touring Broadway production and mental health experts, the organization openly adopted the strategy of using the musical's "celebrity to combat stigma and drive home the message that mental illnesses are illnesses like any other and treatment works and recovery is possible."[33] Following this model, regional professional and amateur companies across the country teamed up with local chapters of NAMI to mount *Next to Normal* in an effort to educate their communities about mental health and raise funds for support programs.

But the show also presents a problem for organizations like NAMI, which supports the biomedical model of distress. The psychoanalytically inflected dramatic formula to which the musical adheres does not require that the mystery of the mad character be solved conclusively. (Many enigmatic protagonists are in fact written to remain enigmatic.) Yet because this type of play is designed to grant the audience a measure of satisfaction in knowing—or in thinking that they know—it invariably proceeds if not by providing absolute explanations then by outlining a range of possibilities as to the cause and nature of the mental crisis on the stage. Thus, Kitt and Yorkey's disclaimers notwithstanding, *Next to Normal* does not stop at pronouncing Diana's illness incurable but prompts the spectator, by the breadcrumbs of the characters' revelations and confessions, to speculate about what might stand in the way of the doctor who "can't cure" her. Yorkey himself acknowledges that while "there are tremendous strides being made in identifying . . . the way the brain works and how that relates to things like depression or schizophrenia and similar mental illnesses, . . . none [of this research] has yet cured one of these diseases, and I don't think any of the treatments has truly helped us to understand how it is that our brain, our body, our souls come to these places of great, great mental injury." Given the current state of psychiatric knowledge, the question that the playwright finds "compelling and worth asking" is "Where exactly do these feelings reside? . . . What part of these things resides in the matter, the tissue, the blood, the chemistry, the circuitry of the brain and what part of these things might be something beyond that, something that's the spirit?"[34]

This query rotates the wheels of the clinical and domestic drama in *Next to Normal*. The questions and techniques through which Kitt and Yorkey articulate and narrativize the "truths" of Diana's "illness" set up a vibrant field of contention that replays the terms of the brain/mind controversy structuring the critical histories of modern psychiatry.[35] By theatricalizing Diana's subjective experience through the language of the unconscious and first suppressing, then revealing the source of her distress in trauma and ungrieved loss, the musical delimits the reigning authority of biomedical definitions of illness and recovery and puts a spotlight on the clinical utility of psychoanalytically derived views of mental health. Indeed, while the authors state that they "didn't want to take a stand one way or the other" in regard to the "plusses and minuses" of somatic remedies, the musical's adjudication between the psychoanalytic and the biomedical is far from evenly balanced.[36] The psychoanalytic imagination prevails on the stage both clinically and aesthetically, as all major clues, if not exhaustive answers, to the puzzle of Diana's condition, come by way of epistemologies that underpin dynamic, rather than biological, psychiatry. In the clinical economy of this musical play, brain science wins some battles over the soul, but loses the war.

The radical suspicion the show harbors with regard to somatic therapies and explanations muddles the desired message of activist organizations whose rhetoric tends to elide the signal differences between biological medicine and psychiatry and between physical and mental disorders. Thus, NAMI has had to qualify its statements of support for *Next to Normal* with disclaimers, stating that "there are parts of the play that do not adequately portray facts about mental illness and mental health treatment." In an effort to address these alleged errors in the musical's narrative, NAMI exhorts the audiences to remember that "correctly diagnosed mental illnesses are medical disorders of the brain" and "modern medications . . . can be vital to recovery."[37]

A critical take on biological psychiatry was, in fact, embedded in the authors' conceit from the beginning, when they set out to write a show about a woman undergoing ECT. The idea for a musical treatment of the topic came to Yorkey when he saw a television report about this treatment. The news story stated that "a disproportionate number of patients who receive shock therapy are women. And a disproportionate number of the doctors who prescribe it are men."[38] This became the kernel for a dramatic story about a woman in search of the right treatment for her depression and all the men in her life who try to "help her get well." Over the course of the long developmental process, the creative team attenuated the drama's attention to clinical controversies, while expanding the dramatic picture of the Goodmans' quotidian experiences. The change in title from *Feeling Electric*, which was used in the early drafts and presentations, to *Next to Normal* was meant to reflect, as well as reinforce, the drift of emphasis from "the particular treatments she goes through" to "Diana and her family."[39] Yet in its final shape, Kitt and Yorkey's case history, especially in portions of the action stylistically realized through rock music and staging, retains the original antiestablishment impulse that inspired it. The show begins with a vague sense of unease and builds to a surge of outrage at the medicalization and pathologization of its heroine's, and, more broadly, the nation's emotional life.

Diagnostic psychiatry gets caught in the rhetorical line of fire early in the show, in a humorous if sobering number called "Who's Crazy / My Psychopharmacologist and I," which caricatures the extremes of the somatic orientation through the "rumpled and world-weary" figure of Dr. Fine (Louis Hobson in the original cast).[40] This extended sequence lampoons the specialty's overriding preference for "objective," testable data, staging Diana's gradual depersonalization and loss of self in a psychiatric realm dominated by positivistic scientism. Stretched over weeks and months, her treatment with Dr. Fine amounts to a quest for the right medication. The focus here is not on etiology (it is tacitly presumed biological) but on the symptomatological picture. Of vivid interest to Dr. Fine are quantifiable manifestations of mental and, especially, physical processes, such as anxiety, headaches, blurry vision, nausea, constipation, weight gain, and lack of appetite, many of which are, ironically, the side effects of the prescribed drugs. Logging these variables methodically into the patient's history, he looks upon her as a challenging mathematical problem rather than a human. Diana's solo singing in this extended ensemble sequence takes the shape of a waltz song that seems to follow a conventional AABA structure ("My Psychopharmacologist and I"). But her return from B to A is thwarted by jazz improvisations issuing from the "Voices" and the stage band, which intervene in the simple design, rerouting the music into unknown territory, turning clarity to murk. "Eventually, we'll get it right," promises Dr. Fine in a tone of rehearsed concern masking indifference. "Not a very exact science, is it?" returns Diana, watching him prescribe an umpteenth combination of pills.[41]

The first half of the number derives much of its humor from the contrast between Diana's vivid inner life, staged as a fantasized tryst with Dr. Fine, and the sterile, impersonal nature of their actual interactions in the external world. But the inner/outer split of the stage picture also draws attention to the order of mental processes dismissed by the doctor, gesturing toward the erasure of subjectivity in diagnostic psychiatry. To Dr. Fine, Diana is only a flat catalog of kaleidoscopically rearranging surface symptoms, to be manipulated and modified by somatic techniques. The notion of an inner conflict—and inner depth—is not viable in his office. Exclusively oriented toward what passes as "hard science," Dr. Fine ignores the contributory role of unconscious processes and trauma at the origin point of her depression, foreclosing any possibility of a meaningful engagement with her psychosocial experience. The end of the number takes a dark turn, concretizing the chilling implications of psychopharmacology. As a harsh spotlight strikes Diana during her final visit to Dr. Fine, the buoyant music loses its polyphonic richness and grinds exhaustedly to a halt. "I don't feel like myself. I mean, I don't feel anything," she utters numbly. "Patient stable," replies Dr. Fine matter-of-factly, the glib finality of his words endorsed by a brusque, hollow chord, which brings the number to a close.[42]

The musical's critical apparatus shifts tracks with the arrival of Dr. Madden (also played by Louis Hobson). An embodiment of the creative team's idea of a well-meaning doctor, he is less an accurate representation of a real-life psychiatrist than a dramatic abstraction of sorts, a kind of composite figure that stands in for the modern mental health care field. From seeing private patients in his office for regular talk therapy sessions to prescribing and administering ECT, the scope of his clinical practice and institutional responsibilities beggars belief. But as a theatrical amalgam of different trends and specialties circulating across the mental health care system, this character usefully highlights the brain/mind divide, operating at the fault lines of the integration of psychoanalytic and biomedical models of madness in an early twenty-first-century clinical context.

Taking a depth-psychological path to Diana's condition, Dr. Madden substitutes talk therapy for medication. "Make up your mind to explore yourself. Make up your mind you have stories to tell," he urges the patient over the lulling sounds of the violin and acoustic guitar, redirecting the locus of clinical and dramatic attention to the space of her suppressed memories and unconscious fantasy.[43] As Diana, hypnotized, begins to open up about herself, she emerges as a modern theatrical counterpart to the fin de siècle trauma patient in early Freudian practice and theory. Deploying analytic tools, albeit in a much-modified and simplified contemporary format, Dr. Madden traces the source of her mental distress to Gabe's death, an unremembered experience she has been carrying in her unconscious, unbeknownst to herself, as a kind of neglected wound in her soul. Steering her introspective trajectory into the past toward the painful events, he arranges conditions under which the patient begins to acknowledge and work through her ungrieved loss.

Gradually, memories of what actually happened take precedence over the alternative history constructed by her mind, a history in which Gabe never died. This psychic trajectory is replayed in act 2, after Diana's memories have been locked away in the unconscious again—not through the mechanisms of repression, the cornerstone of psychoanalytic theory, but through the destructive side-effects of ECT. Prompted by the sounds of Gabe's music box, she retraces her steps to the trauma on her own, without Dr. Madden's assistance. Instrumentalizing the analytic principle of retroactive self-scrutiny, she sings herself back into conscious memories of her son's death in "How Could I Ever Forget?"

In the clinical domain of *Next to Normal*, psychoanalytic thought functions as a carrier of human insight and empathy. Dr. Madden's psychodynamic practice, as staged in "I'm Alive" and "Make Up Your Mind / Catch Me I'm Falling," is contrasted with Dr. Fine's pharmacological remedies, which had flattened and muted Diana's feelings. His consulting room is a place where, as Muriel Dimen might say, "the once known and then repressed" or "the never known and dissociated" is accepted as meaningful, where subjective experiences considered illegitimate and irrational find expression and validation. The psychotherapeutic relationship offers Diana "a chance to say the unspeakable and to think the unthinkable."[44] Gabe, incarnating the unconscious, is present throughout this extended sequence, singing to her, with her, and for her. His status as the rock star of her fantasy in the consulting room is at times shared by Dr. Madden, a sly nod to the dynamic of transference in the analyst-analysand relationship ("Doctor Rock"). Gabe's actions in these and other clinical scenes seem inconsistent; he is now shielding her from remembering the fact of his death ("I'm alive!"), now nudging her to acknowledge the wound and "be free."[45] But contradiction, as Shoshana Felman reminds us, is "the mode of functioning par excellence of the unconscious, and consequently, also of the logic of psychoanalysis."[46]

The talking cure simultaneously functions as a listening cure, as Diana uncovers and shares unwanted parts of her self, filled with grief, guilt, and shame, and gets to be held in someone else's mind—without judgment. This odd regimen of ruthless self-reflection and exposure is fraught with terror and shock. Reaching into the unknown of the unconscious, she sings of "flying headfirst into fate."[47] Yet it is in the process of embracing the uncertainties and risks of analytic inquiry — what Dimen describes as its "subversive opportunity of digging up the ground beneath your feet" — that Diana's soul, paradoxically, begins to heal.[48] By "falling, sinking and sprawling" into self-knowledge, with all its inherent incompleteness guaranteed by psychoanalysis, she arrives at the potential for meaningful change.[49]

Dr. Madden's recourse to ECT rekindles the musical's animosity toward the biological paradigm. Two numbers in particular, "Didn't I See This Movie?" and "The Break," capture Diana's sense of betrayal at the doctor's defection to the somatic camp. Both scenes, perhaps unwittingly, shift the action into a recognizably antipsychiatric register by mobilizing imagery and sounds loaded with resonances and echoes of the cultural attacks on the psych fields from the 1960s and 1970s. The anti-institutional critical strain in these moments is amplified by rock aesthetics, an idiom whose history has been intimately entangled with madness and antipsychiatric thought. The cultural reception of rock and madness in the 1960s and 1970s was mutually constitutive, as both phenomena were actively politicized and romanticized as authentic sites of individual protest, creativity, and challenge to norms. As Nicola Spelman writes, American and British rock artists during that period grappled with the same set of issues that troubled antipsychiatry's intellectuals. A common thematic thread running through songs by David Bowie, Alice Cooper, Pink Floyd, Lou Reed, and many others was "enforced hospitalization . . . as a form of social control wherein the applied medication (drugs) or physical treatment — such as electroconvulsive therapy (ECT) — is intended to eradicate deviant behavior."[50]

The associative train of rock aesthetics in "Didn't I See This Movie" brings out the anti-institutional ethos at the heart of *Next to Normal*. Drawing on rock's ability to signal confrontation and its historical and cultural proximity to critiques of involuntary committal and treatment, the song stages a spectacle of resistance to medical authority. Regaining consciousness in a psychiatric ward after her suicide attempt, Diana delivers an explosive, rock-fueled response to Dr. Madden's suggestion of ECT. The visual setup of this number has some of the basic ingredients of antipsychiatric cultural productions from the 1960s and 1970s: a partially sedated victim in a hospital gown and a menacing doctor figure. Yet while the situation in which this patient finds herself is dire, there is an underlying note of irony in her attitude. "Didn't I see this movie with McMurphy and the nurse?" begins Diana in a tone that shifts between indignation and amusement, her speechlike cadence decorating the persistent rhythm of the cymbals and the bass guitar, which throb together in rapid quaver notes, a countdown to the emotional explosion that comes next. Fully aware that the balance of power in the psychiatrist-patient relationship has changed drastically since the era of *One Flew over the Cuckoo's Nest*, the patient looks upon herself and Dr. Madden as if they were grotesquely antiquated quotations from a kitschy antipsychiatric narrative. Greif's direction intensifies this moment's satiric undertones with exaggerated theatricality, as Diana, atop a hospital bed being pushed by Gabe, cuts off the doctor's protestations, and, as if riding on a blast of angry sound now fully unleashed from the drums and the bass, advances on him, demanding:

> What makes you think I'd lose my mind for you?
> I am no sociopath.
> I'm no Sylvia Plath.
> I'm not some kind of Frances Farmer find for you . . .
> So stay out of my brain—
> I'm no princess of pain.[51]

In some sense, the citing of fictional and historical figures traditionally constructed as tortured rebels playing by their own rules performs a tribute to the anti-institutional ethos of the 1960s and 1970s.[52] Diana's intense vocal delivery, at times approaching a scream, and her aggressive body language suitably situate the antipsychiatric profile of these cultural icons within the performative dimension of rock, whose reception has similarly depended on romantic myths of nonconformist authenticity. Yet by turning down these roles with scenery-chewing gusto, she delimits the relevance of the quoted cultural script in the early twenty-first century. In the post-deinstitutionalization era of *Next to Normal*, it is up to Diana whether to receive treatment or walk out.

"THE BREAK": DIAGNOSTIC PSYCHIATRY AND MAD GRIEF

Diana's ultimate act of spectacular resistance to the authority of diagnostic psychiatry over her emotional life takes place during her last consultation with Dr. Madden in act 2. This climactic scene disambiguates the musical's underlying statement on illness and madness, framing its politics in terms that, while resonating with the cultural echoes of classical antipsychiatry, are much closer to the critical position of the contemporary c/s/x/m (consumer/survivor/ex-patient/mad) movement.[53] Founded on the principles first established by ex-patient and psychiatric survivor groups of the 1970s, the c/s/x/m movement today can be thought of as a broad network of local, national, and international coalitions by and for people living with a diagnosis of mental illness or having a history of psychiatric treatment. Despite their diverse philosophies and programs for social change, these grassroots initiatives have a common basis in the patient's "experience of being on the receiving end of the mental health system." What this means exactly varies from group to group, yet much of their energy prioritizes personal experiences over homogenizing institutional scripts for subjectivity and champions "the right to self-definition" and "respect for the definition so chosen."[54]

Two interconnected numbers, "The Break" and "Make Up Your Mind / Catch Me I'm Falling Reprise," dramatize a turning point in Diana's relationship with Dr. Madden and, by extension, the medical establishment—what can be seen as her figurative passage to the status of a psychiatric survivor. The emotional urgency of "The Break" comes by way of thrash, a style that, as Robert Walser puts it, announces itself through "fast tempos," "frenetic aggressiveness," and "critical or sarcastic lyrics delivered in a menacing growl."[55] Far from being an ironizing gesture, the incursion of hard rock into the clinical realm in this number communicates a desperate sense of pain and protest. In an act of raw and rapid-fire singing, Diana recaps her tortuous medical history of somatically based explanations and treatments. Then, stretching out her words with a half-time feel, she asks:

What happens if the cut, the hurt, the break
was never in my brain or in my blood
but in my soul?

In the last fall and winter of the show's run on Broadway, Marin Mazzie, who portrayed Diana with an eye-opening combination of raw emotionality and razor-sharp intellect, brought this climactic moment to the apogee of theatrical effectiveness. In her rendition, Diana, as if struck by her own question, slumps onto a chair proffered by Dr. Madden. The aggressive music halts expectantly, the patient appearing to reckon with the full meaning of a truth she has stumbled upon, her eyes distant but focused. Slowly, contemplatively, she begins to repeat the question, this time rhetorical, making her way *colla voce* through the emerging terrain of new self-knowledge, peering into frightening vistas cracked open by the insight. With the reprise of the last word, the key to the puzzle, she reaches a clear view of her predicament: if the source of her pain lies in her soul, then the psychiatric establishment, hell-bent on pursuing bodily etiologies and symptoms, is forever treating the wrong "bone."

A startling moment of anagnorisis, Diana's epiphany is, in equal degree, crushing and liberating. Under the diagnostic conditions that govern the staged psychiatric realm, "Grief that continues past four months is pathological and should be medicated."[56] The psychoanalytic trauma model must give way to the biological model, whose somatic therapies paralyze Diana's ability to work through her loss and grieve. Without this ability, her prospects of meaningful improvement or recovery, however distant, are doomed. In a world of quick fixes and superficial solutions instituted by the triumvirate of biological psychiatry and the drug and health insurance industries—forces that install nature over nurture—there are no long-term provisions for her soul.

The discursive match between Dr. Madden and Diana illuminates the philosophic—and political—project that the musical had been diligently working out from its early days as *Feeling Electric*, before it became *Next to Normal*. In the battle of ideas that this scene illuminates, madness passes through oppositional, if not necessarily mutually exclusive, meanings, a rhetorical maneuver that is, on a more implicit plane, rehearsed throughout the whole drama from beginning to end (e.g., "Who's Crazy," "Everything Else," "I Miss the Mountains," "Perfect for You (Reprise)"). Dr. Madden reasserts the idea that Diana's diagnosis names a serious disorder, "a chronic illness. Like diabetes and hypertension." In Diana's emergent understanding, however, her diagnosis, no less seriously, starts to denote a scientized category that upholds arbitrary medical and social norms, a category that essentializes her inner experience through biologically based truth claims, othering her subjectivity as abnormal and her relationship to loss as illegitimate and disproportionate.

The critical stance Diana's character voices in this clinical agon approaches that of psychiatric survivor and Mad Pride self-advocacy groups, which occupy the more radical end of antistigma and disability activism. Members of these communities, many of whom deploy "mad" as a term of self-empowerment, stress that those who grieve too long or too intensely are pathologized because they violate standards of decorum and productivity in Western, late capitalist societies.[57] From this perspective, psychiatry's "disordering" of grief is an act of clinical violence routinely enacted on nonnormative emotional lives through DSM codes. Diana's noisy, messy, unrelenting "mad grief," magnified by the rock vocabulary, breaks the rules of respectability and upsets the smooth functioning of the social order, which expects her to accommodate loss within a "reasonable" period of time prescribed by medical authority: "Four months. For the life of my child. Who makes these decisions?"[58]

Diana's impasse as a grieving patient with the diagnosis of bipolar disorder makes explicit the musical's ongoing commentary about the pathologization of sadness and other negative feelings in the United States, pointing to the role of the mental health system in propping up an abiding cultural hostility to extreme expressions and long-lasting forms of unhappiness. The confrontation comes as a consequence of the musical's underlying loyalty to the psychoanalytic imagination. Dr. Madden's therapeutic emphasis on the unconscious has been a positive source of life-changing epiphanies for Diana, setting her on a course that has led to the new definitions of selfhood, illness, and recovery she is beginning to explore. His defaulting to somatic solutions, such as ECT and "a new drug regimen," by contrast, alienates her, precipitating her decision to reject the therapeutic imperatives of diagnostic psychiatry and take treatment into her own hands. "Maybe I'll let myself fall," resolves Diana. In an act of giving up hope and in the hope of finding, on her own, "another way" to "surviving," she says goodbye to Dr. Madden and walks out.[59]

THE "ORDINARY UNHAPPINESS" OF "LIGHT"

In the end, Kitt and Yorkey's story of Diana's incurable illness is a meditation on the nature of our definitions of both cure and illness. In "Light," which is the musical's closing number styled as an arena rock anthem, Diana appears to be traveling along the psychoanalytic path of self-reflection on her own, diary in hand, as she learns to live with the daily reality, rather than denial, of her loss. Rejecting mainstream biomedical prescriptions, Diana crafts a personal plan for self-care and survival necessitated in large part by the absence of long-term psychiatric provisions for her psychological needs. It is a plan that recognizes the enduring impact of her trauma and embraces alternative notions of what it means to be healthy or sick or convalescing. In her solo verse, which marks the last time we get to hear from her independently of the other voices, she sings of the need to recognize that "some hurts never heal" and of a liberating, life-sustaining insight this admission has brought her:

And you find your way to survive.
And you find out you don't have to be happy at all
To be happy you're alive.[60]

True to the authors' stated position, *Next to Normal* is not a condemnation of psychiatric medicine. Rather than retelling a totalizing antipsychiatric narrative in the style of *One Flew over the Cuckoo's Nest*, which, as Yorkey accurately implies, has become an easy dramatic cliché, the production tests out new directions and positionalities in the space of critical debate concerned with the interface between doctors and patients and between social institutions and individuals. Moments like the Dr. Fine sequence or "Didn't I See This Movie" may paint a disturbing picture of a postasylum network of mental health facilities in which mental patients wearing the "chemical straightjacket" of drug therapies are moved in accordance with the correctness of their behavior.[61] But while the musical revisits traditional narratives of panoptic objectification, it also counters them with a depiction of the patient's critical agency and creative empowerment within and beyond the clinical setting.

Diana's proverbial act of door-slamming does not unambiguously signify a complete break with mental health professionals. For all we know, she might still be seeing Dr. Madden for therapy. Or not. The production does not confirm, nor does it deny, either of these scenarios. But the image of the two of them singing in harmony from the second tier of the stage set, not looking at each other but cooperating vocally at a respectful distance within the same space of humanist meditation, emblematizes the musical's projection of a more equitable distribution of power in the doctor-patient relationship. In this dramatic vision, the patient is not helplessly prey to psychiatry's organizing power over her selfhood but is able to exercise her own modes and norms of self-definition and self-care. The arena rock environment into which "Light" plunges the spectator may be charged with echoes of the music's affinity for narratives of personal rebellion against institutional oppression, but it also updates rock's field of signification with a newly urgent focus on the ways in which mental health patients are capable of rescripting their subjectivities independent of clinical authority in the postasylum landscape.[62]

This brings the dramatic geographies of mental distress in *Next to Normal* close to the orientation of ethnographers who have called for a "reevaluation of the previously static, disciplined and objectified figures" of the mental patient (or ex-patient) and a reimaging of such representational practices through modes of analysis that recognize these people as "active agents" and "resistive workers . . . engaged in different 'fields of contention' in and around psychiatric care."[63] Such post-Foucauldian tactics, emergent in and through grassroots (ex)patient movements and gleaned in *Next to Normal*, outline some correctives to the entrenched tradition of violently polarizing theorizations of the relationship between psychiatry and madness in academic and activist thought. They help us forge new reparative paradigms for authoring and analyzing representations of mental distress or psychiatric disability so that the concepts of stigma and othering "do not always dominate our frames of reference."[64]

Madness has historically thwarted all medical and philosophic attempts to capture it within a totalizing explanatory framework. *Next to Normal* recreates this age-old dynamic on the stage and profits by it in different ways. The ascendancy of a revitalized diagnostic psychiatry has established new priorities in the field of dramatic writing, where the presence of a legible psychiatric diagnosis is now regarded as a welcome sign of positive, ethical representation. DSM-derived names for disorders and symptoms often serve to authenticate new works as well researched, truthful, and responsible. Even previously existing characters, who were originally portrayed as out of control or unhinged but untied to any specified disease entity, now get revisited empathically within a diagnostic framework and rehabilitated as needing a proper psychiatric evaluation and treatment.[65] *Next to Normal* appears to satisfy these priorities. This musical about mental illness and bipolar disorder owes its good name to the high scientific standing of diagnostic psychiatry. That it deals with such "difficult" topics has also proven a boon to its critical status as serious theater.[66]

But *Next to Normal*, like much mainstream and experimental theater before it, also benefits from the prolific ability of madness to deliver both conflict and spectacle through identification with an alterity that defies norms and regulations. Absorbed into the biomedical paradigm of mental health regnant in the world on the stage, madness soon begins to clamor for release. Refusing to be contained within one totalizing explanation, it wreaks havoc within the neatly packaged logic of scientific rationalizations to show diagnostic psychiatry wanting in something vital. Psychoanalysis uncovers and fills that lack in the musical. It is done in part by presenting the talking cure as a therapeutic alternative on the stage and in part through the ample use of the modernist conventions of American bourgeois tragedy, a formula that cannot help but reproduce the conditions and effects of the psychoanalytic imagination that structures it. As a mode of treatment and critical thought, psychoanalysis has its own history of being applied as an all-encompassing, absolutist expert science. But in this musical it is deployed to mirror its other, parallel history as a philosophic and medical site for championing a dissenting individuality and psychic plurality. It is positioned as a more potent therapeutic—and dramatic—alternative to the biomedical paradigm on the stage because it possesses what the latter lacks: a desire and an ability to listen to the human soul and communicate in its riddling language.

Presiding over the finale from the top tier of the set is the invincible, omnipresent Gabe, who instantiates the rhetorical and structural inseparability of the unconscious from the musical's philosophic and dramatic ethos. His tenor voice soaring, he affirms the prospect of reaching a "brand-new," brighter future.[67] Notably, this prospect is not granted to the family on the stage until they have all conceded and begun to make peace with the reality and permanence of Gabe as a wound that never heals. It is, then, through the acceptance of the unconscious and its lessons that the musical forges a passkey to a future where things *can* be better than before. This might seem like a doomed proposition, for it predicates hope on seeking a kind of knowledge that by definition "does not allow for knowing that one knows." Yet, as Felman (following Jacques Lacan) notes, the subject can get hold on the knowledge of the unconscious "by the intermediary of his mistakes."[68] This is, then, *Next to Normal*'s real condition for entering the promised land of "better than before": the commission and the admission of the human mistakes that the musical dramatizes, the mistakes of not remembering and dis-remembering, of not feeling one's feelings, of denying one's past and disavowing one's pain.

The musical's persistent injunction to explore yourself, to disinter what has been forgotten, to make up your mind seems laden with curative rewards. Yet the range of foreseeable improvement intimated in the finale extends no further than Freud's famously reserved prognosis, promising little beyond transformation from "hysterical misery" to "ordinary unhappiness."[69] According to the Goodmans' verbal recollections dispersed through different songs in the show, the edges of their days have always been submerged in chronically "gray and rainy weather," from wedding and vacation to Gabe's death and Natalie's birth. In the end we see the family accept these storms as inevitable, integral part of the vicissitudes of an authentic life: "Give me pain if that's what's real— it's the price we pay to feel."[70]

The musical's effort to find the "sun" and "let it shine" among the "darkest skies" without dispelling the latter marks the distance musical theater-makers have come since the early experiments with madness in the golden age. Importantly, this invocation of "light" does not mean the destruction of madness through cure (as in *Lady in the Dark* or similar projects), but, rather, its absorption into the continuum of the acceptable, which, at the same time and conversely, revises and broadens the existing norms of the acceptable. In this musical, the grooves left by the acts of madness in the social fabric of the world lead to new definitions of one's self-worth and well-being, to which the light of the final song brings visibility and respect. In the closing verses, the characters shed their shame about depression and, addressing the world, come out as emotionally and mentally wounded. Standing in the dazzling sunbeams of the projectors, they embrace the full spectrum of their feelings and invite the audience to "open up" and join forces in the "fight" against the stigmatization of madness, illness, and, yes, unhappiness in American culture.[71]

Conclusion

Contemporary Visions of Madness as Depth Theater

However precarious the status of unconscious conflict may be in mainstream psychiatry today, the presence of a character torn apart by contradictory forces within is still seen as a prerequisite for plays, operas, ballets, or musicals aiming to capture the elusive, vaguely defined tragic sense of life identified with that weighty, if similarly vague, concept, the human condition. The "universal" language of the anguished soul that proliferates through countless theatrical productions, often serving as the index of a work's philosophic heft and artistic excellence, is a historically and geographically specific vernacular of the mind, derived from the psychoanalytic imagination about interiority and madness. The use of this language need not imply any formed opinion on the part of specific theater artists about psychoanalysis or psychotherapy, nor any deliberate attempt to endorse either. More often than not, the psychoanalytic vocabulary comes in the form of readily available theatrical, literary, or cinematic conventions, seemingly with no ties to the clinical. Yet embedded in these conventions are rudimentary psychoanalytic postulations of inner conflict that necessarily reflect and reinforce the steady cultural reign of the psychological as a truth discourse, an authoritative if diffuse knowledge base in which the concept of the unconscious serves as the main motivator and explicator of human behavior, and madness is always in sight or just around the corner.

Contemporary producers of "prestige" or "indie" musicals often rely on the authority of these canonized psychological conventions to construct and market their products as "serious" theater, resorting to rhetorical and creative strategies going back to the midcentury. Benj Pasek, Justin Paul, and Steven Levenson, for example, extol their own creation, *Dear Evan Hansen*, for telling a story of "depth" and "humanity" that is "more real" than is "typical" for a musical, with "an authenticity to every note and every lyric."[1] The show's director, Michael Greif, of *Next to Normal* fame, promises that "everything Evan does in this play has emotional credibility."[2] To deliver on these highly sought-after theatrical truth-values, the musical's authors funnel contemporary situations and musical styles into the psychodynamic character model that was codified during the concurrent golden ages of the Broadway musical and psychoanalysis. Much of Evan's inner life is presented through psychic mimesis. Whether it is his talking to the dead Connor or "being bombarded with thoughts about what other people are saying" through projected images of social media in "Waving through a Window," the musical aestheticizes the experience of "not being able to escape the prison of your mind" in a way that resembles only too well the classic neurotic character of the midcentury.[3] Evan's psychological prototype could be Willie the Weeper from John Latouche and Jerome Moross's experimental musical *Ballet Ballads* (1947), the "undecided, always divided" hero, who is "small, shabby," and "insignificant" but has a vividly intense, conflicted inner life. Willie's character brief in the script all but encapsulates Evan's modern struggles: "He is lost in the fears and doubts that cloud his mind, a mind defeated by the rigors and anxieties of contemporary life."[4]

At the present moment in the history of madness, the reception of musicals featuring distress, especially those with a contemporary setting and clinical references, is conditioned by the impressive cultural capital of diagnostic psychiatry. What might once have been thought of as a case of neurosis, extreme shyness or simple eccentricity, now tends to be perceived as a medical disorder. In this cultural climate, the character of Evan, whose diagnosis remains unnamed in the musical, invited speculation by the critics and fans as to what his condition actually is from a psychiatric standpoint. Some reviewers even accused the musical's authors of trivializing his "mental illness."[5] What do the efforts to diagnose this dramatic character seek to redress? Is there only one correct, scientifically established interpretation of human behavior and feelings that the authors somehow missed? Can a DSM code make the representation of his emotional life more truthful? The attribution of "neurosis" to Evan would come off as passé and naive these days, as the term no longer carries the scientific weight it had at midcentury. But how different is the stage vision of Evan's psychology from "Willie's untidy mind"?[6] Do prescription drugs make him into a character who is more ill? How much more does this contemporary musical actually know about the nature of its hero's suffering? How much do we?

Although this musical has been charged with psychiatric negligence, it has also been acclaimed for its convincing technologies of authenticity and "real-life depth."[7] In the words of an ecstatic *New York Times* critic, *Dear*

Evan Hansen is "more complex than the usual sugary diversions"; this musical drama "draws us so deeply into the character's psyche that it would be like looking in a mirror and trying not to see your reflection."[8] Even some of the critics who fault the musical for "sugarcoat[ing] mental illness" still praise it as important, innovative, and viscerally affecting.[9] The effect of inner truth and sincerity in this brand of the "serious" musical hinges, in large part, on the enduring public faith in the psychological conventions that came into their own during a century marked by the cultural explosion of the dynamic unconscious. On a thematic and plot level, *Dear Evan Hansen* shows little overt interest in psychoanalysis and might even be subtly biased against psychotherapy.[10] But in its presentation of an anguished human interior, the musical recycles models of mind and distress from the midcentury experiments, which depended on psychoanalysis for their claims to significance, credibility, and sophistication.

While such conventions of psychological depth persist in coding musical theater as serious and consequential art, they also continue to get reshaped and repurposed in interesting ways. For example, the 2016 Broadway production of *American Psycho*, with music and lyrics by Duncan Sheik and book by Roberto Aguirre-Sacasa, used these conventions not only to gaze inward and outward through madness, but also to interrogate cultural assumptions of an obligatory inner self, always distinct from and somehow more authentic than one's public persona. On the outside, the musical's antihero, Patrick Bateman, a Wall Street banker and serial killer, is an amalgam of surfaces, his sleek, status-conscious identity composed of elite brand names, designer clothes, ultramodern gadgets, and prescription drugs. The musical's exterior location is Manhattan, a feast for the senses, brimming with opportunities for Patrick's daily self-gratification to the drone of 1980s synth-pop. This gaudy urban playground, however, gets gradually absorbed into a kind of twilight zone, which seems to serve as an abstractly rendered spectacle of his daydreams. Or does it? The Broadway production, directed by Rupert Goold, used psychomachic techniques in a way that made it impossible to tell precisely if the proceedings on the stage, including the lavishly realized blood scenes, are a presentation of actual events taking place in New York City, a symbolic expression of Patrick's inner experience, or both. By collapsing the exterior and the interior into each other, *American Psycho* seems to call into question the necessity for such distinctions in the first place. Can't the book be judged by its cover? Are there always redeeming deposits of psychological gold to be found beneath one's public facade? What if Patrick, both outside and inside, is precisely what we see: an affluent, educated white American male getting away with murder on a daily basis, his reputation kept clean by the machinery of systemic privilege? *American Psycho* uses the antihero's sociopathy as a metaphor for an ailing society. But unlike its not-so-distant relation, *Sweeney Todd*, this musical avoids constructing an extenuating psychological or clinical rationale for the madman's actions. This may be *American Psycho*'s main point: that the Wall Street Everyman does not need hidden depths to thrive in this world, for his violence is not a matter of personal trauma or biology, but, in Patrick's own words, "a symptom of late capitalism."[11]

Michael R. Jackson's *A Strange Loop* (2019), which received the 2020 Pulitzer Prize for Drama, also calls attention to the cultural conventions of a deep self *as* conventions but it does so in a deliberately self-conscious, metatheatrical way, with intriguing philosophical implications. The story's psychomachic setting, "a loop within a loop within a loop inside a perception of one man's reality," doubles as a literal stage for its hero, Usher, "a fat American Black gay man of high intelligence, low self-image, and deep feelings," who is an aspiring musical theater writer and an usher on Broadway.[12] Composing an autobiographical musical in real time, he is immersed in self-examination—and in an examination of his self-examination. His self-apostrophizing songs and scenes with the other characters, all of whom are his Thoughts, annotate and expose his hopes, doubts, fears, and agonies as an outsider in the world of gay men, the theater industry, and his own family. The psychomachia on the stage is not only a site of introspection and compulsive reenactment, which merge with his creative process, but also a site of *A Strange Loop*'s own self-reflexivity. The established tradition of psychological drama, in which Usher is ensnared as a playwright and as a character, calls for some kind of breakthrough or transformation in the finale: "But is he okay? Does he make it? Does he get the change he wants so badly?"[13] Yet Usher—and Jackson—sabotage the running of the theatrical machinery of inner depth in its standard final phase of operation, refusing even the slightest glimmer of progress, let alone cure, as closure. On one important level, this is the musical's means of highlighting what traditional dramatic teleology of personal change, amplified by the popular inspirational rhetoric of individual self-empowerment and pride, obscures in the realm of social relations. If Usher's distress is rooted in and endlessly prolonged by systemic racism and homophobia, then the onus of ending the agony he is living through on the stage cannot be left up to him. To conclude his story with an epiphanic breakthrough of self-confidence as resolution would be only to conclude with a theatrical illusion of social progress, to celebrate a fictional remedy for the real problem that remains unresolved in the outside world. Yet on another signal level, Usher is unable to complete his story because he comes to define his own self as an illusion, a kind of linguistic construct that only exists in the personal and cultural narratives that hold it. To stop the telling of the self is to let the self disappear. This is, of course, what happens on a phenomenological level when the performance of *A Strange Loop* is over. But the internal impasse of the story's last minutes, which leave the character of Usher forever stuck in the vertiginous hall of mirrors that is his psyche, suspends him in a perpetual act of self-reflection and self-construction, which also serves as a way of keeping his self alive and real in the world enclosed by the narrative.

The nonfinality of *A Strange Loop*'s finale raises questions for the ongoing relationship between madness and musical theater. Has Usher's story taken the expressive and rhetorical functions of madness in the art form to the limits of their logical consequences? Or is it just another loop in the musical's history of using madness to accommodate tragedy, to displace happy endings? Another iteration of madness as socially disordered behavior irrecuperable within civilized norms? Another rendering of it as refusal to make up one's mind? Whatever the answers, this musical epitomizes the continued utility of madness in defining the dynamic interrelations between subjectivity and sociality. These dramatic emphases and strategies settled into the art form over the course of numerous experiments with psychodynamic, environmental, and social-constructionist epistemologies. What happens next? If the currently dominant biomedical model, with its vision of distress as a somatically explainable event, has distinctly new lyrical techniques to offer musical theater, we have yet to see them. Or do the techniques forged in dialogue with madness in the twentieth century constitute the contemporary musical's way of guarding against reductive scientization when it comes to dramatizing the inexhaustibly unique traumas of individual subjectivity? Perhaps musical theater already has all the basic tools it needs to speak of madness? Or is it simply that the art form already discovered the most important thing that madness can give to the theater?

Contemporary musical dramas of mental distress tend to set up oppositions and divisions pointing to power imbalances in our society, madness figured as an extreme to be stigmatized or romanticized as an instructive exception to the rule. But on a parallel track, especially when conceived within a psychoanalytic register, madness also operates as a connecting link between people. Once stripped of historically contingent medical diagnoses, it becomes more than just a potentiality; it can be imagined on a continuum, as something that resides, in different forms and to different degrees, in all of us. Perhaps it is this utopian view of human interiority, lit up by the psychoanalytic imagination, that can best explain Broadway's abiding attraction to madness as a coup de théâtre and a doorway into a deeper self.

Notes

INTRODUCTION

1. Ian Hacking, *Mad Travelers: Reflections on the Reality of Transient Mental Illnesses* (Charlottesville: University Press of Virginia, 1998), 1.

2. I use the term "golden age" with caution, paying attention to its ideological implications in musical theater criticism in the context of the broader problems associated with historical periodization. For a discussion of some issues arising from the "golden age" category in musical theater historiography, see Jessica Sternfeld and Elizabeth L. Wollman, "After the 'Golden Age,'" in *The Oxford Handbook of the American Musical*, ed. Raymond Knapp, Mitchell Morris, and Stacy Wolf (New York: Oxford University Press, 2011). On periodization, see Thomas Postlewait, "The Criteria for Periodization in Theatre History," *Theatre Journal* 40, no. 3 (October 1988).

3. This piece of my book's argument dovetails with some of the ideas proposed by David T. Mitchell and Sharon L. Snyder in their seminal work *Narrative Prosthesis: Disability and the Dependencies of Discourse* (Ann Arbor: University of Michigan Press, 2000). Theorizing representations of the disabled body as "a potent symbolic site of literary investment," they deploy their notion of "narrative prosthesis" to demonstrate how "disability has been used throughout history as a crutch upon which literary narratives lean for the representational power, disruptive potentiality, and analytic insight" (49). My reflections on the cultural function and prestige of madness in theatrical arts follow a similar direction. This part of my thesis about madness, however, is specific to the career of psychological notions of human interiority underwritten by the high-cultural authority of psychoanalysis. Thus, in developing this line of thought, I build upon the work of cultural historians like Raymond Williams and Joel Pfister, as I implicate madness in the wide field of cultural influence exercised by the often invisible power of psychological discourses in US-American and Western European cultures. For an overview of this theoretical framework, see Joel Pfister, "On Conceptualizing the Cultural History of Emotional and Psychological Life in America," in *Inventing the Psychological: Toward a Cultural History of Emotional Life in America*, ed. Joel Pfister and Nancy Schnog (New Haven, CT: Yale University Press, 1997).

4. I follow in the footsteps of researchers who have chronicled the social, cultural, and institutional histories of madness, psychiatric medicine, and psychoanalysis in Western European and Northern American locations. My histo-

riographic positionalities and specific claims rest on a foundation built by Michel Foucault, Sander L. Gilman, Gerald N. Grob, Nathan G. Hale, Allan V. Horwitz, Elizabeth Lunbeck, Mark S. Micale, Roy Porter, Benjamin Reiss, Dorothy Ross, Andrew Scull, Michael E. Staub, and many others.

5. Brenda A. Lefrançois, Robert Menzies, and Geoffrey Reaume, eds., *Mad Matters: A Critical Reader in Canadian Mad Studies* (Toronto: Canadian Scholars' Press, 2013), 10.

6. Stephen Harper, *Madness, Power and the Media: Class, Gender and Race in Popular Representations of Mental Distress* (New York: Palgrave Macmillan, 2009), 25.

7. My terminological model is inspired by studies like Caroline Knowles, *Bedlam on the Streets* (London: Routledge, 2000); Harper, *Madness, Power and the Media*; Emily Martin, *Bipolar Expeditions: Mania and Depression in American Culture* (Princeton, NJ: Princeton University Press, 2009), and Carol Thomas Neely, *Distracted Subjects: Madness and Gender in Shakespeare and Early Modern Culture* (Ithaca, NY: Cornell University Press, 2004).

8. Harper, *Madness, Power and the Media*, 14.

9. The question of parallels and interrelations between madness and disability activism has been a subject of academic discussion since at least the 1990s. Peter Beresford, "What Have Madness and Psychiatric System Survivors Got to Do with Disability and Disability Studies?," *Disability & Society* 15, no. 1 (2000): 167–72.

10. Bradley Lewis, "A Mad Fight: Psychiatry and Disability Activism," in *The Disability Studies Reader*, ed. Lennard J. Davis, 5th ed. (London: Routledge, 2017), 104.

11. Lewis, "A Mad Fight," 103. In discussing discourses of individualism, Lewis draws on Michael Oliver's discussion of pervasive themes in representations of disability. For more, see Michael Oliver, *The Politics of Disablement* (London: Palgrave, 1990) and *Understanding Disability: From Theory to Practice* (London: Macmillan, 1996), 130–34.

12. Margaret Price, *Mad at School: Rhetorics of Mental Disability and Academic Life* (Ann Arbor: University of Michigan Press, 2011), 3–4.

13. Shoshana Felman, *Writing and Madness: Literature/Philosophy/Psychoanalysis*, trans. Martha Noel Evans and Shoshana Felman (Ithaca, NY: Cornell University Press, 1985), 27.

14. The increasing importance of this principle to the history of mad and mentally disabled activism can be observed in the internal organization of groups and campaigns within the ex-patient movement, which began in the 1970s. Springing up on the West and East Coasts, the Insane Liberation Front (Portland, Oregon), the Mental Patients' Liberation Project (New York City), the Mental Patients Liberation Front (Boston), the Network Against Psychiatric Assault (San Francisco), and other such local initiatives pursued activism independently yet communicated with each other on common issues through the newspaper *Madness Network News* (1972–86) and the annual Conference on Human Rights and Psychiatric Oppression, which was first held in 1973. As one of the movement's leaders, Judi Chamberlin, writes, both the newspaper and the conference were initially run by mixed groups consisting of "self-styled 'radical' mental health professionals and ex-patients" but were later reorga-

nized into entities "operated and controlled solely by ex-patients." Judi Chamberlin, "The Ex-Patients' Movement: Where We've Been and Where We're Going," *Journal of Mind and Behavior* 11, nos. 3–4 (1990): 327–28.

15. In some theatrical texts, madness, rather than being assigned explicitly to a specific character, is diffused thematically through different forms, figures, and locations on the stage. The heroines of *Oklahoma!* and *The Day before Spring*, for instance, are not spoken of as mad in the texts, at least not explicitly so. But in reading these musicals in my chosen historical context, I highlight the ways in which madness is imbricated into the authors' conceptions of human psychology and interior environment, shaping the dramatic economy of these and other characters on the stage.

16. For a historical examination of the conflict between madness and logos, see Allen Thiher, *Revels in Madness: Insanity in Medicine and Literature* (Ann Arbor: University of Michigan Press, 1999). On the conflict between music and language, see Carolyn Abbate's writing, in particular *Unsung Voices: Opera and Musical Narrative in the Nineteenth Century* (Princeton, NJ: Princeton University Press, 1991) as well as Vladimir Jankélévitch, *Music and the Ineffable*, trans. Carolyn Abbate (Princeton, NJ: Princeton University Press, 2003).

17. See Michel Foucault, "Preface to the 1961 Edition," in *History of Madness*, ed. Jean Khalfa, trans. Jonathan Murphy and Jean Khalfa (London: Routledge, 2006), and Jacques Derrida, "Cogito and the History of Madness," in *Writing and Difference*, trans. Alan Bass (Chicago: University of Chicago Press, 1980).

18. John T. Hamilton, *Music, Madness, and the Unworking of Language* (New York: Columbia University Press, 2008), 9–10.

19. Susan McClary, *Feminine Endings: Music, Gender, and Sexuality* (Minneapolis: University of Minnesota Press, 1991), 85.

20. McClary, *Feminine Endings*, 85.

21. Elin Diamond, *Unmaking Mimesis: Essays on Feminism and Theatre* (London: Routledge, 1997), 6.

22. Christina Wald, *Hysteria, Trauma, and Melancholia: Performative Maladies in Contemporary Anglophone Drama* (New York: Palgrave, 2007), 34.

23. Diamond, *Unmaking Mimesis*, 7.

24. Raymond Knapp and Zelda Knapp, "Musicals and the Envoicing of Mental Illness and Madness: From *Lady in the Dark* to *Man of La Mancha* (and Beyond)," *Journal of Interdisciplinary Voice Studies* 4, no. 2 (2019): 210.

25. Peter Brooks, "Body and Voice in Melodrama and Opera," in *Siren Songs: Representations of Gender and Sexuality in Opera*, ed. Mary Ann Smart (Princeton, NJ: Princeton University Press, 2000).

26. D. A. Miller, *Place for Us: [Essay on the Broadway Musical]* (Cambridge, MA: Harvard University Press, 1998), 83–84.

27. Andrew Lloyd Webber, Don Black, and Christopher Hampton, *Sunset Boulevard: Vocal Selections* (Milwaukee, WI: Hal Leonard Corporation, 1994), 85.

28. "I'll return to my glory days" is a phrase sung by Norma earlier in "With One Look." Webber, Black, and Hampton, *Sunset Boulevard*, 35.

29. Stephen Sondheim, *Finishing the Hat: Collected Lyrics (1954–1981) with Attendant Comments, Principles, Heresies, Grudges, Whines and Anecdotes* (New York: Alfred A. Knopf, 2010), 77.

30. For a brief overview of the historical relationship between psychody-

namic and biological paradigms in American psychiatry, see Elizabeth Lunbeck, "Psychiatry," in *The Cambridge History of Science*, vol. 7, *The Modern Social Sciences*, ed. Theodore M. Porter and Dorothy Ross (Cambridge: Cambridge University Press, 2003).

31. For more on the history of psychodynamic models of the mind, see Eugene Taylor, *The Mystery of Personality: A History of Psychodynamic Theories* (London: Springer, 2009).

32. Recent reappraisals of the iconic events of 1909 in the literature about the early years of the psychoanalytic movement in the United States have stressed a range of previously ignored local disciplinary and institutional factors that, along with Freud's lectures and publications, stimulated the growth of psychodynamic thinking across medical and cultural discourses. As Richard Skues, among others, explains, "Psychoanalysis did not enter America as a brand-new element in an uncontaminated environment; American culture was already heavily populated by comparable and potentially competitive therapeutic and psychological enterprises as well as its own distinctive cultural conditions." Some of these enterprises were already actively developing dynamic theories of the mind. Richard Skues, "Clark Revisited: Reappraising Freud in America," in *After Freud Left: A Century of Psychoanalysis in America*, ed. John Burnham (Chicago: University of Chicago Press, 2012), 80. For the history of dynamic psychologies in the United States before 1909, also see Nathan J. Hale, *Freud and the Americans: The Beginnings of Psychoanalysis in the United States, 1876–1917* (New York: Oxford University Press, 1995), Robert Fuller, *Americans and the Unconscious* (New York: Oxford University Press, 1986); G. E. Gifford, ed., *Psychoanalysis, Psychotherapy, and the New England Medical Scene, 1894–1944* (New York: Science History Publications, 1978).

CHAPTER 1

1. George S. Kaufman, "Musical Comedy—or Musical Serious?," *New York Times*, November 3, 1957, 223.

2. Kaufman, "Musical Comedy," 223.

3. Nathan J. Hale, *The Rise and Crisis of Psychoanalysis in the United States: Freud and the Americans, 1917–1985* (New York: Oxford University Press, 1995), 276–77.

4. Frederic Wertham, "Freud Now," *Scientific American* 181 (October 1949): 50, 51.

5. Dorothy Ross shows that the "golden age" of psychoanalysis within US psychiatry coincided with the high point of Freud's authority among modernist intellectuals and cultural critics, "reaching a peak in the 1950s and early 1960s and declining thereafter with the resurgence of biological psychiatry." See Dorothy Ross, "Freud and the Vicissitudes of Modernism in the United States, 1940–1980," in *After Freud Left: A Century of Psychoanalysis in America*, ed. John Burnham (Chicago: University of Chicago Press, 2012). Cited material appears on page 164.

6. William Barrett, "Writers and Madness," *Partisan Review* 14 (1947): 7.

7. Freud writes: "Like other neuropathologists, I was trained to employ local diagnoses and electro-prognosis, and it still strikes me myself as strange that the case histories I write should read like short stories and that, as one might say, they lack the serious stamp of science. I must console myself with the reflection that the nature of the subject is evidently responsible for this, rather than any preference of my own. The fact is that local diagnosis and electrical reactions lead nowhere in the study of hysteria, whereas a detailed description of mental processes such as we are accustomed to find in the works of imaginative writers enables me, with the use of a few psychological formulas, to obtain at least some kind of insight into the course of that affection." Sigmund Freud and Josef Breuer, *Studies on Hysteria*, ed. and trans. James Strachey with the collaboration of Anna Freud (New York: Basic Books, 2000), 160.

8. Fredric Jameson, *Marxism and Form: Twentieth-Century Dialectical Theories of Literature* (Princeton, NJ: Princeton University Press, 1971), 27 (italics mine).

9. Dorothy Hart and Robert Kimball, eds., *The Complete Lyrics of Lorenz Hart* (New York: Alfred A. Knopf, 1986), 222.

10. "Ordinary unhappiness" is my preferred translation. In the standard translation edited by Strachey, it is "common unhappiness." Joseph Breuer and Sigmund Freud, *Studies on Hysteria*, in vol. 2 of *The Standard Edition of the Complete Psychological Works of Sigmund Freud*, trans. under the general editorship of James Strachey, in collaboration with Anna Freud (London: Hogarth Press, 1955), 305.

11. Allen Thiher, *Revels in Madness: Insanity in Medicine and Literature* (Ann Arbor: University of Michigan Press, 1999), 242.

12. I do not characterize these musicals as artworks exhibiting internal stylistic uniformity or medium autonomy, features so crucial to proponents of high modernism. My analysis is confined to expressions of modernism that have been understood to constitute its inward turn. The musicals in this part of the book promote and borrow from modernist agendas and stage techniques when prioritizing and representing subjective psychological realities, despite the often eclectic blend of musical and dance vocabularies circulating in the fantasy sequences.

13. Adam Philips, *Missing Out: In Praise of the Unlived Life* (New York: Farrar, Straus and Giroux, 2012), 116.

14. Ethan Mordden, *Beautiful Mornin': The Broadway Musical in the 1940s* (New York: Oxford University Press, 1999), 3.

15. Lehman Engel, *The American Musical Theater*, rev. ed. (New York: Collier Books, 1975), 38–41.

16. John M. Clum, "Acting," in *The Oxford Handbook of the American Musical*, ed. Raymond Knapp, Mitchell Morris, and Stacy Wolf (New York: Oxford University Press, 2011), 316.

17. Mark N. Grant, *The Rise and Fall of the Broadway Musical* (Boston: Northeastern University Press, 2004), 262.

18. Scott McMillin, *The Musical as Drama: A Study of the Principles and Conventions behind Musical Shows from Kern to Sondheim* (Princeton, NJ: Princeton University Press, 2006), 20, 19, 15, 21–22, 54, italics mine.

19. Joel Pfister, *Staging Depth: Eugene O'Neill and the Politics of Psychological Discourse* (Chapel Hill: University of North Carolina Press, 1995), and "Glamorizing the Psychological: The Politics of the Performances of Modern Psychological Identities," in *Inventing the Psychological: Toward a Cultural History of Emotional Life in America,* ed. Joel Pfister and Nancy Schnog (New Haven, CT: Yale University Press, 1997); David Savran, *Highbrow/Lowdown: Theater, Jazz, and the Making of the New Middle Class* (Ann Arbor: University of Michigan Press, 2009).

20. Pfister, *Staging Depth,* 6.

21. Savran, *Highbrow/Lowdown,* 165.

22. Christopher Herbert, *Culture and Anomie: Ethnographic Imagination in the Nineteenth Century* (Chicago: University of Chicago Press, 1991), 255.

23. Herbert, *Culture and Anomie,* 258.

24. Andrea Most, *Making Americans: Jews and the Broadway Musical* (Cambridge, MA: Harvard University Press, 2004), 30–31.

25. David Savran, *Communists, Cowboys, and Queers: The Politics of Masculinity in the Work of Arthur Miller and Tennessee Williams* (Minneapolis: University of Minnesota Press, 1992), 30.

26. Emma Smith, "Approaching Shakespeare: Macbeth," lecture, Oxford University, November 2, 2010, iTunes.

27. Macklin Smith, *Prudentius' Psychomachia: A Re-examination* (Princeton, NJ: Princeton University Press, 1976), 114.

28. David M. Lubin, "Modern Psychological Selfhood in the Art of Thomas Eakins," in *Inventing the Psychological,* ed. Pfister and Schnog, 134–35. For a brief history of the word "psychological" in the English language, see Raymond Williams, *Keywords: A Vocabulary of Culture and Society,* rev. ed. (New York: Oxford University Press, 1983), 246–48. For a historical discussion of the conceptual shift from "soul" to "mind," see George Makari, *Soul Machine: The Invention of the Modern Mind* (New York: Norton, 2015).

29. Mark S. Micale, ed., *The Mind of Modernism: Medicine, Psychology, and the Cultural Arts in Europe and America, 1880–1940* (Stanford, CA: Stanford University Press, 2004), 3.

30. Micale, *The Mind of Modernism,* 369, 15.

31. That is not to insist that Freud generated ideas that were then picked up by the artists of his time. As the work of historians like Micale shows, the ideas circulating within psychological and artistic modernisms developed through cross-pollination, with multidirectional flows of influence running between clinical and cultural spaces and informing both realms. For more see Mark S. Micale, "The Modernist Mind: A Map," in *The Mind of Modernism,* 1–68.

32. On the literary-dramatic nature of Freudian psychoanalysis, see Steven Marcus, "Freud and Dora: Story, History, Case History," in *In Dora's Case: Freud—Hysteria—Feminism,* ed. Charles Bernheimer and Clare Kahane, 2nd ed. (New York: Columbia University Press, 1990); Peter Brooks, "Freud's Masterplot," in *Literature and Psychoanalysis, The Question of Reading: Otherwise,* ed. Shoshana Felman (Baltimore: John Hopkins University Press, 1982).

33. Françoise Meltzer, "Unconscious," in *Critical Terms for Literary Study,* ed. Frank Lentricchia and Thomas McLaughlin (Chicago: University of Chicago

Press, 1995), 150. Meltzer also describes other models of the psyche, such as dynamic and systematic, in Freud's theory.

34. Sigmund Freud, *Introductory Lectures on Psycho-Analysis*, trans. and ed. James Strachey (London: Hogarth Press, 1953), 295.

35. Sigmund Freud, *The Interpretation of Dreams* (1900), in *The Standard Edition of the Complete Psychological Works of Sigmund Freud*, vol. 5, trans. under the general editorship of James Strachey, in collaboration with Anna Freud (London: Hogarth Press, 1953), 608.

36. The American psychologist William James's writing on the "stream of thought" predated Freud's implementation of free association techniques and directly influenced Gertrude Stein and other American modernist writers. See William James, *The Principles of Psychology*, vol. 1 (New York: Henry Holt, 1890), chap. 9.

37. August Strindberg, *A Dream Play and Four Chamber Plays*, trans. Walter Johnson (Seattle: University of Washington Press, 1973), 19.

38. Sigmund Freud, *The Interpretation of Dreams*, trans. Joyce Crick (New York: Oxford University Press, 1999), 5, 75.

39. Edna Kenton, *The Provincetown Players and the Playwrights' Theatre, 1915–1922*, ed. Travis Bogard and Jackson R. Bryer (Jefferson, NC: McFarland, 2004), 82.

40. For the use of sonic and movement vocabularies in US dramatic modernism, see Julia A. Walker, *Expressionism and Modernism in the American Theatre: Bodies, Voices, Words* (Cambridge: Cambridge University Press, 2005).

41. Some examples of musical shows with psychomachic techniques from the 1910s to the 1930s are *Tillie's Nightmare* (1910), *Peggy-Ann* (1926), *A Connecticut Yankee* (1927), *Strike Up the Band* (1930), *The Bandwagon* (1931), and *Babes in Arms* (1937).

42. Stephen Sondheim, *Finishing the Hat: Collected Lyrics (1954–1981) with Attendant Comments, Principles, Heresies, Grudges, Whines and Anecdotes* (New York: Alfred A. Knopf, 2010), xx.

43. Bruce Kirle, *Unfinished Show Business: Broadway Musicals as Works-in-Process* (Carbondale: Southern Illinois University Press, 2005), 77.

44. Examples of their experiments with psychomachic staging include dream sequences in *The Bandwagon* (1931) and *Face the Music* (1932). Rasch had also contributed a dream ballet to Kern's *The Cat and the Fiddle* (1931), with a book and lyrics by Otto Harbach. On Rasch's collaborations with Short, see Frank W. D. Ries, "Albertina Rasch: The Broadway Career," *Dance Chronicle* 6, no. 2 (1983): 95–137.

45. Jerome Kern and Oscar Hammerstein II, *Very Warm for May: A Musical Comedy*, AEI Records 008, 1985, compact disc.

46. This allegory anticipates Thornton Wilder's *The Skin of Our Teeth* (1942) and Weill and Lerner's *Love Life* (1948), but also follows and perhaps gives a nod to Arnold Sundgaard and Marc Connelly's *Everywhere I Roam* (1938), with lyrics and music by Fred Stewart, which had a short run at Broadway's National Theatre in the previous season.

47. Stephen Banfield, *Jerome Kern* (New Haven, CT: Yale University Press, 2006), 250.

48. Oscar Hammerstein II, *Very Warm for May: A Musical Play*, typescript, 1939, New York Public Library, Performing Arts Research Collections Theatre, NCOF+ (Hammerstein, O. Very Warm for May), 2.1.13.

49. Hammerstein, *Very Warm for May*, 2.1.12–13, 1.2.1, 2.3.5.

50. Hammerstein, *Very Warm for May*, 2.1.13–15.

51. Hammerstein, *Very Warm for May*, 2.1.13–15.

52. Pfister, "Glamorizing the Psychological," 169, 199.

53. Brooks Atkinson, "The Play: 'Very Warm for May,' with Score by Jerome Kern and Book by Oscar Hammerstein 2nd," review of *Very Warm for May*, Alvin Theatre, New York, *New York Times*, November 18, 1939, 23.

54. Hammerstein, *Very Warm for May*, 1.2.11–14.

55. The psychological topography of this scene as well as other parts of Ogdon's opus involving the externalization of internal states may also be indebted to Hammerstein's collaborations with librettist and lyricist Otto Harbach in the 1920s and the 1930s, including *Gentlemen Unafraid* (1938). Bradley Rogers's recent study of Harbach charts the influence of the Emersonian method of the psychological development of expression on Harbach's dramaturgy for musical theater, with important implications for Hammerstein's writing style and his participation in the aesthetic integration movement. Bradley Rogers, "The Emergence of Integrated Musical: Otto Harbach, Oratorical Theory, and the Cinema," *Theatre Survey* 63, no. 2 (May 2022): 160–82.

56. Hammerstein, *Very Warm for May*, 1.2.3, 2.3.13.

57. Gerald Bordman, liner notes for Jerome Kern and Oscar Hammerstein II, *Very Warm for May*, AEI Records 008, 1985, compact disc; "New Musical in Manhattan," unsigned review of *Very Warm for May*, *Time*, November 27, 1939. Banfield notes that Ogdon Quiler's name is "all too suggestive of the 'odd' 'queer' he most certainly is." Banfield, *Jerome Kern*, 243.

58. "New Musical in Manhattan," unsigned review of *Very Warm for May*, Alvin Theatre, New York, *Time*, November 27, 1939.

59. Hammerstein, *Very Warm for May*, 1.2.7–9. While the obvious parallels between *Very Warm for May* and *Babes in Arms* did not escape the critics, Ogdon's search for realism also invoked associations with the Group Theatre, whose history, like that of his company, began in a Connecticut barn. For more on this period in the Group Theatre's history, see Wendy Smith, *Real Life Drama: The Group Theatre and America, 1931–1940* (New York: Grove Weidenfeld, 1990), 32–34.

60. Hammerstein, *Very Warm for May*, 1.2.4.

61. Hammerstein, *Very Warm for May*, 2.3.7–12.

CHAPTER 2

1. Eli Zaretsky, *Political Freud: A History* (New York: Columbia University, 2015), 149, 158.

2. Stephen Frosh, *Psychoanalysis outside the Clinic: Interventions in Psychosocial Studies* (New York: Palgrave Macmillan, 2010), 6.

3. Eve Kosofsky Sedgwick, *Touching Feeling: Affect, Pedagogy, Performativity* (Durham, NC: Duke University Press, 2003), 150–51.

4. Wolcott Gibbs, "Crying in the Wilderness," review of *Lady in the Dark*, Alvin Theatre, New York, *New Yorker*, February 1, 1941, 27.

5. Kurt Weill, liner notes for *Street Scene: Original Cast Recording*, Columbia Masterworks set M-MM-683, 1947.

6. While Harry Horner designed the sets, the idea of using a revolving stage for Liza dreams has been traced to Short. See Jack Paul Sederholm, "The Musical Directing Career and Stagecraft Contributions of Hassard Short, 1919–1952," PhD diss., Wayne State University, 1974. Short's critically lauded collaboration with Rasch on *The Bandwagon* in 1931, for instance, included a number called "The Beggar Waltz," in which, Fred Astaire recalls, the hero "falls asleep and the revolving stage moves around to disclose his dream. . . . At the conclusion of our specialty ballet number the lights dim out as the stage revolves back to where I am just waking from my dream." Fred Astaire, *Steps in Time* (New York: Da Capo Press, 1979), 169. Moss Hart had firsthand knowledge of Rasch and Short's inventive staging with moving scenic units from his own collaborations with them (e.g., *Face the Music*, 1932; *The Great Waltz*, 1934).

7. Bruce D. McClung, *"Lady in the Dark": Biography of a Musical* (New York: Oxford University Press, 2007), 44.

8. In this paragraph I quote from two reviews by Brooks Atkinson, "The Play in Review: Gertrude Lawrence Appears in Moss Hart's Musical Drama, 'Lady in the Dark,' with a Score by Kurt Weill and Lyrics by Ira Gershwin," *New York Times*, January 24, 1941, and *"Lady in the Dark," New York Times*, February 2, 1941, xi.

9. Elinor Hughes, "Gertrude Lawrence in Hart-Weill-Gershwin Musical," review of *Lady in the Dark*, Colonial Theatre, Boston, *Boston Herald*, December 31, 1940.

10. Atkinson, "Lady in the Dark."

11. Brooks Atkinson, "Struck by Stage Lightning: Comments on the Theatre Wonders of *Lady in the Dark* with Special Reference to Kurt Weill and Gertrude Lawrence," *New York Times*, September 7, 1941.

12. Atkinson, "The Play in Review."

13. Land, "Play on Broadway: *Lady in the Dark*," review of *Lady in the Dark*, Alvin Theatre, New York, *Variety*, January 29, 1941.

14. Land, "Play on Broadway."

15. Nathan J. Hale, *The Rise and Crisis of Psychoanalysis in the United States: Freud and the Americans, 1917–1985* (New York: Oxford University Press, 1995), 128.

16. George Makari, *"Mitteleuropa* on the Hudson," in *After Freud Left: A Century of Psychoanalysis in America*, ed. John Burnham (Chicago: University of Chicago Press, 2012), 113–15.

17. Steven Bach, *Dazzler: The Life and Times of Moss Hart* (New York: Alfred A. Knopf, 2001), 215–16, 218, 229. Bach quotes Glen Boles, a longtime friend of Hart's, saying, "It [*Lady in the Dark*] grew directly out of the sessions with Kubie as an extension of the therapy, a reinforcement of it." According to McClung,

Hart was Kubie's patient from about 1937 to 1959. McClung, *Lady in the Dark*, 45.

18. McClung, *Lady in the Dark*, 105.

19. Dr. Brooks [Lawrence Kubie], "Preface," in Moss Hart, Ira Gershwin, and Kurt Weill, *Lady in the Dark* (New York: Random House, 1941), vii–xiv.

20. Hart, Gershwin, and Weill, *Lady in the Dark*, 13, 5–8, 10, 14, 17, 84, 115, 38, 106, 71, 60, 61, 115, 116, 106, 62, 115.

21. Elin Diamond, *Unmaking Mimesis: Essays on Feminism and Theatre* (London: Routledge, 1997), 6, 4.

22. Diamond, *Unmaking Mimesis*, 29. "To be watched with interest" is a quotation from critic A. B. Walkley's description of Hedda Gabler, which Diamond reproduces in her essay, comparing him to the medical observers at Jean-Martin Charcot's Tuesday lectures on hysteria at the Salpêtrière Hospital in Paris.

23. Sigmund Freud, "A Metapsychological Supplement to the Theory of Dreams," vol. 14 of *The Standard Edition of the Complete Psychological Works of Sigmund Freud*, ed. James Strachey (London: Hogarth Press, 1955), 223.

24. Hart, Gershwin, and Weill, *Lady in the Dark*, 34.

25. Dianne Hunter, "Hysteria, Psychoanalysis, and Feminism: The Case of Anna O," *Feminist Studies* 9, no. 3 (Autumn 1983): 464–88. For a detailed examination of Breuer and Freud's writings about this case and a review of related psychoanalytic literature, see Richard A. Skues, *Sigmund Freud and the History of Anna O.: Reopening a Closed Case* (London: Palgrave Macmillan, 2006).

26. Hart, Gershwin, and Weill, *Lady in the Dark*, 37, 4, 81, 84.

27. McClung, *Lady in the Dark*, especially 149–53. This direction of analysis in the critical literature on *Lady in the Dark* continues in Stephen Hinton, *Weill's Musical Theater: Stages of Reform* (Berkeley: University of California Press, 2012), chap. 9, and Maya Cantu, *American Cinderellas on the Broadway Stage: Imagining the Working Girl from "Irene" to "Gypsy"* (New York: Palgrave, 2015).

28. Kubie, "Preface," x.

29. The new spatial configuration of the playing area in this scene was achieved by rotating only one of the bigger turntables and revealing/concealing it through lighting. This scenic solution split the stage into two halves: one with the doctor's office, the other with the space assigned to Liza's internal reality. Liza crossed over from one dimension to the other without costume change, in full view of the audience.

30. Hart, Gershwin, and Weill, *Lady in the Dark*, 182.

31. Ralph E. Locke, "What Are These Women Doing in Opera?," in *En Travesti: Women, Gender Subversion, Opera*, ed. Corinne E. Blackmer and Patricia Juliana Smith (New York: Columbia University Press, 1995), 63.

32. Hart, Gershwin, and Weill, *Lady in the Dark*, 62–73, 108–9.

33. Naomi Graber, *Kurt Weill's America* (New York: Oxford University Press, 2021), 183.

34. Land, "Play on Broadway."

35. Raymond Knapp and Zelda Knapp, "Musicals and the Envoicing of Mental Illness and Madness: From *Lady in the Dark* to *Man of La Mancha* (and Beyond)," *Journal of Interdisciplinary Voice Studies* 4, no. 2 (2019): 213.

36. Moss Hart and George S. Kaufman's 1939 hit play *The Man Who Came to*

Dinner had characters loosely based on Lawrence (Lorraine Sheldon) and Coward (Beverly Carlton). Coward even contributed a song called "What Am I to Do?" to be sung by the character intended to parody him. *Lady in the Dark* also echoes Coward's *Shadow Play: A Fantasy with Music*, which was part of a cycle of one-act plays titled *Tonight at 8:30* produced on Broadway during the 1936–37 season and revived in 1948. Starring Lawrence and Coward, *Shadow Play* explored the dream life of a depressed woman through dramatic elements that would resurface later in *Lady in the Dark* (e.g., music introducing transitions from the realist action to the realm of the unconscious, which included singing, dancing, intricate lighting design, and moving flats; the heroine's fixation on a half-forgotten song; the self-conscious acts of re-remembering, disavowing, and reconstructing the past). The abstract action occurring in the realm of fantasy allowed for a playful exploration of the fluidity of gender and sexuality. For a discussion of the queer dimension in another Coward play, *Private Lives*, which starred this duo, see Penny Farfan, *Performing Queer Modernism* (New York: Oxford University Press, 2017), chap. 4.

37. Hart, Gershwin, and Weill, *Lady in the Dark*, 134.

38. David Savran, "The Do-Re-Mi of Musical Historiography," in *Changing the Subject: Marvin Carlson and Theater Studies, 1959–2009*, ed. Joseph Roach (Ann Arbor: University of Michigan Press, 2009), 235.

39. Toril Moi, "Patriarchal Thought and the Drive for Knowledge," in *Between Feminism and Psychoanalysis*, ed. Teresa Brennan (London: Routledge, 1989), 196–97.

40. Moi, "Patriarchal Thought," 196–97.

41. Oscar Hammerstein II, "In Re 'Oklahoma!': The Adaptor-Lyricist Describes How the Musical Hit Came into Being," *New York Times*, May 23, 1943, X1.

42. Hammerstein, "In Re 'Oklahoma!,'" X1.

43. Susan Jones, *Literature, Modernism, and Dance* (New York: Oxford University Press, 2013).

44. Agnes de Mille, *Dance to the Piper* (Boston: Little, Brown, 1951), 168. Balanchine's interest in psychomachic ballet also began in Europe, as is evident, for instance, in his work with Ballet Russe de Monte Carlo (e.g., *L'enfant et les Sortileges*). Martha Graham's ballet *Every Soul Is a Circus*, which premiered in 1939 at the St. James Theatre, is a direct precursor not only to Laurey's dreams but also to Liza's "Circus Dream" in *Lady in the Dark*.

45. Sigmund Freud, *The Standard Edition of the Complete Psychological Works of Sigmund Freud*, vol. 4, ed. James Strachey (London: Hogarth Press, 1953), 102.

46. Freud, *Standard Edition*, 4:102.

47. Agnes de Mille, quoted in Max Wilk, *OK! The Story of Oklahoma! A Celebration of America's Most Loved Musical*, 2nd ed. (New York: Applause, 2002), 152.

48. De Mille, quoted in Rosemary Tauris, "Oklahoma! It's Still Ok," *Cue New York*, December 21, 1979.

49. Oscar Hammerstein's draft, quoted in Tim Carter, *"Oklahoma!": The Making of an American Musical* (New Haven, CT: Yale University Press, 2007), 129.

50. De Mille, quoted in Wilk, *OK!*, 118.

51. Wilk, *OK!*, 153; Carter, *Oklahoma!*, 129.

52. De Mille, quoted in Wilk, *OK!*, 153; de Mille, quoted in Jay Carr, "Agnes De Mille Steps Out with an Old Friend—'Oklahoma!,'" *New York Times*, December 9, 1979.

53. Freud, *Standard Edition*, 4:50.

54. Freud, *Standard Edition*, 4:50.

55. Hammerstein, "In Re 'Oklahoma!'"

56. Quoted in Carr, "Agnes De Mille Steps Out." For the relationship between American feminists and psychoanalysis in the 1920s and 1930s, see Mari Jo Buhle, *Feminism and Its Discontents: A Century of Struggle with Psychoanalysis* (Cambridge, MA: Harvard University Press, 1998), chap. 1.

57. Agnes de Mille, quoted in Kara Anne Gardner, *Agnes de Mille: Telling Stories in Broadway Dance* (New York: Oxford University Press, 2016), 24.

58. Gardner, *Agnes de Mille*, 32, 31.

59. Gardner, *Agnes de Mille*, 31.

60. The term "conversion hysteria" was still an active clinical category. It would appear in DSM-I (1952).

61. Felicia McCarren, "The 'Symptomatic Act' circa 1900: Hysteria, Hypnosis, Electricity, Dance," *Critical Inquiry* 21, no. 4 (Summer 1995): 752–53.

62. Olin Downes, "Broadway's Gift to Opera: *Oklahoma!* Shows One of the Ways to an Integrated and Indigenous Form of American Lyric Theatre," *New York Times*, June 6, 1943, X5.

63. Richard Rodgers and Oscar Hammerstein II, *6 Plays by Rodgers and Hammerstein* (New York: Random House, 1958), 39.

64. Carter, *Oklahoma!*, 205.

65. Oscar Hammerstein, "Note on Lyrics," in *Lyrics by Oscar Hammerstein II* (New York: Simon and Schuster, 1949), 19.

66. Lawrence Langner, *The Magic Curtain: The Story of a Life in Two Fields, Theatre and Invention, by the Founder of the Theatre Guild* (New York: Dutton, 1951), 376–77.

67. Carter, *Oklahoma!*, 208.

68. Downes, "Broadway's Gift to Opera."

69. Downes, "Broadway's Gift to Opera."

70. George Beiswanger, "Theatre Today: Symptoms and Surmises," *Journal of Aesthetics and Art Criticism* 3, no. 9–10 (1944): 25.

71. Burton Rasco, "The Guild's *Oklahoma!* Opens at the St. James," *New York World Telegram*, as quoted in Wilk, *OK!*, 232.

72. Downes, "Broadway's Gift to Opera."

73. Downes, "Broadway's Gift to Opera."

74. Downes, "Broadway's Gift to Opera."

75. Alan Jay Lerner, *The Musical Theatre: A Celebration* (New York: Da Capo Press, 1986), 153.

76. Quoted in Gene Lees, *Inventing Champagne: The Worlds of Lerner and Loewe* (New York: St. Martin's Press, 1990), 62; Lerner, *The Musical Theatre*, 151.

77. In Lerner's words, "Kurt did it, and I think we all owe him a debt." Quoted in Lees, *Inventing Champagne*, 63.

78. Dan Dietz, *The Complete Book of 1940s Broadway Musicals* (Lanham, MD: Rowman & Littlefield, 2015), 309.

79. Jones, *Literature, Modernism, and Dance*, 256.

80. Alan Jay Lerner and Frederick Loewe, *The Day before Spring*, typescript, New York Public Library, Performing Arts Research Collections Theatre, NYPL, RM2326, 1.1.1. All references to and quotations from the libretto in this section, unless otherwise noted, come from this typescript.

81. Shoshana Felman, *Writing and Madness: Literature/Philosophy/Psychoanalysis*, trans. Martha Noel Evans and Shoshana Felman (Ithaca, NY: Cornell University Press, 1985), 30.

82. Lerner and Loewe, *The Day before Spring*, 1.5.62–70.

83. Lerner and Loewe, *The Day before Spring*, 1.5.62–70.

84. Lerner and Loewe, *The Day before Spring*, 2.1.16–23.

85. Lerner and Loewe, *The Day before Spring*.

86. In crafting the lyrics, for instance, Lerner deliberately imitated the witty sensibility of Lorenz Hart. See Alan Jay Lerner, *The Street Where I Live* (New York: Norton, 1978), 33–34.

87. Lewis Nichols, "The Play," review of *The Day before Spring*, National Theatre, New York, *New York Times*, November 23, 1945, 27.

88. Walcott Gibbs, "Such a Pretty Piece," review of *The Day before Spring*, National Theatre, New York, *New Yorker*, December 1, 1945, 52.

89. Howard Taubman, "Musicians Return to the Theatre," *New York Times*, October 26, 1947; Lerner, *Musical Theatre*, 162.

90. Gerald Grob, "The Forging of Mental Health Policy in America: World War II to the New Frontier," *Journal of the History of Medicine and Allied Sciences* 42 (1987): 417.

91. Irving Berlin, Howard Lindsay, and Russel Crouse, *Call Me Madam* (New York: Irving Berlin Music Corporation, n.d.), 119–20.

92. Frank Loesser, Jo Swerling, and Abe Burrows, *Guys and Dolls: A Musical Fable on Broadway*, in *American Musicals, 1950–1969*, ed. Laurence Maslon (New York: Library of America, 2014), 32.

93. Terrence McNally, Arthur Laurents, Stephen Sondheim, and Jule Styne, "Landmark Symposium: The Genesis of *Gypsy*," *Dramatists Guild Quarterly* 18, no. 3 (Autumn 1981): 25.

94. Brooks Atkinson, "Theatre: Good Show," review of *Gypsy*, Broadway Theatre, New York, *New York Times*, May 22, 1959, 31.

95. McNally, "Landmark Symposium," 26.

96. Sondheim said on multiple occasions that he was indelibly influenced by *Oklahoma!* and especially *Allegro* (which critic George Jean Nathan, writing in the 1940s, jokingly compared to Strindberg's *A Dream Play*). He also credited *Very Warm for May* with inspiring him to become a theater artist. Among his Broadway shows, *Company* and *Follies* are the most obvious inheritors of the modernist psychomachic techniques discussed in this part of the book. *Company*'s hero, according to Sondheim, "has a combination of breakdown and epiphany. The show really takes place in one second. His friends are there but they're not there. . . . They're all fragments of his consciousness." Neil Patrick

Harris, who played Bobby in the New York Philharmonic's concert staging of *Company* in 2011, recalls Sondheim advising him that "the plot is all in [Bobby's] mind and you're sort of looking at all these photos on the wall. It totally is the existential musical." In *Follies*, the four principal characters, experiencing "a sort of group nervous breakdown," are transported to the hypertheatrical land of unconscious fantasy, at once glamorous and sinister, echoing *Lady in the Dark*'s dream operas. George Jean Nathan, *The Theatre Book of the Year, 1947–1948: A Record and an Interpretation* (New York: Alfred A. Knopf, 1948), 102. In this paragraph I refer to and quote Sondheim's statements from his interview by Max Wilk, audio CD, 1991, NYPL, Performing Arts Research Collections Recorded Sound, LDC 52502; "Stephen Sondheim: The Art of the Musical," *Paris Review* 39, no. 142 (Spring 1997): 268; Robert Sokol, "Good and Crazy: Neil Patrick Harris Describes Being Very Alive in *Company*," *Sondheim Review* 18, no. 1 (Fall 2011): 29–30; and *Finishing the Hat: Collected Lyrics (1954–1981) with Attendant Comments, Principles, Heresies, Grudges, Whines and Anecdotes* (New York: Alfred A. Knopf, 2010), 231.

97. Stephen Sondheim, "In Conversation with Stephen Sondheim," interview by Craig Carnelia, *Dramatist* 9, no. 5 (May–June 2007): 16.

98. Ben Brantley, "Stephen Sondheim: The Man Who Felt Too Much," *New York Times*, March 12, 2020.

99. On the role of psychological discourse in the canonization of Eugene O'Neill, see Joel Pfister, *Staging Depth: Eugene O'Neill and the Politics of Psychological Discourse* (Chapel Hill: University of North Carolina Press, 1995).

100. Jesse Green, "The Essential Musical Dramatist Who Taught Us to Hear," *New York Times*, November 26, 2021.

101. Sondheim, "In Conversation," 19.

CHAPTER 3

1. While some reviewers referred to *Reuben Reuben* as an "opera" or "folk opera," the work was billed as a "new musical" and, for the most part, promoted as such by its producers. Blitzstein calls it "a musical play" in the finished typescript. Marc Blitzstein, *Reuben Reuben: A Musical Play*, typescript, 1955, New York Public Library, Performing Arts Research Collections Music, JPB91-86.

2. For a detailed account of Blitzstein's experimentation and highbrow aspirations and influences in this work, see Howard Pollack, *Marc Blitzstein: His Life, His Work, His World* (New York: Oxford University Press, 2012), chap. 20.

3. Igor Stravinsky's 1951 opera *The Rake's Progress*, which premiered at the Metropolitan Opera in 1953, also included a scene set in an asylum.

4. Elinor Hughes, "Theater," review of *Reuben Reuben*, Shubert Theater, Boston, *Boston Herald*, October 11, 1955; Alta Maloney, "*Reuben Reuben* Opens, New Musical at Shubert," review of *Reuben Reuben*, *Boston Traveler*, October 11, 1955, 59.

5. Blitzstein, *Reuben Reuben*, 2.1.1–5.

6. In the external world, Reuben has trouble speaking and communicates in most cases by writing notes. In addition to interpreting Reuben's condition as "a suicide complex inherited from his father," some of the reviewers traced it to his combat experience in the war, borrowing explanations from psychosomatic medicine, which rose to prominence in the post–World War II climate. For instance, the drama editor of the *Boston Record* judged that the musical was meant to "tell in song and story the plight of a shell-shocked solider suddenly released into civilian life." The *Boston Traveler*'s critic observed that these and other "symptoms of poor health, . . . we are led to believe, are only mental." Hughes, "Theater"; L. G. Gaffney, "*Reuben Reuben*, at Shubert, Misses Fire," a review of *Reuben Reuben*, Shubert Theatre, Boston, *Boston Record*, October 11, 1955; Maloney, "*Reuben Reuben* Opens."

7. David J. Rissmiller and Joshua H. Rissmiller, "Evolution of the Antipsychiatry Movement into Mental Health Consumerism," *Psychiatric Services* 57, no. 6 (June 2006), 863.

8. Gerald Grob, "Psychiatry and Social Activism: The Politics of a Specialty in Postwar America," *Bulletin of the History of Medicine* 60, no. 4 (Winter 1986): 477–501.

9. Michael E. Staub, *Madness Is Civilization: When the Diagnosis Was Social, 1948–1980* (Chicago: University of Chicago Press, 2011), 4.

10. Staub, *Madness Is Civilization*, 5.

11. On the sacralization of Artaud and his madness, see Kimberly Jannarone, *Artaud and His Doubles* (Ann Arbor: University of Michigan Press, 2010), 15–21.

12. Antonin Artaud, quoted in Martin Esslin, *Artaud* (Glasgow: Fontana Collins, 1976), 96.

13. For examples of this trend in other creative genres, see Alexander Dunst, *Madness in Cold War America* (New York: Routledge, 2017).

14. Jerry Herman, *Dear World*, typescript, 1967, New York Public Library, Performing Arts Research Collections Theatre, RM4475A, 1.5.56.

15. Herman, *Dear World* (1967), 2.3.28.

16. Philip Rieff, *Freud: The Mind of the Moralist* (Chicago: University of Chicago Press, 1971), 362.

17. Jean-Christoph Agnew, "The Walking Man and the Talking Cure," in *After Freud Left*, ed. John Burnham (Chicago: University of Chicago Press, 2012), 235.

18. Bob Merrill and Jule Styne, *Rape of Prettybelle*, typescript, New York Public Library, Performing Arts Research Collections Theatre, RM7381, 1.53.

19. John F. Kennedy, "Special Message on Mental Illness and Mental Retardation," February 5, 1963, Papers of John F. Kennedy, President's Office Files, 1–3, https://www.jfklibrary.org/Asset-Viewer/Archives/JFKPOF-052-012.aspx, accessed February 23, 2018.

20. Kennedy, "Special Message," 1.

21. Philip M. Boffey, "Community Care for Mentally Ill Termed a Failure: Study Says Discharges from Hospitals to Unprepared Centers Are a 'Tragedy,'" *New York Times*, September 13, 1984.

22. Albert Q. Maisel, "Bedlam 1946," *Life*, May 6, 1946, 102–3.

23. Pollack, *Marc Blitzstein*, 384.

24. Gerald Grob, *The Mad among Us: The History of the Care of America's Mentally Ill* (New York: Free Press, 1994), 207.

25. Kennedy, "Special Message on Mental Illness," 3.

26. All generalizations about the growth of a socially oriented psychiatry after World War II in this and subsequent paragraphs come from the seminal scholarship of Gerald N. Grob, especially his books *From Asylum to Community: Mental Health Policy in Modern America* (Princeton, NJ: Princeton University Press, 1991) and *The Mad among Us*.

27. William C. Menninger, "Psychiatric Experience in the War, 1941–1946," *American Journal of Psychiatry* 103, no. 5 (March 1947): 580.

28. Grob, *From Asylum to Community*, 7.

29. Menninger, "Psychiatric Experience," 580, 581.

30. Menninger, "Psychiatric Experience," 583.

31. Arthur Laurents, Leonard Bernstein, Stephen Sondheim, and Jerome Robbins, *West Side Story: A Musical* (New York: Random House, 1958), 116.

32. Grob, *From Asylum to Community*, 241.

33. For more on the role of psychiatrists in the creation of the national mental health policy in the 1960s, see Grob, *From Asylum to Community*, chap. 9.

34. Jack R. Ewalt and Patricia L. Ewalt, "History of the Community Psychiatry Movement," *American Journal of Psychiatry* 126, no. 1 (July 1969): 51.

35. Grob, *The Mad among Us*, 223–24.

36. Kennedy, "Special Message," 5.

37. Grob, *The Mad among Us*, 251.

38. Michael J. Dear and Jennifer R. Wolch, *Landscapes of Despair: From Deinstitutionalization to Homelessness* (Princeton, NJ: Princeton University Press, 1987), 175.

39. Kennedy, "Special Message," 3.

40. Craig Zadan, *Sondheim & Co.*, 2nd ed. (New York: Harper and Row, 1986), 92, 87.

41. Pollack, *Marc Blitzstein*, 396.

42. Arthur Laurents and Stephen Sondheim, *Anyone Can Whistle: A Musical Fable* (New York: Random House, 1965), 33.

43. Laurents and Sondheim, *Anyone Can Whistle*, 35.

44. Laurents and Sondheim, *Anyone Can Whistle*, 34–36, 38.

45. Laurents and Sondheim, *Anyone Can Whistle*, 34.

46. David Savran and Daniel Gundlach, "*Anyone Can Whistle* as Experimental Theater," in *The Oxford Handbook of Sondheim Studies*, ed. Robert Gordon (New York: Oxford University Press, 2015), 84.

47. Zadan, *Sondheim & Co.*, 92.

48. Stephen Sondheim, quoted in Mark Eden Horowitz, *Sondheim on Music: Minor Details and Major Decisions*, 2nd ed. (Lanham, MD: Scarecrow Press, 2010), 78.

49. On the gradual, if delayed, absorption of Foucault's *Folie et déraison* into the American academic and intellectual climate, see Arthur Still and Irving Velody, "Introduction," in *Re-writing the History of Madness: Studies in Foucault's*

"Histoire de le folie", ed. Arthur Still and Irving Velody (London: Routledge, 1992), 1–16.

50. Staub, *Madness Is Civilization*, 3.

51. Erving Goffman, *Asylums: Essays on the Social Situation of Mental Patients and Other Inmates* (Chicago: Aldine, 1961), 135.

52. R. D. Laing, *The Politics of Experience* (New York: Pantheon Books, 1967), 83, 90, 79.

53. Laurents and Sondheim, *Anyone Can Whistle*, 83.

54. Zadan, *Sondheim & Co.*, 107.

55. Savran and Gundlach, "*Whistle* as Experimental Theater," 87, 86.

56. Laurents and Sondheim, *Anyone Can Whistle*, 79–80. Hapgood's breaking the fourth wall and making direct contact with the audience at the end of "Simple" prefigures Sondheim's anti-illusionist tactics in the mad scenes of *Follies* ("Live, Laugh, Love") and *Sweeney Todd* ("Epiphany"). Sondheim characterizes Sweeney's address to the audience as "a truly mad gesture." Stephen Sondheim, *Finishing the Hat: Collected Lyrics (1954–1981) with Attendant Comments, Principles, Heresies, Grudges, Whines and Anecdotes* (Alfred A. Knopf: New York, 2010), 355.

57. Thomas Szasz, "The Therapeutic State: The Tyranny of Pharmacy," *Independent Review* 5, no. 4 (Spring 2001): 486.

58. Thomas Szasz, *Law, Liberty, and Psychiatry: An Inquiry into the Social Uses of Mental Health Practices* (New York: Macmillan, 1963), 254, 251, 240.

59. Thomas Szasz, *Myth of Mental Illness: Foundations of a Theory of Personal Conduct* (New York: Harper and Row, 1961), 296.

60. Laurents and Sondheim, *Anyone Can Whistle*, 69.

61. Savran and Gundlach, "*Whistle* as Experimental Theatre," 88; Stephen Sondheim, *Anyone Can Whistle: Vocal Score* (N.p.: Burthen Music, 1968), 77–79.

62. Laurents and Sondheim, *Anyone Can Whistle*, 69, 83.

63. Endorsing the literary-philosophic values of Freud's project, Szasz viewed the analytic situation as a site of self-discovery designed for "student[s] of human living," a "beacon" offering useful modes of inquiry into oneself and society. Szasz, *Myth of Mental Illness*. 310 Some of R. D. Laing's most influential critical texts, such as *The Divided Self: A Study in Sanity and Madness* (1960), have been described as essentially works of psychoanalysis.

64. Eli Zaretsky, *Secrets of the Soul: A Social and Cultural History of Psychoanalysis* (New York: Alfred A. Knopf), 277. Zaretsky writes: "Simultaneously normalizing and fueled by charismatic sources, then, US analysis was at the center of both the growing rationalization of personal life unfolding in the 1950s *and* the looming critique of rationalization, the charismatic rejection of the mundane, that came to the fore in the 1960s." For more, see Zaretsky, chap. 11.

65. While Szasz's theories were taken up by writers of the New Left, he was committed to a libertarian ideology, which also made him popular with champions of conservative and right-wing causes. For more on this, see Staub, *Madness Is Civilization*, chap. 4. For more on the attractiveness of Freud to political theory in the 1960s, see Eli Zaretsky, *Political Freud: A History* (New York: Columbia University Press, 2015).

66. Schub says about Hapgood: "If he weren't a psychiatrist, I'd swear he knew what he was doing," Laurents and Sondheim, *Anyone Can Whistle*, 113.

67. Laurents and Sondheim, *Anyone Can Whistle*, 172, 34.

68. Zaretsky, *Political Freud*, 161. Zaretsky explains that "New Leftists felt they had a choice in regard to psychoanalysis: to condemn it wholesale or to locate a critical strain within it. They responded by developing what might be called the theory of the two Freuds. One Freud was an apolitical, sexist medical doctor. The other was a theorist of suppressed longings, utopia and desire, surrealism and the Situationist International, in a word, of revolution. One Freud authorized American world hegemony, the sanctified middle-class family, and the classifying regimes of the welfare state. The other held that reason arose from madness and encouraged the lib[e]ratory explosions of the 1960s. The fact that neither corresponded to the historical Freud was less important than the uses to which Freud's powerful imago could be put."

69. Sondheim says that the character of mayoress "sang in musical comedy terms because she was a lady who dealt in attitudes instead of emotions." Zadan, *Sondheim & Co.*, 83.

70. Stephen Banfield, *Sondheim's Broadway Musicals* (Ann Arbor: University of Michigan Press, 1993), 134.

71. Sondheim, *Finishing the Hat*, 116.

72. Laurents and Sondheim, *Anyone Can Whistle*, 104.

73. Joanne Gordon, *Art Isn't Easy: The Achievement of Stephen Sondheim* (Carbondale: Southern Illinois University Press, 1990), 35. For Banfield the title song "has a *timeless* quality of intimacy." Banfield, *Sondheim's Broadway Musicals*, 144, italics mine.

74. Sondheim, *Anyone Can Whistle: Vocal Score*, 219. "I'm like the Bluebird" can be read as an allusion to Cole Porter's song "Be Like a Blue Bird" (*Anything Goes*), which is sung by a character named Moon during his confinement in the cell of a brig. For a discussion of other intertextual references to Broadway musicals, see Banfield, *Sondheim's Broadway Musicals*, 143–44.

75. Laurents and Sondheim, *Anyone Can Whistle*, 120–30.

76. Sondheim says: "Our two principal characters were an idealist who turns out to be a cynic and a cynic who turns out to be an idealist." The people's need for a miracle "not explainable in terms of human activity" is "another form of idealism or romanticism, contrasted with that of the two characters" in the musical. Zadan, *Sondheim & Co.*, 88.

77. Laurents and Sondheim, *Anyone Can Whistle*, 128, 129, 173.

CHAPTER 4

1. Dale Wasserman, Joe Darion, and Mitch Leigh, *Man of La Mancha: A Musical Play* (New York: Random House, 1966), 7, 82, 3, vii-viii.

2. Howard Taubman, "Theater: Don Quixote, Singing Knight," review of *Man of La Mancha*, ANTA Washington Square Theatre, *New York Times*, November 23, 1965, 52.

3. Taubman, "Theater," 52; Wasserman, Darion, and Leigh, *Man of La Mancha*, 61.

4. Dale Wasserman, *The Impossible Musical: The "Man of La Mancha" Story* (New York: Applause, 2003), 71, 68.

5. Erving Goffman, *Asylums: Essays on the Social Situation of Mental Patients and Other Inmates* (Chicago: Aldine, 1961), 84.

6. Wasserman, Darion, and Leigh, *Man of La Mancha*, 6.

7. Wasserman, Darion, and Leigh, *Man of La Mancha*, 29, 11, 12, 67.

8. Wasserman, Darion, and Leigh, *Man of La Mancha*, 25–31.

9. Goffman, *Asylums*, 143.

10. Wasserman, Darion, and Leigh, *Man of La Mancha*, 26–31.

11. Wasserman, Darion, and Leigh, *Man of La Mancha*, 45, 69, 70.

12. Wasserman, Darion, and Leigh, *Man of La Mancha*, 69, 71–72, 75, 46, 72.

13. Joe Darion, quoted in Wasserman, *The Impossible Musical*, 101.

14. Raymond Knapp, *The American Musical and the Performance of Personal Identity* (Princeton, NJ: Princeton University Press, 2009), 181.

15. Wasserman, Darion, and Leigh, *Man of La Mancha*, 49.

16. Wasserman, Darion, and Leigh, *Man of La Mancha*, 82.

17. Jerry Herman, *Showtune: A Memoir*, with Marilyn Stasio (New York: Donald I. Fine Books, 1996), 170.

18. Herman, *Showtune*, 171.

19. Angela Lansbury, interview by Howard Sherman and John von Soosten, "Angela Lansbury (#105)," *Downstage Center*, American Theater Wing, iTunes, June 16, 2006.

20. Richard L. Coe, "Angela Shines; Show Dim," review of *Dear World*, Mark Hellinger Theatre, New York, *Washington Post*, February 7, 1969, B11.

21. Jerry Herman, *Dear World*, typescript, 1968, 1.4.56, New York Public Library, Performing Arts Library Research Collections Theatre, RM4475B.

22. Jerry Herman, *Dear World*, typescript, 1967, New York Public Library, Performing Arts Library Research Collections Theatre, RM4475A.

23. Martin Gottfried, review of *Dear World*, Mark Hellinger Theatre, New York, *Women's Wear Daily*, February 7, 1969, 33.

24. Wasserman, Darion, and Leigh, *Man of La Mancha*, 46, 60.

25. Herman, *Showtune*, 171.

26. Walter Kerr, "When Angela Sings 'I Will Not Have It,'" *New York Times*, February 16, 1969, D1.

27. Herman, *Dear World* (1968), 2.2.15.

28. Wasserman, Darion, and Leigh, *Man of La Mancha*, ix.

29. Herman, *Showtime*, 179.

30. Herman, *Dear World* (1968), 1.3.42.

31. Kerr, "When Angela Sings."

32. Herman, *Showtime*, 180.

33. David Savran and Daniel Gundlach, "*Anyone Can Whistle* as Experimental Theater," in *The Oxford Handbook of Sondheim Studies*, ed. Robert Gordon (New York: Oxford University Press, 2015), 85, 91.

34. Herman, *Dear World* (1968), 1.4.61.

35. Hobe, "Show on Broadway: *Dear World*," review of *Dear World*, Hellinger Theatre, New York, *Variety*, February 12, 1969.

36. In describing the "One Person" sequence, I quote from two rehearsal scripts, Herman, *Dear World* (1967), 1.5.59–65, and Herman, *Dear World* (1968),

1.4.58–67. By opening night, "Dear World" took the place of "One Person" at the end of the first act, and "One Person" was moved to the show's finale.

37. R. D. Laing, *The Politics of Experience* (New York: Pantheon Books, 1967), 90.

38. Rebecca Morehouse, "*Prettybelle*'s Realism Lures Champion Back," *Boston Globe*, January 31, 1971, A81. See also John Anthony Gilvey, *Before the Parade Passes By: Gower Champion and the Glorious American Musical* (New York: St. Martin's Press, 2005), 210–11.

39. Elliot Norton, quoted in Gilvey, *Before the Parade*, 215.

40. Star, "Show Out of Town: *Prettybelle*," review of *Prettybelle*, Shubert Theatre, Boston, *Variety*, February 3, 1971; Kevin Kelly, "*Prettybelle* Opens at Shubert," *Boston Globe*, February 2, 1971, 33.

41. "*Prettybelle* Won't Reach New York," *Boston Globe*, March 2, 1971, 35.

42. Merrill and Styne, *Prettybelle*, "Cast of Characters." Howard is also referred to in the typescript as Henry and was listed as such in the program.

43. Star, "Show Out of Town."

44. For more on the dramaturgy of madness in *Follies*, see Aleksei Grinenko, "*Follies* Embodied: A Kleinian Perspective," *Studies in Musical Theatre* 6, no. 3 (2012): 317–24.

45. Laing, *Politics of Experience*, 79.

46. Angela Lansbury, interview, MasterworksbwayVEVO, Sony Music Entertainment published August 15, 2012, https://www.youtube.com/watch?v=hqtH0sVU8_8

47. Merrill and Styne, *Prettybelle*, 1.5, 1.23.

48. Laing, *Politics of Experience*, 78–79.

49. Merrill and Styne, *Prettybelle*, 2.20.

50. Merrill and Styne, *Prettybelle*, 1.25.

51. Gilvey, 213; Merrill and Styne, *Prettybelle*, 2.18.

52. Laing, *Politics of Experience*, 79–80.

53. Merrill and Styne, *Prettybelle*, 1.40.

54. Prettybelle offers sex as reparation to people of color, framing each such act, though consensual, as "therapeutic rape." We are given to understand that on a psychological level these measures serve as her means of atoning for the irreparable harm done by her dead husband, clearing her compromised conscience, and, in a final twist, punishing the parts of LeRoy that are still painfully and powerfully alive inside her mind.

55. Merrill and Styne, *Prettybelle*, 1.50.

56. Laing, *Politics of Experience*, 71.

57. Merrill and Styne, *Prettybelle*, 1.63, 1.64, 2.13, 2.24, 1.49.

58. Laing, *Politics of Experience*, 84.

59. Merrill and Styne, *Prettybelle*, 2.37.

60. Merrill and Styne, *Prettybelle*, 2.18–19.

61. Gilvey, *Before the Parade*, 214.

62. Merrill and Styne, *Prettybelle*, 2.19.

63. This link in the musical's chain of signification around the asylum also plugs into the histories of women who welcomed asylum treatment as a refuge from abusive husbands and overwork. Mark S. Micale and Roy Porter, eds.,

Discovering the History of Psychiatry (New York: Oxford University Press, 1994), 359–61.

64. Merrill and Styne, *Prettybelle*, 2.40.

65. Aljean Harmetz, "'*King of Hearts*'—a Film That Refused to Die," *Los Angeles Times*, August 11, 1974.

66. Kevin Kelly, "'King of Hearts,' It's Not Just Another Mindless Musical," review of *King of Hearts*, Colonial Theatre, Boston, *Boston Globe*, October 5, 1978, B9.

67. Peter Link, *King of Hearts*, typescript, 1978, New York Public Library, Performing Arts Research Collections Theatre, RM1838.

68. Walter Kerr, "*King of Hearts* Swings on Spectacle, Not Plot," review of *King of Hearts*, Minskoff Theatre, New York, *The Sun*, October 29, 1978, D7.

69. Howard Kissel, "'King of Hearts': The Theater," review of *King of Hearts*, Minskoff Theatre, New York, *Women's Wear Daily*, October 24, 1978, 40.

70. Link, *King of Hearts*, 1.4–24.

71. Laing, *Politics of Experience*, 90, 85.

72. Daniel Henninger, "Why Make a War Musical without War?," review of *King of Hearts*, Minskoff Theatre, New York, *Wall Street Journal*, October 24, 1978, 24. See also Allan Wallach, "Theater Review: Musical '*King of Hearts*,'" *Newsday*, October 23, 1978, 32A.

73. Kelly, "*King of Hearts*."

CHAPTER 5

1. Stephen Sondheim and Hugh Wheeler, *Sweeney Todd: The Demon Barber of Fleet Street* (New York: Applause Theatre Book Publishers, 1991), 37. The lyric quoted in the chapter title appears on page 35.

2. Sondheim and Wheeler, *Sweeney Todd*, 23, 34–35, 46, 156. These visual elements, described in the published script, can also be seen in the video recording of the original production, videotaped by the New York Public Library's Theatre on Film and Tape Archive at the Uris Theatre on May 23, 1979. This video document should not be conflated with the widely available made-for-television video recording of the show on tour in Los Angeles in 1981, as the latter diverges from the script and staging of the show's original run at the Uris. For instance, the gravediggers shoveling real dirt on stage at the opening of the show were excised from the production filmed in LA. In light of these and other changes, I use the 1979 recording as my primary source throughout the chapter. The New York Public Library's Theatre on Film and Tape Archive, *Sweeney Todd: The Demon Barber of Fleet Street* (New York: Theatre on Film and Tape Archive, 1979), DVD, 157 min.

3. Sondheim and Wheeler, *Sweeney Todd*, 177, 55–56.

4. Sondheim and Wheeler, *Sweeney Todd*, 33.

5. Judith Schlesinger, "Psychology, Evil, and *Sweeney Todd*, or 'Don't I Know You, Mister?,'" in *Stephen Sondheim: A Casebook*, ed. Joanne Gordon (New York: Routledge, 2014), 129, 130.

6. Bruce Kirle, *Unfinished Show Business: Broadway Musicals as Works-in-*

Process (Carbondale: Southern Illinois University Press, 2005), 117. The connections were evident to the critics reviewing the original production. Thus, Brendan Gill wrote in the *New Yorker*: "We are invited to see Sweeney Todd not as a man obsessed with an insane desire for revenge but as a sorry victim of the workings of a vicious society—that nineteenth-century England which was reaping the rich fruits of the Industrial Revolution by dint of ignoring the cost of human suffering." Brendan Gill, "A Barber's Revenge," review of *Sweeney Todd*, Uris Theatre, New York, *New Yorker*, March 12, 1979.

    7. Harold Prince, "Harold Prince (#200)," interview by Howard Sherman and John von Soosten, *Downstage Center*, American Theater Wing, iTunes, May 2, 2008. Prince's earlier statement to this effect appears in Martin Gottfried, *Sondheim* (New York: Harry N. Abrams, 1993), 127.

    8. David Savran, "Toward a Historiography of the Popular," *Theatre Survey* 45, no. 2 (November 2004): 215.

    9. Dale Wasserman, Joe Darion, and Mitch Leigh, *Man of La Mancha: A Musical Play* (New York: Random House, 1966), 49.

    10. See, for instance, Joanne Gordon, *Art Isn't Easy: The Achievement of Stephen Sondheim* (Carbondale: Southern Illinois University Press, 1990); John Bush Jones, *Our Musicals, Ourselves: A Social History of the American Musical Theatre* (Hanover, NH: University Press of New England, 2003); Raymond Knapp, *The American Musical and the Performance of Personal Identity* (Princeton, NJ: Princeton University Press, 2006).

    11. For Sondheim's and Prince's position on Brecht, see David Savran, *In Their Own Words: Contemporary American Playwrights* (New York: Theatre Communications Group, 1988), 228–29; Carol Ilson, *Harold Prince: A Director's Journey* (New York: Limelight Editions, 2000), 144.

    12. For texts central to this interdisciplinary dialogue but not discussed here for reasons of space, see Julia Kristeva, *Powers of Horror: An Essay on Abjection*, trans. Leon S. Roudiez (New York: Columbia University Press, 1982); Peter Stallybrass and Allon White, *The Politics and Poetics of Transgression* (Ithaca, NY: Cornell University Press, 1986); Susan Strasser, *Waste and Want: A Social History of Trash* (New York: Metropolitan Books, 1999); Ben Campkin and Rosie Cox, eds., *Dirt: New Geographies of Cleanliness and Contamination* (London: I.B. Tauris, 2007); Robin Nagle, *Picking Up: On the Streets and behind the Trucks with the Sanitation Workers of New York City* (New York: Farrar, Straus and Giroux, 2013); and Annabel L. Kim, *Cacaphonies: The Excremental Canon of French Literature* (Minneapolis: University of Minnesota Press, 2022).

    13. William A. Cohen, "Introduction: Locating Filth," in *Filth: Dirt, Disgust, and Modern Life*, ed. William A. Cohen and Ryan Johnson (Minneapolis: University of Minnesota Press, 2005), viii.

    14. Cohen, "Introduction," x.

    15. Michelle Allen, *Cleansing the City: Sanitary Geographies in Victorian London* (Athens: Ohio University Press, 2008), 9.

    16. Stephen Banfield, "Sondheim's Genius," in *The Oxford Handbook of Sondheim Studies*, ed. Robert Gordon (New York: Oxford University Press, 2014), 16.

    17. Dominique Laporte, *History of Shit*, trans. Nadia Benabid and Rodolphe el-Khoury (Cambridge, MA: MIT Press, 2000), 32.

18. Len Cariou, quoted in Craig Zadan, *Sondheim & Co.*, 2nd ed. (New York: Harper and Row, 1986), 289.

19. See, for example, Elizabeth L. Wollman, *Hard Times: The Adult Musical in 1970s New York City* (New York: Oxford University Press, 2012).

20. I borrow the useful notion of a "vortex of behavior" in relation to performance from Joseph Roach, *Cities of the Dead: Circum-Atlantic Performance* (New York: Columbia University Press, 1996), 26.

21. Richard J. Hand and Michael Wilson, *Grand-Guignol: The French Theatre of Horror* (Exeter: University of Exeter Press, 2002), 66.

22. Sondheim found these horror shows, with their central emphasis on staged bloodshed and violence, dramatically ineffective. This experience would help him define his own approach to adapting *Sweeney Todd* in the 1970s. For more on Sondheim's ideas about *Sweeney Todd* as a Grand Guignol melodrama, see Daniel Gerould, ed., *Melodrama* (New York: New York Literary Forum, 1980), 3–7.

23. Angela Lansbury, quoted in Zadan, *Sondheim & Co.*, 254.

24. Walter Kerr, "Is 'Sweeney' on Target?," review of *Sweeney Todd*, Uris Theatre, New York, *New York Times*, March 11, 1979.

25. Sondheim, quoted in Gerould, *Melodrama*, 11.

26. Eugene Lee was known for his mastery of large-scale environmental staging concepts from his previous collaboration with Prince, Wheeler, and Sondheim on the 1974 Broadway revival of *Candide*.

27. Eugene Lee, interview by Howard Sherman, "Eugene Lee (#328)," *Downstage Center*, American Theater Wing, iTunes, July 27, 2011.

28. Harold Prince, quoted in "On Collaboration between Authors and Directors," *Dramatists Guild Quarterly* 16, no. 2 (Summer 1979): 19.

29. Jack Kroll, "The Blood Runs Cold," review of *Sweeney Todd*, Uris Theatre, New York, *Newsweek*, March 12, 1979, 101.

30. Prince, "Harold Prince (#200)."

31. Sondheim, quoted in Gerould, *Melodrama*, 11.

32. Stephen Sondheim, quoted in Zadan, *Sondheim & Co.*, 249.

33. Stephen Banfield, *Sondheim's Broadway Musicals* (Ann Arbor: University of Michigan Press, 1993), 285.

34. Zadan, *Sondheim & Co.*, 255.

35. Mary Douglas, *Purity and Danger: An Analysis of Concept of Pollution and Taboo*, with a new preface by the author (New York: Routledge, 2002), 44, xvii.

36. The image on the prologue's front drop is a reproduction of George Cruikshank's *British Bee Hive* drawing. See production image in Sondheim and Wheeler, *Sweeney Todd*, 113.

37. Josh Alan Friedman, *Tales of Times Square* (New York: Delacorte Press, 1986), 187.

38. Wollman, *Hard Times*, 198.

39. Graduate School and University Center of the City University of New York, *West 42nd Street: "The Bright Light Zone"* (New York: Graduate School and University Center of the City University of New York, 1978), 42.

40. Cohen, "Locating Filth," ix.

41. Douglas, *Purity and Danger*, 45.

42. Samuel R. Delany, *Times Square Red, Times Square Blue*, 20th Anniversary Edition (New York: New York University Press, 2019), xxi.

43. Michael J. Dear and Jennifer R. Wolch, *Landscapes of Despair: From Deinstitutionalization to Homelessness* (Princeton, NJ: Princeton University Press, 1987), 175–79.

44. Philip M. Boffey, "Community Care for Mentally Ill Termed a Failure," *New York Times*, September 13, 1984.

45. Gerald N. Grob, *From Asylum to Community: Mental Health Policy in Modern America* (Princeton, NJ: Princeton University Press, 1991), 303–4.

46. Boffey, "Community Care."

47. Dear and Wolch, *Landscapes of Despair*, 68.

48. Robin Herman, "Carey Says City Worsens Plight of the Homeless: Defends State on Releases from Mental Hospitals," *New York Times*, December 29, 1980, 1.

49. "The Danger of Dumping the Mentally Ill," *New York Times*, December 26, 1979, A26.

50. For an example of contemporaneous criticisms of the deinstitutionalization policy and its makers, see Richard D. Lyons, "How Release of Mental Patients Began: Policy Makers Recall Their Reasoning and Reflect on Outcome," *New York Times*, October 30, 1984. Also see Leona L. Bachrach, *Deinstitutionalization: An Analytical Review and Sociological Perspective* (Rockville, MD: US Department of Health, Education, and Welfare, 1976); Kim Hopper, Ellen Baxter, Stuart Cox, and Laurence Klein, *One Year Later: The Homeless Poor in New York City, 1982* (New York: Institute for Social Welfare Research, 1982).

51. "Careless of the Mentally Ill," *New York Times*, October 24, 1979, A30.

52. Musically, the Beggar Woman's expression here inherits the old conventions of the operatic mad scene. Ellen Rosand observes that in eighteenth-century operas "the rapid emotional changes associated with mental instability are portrayed by the unexpected and the inappropriate on a larger scale—by formal or affective improprieties: by unpredictable juxtapositions of recitative and aria or of arias of wildly contrasting moods or irregular form." Ellen Rosand, "Operatic Madness: A Challenge to Convention," in *Music and Text: Critical Inquiries*, ed. Steven Paul Scher (Cambridge: Cambridge University Press, 1992), 265.

53. Sondheim and Wheeler, *Sweeney Todd*, 30–31.

54. Sondheim, quoted in Zadan, *Sondheim & Co.*, 252.

55. Christopher G. Bond, *Sweeney Todd: The Demon Barber of Fleet Street* (London: Samuel French, 1974), 1, 42.

56. While this flash of nudity was not without its shock value, it was also part of the larger trends of the period. For more on nudity in 1970s musicals, see Wollman, *Hard Times*. Sondheim's reference to "dirty Cockney slang" appears in Mark Eden Horowitz, *Sondheim on Music: Minor Details and Major Decisions*, Less Is More Edition (Lanham, MD: Rowman and Littlefield, 2019), 133.

57. Sondheim and Wheeler, *Sweeney Todd*, 148, 197, 156.

58. Cohen, "Locating Filth," ix.

59. In the 1960s and 1970s, the image of a mad streetwalker appeared on and off Broadway with some consistency. Examples of other songs dramatizing this

image include "Timid Frieda" in *Jacques Brel Is Alive and Well and Living in Paris* (1968) and "Minnesota Strip / Song of a Child Prostitute" in *Runaways* (1978).

60. Sondheim and Wheeler, *Sweeney Todd*, 148, 73, 144.

61. Clayton Riley, "A New Black Magic—and They Weave It Well," review of *Ain't Supposed to Die a Natural Death*, Ethel Barrymore Theatre, New York, *New York Times*, November 7, 1971.

62. Melvin van Peebles, *Aint Supposed to Die a Natural Death* (Toronto: Bantam Books, 1973), 13.

63. Peebles, *Aint Supposed to Die*, 12.

64. Peebles, *Aint Supposed to Die*, 150–56.

65. For joint analyses of madness, race/Blackness, and political and cultural protest in the United States, see Jonathan M. Metzl, *The Protest Psychosis: How Schizophrenia Became a Black Disease* (Boston: Beacon Press, 2009), and La Marr Jurelle Bruce, *How to Go Mad without Losing Your Mind: Madness and Black Radical Creativity* (Durham, NC: Duke University Press, 2021). For reflections on the role of the sociogenic paradigm of madness in critical analyses of Blackness and aesthetic representation, also see Therí Alyce Pickens, *Black Madness :: Mad Blackness* (Durham, NC: Duke University Press, 2019), 52–54.

66. Sondheim and Wheeler, *Sweeney Todd*, 118, 120.

67. "Danger of Dumping."

68. Philip Jenkins, *Decade of Nightmares: The End of the Sixties and the Making of Eighties America* (New York: Oxford University Press, 2006), 45–46.

69. Sondheim and Wheeler, *Sweeney Todd*, 186.

70. Sondheim and Wheeler, *Sweeney Todd*, 189.

71. Graduate School and University Center of CUNY, *West 42nd Street*, 190.

72. Sondheim and Wheeler, *Sweeney Todd*, 179.

73. Sondheim and Wheeler, *Sweeney Todd*, 81.

74. Stephen Sondheim, *Finishing the Hat: Collected Lyrics (1954–1981) with Attendant Comments, Principles, Heresies, Grudges, Whines and Anecdotes* (New York: Alfred A. Knopf, 2010), 355.

75. Sondheim and Wheeler, *Sweeney Todd*, 33.

76. Gordon, *Art Isn't Easy*, 233; Sondheim, *Finishing the Hat*, 355.

77. Quoted in Horowitz, *Sondheim on Music*, 149; Sondheim, *Finishing the Hat*, 355.

78. Quoted in Horowitz, *Sondheim on Music*, 149.

79. Sondheim, *Finishing the Hat*, 355.

80. Quoted in Horowitz, *Sondheim on Music*, 149, 140.

81. Sondheim, *Finishing the Hat*, 355. Sondheim defines his hero as a schizophrenic yet draws his model for schizophrenia from *The Three Faces of Eve*, a 1957 movie whose heroine suffers from a dissociative identity disorder. Horowitz, *Sondheim on Music*, 140.

82. Quoted in Horowitz, *Sondheim on Music*, 140.

83. Eve Kosofsky Sedgwick, "Melanie Klein and the Difference Affect Makes," *South Atlantic Quarterly* 106, no. 3 (Summer 2007): 629.

84. Jacques Lacan quoted in Julia Kristeva, *Melanie Klein*, trans. Ross Guberman (New York: Columbia University Press, 2001), 230.

85. Melanie Klein, "Notes on Some Schizoid Mechanisms," in *Envy and Grat-*

itude and Other Works, 1946–1963, vol. 3 of *The Writings of Melanie Klein* (New York: Free Press, 1984), 8.

86. Sedgwick, "Melanie Klein," 633.

87. Sondheim and Wheeler, *Sweeney Todd*, 101.

88. Quoted in Horowitz, *Sondheim on Music*, 139.

89. Sondheim, *Finishing the Hat*, 355.

90. Graduate School and Center of CUNY, *West 42nd Street*, 45.

91. Stephen Sondheim and Hugh Wheeler, *Sweeney Todd: The Demon Barber of Fleet Street*, vocal score (New York: Rilting Music, 1997), 173, 21, 321. For a close analysis of the nature and function of the Herrmann chord in the musical, see Craig M. McGill, "Sondheim's Use of the 'Herrmann Chord' in *Sweeney Todd*," *Studies in Musical Theatre* 6, no. 3 (2012): 291–312.

92. Stephen Sondheim, "The Art of the Musical," *Paris Review* 39, no. 142 (Spring 1997): 274.

93. Sondheim and Wheeler, *Sweeney Todd*, 3.

94. Michael Fleming and Roger Manvell, *Images of Madness: The Portrayal of Insanity in the Feature Film* (Cranbury, NJ: Associated University Press, 1985), 308.

95. *Taxi Driver*, directed by Martin Scorsese (1976; Culver City, CA: Sony Pictures Home Entertainment, 2007), DVD.

96. Sondheim and Wheeler, *Sweeney Todd*, 2.

97. Cohen, "Locating Filth," x.

98. Cohen, "Locating Filth," x.

99. Cohen, "Locating Filth," x.

100. Jerry Herman, *Dear World*, typescript, 1968, New York Public Library, Performing Arts Research Collections Theatre, RM4475B, 1.4.53–54.

101. Klein, "Notes on Some Schizoid Mechanisms," 8–9.

102. Knapp, *The American Musical and the Performance of Personal Identity*, 333. Sweeney Todd's critical history has consistently featured discussions of anthropophagy as a descriptor of capitalistic modernity. For a detailed analysis of cannibalism in the musical, see Anette Pankratz, "The Pleasures in the Horrors of Eating Human Flesh: Stephen Sondheim and Hugh Wheeler's *Sweeney Todd*," in *The Pleasures and Horrors of Eating: The Cultural History of Eating in Anglophone Literature*, ed. Marion Gymnich and Norbert Lennartz (Göttingen: V&R Unipress, 2010), 387–407.

103. Sondheim and Wheeler, *Sweeney Todd*, 105.

104. *Taxi Driver*, DVD.

105. Sondheim and Wheeler, *Sweeney Todd*, 200–201.

106. Sedgwick, "Melanie Klein," 630.

107. Klein, "Notes on Some Schizoid Mechanisms," 3.

108. Stephen Sondheim and George Furth, *Company: A Musical Comedy* (New York: Theatre Communications Group, 1996), 33.

109. James Goldman and Stephen Sondheim, *Follies: A Musical* (New York: Random House, 1971), 110.

110. In Klein, the primary anxiety against which the self defends itself has an endogenous origin; it is there from the beginning, even before environmental etiological factors may kick in.

111. Julia Kristeva, *Melanie Klein*, trans. Ross Guberman (New York: Columbia University Press, 2001), 232.

112. Sondheim and Wheeler, *Sweeney Todd*, 32.

113. Eugene Victor Wolfestein, *Psychoanalytic Marxism: Groundwork* (London: Free Association Books, 1993), 348.

114. Kristeva, *Melanie Klein*, 200, 234.

115. Kristeva, *Melanie Klein*, 234.

116. Richard Eder, "Critic's Notebook: 'Sweeney's' Dark Side," *New York Times*, March 29, 1979, C16. Lansbury recalls: "We didn't know for quite a long time whether we were going to run. And it was only when we got the Tonys that we started to do land-office business. . . . Finally . . . the theatergoing public were told by the Tonys that this was a great show. And then they started to enjoy it and become non-critical." Angela Lansbury, "Angela Lansbury (#105)," interview by Howard Sherman and John von Soosten, *Downstage Center*, American Theater Wing, iTunes, June 16, 2006.

117. Eder, "Critic's Notebook."

118. John Simon, "A Little Knife Music," review of *Sweeney Todd*, Uris Theatre, New York, *New Yorker*, March 19, 1979.

119. Sondheim and Wheeler, *Sweeney Todd*, 177; Sondheim and Wheeler, *Sweeney Todd*, vocal score, 370–72.

120. T. E. Kalem, Gerald Rabkin, and William Wolf, "Critics' Roundtable Discuss Sweeney Todd," *New York Theatre Review*, April 1979, 13–20. For similar critical reactions, see Richard Eder, "Stage: Introducing 'Sweeney Todd,'" *New York Times*, March 2, 1979, C3; James Fenton, "The Barberous Crimes of Sondheim and Prince," *Sunday Times* (London), July 6, 1980, 40; Gill, "A Barber's Revenge"; and Foster Hirsch, *Harold Prince and the American Musical* (New York: Cambridge University Press, 1989), 129–30.

121. Quoted in Gerould, *Melodrama*, 10.

122. For an account of the sanitary efforts in Times Square before the 1990s, see Friedman, *Tales of Times Square*.

123. Delany, *Times Square Red*, xxi–xxii.

124. Sondheim and Wheeler, *Sweeney Todd*, 2, 176.

125. William A. Cohen, "Victorian Dirt," *Victorian Network* 6, no. 8 (Winter 2015): 6.

CHAPTER 6

1. Gerald Klerman, George Vaillant, Robert Spitzer, and Robert Michaels, "Commentary: A Debate on DSM-III," *American Journal of Psychiatry* 141, no. 4 (April 1984): 544.

2. Klerman et al., "Commentary," 545.

3. Rick Mayes and Allan V. Horwitz, "DSM-III and the Revolution in the Classification of Mental Illness," *Journal of the History of the Behavioral Sciences* 41, no. 3 (Summer 2005): 250.

4. Mayes and Horwitz, "DSM-III," 258.

5. Allan V. Horwitz, *Creating Mental Illness* (Chicago: University of Chicago Press, 2002), 134.

6. Allen Thiher, *Revels in Madness: Insanity in Medicine and Literature* (Ann Arbor: University of Michigan Press, 1999), 226.

7. Oliver Sacks, "The Other Road: Freud as Neurologist," in *Freud: Conflict and Culture*, ed. Michael S. Roth (New York: Alfred A. Knopf, 1998), 229.

8. Elizabeth Wright, ed., *Feminism and Psychoanalysis: A Critical Dictionary* (Cambridge, MA: Blackwell, 1992), 22–23.

9. Mitchell Wilson, "DSM-III and the Transformation of American Psychiatry: A History," *American Journal of Psychiatry* 150, no. 3 (March 1993): 400.

10. Mayes and Horwitz, "DSM-III," 250.

11. The term "cognitive modernism," as defined by Dorothy Ross, refers to "the turn-of-the century recognition of the subjectivity of perception and cognition" in social theory, philosophy of science, and the arts. Dorothy Ross, ed., *Modernist Impulses in the Human Sciences, 1870–1930* (Baltimore: John Hopkins University Press, 1994), 8.

12. In *Passion*, biological thinking manifests itself in the medical emphasis on Fosca's "physical state." Modeled on an epileptic, the character is said to be suffering from "hysterical convulsions." The doctor explains that "her nerves are exposed, where ours are protected by a firm layer of skin." Stephen Sondheim and James Lapine, *Passion: A Musical* (New York: Theatre Communications Group, 1994), 17–19; I. U. Tarchetti, *Passion*, trans. Lawrence Venuti (San Francisco: Mercury House, 1994), vi. *The Light in the Piazza* traces Clara's "mental and emotional capacities" to a head injury. Craig Lucas and Adam Guettel, *The Light in the Piazza* (New York: Theatre Communications Group, 2007), 47. In *Be More Chill*, Jeremy changes his personality by ingesting a pill with a computerized implant device for the brain, which functions as an allegory for psychoactive medication.

13. "Just something you were born with," explains the doctor. William Finn and James Lapine, *A New Brain* (New York: Samuel French, 1999), 40.

14. The press about the US production used the term "mental retardation" to define the musical's hero and theme.

15. Brian Yorkey, interview by Steve Paikin, *The Agenda with Steve Paikin*, TVOntario, published on YouTube on June 29, 2011, https://www.youtube.com/watch?v=_TqBTdWgsh4, accessed January 8, 2014.

16. Alice Ripley, interview by Eden Lane, *In Focus with Eden Lane*, PBS, https://www.youtube.com/watch?v=RTcBaVVfZ94&t=1337s, accessed March 20, 2018.

17. Mayes and Horwitz, "DSM-III," 249.

18. Horwitz, *Creating Mental Illness*, 132.

19. Horwitz, *Creating Mental Illness*, 155.

20. Klerman et al., "Commentary," 542.

21. Dorothy Ross, "Freud and the Vicissitudes of Modernism in the United States, 1940–1980," in *After Freud Left: A Century of Psychoanalysis in America*, ed. John Burnham (Chicago: University of Chicago Press, 2012), 188, 182–83.

22. Mayes and Horwitz, "DSM-III," 250.

23. DSM-III's approach to nosology revived Emil Kraepelin's methods of classification, which dominated the field before the ascendance of Freud's psychodynamic paradigm. Kraepelian psychiatry is driven by "three ideas: that

mental disorders are best understood as analogues with physical diseases; that the classification of mental disorders demands careful observation of visible symptoms instead of inferences based on unproven causal theories; and that empirical research will eventually demonstrate the organic and biochemical origins of mental disorders," Mayes and Horwitz, "DSM-III," 260. For more, see Allan Young, *The Harmony of Illusions: Inventing Post-traumatic Stress Disorder* (Princeton, NJ: Princeton University Press, 1995), 95–98.

24. Klerman et al., "Commentary," 540.

25. Mayes and Horwitz, "DSM-III," 265.

26. Klerman et al., "Commentary," 539.

27. T. M. Luhrmann, *Of Two Minds: The Growing Disorder in American Psychiatry* (New York: Alfred A. Knopf, 2001), 250.

28. Leon Eisenberg, "Mindlessness and Brainlessness in Psychiatry," *British Journal of Psychiatry* 148 (1986): 497–508; Morton F. Reiser, "Are Psychiatric Educators 'Losing the Mind?,'" *American Journal of Psychiatry* 145, no. 2 (February 1988): 148–53.

29. Klerman et al., "Commentary," 542–43. For a brief description of the battle over the category of "neurosis" in the making of DSM-III, see Mayes and Horwitz, "DSM-III," 261–63.

30. Laura L. Hall reports in 1993 that between 1980 and 1992, the National Institute of Mental Health increased its funding of mental disorders research by nearly 7 percent annually. She stresses that "the greatest gains in funding were seen in basic biological research and clinical research focused on schizophrenia and major mood and anxiety disorders." Laura Lee Hall, "The Biology of Mental Disorders," *Journal of the American Medical Association* 269, no. 7 (February 1993): 844.

31. Luhrmann, *Of Two Minds*, 208, 203, 238.

32. Michael E. Staub, *Madness Is Civilization: When the Diagnosis Was Social, 1948–1980* (Chicago: University of Chicago Press, 2011), 186.

33. In this paragraph I quote from the surrounding dialogue and lyrics of the following songs: "Lost in the Darkness," "Jekyll's Plea," and "Obsession." *Jekyll & Hyde: The Musical*, music by Frank Wildhorn, book and lyrics by Leslie Bricusse, stage direction by Robin Phillips, directed for television by Don Roy King, Broadway Television Network Presents, 2001, DVD.

34. "Jekyll's Plea."

35. Nancy C. Andreasen, "Editorial: Body and Soul," *American Journal of Psychiatry* 153, no. 5 (May 1996): 589.

36. Andreasen, "Editorial," 589.

37. Frank Rich, "Theater: Charlie and Algernon," review of *Charlie and Algernon*, Helen Hayes Theater, New York, *New York Times*, September 15, 1980, C17; Douglas Watt, review of *Charlie and Algernon*, *New York Daily News*, as quoted in Dan Dietz, *The Complete Book of 1980s Broadway Musicals* (Lanham, MD: Rowman & Littlefield, 2016), 46.

38. Ken Mandelbaum, *Not since "Carrie": Forty Years of Broadway Musical Flops* (New York: St. Martin's Press, 1991).

39. David Rogers and Charles Strouse, *Charlie and Algernon* (Chicago: Dramatic Publishing Company, 1981), 5, 22, 69.

40. Rogers and Strouse, *Charlie and Algernon*, 56.

41. Charles Strouse and David Rogers, *Charlie and Algernon*, typescript, 1980, New York Public Library, Performing Arts Research Collections Theatre, NCOF+ 83-1024, 1.

42. Strouse and Rogers, *Charlie and Algernon*, typescript, 4.

43. Rogers and Strouse, *Charlie and Algernon*, 66, 48, 8.

44. Gerald N. Grob, *Mad among Us: A History of the Care of America's Mentally Ill* (New York: Free Press, 1994), 202.

45. Gerald N. Grob, *From Asylum to Community: Mental Health Policy in Modern America* (Princeton, NJ: Princeton University Press, 1991), 301.

46. John Beaufort, "A Mouse Goes Musical," review of *Charlie and Algernon*, Helen Hayes Theatre, New York, *Christian Science Monitor*, September 16, 1980.

47. Rogers and Strouse, *Charlie and Algernon*, 53.

48. Rogers and Strouse, *Charlie and Algernon*, 78. In "Production Notes," Rogers characterizes the maze used in the Broadway production as a "real maze" as opposed to other, more pared-down options he recommends as possible substitutes for the design.

49. Rogers and Strouse, *Charlie and Algernon*, 33.

50. Daniel Keyes, *Algernon, Charlie, and I: A Writer's Journey* (Boca Raton, FL: Challenge Press, 1999), 164–65.

51. Keyes, *Algernon, Charlie, and I*, 86–87.

52. Rogers and Strouse, *Charlie and Algernon*, 39–44.

53. Glen O. Gabbard and Krin Gabbard compare a similar function of the psychiatrist figure in movies to what Henry James calls a *ficelle*: "the colorless confidants and confidantes to whom several centuries of stage heroes and heroines have explained their thoughts for the benefit of the audience." As these writers point out, "The invention of psychotherapy has presented filmmakers with the ideal *ficelle*, one that need not even speak, yet whose presence allows a character to engage in intense self-scrutiny before the cameras." Glen O. Gabbard and Krin Gabbard, *Psychiatry and the Cinema*, 2nd ed. (Washington, DC: American Psychiatric Press, 1999), 7.

54. Keyes, *Algernon, Charlie, and I*, 216.

55. Rogers and Strouse, *Charlie and Algernon*, 59.

56. Rogers and Strouse, *Charlie and Algernon*, 70–71.

57. Rogers and Strouse, *Charlie and Algernon*, 50, 53.

58. Rogers and Strouse, *Charlie and Algernon*, 54. Strouse says that in composing *Annie*'s score he "tried very hard to reflect the twenties and thirties.... But this ["Tomorrow"] and one other song, 'Hard-Knock Life' were definitely not of the twenties.... The chords there are ... guitar chords, they're very influenced by rock." According to Keyes, *Annie*'s song "Tomorrow" was initially intended for Charlie. If Keyes's account is correct, it clarifies the genealogy of the song's contemporary sound, as it sounds very much like the rest of Strouse's score for *Charlie and Algernon*. Charles Strouse, "Theater Talk: Legendary Composer Charles Strouse, Pt. 2," interview by Susan Haskins and Michael Riedel, posted on May 12, 2011, https://www.youtube.com/watch?v=YCxZV -uhBEg; Keyes, *Algernon, Charlie, and I*, 162.

59. Rogers and Strouse, *Charlie and Algernon*, 57.

60. Rogers and Strouse, *Charlie and Algernon*, 50, 53, 57.

61. Rogers and Strouse, *Charlie and Algernon*, 61, 74.

62. Mel Gussow, "Theater: A Man, a Mouse and Making of a Genius," review of *Charlie and Algernon*, Terrace Theater, Washington DC, *New York Times*, March 12, 1980.

63. Gussow, "Theater."

64. In "Just Another Day," Natalie appears with a stack of books in her hands and mentions *Flowers for Algernon* when listing her school assignments. Tom Kitt and Brian Yorkey, *Next to Normal* (New York: Theatre Communications Group, 2010), 9. Yorkey's adapted version of *Next to Normal*'s script that was serialized on Twitter in 2009 includes additional references to Keyes's story.

CHAPTER 7

1. Tom Kitt and Brian Yorkey, *Next to Normal* (New York: Theatre Communications Group, 2010), 74–76.

2. Brian Yorkey, interview by Steve Paikin, *The Agenda with Steve Paikin*, TVOntario, published on YouTube on June 29, 2011, https://www.youtube.com/watch?v=_TqBTdWgsh4, accessed January 8, 2014.

3. Yorkey, *Agenda with Steve Paikin*.

4. "The 2010 Pulitzer Prize Winner in Drama," official website for the Pulitzer Prize, http://www.pulitzer.org/winners/tom-kitt-and-brian-yorkey, accessed June 13, 2018.

5. The musical has since received stagings with a multiracial casting, which broadened the referential capacity of Yorkey and Kitt's story, as in for example, the limited-engagement production at the Eisenhower Theater in Washington, DC, in 2020.

6. "The 2010 Pulitzer Prize Winner in Drama."

7. David Rooney, "*Next to Normal*: This Original New Pop-Rock Musical Has Benefited Unequivocally from Treatment," review of *Next to Normal*, Booth Theatre, New York, *Variety*, April 15, 2009.

8. Ben Brantley, "Fragmented Psyches, Uncomfortable Emotions: Sing Out!," review of *Next to Normal*, Booth Theatre, New York, *New York Times*, April 15, 2009.

9. Michael Kuchwara, "Mental Illness Shatters Family in *Next to Normal*," review of *Next to Normal*, Booth Theatre, New York, *Associated Press*, April 15, 2009.

10. Peter Marks, "Theatre Review of *Next to Normal* and *Hair* on Broadway," review of *Next to Normal*, Booth Theatre, New York, *Washington Post*, April 16, 2009.

11. Alice Ripley, quoted in Peter Marks, "After a New York Run, an Unusual 'Next' Step," *Washington Post*, November 23, 2008; Kuchwara, "Mental Illness Shatters Family."

12. Brantley, "Fragmented Psyches."

13. Tom Kitt and Brian Yorkey, "Conversation: Pulitzer Prize Winners in

Drama, Tom Kitt and Brian Yorkey of *Next to Normal*," interview by Murrey Jacobson, *NewsHour*, PBS, April 14, 2010, https://www.pbs.org/newshour/arts/co nversation-pulitzer-prize-winners-in-drama-tom-kitt-and-brian-yorkey-of-ne xt-to-normal, accessed October 3, 2018.

14. Drawing on Elizabeth Wollman's discussion of Scott Warfield's classification, *Next to Normal* can be best described as the type of rock musical that, while never billed as such, "reveals enough influence from contemporary popular genres to earn the label in the press, in theater histories, and among theater aficionados." As Wollman's scholarship has shown, most musical theater scores composed in this vein comprise a blend of rock and other music styles. *Next to Normal* is no exception. This has to do not only with rock's historical fragmentation into multiple subtypes and the elusive distinctions between rock and other popular musics, but also with a certain kind of softening or *smoothing out* that occurs in the process of translating rock to the production apparatus and performance conventions of the stage musical. Elizabeth L. Wollman, *The Theater Will Rock: A History of the Rock Musical from "Hair" to "Hedwig"* (Ann Arbor: University of Michigan Press, 2006), 3–4. See also Scott Warfield, "From *Hair* to *Rent*: Is 'Rock' a Four-Letter Word on Broadway?," in *The Cambridge Companion to the Musical*, ed. William E. Everett and Paul R. Laird, 2nd ed. (Cambridge: Cambridge University Press, 2002).

15. As Wollman tells us, Greif similarly instructed Adam Pascal to "use exaggerated physical gestures . . . as if he were a rock star singing during a concert in a huge venue." Wollman, *The Theater Will Rock*, 207.

16. Wollman, *The Theater Will Rock*, 72.

17. Michael Greif, quoted in Marks, "After a New York Run."

18. Brian Yorkey, Tom Kitt, Michael Greif, and David Stone, "*Next to Normal*: The Road to Broadway," interview by Ted Chapin, *Working in the Theatre* 384, American Theatre Wing, filmed November 2009, https://www.youtube.com/wa tch?v=6t0tI4IhJSU&t=1714s, accessed January 4, 2017.

19. The structural analogies between *A Doll's House* and *Next to Normal* are particularly striking. Echoing Ibsen's Nora, Diana forces her husband to have a conversation about a subject they have avoided for many years in "How Could I Ever Forget? / What Was His Name?" Dan's characteristic unwillingness to let her speak about their son's death throughout the musical and his renewed attempts to silence her at the end of the scene precipitate this American housewife's decision to walk out on him shortly after, in an open-ended finale.

20. Brantley, "Fragmented Psyches."

21. Françoise Meltzer, "Unconscious," in *Critical Terms for Literary Study*, ed. Frank Lentricchia and Thomas McLaughlin (Chicago: University of Chicago Press, 1995), 150–51.

22. Alice Ripley, "Depth Interview: Alice Ripley on *Next to Normal*: Tour and Career Retrospective," interview by Pat Cerasaro, Broadwayworld.com, December 11, 2010, https://www.broadwayworld.com/article/InDepth-InterVi ew-Alice-Ripley-on-NEXT-TO-NORMAL-Tour-A-Career-Retrospective-2010 1211, accessed September 15, 2018. The other two influences Ripley cites in this interview are *Long Day's Journey into Night* and *Buried Child*: "All of these I carry with me everywhere I go when I am doing work on Diana."

23. Marin Mazzie, "Marin Mazzie on the Irresistible Pull of *Next to Normal*," interview by Kathy Henderson, Broadway.com, July 26, 2010, https://www.bro adway.com/buzz/153099/marin-mazzie-on-the-irresistible-pull-of-next-to-nor mal/

24. Tveit continues: "They even did something with my T-shirts. . . . The color of my T-shirt . . . would match the character that I was influencing at that time." "*Next to Normal*, Cast Reunion," *Stars in the House with Seth Rudetsky and James Wesley*, YouTube, livestreamed on September 15, 2020, https://www.yout ube.com/watch?v=tLK_bXZjT_4&feature=youtu.be

25. Charles McNulty, "Theater Review: *Next to Normal* at the Ahmanson Theatre," *Los Angeles Times*, November 29, 2010.

26. Kuchwara, "Mental Illness Shatters Family"; Marks, "*Next to Normal* and *Hair* on Broadway"; Peter Marks, "Theater Review: *Next to Normal* at Kennedy Center," review of *Next to Normal*, John F. Kennedy Center for the Performing Arts, Washington, DC, *Washington Post*, June 30, 2011. The adjectives quoted at the end of the sentence abound in reviews (including but not limited to the ones cited in this chapter) as well as printed interviews, radio and TV broadcasts, podcasts, and other materials relating to *Next to Normal*.

27. John Lahr, "Innocence Abroad: Adam Guettel's Italian Romance," *New Yorker*, February 2, 2004.

28. Brooks Atkinson, "The Play in Review: Gertrude Lawrence Appears in Moss Hart's Musical Drama, 'Lady in the Dark,' with a Score by Kurt Weill and Lyrics by Ira Gershwin," review of *Lady in the Dark*, Alvin Theatre, New York, *New York Times*, January 24, 1941; Brooks Atkinson, "Lady in the Dark," *New York Times*, February 2, 1941, xi; Marks, "*Next to Normal* at Kennedy Center"; Marks, "*Next to Normal* and *Hair* on Broadway."

29. Yorkey, *Agenda with Steve Paikin*.

30. Yorkey, *Agenda with Steve Paikin*.

31. Brian Yorkey, "An Interview with *Next to Normal* Writer/Lyricist Brian Yorkey," interview by Marcia Purse, published in 2009, updated on September 14, 2016, https://www.verywell.com/brian-yorkey-interview-380335, accessed on October 15, 2018. Ripley recalls that Yorkey gave her two books, *Darkness Visible* and *Noonday Demon*, to help her prepare for the role. "*Next to Normal*, Cast Reunion."

32. Yorkey, *Agenda with Steve Paikin*.

33. Michael Fitzpatrick, executive director of NAMI, "Voices" (blog post), Kimmel Center for the Performing Arts, June 21, 2011, http://blog.kimmelcenter .org/post/6761990169/todays-voices-comes-from-special-guest-michael, accessed October 10, 2018.

34. Fitzpatrick, "Voices."

35. See, for example, Elizabeth Lunbeck, "Psychiatry," in *The Cambridge History of Science*, vol. 7, *The Modern Social Sciences*, ed. Theodore M. Porter and Dorothy Ross (Cambridge: Cambridge University Press, 2003).

36. Kitt and Yorkey, "Conversation."

37. "Fundraiser: Next to Normal," National Alliance for Mental Illness, Georgia, https://namiga.org/fundraiser-next-to-normal/, accessed October 1, 2018. It is probably *Next to Normal*'s mainstream success as a musical about

bipolar disorder and its much-publicized involvement with the cause of mental health awareness that has prompted accusations of it being too pro-establishment in academic scholarship. Thus, in Scott Wallin's opinion, the creative team's framing of the lead character's distress as a "mental illness" yields a pathologizing narrative, which endorses the biomedical paradigm, reduces psychosocial disability to a "biological condition located within the individual," and "deprives Diana of agency to be more than a poster child for psychiatry." My reading of the musical, however, argues for a vastly different perspective: the show situates its lead character within a system of relations overdetermined by diagnostic psychiatry and then proceeds to dismantle this system, recanting its authority. Scott Wallin, "*Next to Normal* and the Persistence of Pathology in Performances of Psychosocial Disability," *Disability Studies Quarterly* 33, no. 1 (2013), http://dsq-sds.org/article/view/3428, accessed January 5, 2018.

38. Brian Yorkey, "Road to Broadway."

39. Yorkey, *Agenda with Steve Paikin.*

40. Kitt and Yorkey, *Next to Normal*, 16.

41. Kitt and Yorkey, *Next to Normal*, 18.

42. Kitt and Yorkey, *Next to Normal*, 22.

43. Kitt and Yorkey, *Next to Normal*, 45.

44. Muriel Dimen, "Strange Hearts: On the Paradoxical Liaison between Psychoanalysis and Feminism," in *Freud: Conflict and Culture*, ed. Michael S. Roth (New York: Alfred A. Knopf, 1998), 219.

45. Kitt and Yorkey, *Next to Normal*, 44, 91.

46. Shoshana Felman, *Writing and Madness: Literature/Philosophy/Psychoanalysis*, trans. Martha Noel Evans and Shoshana Felman (Ithaca, NY: Cornell University Press, 1985), 120.

47. Kitt and Yorkey, *Next to Normal*, 49.

48. Dimen, "Strange Hearts," 220.

49. Kitt and Yorkey, *Next to Normal*, 91.

50. Nicola Spelman, *Popular Music and the Myths of Madness* (Burlington, VT: Ashgate, 2012), 3.

51. Kitt and Yorkey, *Next to Normal*, 56–57.

52. The Broadway production's field of allusions to the cultural history of madness and disability also included a song about "crazy" Mozart, a mention of *Flowers for Algernon*, and a nod to J. D. Salinger's 1951 novel *The Catcher in the Rye*. The latter work was not referred to verbally but was present physically on the third level of the stage set, where Gabe sat reading it, while Diana sang "I Miss the Mountains." Actor Kyle Dean Massey shows the location of the book on the production's set in his video blog. "Normal Life with Kyle Dean Massey—Video Blog #10," Broadway.com, YouTube, published on April 5, 2010, https://youtu.be/pb3m_vE5zrE. Intertextually, *Catcher* and *Next to Normal* communicate with each other not only by sharing the theme of loss and grief for a dead child but also by critiquing and resisting the cure-or-kill teleology common to disability narratives in popular entertainment mediums. As my discussion further in this chapter shows, this musical rejects that teleology. For a discussion of *Catcher*'s strategy of resistance, see David T. Mitchell and Sharon

L. Snyder, *Narrative Prosthesis: Disability and the Dependencies of Discourse* (Ann Arbor: University of Michigan Press, 2000), 169–71.

53. Historically, antipsychiatry's impact on the patient-led liberation movement cannot be underestimated. Not only did the former help launch a cultural momentum for the latter but it also provided concepts and language of empowerment for those who suffered from the defects of the mental health system. In the 1970s, major components of antipsychiatry's arguments against the medicalization of madness undergirded the rhetoric of ex-patients, who described themselves as psychiatrically labeled and stigmatized. The movement's newspaper, *Madness Network News*, intermixed patient narratives and art with texts by and references to Szasz, Goffman, Foucault, and Laing. Today groups like Mad Pride can be seen as the most direct descendants of antipsychiatric thought; they often assert that heritage themselves. Yet even during the early years of the movement some ex-patients and psychiatric survivors also criticized antipsychiatry for claiming exclusive insight into the experiences of the mad. In Judi Chamberlin's opinion, for example, antipsychiatry was "largely an intellectual exercise of academics and dissident mental health professionals" who did not care to "reach out to struggling ex-patients or to include their perspectives." The exclusion of nonpatients, no matter how sympathetic, from leading positions eventually became a guiding principle of the ex-patient movement, as its members insisted on the importance of defining their experiences on their own terms and speaking for themselves. Notably, Chamberlin is also critical of pro-psychiatry, antistigma groups that "claim to speak 'for' patients, that is, to be patients' advocates." NAMI, she writes, "enthusiastically embraces the medical model and promotes the expansion of involuntary commitment and the lifetime control of people labeled 'mentally ill.'" Thus, some of antipsychiatry's leading tenets continue to reside within the politics of the c/s/x/m movement. Judi Chamberlin, "The Ex-Patients' Movement: Where We've Been and Where We're Going," *Journal of Mind and Behavior* 11, nos. 3–4 (1990): 324, 334. Also see Sherry Hirsch et al., eds., *Madness Network News Reader* (San Francisco: Glide Publications, 1974).

54. John Cromby, David Harper, and Paula Reavey, *Psychology, Mental Health and Distress* (London: Palgrave, 2013), 49–52.

55. Robert Walser, *Running with the Devil: Power, Gender and Madness in Heavy Metal Music* (Hanover, NH: Wesleyan University Press, 1993), 15.

56. Kitt and Yorkey, *Next to Normal*, 92.

57. See, for example, Jennifer M. Poole and Jennifer Ward, "'Breaking Open the Bone': Storying, Sanism, and Mad Grief," in *Mad Matters: A Critical Reader in Canadian Mad Studies*, ed. Brenda A. Lefrançois, Robert Menzies, and Geoffrey Reaume (Toronto: Canadian Scholars' Press, 2013), 94–104.

58. Poole and Ward, "Breaking Open the Bone"; Kitt and Yorkey, *Next to Normal*, 92.

59. Kitt and Yorkey, *Next to Normal*, 89–92.

60. Kitt and Yorkey, *Next to Normal*, 101.

61. I am referencing Judi Chamberlin's take on the postasylum geographies of psychiatric control. Her characterization of psychiatric medication in the quoted text also serves as an example of classic antipsychiatry's influence on

the early writing by the patient-led liberation movement in the 1970s. Judy Chamberlin, *On Our Own: Patient-Controlled Alternatives to the Mental Health System* (New York: Hawthorn Books, 1978), xvi, 13.

62. The use of rock in "Light," "The Break," and "Didn't I See the Movie?" also calls to mind the aesthetics of awareness-raising events by Mad Pride or other activist groups that have utilized live rock performance as a means of disseminating and bonding over their mistrust of the psychiatric establishment. Robert Dellar, *Splitting in Two: Mad Pride and Punk Rock Oblivion* (London: Unkant Publishers, 2014).

63. Hester Parr, *Mental Health and Social Space: Towards Inclusionary Geographies* (Oxford: Blackwell, 2008), 26, 23. For other examples of this type of ethnographically based scholarship, see Caroline Knowles, *Bedlam on the Streets* (London: Routledge, 2000) and Emily Martin, *Bipolar Expeditions: Mania and Depression in American Culture* (Princeton, NJ: Princeton University Press, 2009).

64. Parr, *Mental Health and Social Space*, 184.

65. One example of the trend is the 2019 film *Joker*, which reimagines the eponymous character by medicalizing him. Joaquin Phoenix, who played him, says, "There was something really interesting about the idea of the laugh being rooted in a real condition and the struggle of that." Quoted in Rebecca Keegan, "Making of 'Joker': How Todd Phillips' 'Bold Swing' Became a Study in Madness," *Hollywood Reporter*, December 27, 2019. See also Glenn Close's recent discussion of her film character Alex Forrest from *Fatal Attraction* in "Glenn Close and Patrick Kennedy on the Weight of Mental Illness," conversation with Philip Galanes, *New York Times*, March 11, 2017.

66. Kuchwara, "Mental Illness Shatters Family."

67. Kitt and Yorkey, *Next to Normal*, 103.

68. Felman, *Writing and Madness*, 121.

69. "Ordinary unhappiness" is my preferred translation. In the standard translation edited by Strachey, it is "common unhappiness." Joseph Breuer and Sigmund Freud, *Studies on Hysteria*, in vol. 2 of *The Standard Edition of the Complete Psychological Works of Sigmund Freud*, trans. under the general editorship of James Strachey, in collaboration with Anna Freud (London: Hogarth Press, 1955), 305.

70. Kitt and Yorkey, *Next to Normal*, 10, 102.

71. Kitt and Yorkey, *Next to Normal*.

CONCLUSION

1. Benj Pasek, Justin Paul, and Steven Levenson, quoted in "How *Dear Evan Hansen* Found His Voice," *Playbill*, December 2016.

2. Michael Greif, quoted in Pasek, Paul, and Levenson, "How *Dear Evan Hansen* Found His Voice."

3. Ben Platt, Jennifer Laura Thompson, and Rachel Bay Jones, "Theater Talk: *Dear Evan Hansen* Actors," interview by Susan Haskins and Jesse Green, *Theater Talk*, PBS, January 27, 2017, https://www.youtube.com/watch?v=21Hk7c8rTjk, accessed on March 23, 2017.

4. John Latouche and Jerome Moross, *Ballet Ballads*, typescript, New York Public Library, Performing Arts Research Collections Theatre, RM4553, "Willie the Weeper," 12, 1.

5. See, for instance, critic Linda Winer's take on this show. Linda Winer, "'Dear Evan Hansen' Review: Musical Too Light for Heavy Topics," review of *Dear Evan Hansen*, Second Stage Theatre, New York, *Newsday*, May 1, 2016; Linda Winer, "'Dear Evan Hansen' Review: Endearingly Original," review of *Dear Evan Hansen*, Music Box Theatre, New York, *Newsday*, December 5, 2016; Jessie Green, Linda Winer, and Elizabeth Vincentelli, "Theater Talk: Holiday Critics 2016," interview by Michael Reidel and Susan Haskins, December 9, 2016, *Theater Talk*, PBS, https://www.youtube.com/watch?v=GWGG9YJXsy8, accessed November 28, 2022.

6. "Ballet Ballads: Godkin, Holm, and Litz [Programs]," NYPL, Performing Arts Research Collections Dance, MGZB.

7. Winer, "'Dear Evan Hansen' Review: Endearingly Original."

8. Charles Isherwood, "In *Dear Evan Hansen*, a Lonely Teenager, a Viral Lie and a Breakout Star," review of *Dear Evan Hansen*, Music Box Theatre, New York, *New York Times*, December 4, 2016; Charles Isherwood, "*Dear Evan Hansen* Puts a Twist on Teenage Angst," review of *Dear Evan Hansen*, Second Stage Theatre, New York, *New York Times*, May 1, 2016.

9. Winer, "'Dear Evan Hansen' Review: Endearingly Original."

10. I thank one of my anonymous readers for highlighting the slight undercurrent of mockery in this musical's depiction of psychotherapy.

11. For more on this production, see Aleksei Grinenko, *American Psycho*, review of *American Psycho*, Gerald Schoenfeld Theatre, New York, *Theatre Journal* 68, no. 4 (December 2016): 669–70.

12. Michael R. Jackson, *A Strange Loop: A Musical* (New York: Theatre Communications Group, 2020), "Setting," "Characters."

13. Jackson, *A Strange Loop*, 96.

Bibliography

Abbate, Carolyn. *Unsung Voices: Opera and Musical Narrative in the Nineteenth Century*. Princeton, NJ: Princeton University Press, 1991.

Allen, Michelle. *Cleansing the City: Sanitary Geographies in Victorian London*. Athens: Ohio University Press, 2008.

Andreasen, Nancy C. "Editorial: Body and Soul." *American Journal of Psychiatry* 153, no. 5 (May 1996): 589–90.

Astaire, Fred. *Steps in Time*. New York: Da Capo Press, 1979.

Atkinson, Brooks. "Lady in the Dark." *New York Times*, February 2, 1941, xi.

Atkinson, Brooks. "The Play: 'Very Warm for May,' with Score by Jerome Kern and Book by Oscar Hammerstein II." Review of *Very Warm for May*, Alvin Theatre, New York. *New York Times*, November 18, 1939.

Atkinson, Brooks. "The Play in Review: Gertrude Lawrence Appears in Moss Hart's Musical Drama, 'Lady in the Dark,' with a Score by Kurt Weill and Lyrics by Ira Gershwin." Review of *Lady in the Dark*, Alvin Theatre, New York. *New York Times*, January 24, 1941.

Atkinson, Brooks. "Struck by Stage Lightning: Comments on the Theatre Wonders of *Lady in the Dark* with Special Reference to Kurt Weill and Gertrude Lawrence." *New York Times*, September 7, 1941.

Atkinson, Brooks. "Theatre: Good Show." Review of *Gypsy*, Broadway Theatre, New York. *New York Times*, May 22, 1959, 31.

Bach, Steven. *Dazzler: The Life and Times of Moss Hart*. New York: Alfred A. Knopf, 2001.

Bachrach, Leona L. *Deinstitutionalization: An Analytical Review and Sociological Perspective*. Rockville, MD: US Department of Health, Education, and Welfare, 1976.

"Ballet Ballads: Godkin, Holm, and Litz [Programs]." NYPL, Performing Arts Research Collections Dance, MGZB.

Banfield, Stephen. *Jerome Kern*. New Haven, CT: Yale University Press, 2006.

Banfield, Stephen. *Sondheim's Broadway Musicals*. Ann Arbor: University of Michigan Press, 1993.

Barrett, William. "Writers and Madness," *Partisan Review* 14 (1947): 5–22.

Beaufort, John. "A Mouse Goes Musical." Review of *Charlie and Algernon*, Helen Hayes Theatre, New York. *Christian Science Monitor*, September 16, 1980.

Beiswanger, George. "Theatre Today: Symptoms and Surmises." *Journal of Aesthetics and Art Criticism* 3, nos. 9–10 (1944): 19–29.

Beresford, Peter. "What Have Madness and Psychiatric System Survivors Got to Do with Disability and Disability Studies?" *Disability & Society* 15, no. 1 (2000): 167–72.

Berlin, Irving, Howard Lindsay, and Russel Crouse. *Call Me Madam*. Vocal score. New York: Irving Berlin Music Corporation, n.d.

Blitzstein, Marc. *Reuben Reuben: A Musical Play*. Typescript, 1955. New York Public Library, Performing Arts Research Collections Music, JPB91-86.

Boffey, Philip M. "Community Care for Mentally Ill Termed a Failure: Study Says Discharges from Hospitals to Unprepared Centers Are a 'Tragedy.'" *New York Times*, September 13, 1984.

Bond, Christopher G. *Sweeney Todd: The Demon Barber of Fleet Street*. London: Samuel French, 1974.

Bordman, Gerald. Liner notes for Jerome Kern and Oscar Hammerstein II, *Very Warm for May*. AEI Records 008, 1985. Compact disc.

Brantley, Ben. "Fragmented Psyches, Uncomfortable Emotions: Sing Out!" Review of *Next to Normal*, Booth Theatre, New York. *New York Times*, April 15, 2009.

Brantley, Ben. "Stephen Sondheim: The Man Who Felt Too Much." *New York Times*, March 12, 2020.

Breuer, Joseph, and Sigmund Freud. *Studies on Hysteria*. Edited and translated by James Strachey with the collaboration of Anna Freud. New York: Basic Books, 2000.

Breuer, Joseph, and Sigmund Freud. *Studies on Hysteria*. In vol. 2 of *The Standard Edition of the Complete Psychological Works of Sigmund Freud*, translated under the general editorship of James Strachey, in collaboration with Anna Freud. London: Hogarth Press, 1955.

Brewer, Elizabeth. "Coming Out Mad, Coming Out Disabled." In *Literatures of Madness: Disability Studies and Mental Health*, edited by Elizabeth J. Donaldson, 11–30. London: Palgrave, 2018.

Brooks, Peter. "Body and Voice in Melodrama and Opera." In *Siren Songs: Representations of Gender and Sexuality in Opera*, edited by Mary Ann Smart, 118–34. Princeton, NJ: Princeton University Press, 2000.

Brooks, Peter. "Freud's Masterplot." In *Literature and Psychoanalysis, the Question of Reading: Otherwise*, edited by Shoshana Felman, 280–300. Baltimore: John Hopkins University Press, 1982.

Bruce, La Marr Jurelle. *How to Go Mad without Losing Your Mind: Madness and Black Radical Creativity*. Durham, NC: Duke University Press, 2021.

Buhle, Mari Jo. *Feminism and Its Discontents: A Century of Struggle with Psychoanalysis*. Cambridge, MA: Harvard University Press, 1998.

Burnham, John, ed. *After Freud Left: A Century of Psychoanalysis in America*. Chicago: University of Chicago Press, 2012.

Campkin, Ben, and Rosie Cox, eds. *Dirt: New Geographies of Cleanliness and Contamination*. London: I.B. Tauris, 2007.

Cantu, Maya. *American Cinderellas on the Broadway Stage: Imagining the Working Girl from "Irene" to "Gypsy"*. New York: Palgrave, 2015.

"Careless of the Mentally Ill." *New York Times*, October 24, 1979, A30.

Carr, Jay. "Agnes De Mille Steps Out with an Old Friend—'Oklahoma!'" *New York Times*, December 9, 1979.

Carter, Tim. *"Oklahoma!": The Making of an American Musical*. New Haven, CT: Yale University Press, 2007.

Chamberlin, Judi. "The Ex-Patients' Movement: Where We've Been and Where We're Going." *Journal of Mind and Behavior* 11, nos. 3–4 (1990): 323–36.

Chamberlin, Judi. *On Our Own: Patient-Controlled Alternatives to the Mental Health System.* New York: Hawthorn Books, 1978.

Clum, John M. "Acting." In *The Oxford Handbook of the American Musical*, edited by Raymond Knapp, Mitchell Morris, and Stacy Wolf, 309–19. New York: Oxford University Press, 2011.

Coe, Richard L. "Angela Shines; Show Dim." Review of *Dear World*, Mark Hellinger Theatre, New York. *Washington Post*, February 7, 1969, B11.

Cohen, William A. "Victorian Dirt." *Victorian Network* 6, no. 8 (Winter 2015): 1–6.

Cohen, William A., and Ryan Johnson, eds. *Filth: Dirt, Disgust, and Modern Life.* Minneapolis: University of Minnesota Press, 2005.

Cromby, John, David Harper, and Paula Reavey. *Psychology, Mental Health and Distress.* London: Palgrave, 2013.

"The Danger of Dumping the Mentally Ill." *New York Times*, December 26, 1979, A26.

Dear, Michael J., and Jennifer R. Wolch. *Landscapes of Despair: From Deinstitutionalization to Homelessness.* Princeton, NJ: Princeton University Press, 1987.

Delany, Samuel R. *Times Square Red, Times Square Blue.* 20th Anniversary Edition. New York: New York University Press, 2019.

Dellar, Robert. *Splitting in Two: Mad Pride and Punk Rock Oblivion.* London: Unkant Publishers, 2014.

de Mille, Agnes. *Dance to the Piper.* Boston: Little, Brown, 1951.

Derrida, Jacques. "Cogito and the History of Madness." In *Writing and Difference*, translated by Alan Bass, 31–63. Chicago: University of Chicago Press, 1980.

Diamond, Elin. *Unmaking Mimesis: Essays on Feminism and Theatre.* London: Routledge, 1997.

Dietz, Dan. *The Complete Book of 1940s Broadway Musicals.* Lanham, MD: Rowman & Littlefield, 2015.

Dietz, Dan. *The Complete Book of 1980s Broadway Musicals.* Lanham, MD: Rowman & Littlefield, 2016.

Dimen, Muriel. "Strange Hearts: On the Paradoxical Liaison between Psychoanalysis and Feminism." In *Freud: Conflict and Culture*, edited by Michael S. Roth, 207–20. New York: Alfred A. Knopf, 1998.

Douglas, Mary. *Purity and Danger: An Analysis of Concept of Pollution and Taboo.* With a new preface by the author. New York: Routledge, 2002.

Downes, Olin. "Broadway's Gift to Opera: *Oklahoma!* Shows One of the Ways to an Integrated and Indigenous Form of American Lyric Theatre." *New York Times*, June 6, 1943, X5.

Dunst, Alexander. *Madness in Cold War America.* New York: Routledge, 2017.

Eder, Richard. "Critic's Notebook: 'Sweeney's' Dark Side." *New York Times*, March 29, 1979, C16.

Eder, Richard. "Stage: Introducing 'Sweeney Todd.'" Review of *Sweeney Todd: The Demon Barber of Fleet Street*, Uris Theatre, New York. *New York Times*, March 2, 1979, C3.

Eisenberg, Leon. "Mindlessness and Brainlessness in Psychiatry." *British Journal of Psychiatry* 148 (1986): 497–508.

Engel, Lehman. *The American Musical Theater*. Rev. ed. New York: Collier Books, 1975.

Esslin, Martin. *Artaud*. Glasgow: Fontana Collins, 1976.

Ewalt, Jack R., and Patricia L. Ewalt. "History of the Community Psychiatry Movement." *American Journal of Psychiatry* 126, no. 1 (July 1969): 81–90.

Farfan, Penny. *Performing Queer Modernism*. New York: Oxford University Press, 2017.

Felman, Shoshana. *Writing and Madness: Literature/Philosophy/Psychoanalysis*. Translated by Martha Noel Evans and Shoshana Felman. Ithaca, NY: Cornell University Press, 1985.

Fenton, James. "The Barberous Crimes of Sondheim and Prince." Review of *Sweeney Todd: The Demon Barber of Fleet Street*, Theatre Royal, Drury Lane, London. *Sunday Times* (London), July 6, 1980, 40.

Finn, William, and James Lapine. *A New Brain*. New York: Samuel French, 1999.

Fitzpatrick, Michael. "Voices" (blog post). Kimmel Center for the Performing Arts, June 21, 2011. http://blog.kimmelcenter.org/post/6761990169/todays -voices-comes-from-special-guest-michael, accessed October 10, 2018.

Fleming, Michael, and Roger Manvell. *Images of Madness: The Portrayal of Insanity in the Feature Film*. Cranbury, NJ: Associated University Press, 1985.

Foucault, Michel. *History of Madness*. Edited by Jean Khalfa, translated by Jonathan Murphy and Jean Khalfa. London: Routledge, 2006.

Freud, Sigmund. *The Interpretation of Dreams* (1900). In vol. 5 of *The Standard Edition of the Complete Psychological Works of Sigmund Freud*, translated under the general editorship of James Strachey, in collaboration with Anna Freud. London: Hogarth Press, 1953.

Freud, Sigmund. *The Interpretation of Dreams*. Translated by Joyce Crick. New York: Oxford University Press, 1999.

Freud, Sigmund. *Introductory Lectures on Psycho-Analysis*. Translated and edited by James Strachey. London: Hogarth Press, 1953.

Freud, Sigmund. "A Metapsychological Supplement to the Theory of Dreams." In vol. 14 of *The Standard Edition of the Complete Psychological Works of Sigmund Freud*, translated under the general editorship of James Strachey, in collaboration with Anna Freud. London: Hogarth Press, 1955.

Freud, Sigmund. *The Standard Edition of the Complete Psychological Works of Sigmund Freud*. Vol. 4, translated under the general editorship of James Strachey, in collaboration with Anna Freud. London: Hogarth Press, 1953.

Friedman, Josh Alan. *Tales of Times Square*. New York: Delacorte Press, 1986.

Frosh, Stephen. *Psychoanalysis outside the Clinic: Interventions in Psychosocial Studies*. New York: Palgrave Macmillan, 2010.

Fuller, Robert. *Americans and the Unconscious*. New York: Oxford University Press, 1986.

"Fundraiser: *Next to Normal*." National Alliance for Mental Illness, Georgia. https://namiga.org/fundraiser-next-to-normal/, accessed October 1, 2018.

Gabbard, Glen O., and Krin Gabbard. *Psychiatry and the Cinema*. 2nd ed. Washington, DC: American Psychiatric Press, 1999.

Gaffney, L. G. "*Reuben Reuben*, at Shubert, Misses Fire." Review of *Reuben Reuben*, Shubert Theatre, Boston. *Boston Record*, October 11, 1955.

Gardner, Kara Anne. *Agnes de Mille: Telling Stories in Broadway Dance*. New York: Oxford University Press, 2016.

Gerould, Daniel, ed. *Melodrama*. New York: New York Literary Forum, 1980.

Gibbs, Wolcott. "Crying in the Wilderness." Review of *Lady in the Dark*, Alvin Theatre, New York. *New Yorker*, February 1, 1941, 27.

Gibbs, Wolcott. "Such a Pretty Piece." Review of *The Day before Spring*, National Theatre, New York. *New Yorker*, December 1, 1945, 52.

Gifford, G. E., ed. *Psychoanalysis, Psychotherapy, and the New England Medical Scene, 1894–1944*. New York: Science History Publications, 1978.

Gill, Brendan. "A Barber's Revenge." Review of *Sweeney Todd: The Demon Barber of Fleet Street*, Uris Theatre, New York. *New Yorker*, March 12, 1979.

Gilvey, John Anthony. *Before the Parade Passes By: Gower Champion and the Glorious American Musical*. New York: St. Martin's Press, 2005.

"Glenn Close and Patrick Kennedy on the Weight of Mental Illness." Conversation with Philip Galanes. *New York Times*, March 11, 2017.

Goffman, Erving. *Asylums: Essays on the Social Situation of Mental Patients and Other Inmates*. Chicago: Aldine, 1961.

Goffman, Erving. *Stigma: Notes on the Management of Spoiled Identity*. New York: Simon and Schuster, 1963.

Goldman, James, and Stephen Sondheim. *Follies: A Musical*. New York: Random House, 1971.

Gottfried, Martin. "Dear World." Review of *Dear World*, Mark Hellinger Theatre, New York. *Women's Wear Daily*, February 7, 1969, 33.

Gottfried, Martin. *Sondheim*. New York: Harry N. Abrams, 1993.

Gordon, Joanne. *Art Isn't Easy: The Achievement of Stephen Sondheim*. Carbondale: Southern Illinois University Press, 1990.

Gordon, Robert. *The Oxford Handbook of Sondheim Studies*. New York: Oxford University Press, 2015.

Graber, Naomi. *Kurt Weill's America*. New York: Oxford University Press, 2021.

Graduate School and University Center of the City University of New York. *West 42nd Street: "The Bright Light Zone"*. New York: Graduate School and University Center of the City University of New York, 1978.

Grant, Mark N. *The Rise and Fall of the Broadway Musical*. Boston: Northeastern University Press, 2004.

Green, Jesse. "The Essential Musical Dramatist Who Taught Us to Hear." *New York Times*, November 26, 2021.

Green, Jessie, Linda Winer, and Elizabeth Vincentelli. "Theater Talk: Holiday Critics 2016," interview by Michael Reidel and Susan Haskins, December 9, 2016, PBS. https://www.youtube.com/watch?v=GWGG9YJXsy8

Grinenko, Aleksei. "American Psycho." Review of *American Psycho*, Gerald Schoenfeld Theatre, New York. *Theatre Journal* 68, no. 4 (December 2016): 669–70.

Grinenko, Aleksei. "The Eye of the Storm: Reading *Next to Normal* with Psychoanalysis." In *The Routledge Companion to the Contemporary Musical*, edited by Jessica Sternfeld and Elizabeth Wollman, 283–93. London: Routledge, 2019.

Grinenko, Aleksei. "*Follies* Embodied: A Kleinian Perspective." *Studies in Musical Theatre* 6, no. 3 (2012): 317–24.

Grinenko, Aleksei. "'Is That Just Disgusting?': Mapping the Social Geographies of Filth and Madness in *Sweeney Todd.*" *Theatre Journal* 68, no. 2 (2016): 231–48.

Grob, Gerald N. "The Forging of Mental Health Policy in America: World War II to the New Frontier." *Journal of the History of Medicine and Allied Sciences* 42 (1987): 410–46.

Grob, Gerald N. *From Asylum to Community: Mental Health Policy in Modern America.* Princeton, NJ: Princeton University Press, 1991.

Grob, Gerald N. *The Mad among Us: The History of the Care of America's Mentally Ill.* New York: Free Press, 1994.

Grob, Gerald. "Psychiatry and Social Activism: The Politics of a Specialty in Postwar America." *Bulletin of the History of Medicine* 60, no. 4 (Winter 1986): 477–501.

Gussow, Mel. "Theater: A Man, a Mouse and Making of a Genius." Review of *Charlie and Algernon*, Terrace Theater, Washington DC. *New York Times*, March 12, 1980.

Hacking, Ian. *Mad Travelers: Reflections on the Reality of Transient Mental Illnesses.* Charlottesville: University Press of Virginia, 1998.

Hale, Nathan J. *Freud and the Americans: The Beginnings of Psychoanalysis in the United States, 1876–1917.* New York: Oxford University Press, 1995.

Hale, Nathan J. *Freud and the Americans: The Rise and Crisis of Psychoanalysis in the United States, 1917–1985.* New York: Oxford University Press, 1995.

Hall, Laura Lee. "The Biology of Mental Disorders." *Journal of the American Medical Association* 269, no. 7 (February 1993): 844.

Hamilton, John T. *Music, Madness, and the Unworking of Language.* New York: Columbia University Press, 2008.

Hammerstein, Oscar, II. "In Re 'Oklahoma!': The Adaptor-Lyricist Describes How the Musical Hit Came into Being." *New York Times*, May 23, 1943, X1.

Hammerstein, Oscar, II. *Lyrics by Oscar Hammerstein II.* New York: Simon and Schuster, 1949.

Hammerstein, Oscar, II. *Very Warm for May: A Musical Play.* Typescript, 1939. New York Public Library, Performing Arts Research Collections Theatre, NCOF+ (Hammerstein, O. Very Warm for May).

Hand, Richard J., and Michael Wilson. *Grand-Guignol: The French Theatre of Horror.* Exeter: University of Exeter Press, 2002.

Harmetz, Aljean. "King of Hearts'—a Film That Refused to Die." *Los Angeles Times*, August 11, 1974.

Harper, Stephen. *Madness, Power and the Media: Class, Gender and Race in Popular Representations of Mental Distress.* New York: Palgrave Macmillan, 2009.

Hart, Dorothy, and Robert Kimball, eds. *The Complete Lyrics of Lorenz Hart.* New York: Alfred A. Knopf, 1986.

Hart, Moss, Ira Gershwin, and Kurt Weill. *Lady in the Dark.* New York: Random House, 1941.

Henninger, Daniel. "Why Make a War Musical without War?" Review of *King of Hearts*, Minskoff Theatre, New York. *Wall Street Journal*, October 24, 1978, 24.

Herbert, Christopher. *Culture and Anomie: Ethnographic Imagination in the Nineteenth Century*. Chicago: University of Chicago Press, 1991.

Herman, Jerry. *Dear World*. Typescript, 1967. New York Public Library, Performing Arts Research Collections Theatre, RM4475A.

Herman, Jerry. *Dear World*. Typescript, 1968. New York Public Library, Performing Arts Research Collections Theatre, RM4475B.

Herman, Jerry. *Showtune: A Memoir*. With Marilyn Stasio. New York: Donald I. Fine Books, 1996.

Herman, Robin. "Carey Says City Worsens Plight of the Homeless: Defends State on Releases from Mental Hospitals." *New York Times*, December 29, 1980.

Hinton, Stephen. *Weill's Musical Theater: Stages of Reform*. Berkeley: University of California Press, 2012.

Hirsch, Foster. *Harold Prince and the American Musical*. New York: Cambridge University Press, 1989.

Hirsch, Sherry, Joe Kennedy Adams, Leonard Roy Frank, Wade Hudson, Richard Keene, Gail Krawitz-Keene, David Richman, and Robert Roth, eds. *Madness Network News Reader*. San Francisco: Glide Publications, 1974.

Hobe. "Show on Broadway: *Dear World*." Review of *Dear World*, Hellinger Theatre, New York. *Variety*, February 12, 1969.

Hopper, Kim, Ellen Baxter, Stuart Cox, and Laurence Klein. *One Year Later: The Homeless Poor in New York City, 1982*. New York: Institute for Social Welfare Research, 1982.

Horowitz, Mark Eden. *Sondheim on Music: Minor Details and Major Decisions*. 2nd ed. Lanham, MD: Scarecrow Press, 2010.

Horowitz, Mark Eden. *Sondheim on Music: Minor Details and Major Decisions*. Less Is More Edition. Lanham, MD: Scarecrow Press, 2019.

Horwitz, Allan V. *Creating Mental Illness*. Chicago: University of Chicago Press, 2002.

"How *Dear Evan Hansen* Found His Voice." *Playbill*, December 2016.

Howe, Blake, Stephanie Jensen-Moulton, Neil Lerner, and Joseph Straus, eds. *The Oxford Handbook of Musical and Disability Studies*. New York: Oxford University Press, 2016.

Hughes, Elinor. "Gertrude Lawrence in Hart-Weill-Gershwin Musical." Review of *Lady in the Dark*, Colonial Theatre, Boston. *Boston Herald*, December 31, 1940.

Hughes, Elinor. "Theater." Review of *Reuben Reuben*, Shubert Theater, Boston. *Boston Herald*, October 11, 1955.

Hunter, Diane. "Hysteria, Psychoanalysis, and Feminism: The Case of Anna O." *Feminist Studies* 9, no. 3 (Autumn 1983): 464–88.

Ilson, Carol. *Harold Prince: A Director's Journey*. New York: Limelight Editions, 2000.

Isherwood, Charles. "*Dear Evan Hansen* Puts a Twist on Teenage Angst." Review of *Dear Evan Hansen*, Second Stage Theatre, New York. *New York Times*, May 1, 2016.

Isherwood, Charles. "In *Dear Evan Hansen*, a Lonely Teenager, a Viral Lie and a Breakout Star." Review of *Dear Evan Hansen*, Music Box Theatre, New York. *New York Times*, December 4, 2016.

Jackson, Michael R. *A Strange Loop: A Musical*. New York: Theatre Communications Group, 2020.

James, William. *The Principles of Psychology*, Vol. 1. New York: Henry Holt, 1890.

Jameson, Fredric. *Marxism and Form: Twentieth-Century Dialectical Theories of Literature*. Princeton, NJ: Princeton University Press, 1971.

Jankélévitch, Vladimir. *Music and the Ineffable*. Translated by Carolyn Abbate. Princeton, NJ: Princeton University Press, 2003.

Jannarone, Kimberly. *Artaud and His Doubles*. Ann Arbor: University of Michigan Press, 2010.

Jekyll & Hyde: The Musical. Music by Frank Wildhorn, book and lyrics by Leslie Bricusse, stage direction by Robin Phillips, directed for television by Don Roy King. Broadway Television Network Presents, 2001. DVD.

Jenkins, Philip. *Decade of Nightmares: The End of the Sixties and the Making of Eighties America*. New York: Oxford University Press, 2006.

Jones, John Bush. *Our Musicals, Ourselves: A Social History of the American Musical Theatre*. Hanover, NH: University Press of New England, 2003.

Jones, Susan. *Literature, Modernism, and Dance*. New York: Oxford University Press, 2013.

Kalem, T. E., Gerald Rabkin, and William Wolf. "Critics' Roundtable Discuss *Sweeney Todd*." *New York Theatre Review*, April 1979, 13–20.

Kaufman, George S. "Musical Comedy—or Musical Serious?" *New York Times*, November 3, 1957, 223.

Keegan, Rebecca. "Making of 'Joker': How Todd Phillips' 'Bold Swing' Became a Study in Madness." *Hollywood Reporter*, December 27, 2019.

Kelly, Kevin. "'King of Hearts,' It's Not Just Another Mindless Musical." Review of *King of Hearts*, Colonial Theatre, Boston. *Boston Globe*, October 5, 1978, B9.

Kelly, Kevin. "*Prettybelle* Opens at Shubert." Review of *Prettybelle*, Shubert Theatre, Boston. *Boston Globe*, February 2, 1971, 33.

Kennedy, John F. "Special Message on Mental Illness and Mental Retardation." February 5, 1963, Papers of John F. Kennedy, President's Office Files, 1–3. https://www.jfklibrary.org/Asset-Viewer/Archives/JFKPOF-052-012.aspx

Kenton, Edna. *The Provincetown Players and the Playwrights' Theatre, 1915–1922*. Edited by Travis Bogard and Jackson R. Bryer. Jefferson, NC: McFarland, 2004.

Kern, Jerome, and Oscar Hammerstein II. *Very Warm for May: A Musical Comedy*. AEI Records 008. 1985. Compact disc.

Kerr, Walter. "Is 'Sweeney' on Target?" Review of *Sweeney Todd: The Demon Barber of Fleet Street*, Uris Theatre, New York. *New York Times*, March 11, 1979.

Kerr, Walter. "*King of Hearts* Swings on Spectacle, Not Plot." Review of *King of Hearts*, Minskoff Theatre, New York. *The Sun*, October 29, 1978, D7.

Kerr, Walter. "When Angela Sings 'I Will Not Have It.'" *New York Times*, February 16, 1969, D1.

Keyes, Daniel. *Algernon, Charlie, and I: A Writer's Journey*. Boca Raton, FL: Challenge Press, 1999.

Kim, Annabel L. *Cacaphonies: The Excremental Canon of French Literature*. Minneapolis: University of Minnesota Press, 2022.

Kirle, Bruce. *Unfinished Show Business: Broadway Musicals as Works-in-Process*. Carbondale: Southern Illinois University Press, 2005.

Kissel, Howard. "'King of Hearts': The Theater." Review of *King of Hearts*, Minskoff Theatre, New York. *Women's Wear Daily*, October 24, 1978, 40.

Kitt, Tom, and Brian Yorkey. "Conversation: Pulitzer Prize Winners in Drama, Tom Kitt and Brian Yorkey of *Next to Normal*." Interview by Murrey Jacobson. *NewsHour*, PBS, April 14, 2010. https://www.pbs.org/newshour/arts/co nversation-pulitzer-prize-winners-in-drama-tom-kitt-and-brian-yorkey-of -next-to-normal

Kitt, Tom, and Brian Yorkey. *Next to Normal*. New York: Theatre Communications Group, 2010.

Klein, Melanie. *Envy and Gratitude and Other Works, 1946–1963*. Vol. 3 of *The Writings of Melanie Klein*. New York: Free Press, 1984.

Klerman, Gerald, George Vaillant, Robert Spitzer, and Robert Michaels. "Commentary: A Debate on DSM-III." *American Journal of Psychiatry* 141, no. 4 (April 1984): 539–53.

Knapp, Raymond. *The American Musical and the Performance of Personal Identity*. Princeton, NJ: Princeton University Press, 2006.

Knapp, Raymond, and Zelda Knapp. "Musicals and the Envoicing of Mental Illness and Madness: From *Lady in the Dark* to *Man of La Mancha* (and Beyond)." *Journal of Interdisciplinary Voice Studies* 4, no. 2 (2019): 209–23.

Knowles, Caroline. *Bedlam on the Streets*. London: Routledge, 2000.

Kristeva, Julia. *Melanie Klein*. Translated by Ross Guberman. New York: Columbia University Press, 2001.

Kristeva, Julia. *Powers of Horror: An Essay on Abjection*. Translated by Leon S. Roudiez. New York: Columbia University Press, 1982.

Kroll, Jack. "The Blood Runs Cold." Review of *Sweeney Todd: The Demon Barber of Fleet Street*, Uris Theatre, New York. *Newsweek*, March 12, 1979, 101.

Kuchwara, Michael. "Mental Illness Shatters Family in *Next to Normal*." Review of *Next to Normal*, Booth Theatre, New York. *Associated Press*, April 15, 2009.

Lahr, John. "Innocence Abroad: Adam Guettel's Italian Romance." *New Yorker*, February 2, 2004.

Laing, R. D. *The Politics of Experience*. New York: Pantheon Books, 1967.

Land. "Play on Broadway: Lady in the Dark." Review of *Lady in the Dark*, Alvin Theatre, New York. *Variety*, January 29, 1941.

Langner, Lawrence. *The Magic Curtain: The Story of a Life in Two Fields, Theatre and Invention, by the Founder of the Theatre Guild*. New York: Dutton, 1951.

Lansbury, Angela. "Angela Lansbury (#105)." Interview by Howard Sherman and John von Sooste. *Downstage Center*, American Theater Wing. iTunes. June 16, 2006.

Lansbury, Angela. Interview. MasterworksbwayVEVO, Sony Music Entertainment. Published August 15, 2012. https://www.youtube.com/watch?v=hqtH 0sVU8_8

Laporte, Dominique. *History of Shit*. Translated by Nadia Benabid and Rodolphe el-Khoury. Cambridge, MA: MIT Press, 2000.

Latouche, John, and Jerome Moross. *Ballet Ballads*. Typescript. New York Public Library, Performing Arts Research Collections Theatre, RM4553.

Latouche, John, and Jerome Moross. *The Golden Apple*. New York: Random House, 1954.

Laurents, Arthur, Leonard Bernstein, Stephen Sondheim, and Jerome Robbins. *West Side Story: A Musical*. New York: Random House, 1958.

Laurents, Arthur, and Stephen Sondheim. *Anyone Can Whistle: A Musical Fable*. New York: Random House, 1965.

Lee, Eugene. Interview by Howard Sherman. "Eugene Lee (#328)." *Downstage Center*. American Theater Wing. iTunes. July 27, 2011.

Lees, Gene. *Inventing Champagne: The Worlds of Lerner and Loewe*. New York: St. Martin's Press, 1990.

Lefrançois, Brenda A., Robert Menzies, and Geoffrey Reaume, eds. *Mad Matters: A Critical Reader in Canadian Mad Studies*. Toronto: Canadian Scholars' Press, 2013.

Lerner, Alan Jay. *The Musical Theatre: A Celebration*. New York: Da Capo Press, 1986.

Lerner, Alan Jay. *The Street Where I Live*. New York: Norton, 1978.

Lerner, Alan Jay, and Frederick Loewe. *The Day before Spring*. Typescript. New York Public Library, Performing Arts Research Collections Theatre, RM2326.

Lewis, Bradley. "A Mad Fight: Psychiatry and Disability Activism." In *The Disability Studies Reader*, 5th ed., edited by Lennard J. Davis, 102–18. London: Routledge, 2017.

Link, Peter. *King of Hearts*. Typescript, 1978. New York Public Library, Performing Arts Research Collections Theatre, RM1838.

Locke, Ralph E. "What Are These Women Doing in Opera?" In *En Travesti: Women, Gender Subversion, Opera*, edited by Corinne E. Blackmer and Patricia Juliana Smith, 59–98. New York: Columbia University Press, 1995.

Lucas, Craig, and Adam Guettel. *The Light in the Piazza*. New York: Theatre Communications Group, 2007.

Luhrmann, T. M. *Of Two Minds: The Growing Disorder in American Psychiatry*. New York: Alfred A. Knopf, 2001.

Lunbeck, Elizabeth. "Psychiatry." In *The Cambridge History of Science*, vol. 7, *The Modern Social Sciences*, edited by Theodore M. Porter and Dorothy Ross, 663–77. Cambridge: Cambridge University Press, 2003.

Lyons, Richard D. "How Release of Mental Patients Began: Policy Makers Recall Their Reasoning and Reflect on Outcome." *New York Times*, October 30, 1984.

Maisel, Albert Q. "Bedlam 1946." *Life*, May 6, 1946.

Makari, George. *Soul Machine: The Invention of the Modern Mind*. New York: Norton, 2015.

Maloney, Alta. "*Reuben Reuben* Opens, New Musical at Shubert." Review of *Reuben Reuben*, Shubert Theatre, Boston. *Boston Traveler*, October 11, 1955, 59.

Mandelbaum, Ken. *Not since "Carrie": Forty Years of Broadway Musical Flops*. New York: St. Martin's Press, 1991.

Marcus, Steven. "Freud and Dora: Story, History, Case History." In *In Dora's*

Case: Freud—Hysteria—Feminism, 2nd ed., edited by Charles Bernheimer and Clare Kahane, 56–91. New York: Columbia University Press, 1990.

Marks, Peter. "After a New York Run, an Unusual 'Next' Step." *Washington Post*, November 23, 2008.

Marks, Peter. "Theater Review: *Next to Normal* at Kennedy Center." Review of *Next to Normal*, John F. Kennedy Center for the Performing Arts, Washington DC. *Washington Post*, June 30, 2011.

Marks, Peter. "Theatre Review of *Next to Normal* and *Hair* on Broadway." Review of *Next to Normal*, Booth Theatre, New York. *Washington Post*, April 16, 2009.

Martin, Emily. *Bipolar Expeditions: Mania and Depression in American Culture.* Princeton, NJ: Princeton University Press, 2009.

Maslon, Laurence, ed. *American Musicals, 1950–1969: The Complete Books & Lyrics of Eight Broadway Classics.* New York: Library of America, 2014.

Mayes, Rick, and Allan V. Horwitz. "DSM-III and the Revolution in the Classification of Mental Illness." *Journal of the History of the Behavioral Sciences* 41, no. 3 (Summer 2005): 249–67.

Mazzie, Marin. "Marin Mazzie on the Irresistible Pull of *Next to Normal*." Interview by Kathy Henderson. Broadway.com, July 26, 2010. https://www.broadway.com/buzz/153099/marin-mazzie-on-the-irresistible-pull-of-next-to-normal/

McCarren, Felicia. "The 'Symptomatic Act' circa 1900: Hysteria, Hypnosis, Electricity, Dance." *Critical Inquiry* 21, no. 4 (Summer 1995): 748–74.

McClary, Susan. *Feminine Endings: Music, Gender, and Sexuality.* Minneapolis: University of Minnesota Press, 1991.

McClung, Bruce D. *"Lady in the Dark": Biography of a Musical.* New York: Oxford University Press, 2007.

McGill, Craig M. "Sondheim's Use of the 'Herrmann Chord' in *Sweeney Todd*." *Studies in Musical Theatre* 6, no. 3 (2012): 291–312.

McNally, Terrence, Arthur Laurents, Stephen Sondheim, and Jule Styne. "Landmark Symposium: The Genesis of *Gypsy*." *Dramatists Guild Quarterly* 18, no. 3 (Autumn 1981): 10–30.

McMillin, Scott. *The Musical as Drama: A Study of the Principles and Conventions behind Musical Shows from Kern to Sondheim.* Princeton, NJ: Princeton University Press, 2006.

McNulty, Charles. "Theater Review: *Next to Normal* at the Ahmanson Theatre." Review of *Next to Normal*, Ahmanson Theatre, Los Angeles. *Los Angeles Times*, November 29, 2010.

Meltzer, Françoise. "Unconscious." In *Critical Terms for Literary Study*, edited by Frank Lentricchia and Thomas McLaughlin, 147–62. Chicago: University of Chicago Press, 1995.

Menninger, William C. "Psychiatric Experience in the War, 1941–1946." *American Journal of Psychiatry* 103, no. 5 (March 1947): 577–86.

Merrill, Bob, and Jule Styne. *Rape of Prettybelle*. Typescript. New York Public Library, Performing Arts Research Collections Theatre, RM7381.

Metzl, Jonathan M. *The Protest Psychosis: How Schizophrenia Became a Black Disease.* Boston: Beacon Press, 2009.

Micale, Mark S., ed. *The Mind of Modernism: Medicine, Psychology, and the Cultural Arts in Europe and America, 1880–1940*. Stanford, CA: Stanford University Press, 2004.

Micale, Mark S., and Roy Porter, eds. *Discovering the History of Psychiatry*. New York: Oxford University Press, 1994.

Miller, D. A. *Place for Us: [Essay on the Broadway Musical]*. Cambridge, MA: Harvard University Press, 1998.

Mitchell, David T., and Sharon L. Snyder. *Narrative Prosthesis: Disability and the Dependencies of Discourse*. Ann Arbor: University of Michigan Press, 2000.

Moi, Toril. "Patriarchal Thought and the Drive for Knowledge." In *Between Feminism and Psychoanalysis*, edited by Teresa Brennan, 189–205. London: Routledge, 1989.

Mordden, Ethan. *Beautiful Mornin': The Broadway Musical in the 1940s*. New York: Oxford University Press, 1999.

Morehouse, Rebecca. "*Prettybelle*'s Realism Lures Champion Back." *Boston Globe*, January 31, 1971, A81.

Most, Andrea. *Making Americans: Jews and the Broadway Musical*. Cambridge, MA: Harvard University Press, 2004.

Nagle, Robin. *Picking Up: On the Streets and behind the Trucks with the Sanitation Workers of New York City*. New York: Farrar, Straus and Giroux, 2013.

Nathan, George Jean. *The Theatre Book of the Year, 1947–1948: A Record and an Interpretation*. New York: Alfred A. Knopf, 1948.

Neely, Carol Thomas. *Distracted Subjects: Madness and Gender in Shakespeare and Early Modern Culture*. Ithaca, NY: Cornell University Press, 2004.

"New Musical in Manhattan." Unsigned review of *Very Warm for May*, Alvin Theatre, New York. *Time*, November 27, 1939.

"*Next to Normal*, Cast Reunion." *Stars in the House with Seth Rudetsky and James Wesley*. YouTube, September 15, 2020. https://www.youtube.com/watch?v=t LK_bXZjT_4&feature=youtu.be

Nichols, Lewis. "The Play." Review of *The Day before Spring*, National Theatre, New York. *New York Times*, November 23, 1945, 27.

"Normal Life with Kyle Dean Massey—Video Blog #10," Broadway.com, *YouTube*, April 5, 2010. https://youtu.be/pb3m_vE5zrE

Oliver, Michael. *The Politics of Disablement*. London: Palgrave, 1990.

Oliver, Michael. *Understanding Disability: From Theory to Practice*. London: Macmillan, 1996.

"On Collaboration between Authors and Directors." *Dramatists Guild Quarterly* 16, no. 2 (Summer 1979): 14–34.

Pankratz, Anette. "The Pleasures in the Horrors of Eating Human Flesh: Stephen Sondheim and Hugh Wheeler's *Sweeney Todd*." In *The Pleasures and Horrors of Eating: The Cultural History of Eating in Anglophone Literature*, edited by Marion Gymnich and Norbert Lennartz, 387–407. Göttingen: V&R Unipress, 2010.

Parr, Hester. *Mental Health and Social Space: Towards Inclusionary Geographies*. Oxford: Blackwell, 2008.

Pfister, Joel. *Staging Depth: Eugene O'Neill and the Politics of Psychological Discourse*. Chapel Hill: University of North Carolina Press, 1995.

Pfister, Joel, and Nancy Schnog, eds. *Inventing the Psychological: Toward a Cultural History of Emotional Life in America*. New Haven, CT: Yale University Press, 1997.

Philips, Adam. *Missing Out: In Praise of the Unlived Life*. New York: Farrar, Straus, and Giroux, 2012.

Pickens, Therí Alyce. *Black Madness :: Mad Blackness*. Durham, NC: Duke University Press, 2019.

Platt, Ben, Jennifer Laura Thompson, and Rachel Bay Jones, "Theater Talk: *Dear Evan Hansen* Actors." Interview by Susan Haskins and Jesse Green. *Theatre Talk*, PBS, January 27, 2017. https://www.youtube.com/watch?v=21Hk7c8rTjk

Pollack, Howard. *Marc Blitzstein: His Life, His Work, His World*. New York: Oxford University Press, 2012.

Poole, Jennifer M., and Jennifer Ward. "'Breaking Open the Bone': Storying, Sanism, and Mad Grief." In *Mad Matters: A Critical Reader in Canadian Mad Studies*, edited by Brenda A. Lefrançois, Robert Menzies, and Geoffrey Reaume, 94–104. Toronto: Canadian Scholars' Press, 2013.

Postlewait, Thomas. "The Criteria for Periodization in Theatre History." *Theatre Journal* 40, no. 3 (October 1988): 299–318.

"Prettybelle Won't Reach New York." *Boston Globe*, March 2, 1971, 35.

Price, Margaret. *Mad at School: Rhetorics of Mental Disability and Academic Life*. Ann Arbor: University of Michigan Press, 2011.

Prince, Harold. "Harold Prince (#200)." Interview by Howard Sherman and John von Soosten. *Downstage Center*. American Theater Wing. iTunes. May 2, 2008.

Reiser, Morton F. "Are Psychiatric Educators 'Losing the Mind?'" *American Journal of Psychiatry* 145, no. 2 (February 1988): 148–53.

Rich, Frank. "Theater: Charlie and Algernon." Review of *Charlie and Algernon*, Helen Hayes Theater, New York. *New York Times*, September 15, 1980, C17.

Rieff, Philip. *Freud: The Mind of the Moralist*. Chicago: University of Chicago Press, 1971.

Ries, Frank W. D. "Albertina Rasch: The Broadway Career." *Dance Chronicle* 6, no. 2 (1983): 95–137.

Riley, Clayton. "A New Black Magic—and They Weave It Well." Review of *Ain't Supposed to Die a Natural Death*, Ethel Barrymore Theatre, New York. *New York Times*, November 7, 1971.

Ripley, Alice. "Depth Interview: Alice Ripley on *Next to Normal* Tour and Career Retrospective." By Pat Cerasaro. Broadwayworld.com, December 11, 2010. https://www.broadwayworld.com/article/InDepth-InterView-Alice-Ripley-on-NEXT-TO-NORMAL-Tour-A-Career-Retrospective-20101211

Ripley, Alice. *In Focus with Eden Lane*. Interview by Eden Lane. PBS, March 1, 2011. https://www.youtube.com/watch?v=RTcBaVVfZ94&t=1337s

Rissmiller, David J., and Joshua H. Rissmiller. "Evolution of the Antipsychiatry Movement into Mental Health Consumerism." *Psychiatric Services* 57, no. 6 (June 2006): 863–66.

Roach, Joseph. *Cities of the Dead: Circum-Atlantic Performance*. New York: Columbia University Press, 1996.

Rodgers, Richard, and Oscar Hammerstein II. *6 Plays by Rodgers and Hammerstein*. New York: Random House, 1958.

Rogers, Bradley. "The Emergence of Integrated Musical: Otto Harbach, Oratorical Theory, and the Cinema." *Theatre Survey* 63, no. 2 (May 2022): 160–82.

Rogers, David, and Charles Strouse. *Charlie and Algernon*. Chicago: Dramatic Publishing Company, 1981.

Rooney, David. "*Next to Normal*: This Original New Pop-Rock Musical Has Benefited Unequivocally from Treatment." Review of *Next to Normal*, Booth Theatre, New York. *Variety*, April 15, 2009.

Rosand, Ellen. "Operatic Madness: A Challenge to Convention." In *Music and Text: Critical Inquiries*, edited by Steven Paul Scher, 241–87. Cambridge: Cambridge University Press, 1992.

Ross, Dorothy, ed. *Modernist Impulses in the Human Sciences, 1870–1930*. Baltimore: John Hopkins University Press, 1994.

Sacks, Oliver. "The Other Road: Freud as Neurologist." In *Freud: Conflict and Culture*, edited by Michael S. Roth, 221–34. New York: Alfred A. Knopf, 1998.

Savran, David. *Communists, Cowboys, and Queers: The Politics of Masculinity in the Work of Arthur Miller and Tennessee Williams*. Minneapolis: University of Minnesota Press, 1992.

Savran, David. "The Do-Re-Mi of Musical Historiography." In *Changing the Subject: Marvin Carlson and Theater Studies, 1959–2009*, edited by Joseph Roach, 223–37. Ann Arbor: University of Michigan Press, 2009.

Savran, David. *Highbrow/Lowdown: Theater, Jazz, and the Making of the New Middle Class*. Ann Arbor: University of Michigan Press, 2009.

Savran, David. *In Their Own Words: Contemporary American Playwrights*. New York: Theatre Communications Group, 1988.

Savran, David. *A Queer Sort of Materialism*. Ann Arbor: University of Michigan Press, 2003.

Savran, David. "Towards a Historiography of the Popular." *Theatre Survey* 45, no. 2 (2004): 211–17.

Sederholm, Jack Paul. "The Musical Directing Career and Stagecraft Contributions of Hassard Short, 1919–1952." PhD dissertation. Wayne State University, 1974.

Sedgwick, Eve Kosofsky. "Melanie Klein and the Difference Affect Makes." *South Atlantic Quarterly* 106, no. 3 (Summer 2007): 625–42.

Sedgwick, Eve Kosofsky. *Touching Feeling: Affect, Pedagogy, Performativity*. Durham, NC: Duke University Press, 2003.

Schlesinger, Judith. "Psychology, Evil, and *Sweeney Todd*, or 'Don't I Know You, Mister?'" In *Stephen Sondheim: A Casebook*, edited by Joanne Gordon, 125–41. New York: Routledge, 2014.

Sievers, W. David. *Freud on Broadway: A History of Psychoanalysis and the American Drama*. New York: Cooper Square, 1970.

Simon, John. "A Little Knife Music." Review of *Sweeney Todd*, Uris Theatre, New York. *New Yorker*, March 19, 1979.

Skues, Richard A. *Sigmund Freud and the History of Anna O.: Reopening a Closed Case*. London: Palgrave Macmillan, 2006.

Smith, Emma. "Approaching Shakespeare: Macbeth." Lecture, Oxford University. iTunes. November 2, 2010.

Smith, Macklin. *Prudentius' Psychomachia: A Re-examination*. Princeton, NJ: Princeton University Press, 1976.

Smith, Wendy. *Real Life Drama: The Group Theatre and America, 1931–1940*. New York: Grove Weidenfeld, 1990.

Sokol, Robert. "Good and Crazy: Neil Patrick Harris Describes Being Very Alive in *Company*." *Sondheim Review* 18, no. 1 (Fall 2011): 29–30.

Sondheim, Stephen. *Anyone Can Whistle: Vocal Score*. N.p.: Burthen Music, 1968.

Sondheim, Stephen. *Finishing the Hat: Collected Lyrics (1954–1981) with Attendant Comments, Principles, Heresies, Grudges, Whines and Anecdotes*. New York: Alfred A. Knopf, 2010.

Sondheim, Stephen. "In Conversation with Stephen Sondheim." Interview by Craig Carnelia. *Dramatist* 9, no. 5 (May–June 2007): 16–23.

Sondheim, Stephen. Interview by James Lipton. "The Art of the Musical." *Paris Review* 39, no. 142 (Spring 1997): 258–78.

Sondheim, Stephen. Interview by Max Wilk. Audio CD, 1991. New York Public Library, Performing Arts Research Collections Recorded Sound, LDC 52502.

Sondheim, Stephen, and George Furth. *Company: A Musical Comedy*. New York: Theatre Communications Group, 1996.

Sondheim, Stephen, and James Lapine. *Passion: A Musical*. New York: Theatre Communications Group, 1994.

Sondheim, Stephen, and Hugh Wheeler. *Sweeney Todd: The Demon Barber of Fleet Street*. New York: Applause Theatre Book Publishers, 1991.

Sondheim, Stephen, and Hugh Wheeler. *Sweeney Todd: The Demon Barber of Fleet Street*. New York Public Library: Theatre on Film and Tape Archive, 1979, DVD, 157 min.

Sondheim, Stephen, and Hugh Wheeler, *Sweeney Todd: The Demon Barber of Fleet Street*. Vocal score. New York: Rilting Music, 1997.

Spelman, Nicola. *Popular Music and the Myths of Madness*. Farnham: Ashgate, 2012.

Stallybrass, Peter, and Allon White. *The Politics and Poetics of Transgression*. Ithaca, NY: Cornell University Press, 1986.

Star. "Show Out of Town: *Prettybelle*." Review of *Prettybelle*, Shubert Theatre, Boston. *Variety*, February 3, 1971.

Staub, Michael E. *Madness Is Civilization: When the Diagnosis Was Social, 1948–1980*. Chicago: University of Chicago Press, 2011.

Sternfeld, Jessica, and Elizabeth L. Wollman. "After the 'Golden Age.'" In *The Oxford Handbook of the American Musical*, edited by Raymond Knapp, Mitchell Morris, and Stacy Wolf, 111–24. New York: Oxford University Press, 2011.

Still, Arthur, and Irving Velody, eds. *Re-writing the History of Madness: Studies in Foucault's "Histoire de le folie"*. London: Routledge, 1992.

Strasser, Susan. *Waste and Want: A Social History of Trash*. New York: Metropolitan Books, 1999.

Strindberg, August. *A Dream Play and Four Chamber Plays*. Translated by Walter Johnson. Seattle: University of Washington Press, 1973.

Strouse, Charles. "Theater Talk: Legendary Composer Charles Strouse, Pt. 2."

Interview by Susan Haskins and Michael Riedel. Posted on May 12, 2011. https://www.youtube.com/watch?v=YCxZV-uhBEg

Strouse, Charles, and David Rogers. *Charlie and Algernon*. Typescript, 1980. New York Public Library, Performing Arts Research Collections Theatre, NCOF+ 83-1024.

Szasz, Thomas. *Law, Liberty, and Psychiatry: An Inquiry into the Social Uses of Mental Health Practices*. New York: Macmillan, 1963.

Szasz, Thomas. *The Myth of Mental Illness: Foundations of a Theory of Personal Conduct*. New York: Harper and Row, 1961.

Szasz, Thomas. "The Therapeutic State: The Tyranny of Pharmacy." *Independent Review* 5, no. 4 (Spring 2001): 485–21.

Tarchetti, I. U. *Passion*. Translated by Lawrence Venuti. San Francisco: Mercury House, 1994.

Taubman, Howard. "Musical at Majestic is About Madness." Review of *Anyone Can Whistle*, Majestic Theatre, New York. *New York Times*, April 6, 1964, 36.

Taubman, Howard. "Musicians Return to the Theatre." *New York Times*, October 26, 1947.

Taubman, Howard. "Theater: Don Quixote, Singing Knight." Review of *Man of La Mancha*, ANTA Washington Square Theatre. *New York Times*, November 23, 1965, 52.

Tauris, Rosemary. "Oklahoma! It's Still Ok." *Cue New York*, December 21, 1979.

Taxi Driver. Directed by Martin Scorsese. 1976. Culver City, CA: Sony Pictures Home Entertainment, 2007, DVD.

Taylor, Eugene. *The Mystery of Personality: A History of Psychodynamic Theories*. London: Springer, 2009.

Thiher, Allen. *Revels in Madness: Insanity in Medicine and Literature*. Ann Arbor: University of Michigan Press, 1999.

Van Peebles, Melvin. *Aint Supposed to Die a Natural Death*. Toronto: Bantam Books, 1973.

Wald, Christina. *Hysteria, Trauma, and Melancholia: Performative Maladies in Contemporary Anglophone Drama*. New York: Palgrave, 2007.

Walker, Julia A. *Expressionism and Modernism in the American Theatre: Bodies, Voices, Words*. Cambridge: Cambridge University Press, 2005.

Wallach, Allan. "Theater Review: Musical '*King of Hearts*.'" Review of *King of Hearts*, Minskoff Theatre, New York. *Newsday*, October 23, 1978, 32A.

Wallin, Scott. "*Next to Normal* and the Persistence of Pathology in Performances of Psychosocial Disability." *Disability Studies Quarterly* 33, no. 1 (2013). http://dsq-sds.org/article/view/3428

Walser, Robert. *Running with the Devil: Power, Gender and Madness in Heavy Metal Music*. Hanover, NH: Wesleyan University Press, 1993.

Warfield, Scott. "From *Hair* to *Rent*: Is 'Rock' a Four-Letter Word on Broadway?" In *The Cambridge Companion to the Musical*, 2nd ed., edited by William E. Everett and Paul R. Laird, 235–49. Cambridge: Cambridge University Press, 2008.

Wasserman, Dale. *The Impossible Musical: The "Man of La Mancha" Story*. New York: Applause, 2003.

Wasserman, Dale, Joe Darion, and Mitch Leigh. *Man of La Mancha: A Musical Play*. New York: Random House, 1966.

Webber, Andrew Lloyd, Don Black, and Christopher Hampton. *Sunset Boulevard: Vocal Selections*. Milwaukee, WI: Hal Leonard Corporation, 1994.

Weill, Kurt. Liner notes for *Street Scene: Original Cast Recording*. Columbia Masterworks set M-MM-683, 1947.

Wertham, Frederic. "Freud Now." *Scientific American* 181 (October 1949): 50–54.

Wilk, Max. *OK! The Story of Oklahoma! A Celebration of America's Most Loved Musical*. 2nd ed. New York: Applause, 2002.

Williams, Raymond. *Keywords: A Vocabulary of Culture and Society*. Rev ed. New York: Oxford University Press, 1983.

Wilson, Mitchell. "DSM-III and the Transformation of American Psychiatry: A History." *American Journal of Psychiatry* 150, no. 3 (March 1993): 399–410.

Winer, Linda. "'Dear Evan Hansen' Review: Endearingly Original." Review of *Dear Evan Hansen*, Music Box Theatre, New York. *Newsday*, December 5, 2016.

Winer, Linda. "*Dear Evan Hansen*'s Review: Musical Too Light for Heavy Topics." Review of *Dear Evan Hansen*, Second Stage Theatre, New York. *Newsday*, May 1, 2016.

Wollman, Elizabeth L. *Hard Times: The Adult Musical in 1970s New York City*. New York: Oxford University Press, 2012.

Wollman, Elizabeth L. *The Theater Will Rock: A History of the Rock Musical from "Hair" to "Hedwig"*. Ann Arbor: University of Michigan Press, 2006.

Wolfestein, Eugene Victor. *Psychoanalytic Marxism: Groundwork*. London: Free Association Books, 1993.

Wright, Elizabeth, ed. *Feminism and Psychoanalysis: A Critical Dictionary*. Cambridge, MA: Blackwell, 1992.

Yorkey, Brian. *The Agenda with Steve Paikin*. Interview by Steve Paikin. TVOntario, published on YouTube on June 29, 2011. https://www.youtube.com/watch?v=_TqBTdWgsh4, accessed January 8, 2014.

Yorkey, Brian. "An Interview with *Next to Normal* Writer/Lyricist Brian Yorkey." Interview by Marcia Purse. Published in 2009, updated September 14, 2016. https://www.verywell.com/brian-yorkey-interview-380335, accessed October 15, 2018.

Yorkey, Brian, Tom Kitt, Michael Greif, and David Stone. "*Next to Normal*: The Road to Broadway." Interview by Ted Chapin. *Working in the Theatre* 384, American Theatre Wing, November 2009. https://www.youtube.com/watch?v=6t0tI4IhJSU&t=1714s, accessed January 4, 2017.

Young, Allan. *The Harmony of Illusions: Inventing Post-traumatic Stress Disorder*. Princeton, NJ: Princeton University Press, 1995.

Zadan, Craig. *Sondheim & Co.* 2nd ed. New York: Harper and Row, 1986.

Zaretsky, Eli. *Political Freud: A History*. New York: Columbia University, 2015.

Zaretsky, Eli. *Secrets of the Soul: A Social and Cultural History of Psychoanalysis*. New York: Alfred A. Knopf, 2004.

Index